Education and the Scandinavian Welfare State in the Year 2000

I0425809

REFERENCE BOOKS IN INTERNATIONAL EDUCATION
VOLUME 39
GARLAND REFERENCE LIBRARY OF SOCIAL SCIENCE
VOLUME 1129

EDUCATION AND THE SCANDINAVIAN WELFARE STATE IN THE YEAR 2000

EQUALITY, POLICY, AND REFORM

EDITED BY
ARILD TJELDVOLL

Routledge
Taylor & Francis Group

LONDON AND NEW YORK

First published 1998 by Garland Publishing, Inc.

2 Park Square, Milton Park, Abingdon, Oxon OX14 4RN
711 Third Avenue, New York, NY 10017, USA

Routledge is an imprint of the Taylor & Francis Group, an informa business

First issued in paperback 2016

Library of Congress Cataloging-in-Publication Data

Education and the Scandinavian welfare state in the year 2000 :
     equality, policy, and reform / edited by Arild Tjeldvoll.
          p.   cm. — (Garland reference library of social science ;
     v. 1129. Reference books in international education ; v. 39)
          Includes bibliographical references and index.
          1. Education—Social aspects—Scandinavia.   2. Educational
     change—Scandinavia.   3. Education and state—Scandinavia.
     I. Tjeldvoll, Arild.   II. Series: Garland reference library of social
     science ; v. 1129.   III. Series: Garland reference library of social
     science. Reference books in international education ; vol. 39.
     LC191.8.S34E36   1998
     379.48—dc21   97-8635
                                                                        CIP
ISBN 13: 978-0-8153-2476-8 (hbk)
ISBN 13: 978-1-138-96838-7 (pbk)

Contents

Series Editor's Foreword

This series of scholarly works in comparative and international education has grown well beyond the initial conception of a collection of reference books. Although retaining its original purpose of providing a resource to scholars, students, and a variety of other professionals who need to understand the role played by education in various societies or world regions, it also strives to provide accurate, relevant, and up-to-date information on a wide variety of selected educational issues, problems, and experiments within an international context.

Contributors to this series are well-known scholars who have devoted their professional lives to the study of their specializations. Without exception these men and women possess an intimate understanding of the subject of their research and writing. Without exception they have not only studied their subject in dusty archives, but have lived and traveled widely in their quest for knowledge. In short, they are "experts" in the best sense of that often overused word.

In our increasingly interdependent world, it is now widely understood that it is a matter of military, economic, and environmental survival not only that we understand better what makes other societies tick, but also that we make a serious effort to understand how others, be they Japanese, Hungarian, South African, or Chilean, attempt to solve the same kinds of educational problems that we face in North America. As the late George Z.F. Bereday wrote more than three decades ago: "(Education) is a mirror held against the face of a people. Nations may put on blustering shows of strength to conceal public weakness, erect grand façades to conceal shabby backyards, and profess peace while secretly arming for conquest, but how they take care of their children tells unerringly who they are" (*Comparative Methods in Education,* New York: Holt, Rinehart and Winston, 1964, p. 5).

Perhaps equally important, however, is the valuable perspective that studying another education system (or its problems) provides us in understanding our own system (or its problems). When we step beyond our own limited experience and our commonly held assumptions about schools and learning in order to look back at our system in contrast to another, we see it in a very different light. To learn, for example, how China or Belgium handles the education of a multilingual society; how the French provide for the funding of public education; or how the Japanese control access to their universities enables us to better understand that there are reasonable alternatives to our own familiar way of doing things. Not that we can *borrow* directly from other societies. Indeed, educational arrangements are inevitably a reflection of deeply embedded political, economic, and cultural factors that are unique to a particular society. But a conscious recognition that there are other ways of doing things can serve to open our minds and provoke our imaginations in ways that can result in new experiments or approaches that we may not have otherwise considered.

Since this series is intended to be a useful research tool, the editor and contributors welcome suggestions for future volumes, as well as for ways in which this series can be improved.

Edward R. Beauchamp
University of Hawaii

Preface

An educational expedition to China can have unexpected consequences, especially when the delegation leader is Edward Beauchamp, from the University of Hawaii. He inspired me to put together this volume on Scandinavian education. Other sources of encouragement have been several of my fellow members in CIES—the Comparative and International Education Society (North America). In particular, William K. Cummings, at State University of New York at Buffalo, and Philip G. Altbach, Boston College, have challenged me to make a Scandinavian contribution to the field of comparative education.

In the practical work of making this volume "camera ready" in order to meet Garland Publishing's requirement, Dr. Içara da Silva Holmesland from ELI Group—the Educational Leadership International, Oslo—has been of immense help.

Colleagues from Denmark, Finland, Iceland, Norway and Sweden have taken the challenge together with me and put forth strong efforts to make this work ready on time.

I thank you all for having contributed to the content, and I thank Garland Publishing Senior Editor Marie Ellen Larcada for cooperation and support.

Arild Tjeldvoll
Oslo, May 1998

Introduction
Arild Tjeldvoll

The term "Scandinavia" is often used by the Anglo-American world not only to refer to the peninsula itself but also to the whole northwestern region of Europe which includes Denmark, Finland, Iceland, Norway and Sweden and has a population of about 20 million people. The label "the Nordic Countries" is frequently used by people in the region as well as by continental Europeans. It might be argued that "Nordic countries" are also found in other parts of the world, and that Scandinavia is a better word to identify the region. This volume on Scandinavian education examines the whole region, i.e., all the five countries.

All regions of the world possess their own specific characteristics, usually shared by their member countries and often made visible through similar socio-cultural features. Thus, it seems fair to claim that the Scandinavian region has some distinguishing features. Foremost among these is the model of the welfare state. All five countries have developed a state organization characterized by a considerable degree of social justice. The ideal of creating a democratic society has been a very high priority. This aim has been realized by means of an overall social policy, which was intended to create optimal and equitable life conditions for all social groups, regardless of social background, gender, ethnicity and geographical location. The history of the region has created links that still exist between the different areas and that are maintained today through the policies of The Nordic Council, of which all countries are members. Historically, Denmark and Sweden have been the dominant states. Denmark controlled the areas of today´s Norway (until 1814), Iceland, Greenland and the Faroe Islands, while Sweden was the major partner in a union with Finland until 1814 and with Norway from 1814 until 1905. Except for Finland and the indigenous people of Greenland, all the other countries have a common linguistic root in Old Norse. Today, the peoples of Denmark, Norway, and Sweden speak and read each other's languages fairly easily.

Lutheranism is the dominant religion of the region. In most Scandinavian countries, more than 90 percent of the population belongs to this Protestant church and, until recently, it was the State church in most of them. Socially and culturally, the countries used to be very homogeneous. Recently, however, there have been changes due to significant immigration from Third World countries. The labor movement has been the dominant political force in building up the welfare state, often in an influential alliance with the dominating and socialist-oriented trade unions. On an international scale, all the countries are relatively small and politically stable, and their populations have normally been spread over vast areas. Denmark is the exception, having a greater concentration of inhabitants per square kilometer.

The countries of the Scandinavian region have all used *educational policies* as a strategy for creating social justice. During the twentieth century, the comprehensive school became the dominant model on primary and lower secondary levels. A common content, representing what was seen as a homogeneous culture, was compulsory for all students. Learning the same subject matter and learning it together has been a curriculum principle until now. In practice, all students can continue into upper secondary education and higher education is free—the students pay only student-body membership. Summing up, it seems fair to claim that, by the 1980s, the countries in Scandinavia had achieved most aims of a democratic education policy.

The above description may now sound much like a rosy fairy tale. During the 1980s, the Scandinavian education model started meeting several challenges. The school to which all youngsters had had access became more academically oriented, and many students at the junior secondary level started showing difficulties in coping with the subjects' content. Motivation to attend school seems to be decreasing. The present concern is to find out whether the higher academic demands combined with a situation of growing unemployment, in which an education seems to offer no guarantee for a job, can explain the loss of interest in schooling among young people. Under such circumstances, the quality of teaching and the schools' effectiveness are being questioned by a growing number of parents and employers.

Several current changes in the frame factors of Scandinavian education are being observed in the 1990s. The fall of the Berlin Wall symbolizes a dramatic ideological change in political, social, and cultural life. A more rugged individualism and less concern for collective values and interests are observed in Scandinavia, even though the change is far less dramatic than in, e.g., Russia. The change in values from socialism, social democracy, collectivism, and solidaric cooperation to liberalism, individualism, and competition seems to have had a direct effect upon economic reasoning. Market economy and privatization of previous public services used to be heavily attacked by the left and not very much propagated by the conservatives some years ago. Today, market economy and privatization are regarded more naturally than before and conquer, each day, new areas of society. The presence of a tough, commercialized media world, especially TV, is one of the signs of the new order. Thus, one can state that social change has become more rapid.

The cultural scene has changed significantly as a consequence of immigration and increased international communication. The tension of the change is illustrated by the encounter of rural and poorly educated immigrants from Third World countries with post-modern Scandinavians. Some people see this meeting of different cultures as something positively challenging and fruitful. However, others see the mixture of immigrants and modernists as threats to the established social structures. The neo-Nazists have again become active within Scandinavia. Demonstrations and violent incidents involving immigrants are not uncommon.

The technological revolution, especially in the computer world, and the new economic situation have created unemployment, which, so far, no training measures have been able to counteract. Production and services seem to be changing and developing in a direction which increases the number of people considered unqualified to participate in the world of work. Some persons are not capable of taking the sort of training which would allow them to adapt to the new situation. At the same time, among others, there is an increasing interest in higher education. Education is still assessed as a general good that might give people greater chances in the labor market. However, academic unemployment is already a fact. Higher education, so far, has not been able to adapt rapidly enough to the changed needs of Scandinavia in the 1990s.

What are the educational consequences of these changed social frame factors of welfare state Scandinavia? The principles of equity and equality as social cornerstone values are being challenged and changed. Even though most of the rhetoric of these values is maintained in party programs and policy documents, there is a new and distinct quest for *quality* in education. This quest is not so much concerned with the process as with the products of education. What sort of competence do schools produce? Will the achieved competence help students to survive and succeed in a tight labor market? The great challenge for the policy makers, especially those with an anchoring in a socialist heritage, is to integrate the values of equity/equality with those of quality and competition. Some claim that a certain quality of education is necessary in order to sustain equality and maintain society as a good and human social collectivity. Phrased differently, competition in the market keeps up the quality of equality.

How can this be possible in a comprehensive school? Whether it is possible or not remains an open question. New measures have restructured the leadership function of the education system, making visible the responsibility for goal achievement by target groups. The notion of accountability is not often expressed clearly, but it is really what is required. Accountability and efficiency, also in education, are more and more seen as natural consequences of the recent quality policies. A good example is the adoption of *management by objectives* and *external evaluation* by all schools. Scandinavian teacher trade unions are reluctant to allow the principal to come into the classroom to control the quality of their teaching or to allow external experts to assess the quality of their products—students' achievements.

Principles of funding for education are changing. As a rather dramatic example, Sweden stands out, having introduced the voucher system in the compulsory school. Introduced and established by conservatives, it has, remarkably enough, been kept up by a social-democratic (Labor) government. Put differently, Margaret Thatcher's much-criticized educational policy principles of the 1980s are now found natural by Swedish socialists. The voucher system in Sweden is closely related to a significant increase in private schooling, a tendency that shows signs of expanding to the rest of the region. Finally, internationalization of Scandinavian schooling is strongly expressed in all the countries. International programs and student exchange are encouraged in different ways.

The typical Scandinavian education of the post-World War II decades may be seriously changed by the year 2000. From being a region characterized by equality of access and financing, by progressive pedagogy and by being almost one hundred percent public, it may become more like its European neighbors, more organizationally differentiated by abandoning the principle of comprehensive schooling and more quality oriented in all subjects, be they vocational or academic. Put differently, the progressive student-centered Scandinavian concept of using education as an important means to attain the equality aims professed in general social policies may be facing an end. Instead, there may come quality schooling with early organizational differentiation between the vocationally and the academically oriented. The ultimate criteria of quality might be the ability to reach the most attractive positions in the labor market.

This volume has been put together in order to illuminate Scandinavian education approaching the year 2000. Based on their experiences and research, a number of educators have been asked to present the Scandinavian setting (part I), some reforms of the 1990s (part II) and perspectives on future development (part III).

In the first chapter, Part I, Arild Tjeldvoll sets the scene for this volume by addressing features of the Scandinavian education model and how it is being currently challenged by ideological changes. Based on a description of changes within curriculum, organization, leadership and funding, the author discusses whether the new aim of "quality of equality" is a possibility or a paradox. In chapter 2, "Populism and Education in Norway," Jon Lauglo argues that the Norwegian variety of populism has had an enduring influence on the evolution of education in that country. After an analysis of the concept of populism, signs of this ideology in Norwegian society are traced, prior to being related to Norwegian education. Among the populist characteristics of Norwegian education, Jon Lauglo discusses the common school with a weak academic tradition and the superior authenticity of the vernacular. "Parents' Participation in Danish Schools: Genuine Influence or Pseudo-Legitimation?" is the problem raised by Jens Hoff in chapter 3. His objects of study are the user boards of parents in Danish comprehensive schools. Several voices of the debate have condemned the work of these boards as a pseudo-legitimation of the traditional political-bureaucratic type. Hoff's findings point towards another, and promising, direction. The topic of Kjell Eide, in chapter 4, is "The Impact of Research on Norwegian Educational Policy." He shows how the belief in science and research predominated among central Norwegian politicians after World War II as well as how radical views have more and more challenged the rather positivist understanding of science in the 50s and 60s. Eide presents a critique of traditional economist thinking in education, as well as how the Organization for Economic Cooperation and Development (OECD) has significantly interacted with Norwegian educational policy formulation. In chapter 5, "The Swedish School Reforms: Trends and Issues," Torsten Husén discusses trends and issues within Swedish educational reform policies. After placing the educational policies within the full frame of the development of the Swedish social welfare state from the 1930 onwards, the level of success and influences on the process are discussed. Mina O'Dowd turns to the micro level of the Scandinavian setting, illustrating how female students experience their last compulsory year in the comprehensive school. In chapter 6, titled "School Fatigue and 'Too Many Bad Excuses': Swedish Teenage Girls Talk about Truancy," the following question is investigated and discussed: Is school fatigue an educational problem that has social repercussions or a social problem that has educational repercussions. Or is it both? In the last chapter of Part I, Reijo Raivola compares Finnish teachers' professionalism to that of American, British, and German teachers in "Comparative Perspectives on Professionalism among American, British, German, and Finnish Teachers." He focuses his concern on the teacher proletarianization hypothesis. If teaching is, mainly, either practice or art, what are the consequences for the teaching profession's strategy to be seen as a valid instrument within educational reform policies?

In the second part of the book, three educational reforms are presented and discussed. In chapter 8, Gary Miron's "Restructuring Education in Sweden" places the Swedish reform into an international context by identifying external sources of influence. Because of serious economic problems, Sweden is today characterized as the guinea pig of educational reform. The speed and extent of market oriented changes in this former archetype of a social welfare state are astonishing and have made it a social laboratory. Miron presents arguments for and against the reforms before consciously applying a constructivist view in his general reflections on the reform. Next, in chapter 9, Peder Haug reports on "Political Ideals and Pedagogical Dilemma: On Beginning School for Six-Year-Olds in Norway." His analysis is particularly interesting for showing how different factors influence both process and content of the reform. The third reform presented is "Upper Secondary School Reform in Norway" by Anne-Lise Th. Iván, in chapter 10. While the first two reforms presented in this part concentrated the discussion on the analysis of principles, this chapter goes deeper into practical and organizational aspects of one specific reform. Reform 94 exemplifies several of the general principles of Norwegian educational reforms in the 1990s. This reform is an attempt to extend the comprehensive principle into upper secondary school, contrary to the general trend toward greater differentiation between schools. On the other hand, it also exemplifies the trend towards centralizing the goals (management by objectives), content, and evaluation, while decentralizing decisions about methods and use of resources.

In Part III, the focus is directed toward the future. In chapter 11, "The Future School Manager," Kah Slenning presents findings from a study in which persons in Swedish elite positions assess the competence needs of a professional school manager in the future. In essence, the findings may be seen as a synthesis of operationalized values from both a social/liberal humanist tradition as well as the current efficiency and market-oriented thinking. Chapter 11 takes us to a Swedish setting and two school cases, which, however, are seen as illustrative of future challenges for all the Scandinavian countries. Chapter 12 deals with "The Comprehensive Schools in Norway: Challenged by a Changing Society." Here, Içara da Silva Holmesland points to several challenges facing the Norwegian comprehensive school as we approach the year 2000. Particularly, the challenge to raise academic achievements within an educational culture traditionally indifferent toward a liberal education seems vital to a country desiring to attain international competitiveness. Even more important may be the challenge to solve the problems of cultural collisions following immigration, particularly from Muslim countries. The future perspectives on vocational education in Iceland are the concern of chapter 13, in which Jon Torfi Jónasson identifies "The Foes of Icelandic Vocational Education at the Upper Secondary Level." Contrary to a high level of rhetoric about how important vocational education is, his findings indicate that several foes are operating, and there is, thus, good reason for serious doubts about the future of this type and level of education in Iceland.

Holger Daun's contribution is titled "Comprehensive Schooling at the Intersection of Market, State, and Civil Forces: Two Swedish Case Studies." Daun presents the socio-political background for the current restructuring of Swedish education, before outlining how the function of education systems is conditioned by societal changes and state policies. With this background, three school cases are analyzed, and hypotheses formulated about the effects of current policies on the Scandinavian welfare paradigm in the future. In the last chapter of this volume (15) the topic is "From the Mass to the Elite. Structure, Limits, and the Future of Scandinavian Educational Systems." Osmo Kivinen and Risto Rinne take as their point of departure the questioning of egalitarian educational policies that is taking place in many countries. What is the relationship between elite and mass education? Which alternatives can be found to the traditional state-centralized educational systems? The authors look for alternatives outside Scandinavia and also discuss the role of education towards the end of the century with respect to the labor market and the lives of individuals.

PART I

The Scandinavian Setting

CHAPTER 1

Quality of Equality? Scandinavian Education Towards the Year 2000[1]

Arild Tjeldvoll

INTRODUCTION

Social development of the countries in the Scandinavian region in our century has had a number of common features. Foremost among these is the Scandinavian model of the welfare state. Common for these countries—Denmark, Finland, Iceland, Norway, and Sweden—is that they all, by the 1970s, had developed a state organization characterized by a considerable degree of social justice. The ideal of a democratic society had been attempted and realized by means of an overall social policy, aiming at creating optimal equity of life conditions for all social groups, identified by social background, gender, ethnicity, and/or geographical location. The main implementing mandator of this policy has been an alliance of the Social Democratic Party (Labor) and its Siamese twin—the dominating and socialist-oriented trade union. Through their joint action, these two organizations have advanced what has been termed the Labor Movement.

From being politically more or less revolutionary in the first half of the century, the Movement advanced gradually towards parliamentarism and took over political power after general elections. However, the overall aim continued to be the equalization of social class differences. As part of the struggle for social justice based on socialist principles, the *educational* policy was chosen as a particularly important social change agent (Slagstad 1994). In line with progressive education traditions, equal access to education was both seen as a democratic right for the single individual as well as a tool for making the society more democratic collectively. By the 1970s, all citizens of Scandinavia were legally obliged to participate in a basic comprehensive education of nine years. They were also given the right to go on voluntarily to secondary and higher education. All education was free of tuition fees, and paid by the state or the municipalities. This education policy attained, especially after World War II, a high degree of consensus among the political parties on all principles of equal education for all. By the end of the 1970s most aims of this democratic education policy were achieved in all the Scandinavian countries.

During the 1980s this model faced several challenges. Even though access to schooling had been made steadily more democratic, the content of the junior secondary school remained dominated by academics and was considered difficult by many students. Difficulties in mastering the content of school subjects, coupled with a situation of growing unemployment in which the amount of education seemed not to be a guarantee for having a job after graduation, appear to have negatively influenced the motivation of students. The teaching profession also faced challenges. The recruitment pool and the social status of teachers seemed to have decreased relative to earlier times. A growing number of parents and leading employer organizations started increasingly to question the quality of teaching and the school's productivity.

With this sketch of Scandinavian educational policies as a backdrop, the intention of this chapter is to highlight some essential aspects of the Scandinavian model as it developed itself in the 1980s. Some reflections will be made on how the new ideological signals and international educational trends started affecting this model in the beginning of the 1990s.

THE SCANDINAVIAN EDUCATION MODEL

Various obstacles needed to be overcome by the different Scandinavian countries in order to provide equal education for all citizens. As an illustration, in the case of Norway, whose citizens live spread along fjords, in passes between mountains, or on islands, it has become necessary to have many small schools with, often, very few students (Lauglo 1995). Such a solution certainly imposes high costs on public education systems. Thus, having at the same time the ambition of offering equally good teaching under equal teaching conditions in all schools, the Scandinavian public school had to become expensive. In the three first quarters of this century, the teachers held a strong position and high social status in these countries. In regard to social background, salaries, and social status as seen by others and by themselves, Scandinavian teachers, including those working in the primary schools, ranked highest compared with similar groups in other West European and North American countries (Aubert 1956). Without going deeply into the historical background, it suffices here to mention that Scandinavian teachers have had very strong trade unions, which have been successful in their negotiations for attaining higher salaries and reducing the number of working hours. They have also been members of important commissions that dealt with educational reform questions. The teachers' unions seemed to have worked consciously towards the criteria demanded for an occupation to become a full profession (Wilenski 1964–65).

The educational systems of the Scandinavian countries have, in general, been strongly centralist regarding curriculum, examination and governance. However, it should be noted that Denmark has been a little bit different. The lesser degree of centralism and the greater local pluralism in this country may be due to the previous position and policies of the Lutheran Church. Historically, the State Lutheran Church has had the main responsibility for and control over the educational system in the Scandinavian countries. When theological disputes within the Church developed and created threats to its unity, this problem was solved differently in Denmark as compared to the other countries. The Danish Church solved the problems by rather liberally accepting a more open institution, where different "decentralized" interpretations of Scripture were allowed. In Sweden, however, and in Norway, disputes were solved by segregating from the main church different "free churches." Thus, the State Church continued to significantly influence the education sector. When the strong Labor Movement developed and established clear goals for educating the whole population, it became natural for this new political power in Sweden as well as in Norway to inherit the centralist role of the Lutheran State Church.

The rather strong centralism is expressed in a national curriculum for the primary and secondary school. Even though the national curricula in Scandinavia are always the product of political compromises and designed as "frame plans" expected to be further elaborated and given locally distinct form and content, they are fairly clear in their overall aims, rooted in the legal acts for the different levels of schooling. The specific subjects' goals and content have been very distinct, taking often a more governing role for the implementation than the overall aims. The significant position of the traditional subjects has been consolidated by a centrally designed and operated examination, normally closely following the goal and content of the traditional subjects. In the implementation of the educational reform policies, the overall aims and the subjects' goals have come to send different messages to the schools: while the aims stress democratic values, student-centered teaching and less evaluation as control, the subjects' goals favor a traditional academic content, which means, implicitly, traditional pedagogy.

Until the 1980s, administration was centralist. The ministry of education had governed by means of centrally formulated regulations. Compliance with these rules was controlled by a state representative on the county level. Formally, school boards at the municipality level have had some influence on the implementation of the national educational policy. However, due to the centralization of the national curriculum, planning, examinations, and the fact that the state has covered the main part of the local budgets, local influence has been rather symbolic. As an instrument of goal-directed socialization, the Scandinavian comprehensive school has been more of a centralist nature. To some degree the Danish version can be seen as deviating from this pattern.

Modern Scandinavian schooling mainly represents the same curriculum tradition as previously administered by the Church. Progressivism, socialist-inspired efforts towards justice and democratization, implied mainly that traditional schooling should now be regarded as attainable by all members of the society. Looking, however, at the overall aims, especially of the primary and lower secondary schools, it is obvious that the progressivists intend a more profound change, i.e., towards greater democracy. Not only access to the traditional institution but also a democratic change in direction of content, methods, and forms of evaluation are the aims.

A democratically organized school has been seen as a means for achieving the optimal self-realization of the individual, as well as of specific social groups, and for further democratization of the whole society. From the beginning of the 1980s, this intention has been reinforced because of the substantial immigration from Third World countries and from South/East Europe. An example of how far this progressivism has developed is found in Norway's National Curriculum of 1987. Here it is stated as an overall principle that in the practical work of the classroom, teaching/learning activities shall always have the specific socio-cultural and academic characteristics of the single student as their point of departure—a distinctly student-centered pedagogy (Norwegian Ministry of Education 1987). During the 1970s the "modus operandi" among educationalists was towards a "problem-oriented and project work-pedagogy" (Illeris 1981). These principles were seen as the basis for creating a motivating environment towards what is considered traditional as well as critical knowledge and creating favorable conditions for instilling democratic values and skills. Group work was expected to be a more efficient form of organizing the students and it was, therefore, seen as an important part of a pedagogy with democratic and humanistic educational aims.

The Scandinavian education model at the beginning of the 1980s can be seen as characterized by a considerable degree of general political consensus on the comprehensive school principle. Also, it seems fair to say that a majority of the population prefers humanistic and progressivist pedagogy to the traditional teacher-centered teaching. The radical political critique of the 1960s and 1970s of an academically and traditional knowledge-oriented pedagogy (and, therefore, of a school reproducing social inequalities) had gained significant ground in the national curricula and within the teaching profession. The critique had a considerable impact on the theory and practice of teachers.

There is then a dualism in this model which has on one side a traditional liberal arts curriculum with traditional examinations and a centralist governance but, on the other side, a radical, humanistic and process-oriented understanding of what constitutes a valid school. In Denmark, however, this dualism has been more noticeable than in the other Scandinavian countries. The specific Danish traditionalism may also have been reinforced when the country joined the European Union (EU) in 1972. Even though it is always stressed by the EU that all member countries have absolute independence in their education policies, the Danish membership may very well, indirectly, have brought the country closer to the more academic and conservative continental tradition of what is considered "proper schooling."

In contrast to the public humanistic and democratic image of Scandinavian education defended at the beginning of the 1980s, there is a stronger demand for a more academic type of education from certain groups of parents and students who have been expressing discontent with the quality of the schools. However, the society is confronted with the reality that a larger amount of education is no longer any safe guarantee of finding a position in an ever-shrinking job market which also requires a higher level of intellectual skills. From the conservatives and the extreme right-wing activists one hears an increasingly more distinct critique of the Scandinavian model. It is accused of being too process oriented, too concerned about equality, and not concerned enough about basic knowledge and competition. It is also seen as too expensive. Even though enrollments have been decreasing, the number of teachers has not followed the same curve, implying that more teachers are doing less work than before. The teachers trade unions are seen as having too much power, even to some degree, illegitimate power, both in negotiations over teachers' salaries and over educational policies. If one takes a look outside the Scandinavian scene, it is not difficult to discover what might have reinforced the critique of the humanistic and democratic Scandinavian model.

INTERNATIONAL IDEOLOGICAL CHANGES

The external ideological pressure on Scandinavia may be exemplified by two important documents. One is the American study *A Nation at Risk*, from 1983 (Rydin 1991) and the other is the English document *1988 Educational Reform Act* (Todd 1991). In the United States the lack of quality in the decentralized American education model was seen as seriously threatening the nation's international competitive force and, by that, jeopardizing the position of a superpower. Similarly, Mrs. Thatcher's re-evaluation of the English decentralized, and teacher-dominated system, found that the system was not a valid means for producing the necessary competence to enable the country to fulfill its ambitions in the international economic competition.

After the fall of the Berlin Wall and all the "velvet revolutions" in East/Central Europe, a clear market economy, based on classical liberalist philosophy and political conservatism, replaced Marxist and socialist collective thinking all over this part of Europe (Tjeldvoll 1992). In Russia, the change was seen as logical, not in the direction of some sort of a Scandinavian-style capitalist planned economy and social democracy but as a turn to what the former communist leaders had once labeled their enemy's form of economy—wild capitalism. Many people in the East naturally thought that when communism was gone, the alternative had to be the opposite—"wild capitalism and rugged individualism"—the model of the formerly described enemy.

A substantial part of the ideological house cleaning in East/Central Europe was related to the reformulation of education policies. Education had been seen by whose predecessors as an extremely important means in the struggle to change society. The people that took over power thought similarly. A re-socialization of the teaching profession was seen as an urgent step.

In East/Central Europe one finds both "a return to the past," meaning that the classic liberal education subjects have been brought back to their former position and an early organizational streaming, or differentiation, of the students is again seen as functional. At the same time there is a distinct progressivist American influence—social studies on human rights and student-centered teaching are now introduced in the East as part of the Western cultural support to the new democracies. This rapid shaping of a "neo-conservative educational paradigm" (Kozma 1992) in its geographical neighborhood, has probably influenced the general climate of educational policy making in Scandinavia. The influence of this new paradigm may have been reinforced by an intense and increasing discussion in the region, excluding Denmark, about whether or not to join the European Union.

In summarizing the characteristics of the change process of educational ideology gaining momentum at the beginning of the 1990s, one might claim that a change is taking place, moving from the socio-political and economic ideas of Karl Marx to those of Adam Smith. There is also a change from solitary collective to individual competition as the primary frame of reference for the political power's analysis of social problems, policy formulation, and policy implementation. In the field of education, the effect is a move away from the collectivist view that education should be of equal quality for all individuals, independent of social background. Especially the basic education, primary and lower secondary, should be organized so as to take into account each learner's social, cultural, and academic background. This is seen as a socially, pedagogically and democratically relevant approach. Simultaneously, such an educational policy is expected to function as a socially equalizing policy; thus class distinction should be gradually wiped out.

In contrast to collectivism and equity, the new and emerging neo-liberalist-conservative view has individualism and quality as essential criteria for a relevant educational policy. Quality, therefore, has precedence over equality. Education is a valuable commodity for the single individual in his or her competition for the most attractive career opportunities. According to these views, schools are seen as companies themselves, competing with each other in a free market and trying to attract customers by supplying what they regard individually as high-quality education. Competition based on inequity is the essential new dynamic element. Students are expected to compete with each other, and so are the schools as organizations. This dynamic competition is expected to produce qualitative individual achievements and higher quality schools in general. The collective effect of this dynamic is expected to be an increased level of competence for the country as a totality, almost as if the country itself has become a company. This appears to be the ultimate goal of the governments in charge of nations willing to participate in international competition. In order for these countries to be internationally competitive, the goal of equity and equality for the single individual becomes subordinated to what fosters the competitive power for the country as a whole. The country needs to create a national economic surplus, the government's first precondition for offering welfare to all its members. Using too many resources on equality before enough economically competitive quality is at hand might jeopardize even the basic welfare state rights, i.e., schooling of equal quality.

In an overall social policy perspective, there seems to be a change of opinion as to the basic function of education in a society. Perhaps the main change is from regarding schooling as primarily a socio-political force to seeing its contribution as mainly one of an economic and political order. Thus, the new foci seem to be individual choice, competition, quality, effectiveness, and efficiency.

EDUCATIONAL CONSEQUENCES IN SCANDINAVIA

In Scandinavia, the educational consequences of international ideological changes are illuminated by research (e.g. Telhaug and Tønnessen 1992; Miron 1993; Holmesland 1994), the popular debate in the media, the professional debate in the teacher unions' journals, and the recent versions of the countries' national curricula and legal regulations for their educational systems. The most recent changes of policy directions in national curricula and legal regulations are clearly expressed in the Scandinavian ministries of education's reports to the United Nations Educational, Scientific and Cultural Organization (UNESCO) 44th International Conference on Education in 1994. These reports are used as main sources for the following analysis. Before attempting to identify elements of change in curriculum and structure of the region as a whole, Denmark, as a forerunner in the education change process, will be briefly considered.

Denmark—Setting a Change Agenda for the Region

Most likely due to the Church's role in Denmark as compared to other countries of the region, this country has all the time been more distinctly characterized by both a more structural pluralism and a more prevailing influence on content from conservative and continental traditions. The establishment of a compulsory comprehensive school, for example, came at a later date in Denmark. It was not until 1975 that it was made legal (Telhaug and Tønnessen 1992:26-30). Independent or private schools have reached in this country a significantly higher position (7.4 percent in 1980) than in the others (Telhaug and Tønnessen 1992). A Norwegian comparative education researcher A.O. Telhaug found in his study of recent Danish education policies that the Labor Party, or the Social Democrats in Denmark had, much earlier and differently from the Scandinavian neighbors, adopted a neo-liberalist view in their social policies, the field of education included (Telhaug and Tønnessen 1992). On this part of the Scandinavian educational policy scene appeared, in 1982, a politician said to be an exceptionally competent and dynamic entrepreneur—Mr. Bertel Haarder—as minister of education, representing the Liberal-Conservative Party, within the center-right coalition government (Telhaug and Tønnessen 1992). According to Telhaug and Tønnessen, Mr. Haarder may have to a considerable degree accelerated the change of Danish education in a market economy towards a neo-liberal direction.

In summary, Denmark has historically been closer to the European continental education tradition than the other Scandinavian countries. The influence of this tradition has possibly, indirectly, been reinforced by the country joining the European Union in 1972, and, directly, from having an exceptionally dynamic minister of education from 1982 until 1992.

Curriculum—Back-to-Basics?

A common feature in Scandinavia is the implementation of national curricula, which are now to be managed and assessed by employing clear goals and specific resource frames. At the curriculum level, this seems to reflect a change towards management by objectives as the overall principle for the education system as a whole (Swedish Ministry 1994:10). As a main change from the previous national curricula the present emphasis is on *content*, seen as a rehabilitation of basic *knowledge* (Lauvdal 1994). All countries have in their latest report from their ministries of education to the UNESCO International Conference on Education 44th session, 1994, made this curricular turn clear. Especially science and foreign languages are to be given higher priorities now (Danish Ministry 1994:8). Quality and creativity are frequently mentioned as important objectives of the future policy (Norwegian Ministry 1994, Finnish Ministry 1994). Closely related to knowledge, quality, and creativity, the concept of competence is also applied: "Knowledge and competence are seen as essential for the further enrichment and development of the welfare society" (Norwegian Ministry 1994:10). It is frequently claimed, fairly directly, that small countries, like those in Scandinavia, must utilize their capacities, i.e., their human resources, as knowledge producers, in order to strengthen their competitive force in international cooperation. Concerning teaching methods, not very much has been expressed explicitly. In the public debate, however, some conservative opinions are expressed. There are requests not only for going back to "basic knowledge," but also for a more teacher-dominated "basic pedagogy." Generally, however, prevailing progressivist opinions on teaching methods seem to be accepted by the ministries. But the way progressivism has become accepted is now more directly related to goal achievement. That method leading to the highest achievement by students seems to be the desired pedagogy. At the same time the curricula express the radical process-oriented tradition. Project work and group work are accepted, but there are also signals indicating that these methods ought to be based on clearer goals and duties for the participants, the opposite of the past's ideal of "the goal emerging during the process" (Norwegian Ministry 1993).

Evaluation, as the final stage of any organized learning activity, has now gained a new and general importance and is frequently a central element of the new policies. This could also be seen as a reflection of the education systems' overall change from management by rules and directives to management by objectives. Such a change seems to make evaluation, as a means of control and monitoring, unavoidable. At the same time as the ministry's bodies at different system levels are accepting the principle and function of evaluation as simply a rational consequence of the logic of goals and accountability, others strongly criticize the evaluation means (Tjeldvoll 1992). The reactions against goal and accountability-based external evaluations of schools coming from traditionally radical and progressivist circles can exemplify the general resistance to current educational changes rooted in market economy and neo-liberalism. The resistance is most clearly expressed by the teaching profession, but followed by a considerable faction of the scholars in the area of education. The latter has joined interest with the teacher trade unions and is taking the teachers' stand from a humanistic and student-centered perspective as the overall frame of reference for education activities (Telhaug and Tønnessen 1992:115–125).

For the upper secondary level, the most conspicuous curriculum change is the reduced number of early special subject branches, or subject differentiation. The focus now is giving the whole cohort more general, academic subjects so that all students will be optimally prepared for lifelong education, which is seen as necessary because of the rapid changes in work life. Another distinct feature of the vocational branches of upper secondary school is their declared effort to strengthen the connection with business by establishing cooperating agreements and "social partnerships." The ambition is to utilize the working life more efficiently in training capacities. This strategy seems to be, first, plainly pedagogical, i.e., a lot of students are expected to be more motivated to learn "by doing" in real life. Second, it is expected that by opening open channels to business life and shifting competence needs, the education system may be better prepared to cope with the changing qualifications in business and working life in general.

Higher education has especially two marked features regarding curriculum. First, different institutions' course offerings are coordinated on the national level, in order to obtain improved subject concentration, quality, and cost-effectiveness. Here it should be kept in mind that most higher education institutions in Scandinavia are state owned and managed. A recent example of one type of state efficiency strategy for higher education is provided by Norway, where the number of higher education institutions has been reduced, or reorganized from 110 to 26. These 26 institutions are expected to coordinate their research and teaching within a "Norway-network" of competence building within higher education and research (Norwegian Ministry 1994). Second, there is a definite goal of improving the quality of teaching within higher education, especially at the traditional research universities. Improved quality of teaching within these institutions is seen as a primary strategy for increasing efficiency and producing a highly qualified professional labor force.

Structure, Organization and Leadership

A short time ago schooling in Scandinavia typically started at the age of seven. Recently all the countries began offering "pedagogical activities" for the six-year-olds, on a voluntary basis. Iceland (1990) and Norway (1994) have already made admission at the age of six compulsory. There are indications that the other countries will be following very soon. Also, it seems to be just a matter of time before all the countries expand the number of compulsory schooling years to ten, as Iceland and Norway have recently done.

In Norway the latest legal reform gives everyone graduating from lower secondary, or basic school, the right to attend three years of schooling at the upper secondary level. Presently, in all the Scandinavian countries, more than 90 percent of graduates from the lower secondary schools take one or more years of schooling at the upper secondary level.

For the vocational part of secondary schooling, two new trends are visible. More importance is being placed on training at workplaces, also known as the apprenticeship system. Simultaneously, the time in vocational schooling is being reduced, and the organizational differentiation between different vocational branches is being delayed to the second year. Whereas earlier there was a choice of 109 different branches (in the first year of the secondary vocational school in Norway), the number has now been reduced to 13. In the first year the main concentration will be on general academic subjects, with the emphasis on an optimal broad knowledge base for later specialization, retraining, and lifelong education (Norwegian Ministry 1994). Both these reforms obviously aim at producing a qualified labor force, more in harmony with what is required. For a learner who is not particularly interested in academic subjects, the new emphasis on academic knowledge might create a motivation problem.

Management by objectives, accountability, and evaluation has become the new dogma for educational policy implementation in Scandinavia. A few protests were heard (Tjeldvoll 1992) but, on the whole, these principles, prevalent and natural for profit-based business life, have been accepted by the professional educators' community with relative silence. These principles imply that the previous form of management by regulations and earmarked resources has been abandoned. Instead, the organization level now responsible for implementation has goals and some specified frame factors. Then it is the responsibility of the operating agent to decide how to reach the goals. Later, external evaluations will verify whether the implementation has been goal-effective and accountable. The level of effectiveness, efficiency, and accountability will then constitute the basis for the supreme mandator's total assessment of goal achievements and the operative agent's competence and capability, in general, and its leadership competence, in particular.

At the ministerial level these new management principles have had as an important consequence the strengthening of political leadership of the ministries at the cost of a reduced position for trade unions and educational advisory bodies or directorates. Several influential professional councils have recently been closed down. Together with the introduction of management by objectives, a fairly consistent decentralization of decision-making power has followed. However, it seems fair to claim that there has been, at the same time, a clear strengthening of central-level political decision-making power and a decentralization of decision-making power regarding the implementation at the operational level.

All the countries seem to be undergoing a dramatic transformative phase, especially because most school leaders seem not to be prepared for a new managerial responsibility, i.e., verifying whether classroom activities are goal effective and goal efficient. This logically implies that the school principal is expected to intrude into classrooms, which up to now have been the Scandinavian teachers' autonomous arena. In fact, the principal will have to evaluate whether the teacher's teaching is goal-efficient or not and impose the necessary sanctions when not satisfied with the results (Nytell 1994). Neither the principals nor the teachers seem to be prepared for being exposed to the threats of external evaluations.

Funding and Privatization

Traditionally all compulsory education in Scandinavia has been tuition free. Also post-compulsory and higher education have not charged fees of any significance. For upper secondary and higher education the costs of living have been supported by the State fairly generously through loans and stipends. In reality, it is fair to say that no Scandinavian has been prevented from entering his or her preferred field of further studies because of economic reasons.

A new trend of the 1990s, has been the various initiatives for establishing private or independent schools within the region. Denmark, which has traditionally been an indisputable leader, with 7–8 percent of private schooling at the compulsory level, has, however, experienced a weak downward trend. Norway is experiencing a growing interest for private schooling at all three levels (Holmesland 1994). The previous conservative/center Swedish government (1991–93) made a fundamental change in the acts of education, in favor of independent/private schools, and introduced the voucher system. Under this system, whatever resources budgeted for education by the authorities can be used by students in whichever institution they choose to be enrolled. The students and the parents are allowed to make their own choice (Miron 1992, 1993). The number of independent schools in Sweden has shown a marked increase since 1991. After the Social Democratic Party's victory in the general elections of September 1994, the market liberal arrangements introduced by its predecessors have been maintained. In all Scandinavian countries, independent or private schools at present need to be approved by the education authorities of the country. Normally such schools will have 80–85 percent of their expenses covered by the State.

Internationalization

Internationalizing education is increasingly becoming an aim of the Scandinavian countries. Denmark, as a member of the European Union (EU), seems to have been particularly active in this area. While the country held the EU presidency in the first half of 1993, it launched the idea of "an open space for cooperation within higher education." The idea was that students should be given opportunity to attend parts of or their entire course of education, in another EU-member state. This Danish idea has become a generally accepted concept and seems to have become one of the overall objectives of the educational policy at European level (Danish Ministry 1994). The other Scandinavian states, whether joining EU as members or not, appear to be in favor of this sort of international cooperation (Norwegian Ministry 1994; Swedish Ministry 1994).

The Scandinavian countries have always been in favor of internationalization, and now the content and the structure of the countries' education systems are being analyzed and assessed to be internationally compatible. There is also a new importance associated with the exchange of students and staff with other countries outside Scandinavia. The study of foreign languages, particularly English, has been given extra stimulus, as a consequence of the recent discussions about more countries of the region joining EU.[2]

DISCUSSION

At the same time as a new market-oriented and neo-liberal/conservative profile of curriculum and structure of educational systems emerges in Scandinavia, it is also clear that the governments are concerned with keeping up the language of traditional social democratic progressivism in their presentation of educational policies for the future. There will be equal access to education and training for all, independent of sex, ethnic origin, geographical location or social background. Common values and culture will be the basis for the education of all. In the Norwegian UNESCO report, it is even maintained explicitly that secondary education must avoid class distinctions (Norwegian Ministry 1994:22). Expansion is seen as important because education will become accessible to more people. In general, the welfare state principles of education are to be maintained.

The most clear rationale for the bridge between the former social democratic policy of solidarity and the recent adaptation to an international market and competitive situation is expressed on the Norwegian side by the Labor government's new slogan: "Quality of Equality" (Norwegian Ministry 1994: 20). By improving the education policy for an individual's attainment of relevant competence and the collective competence of value for the economic policies of the country, the educational policy itself is seen as a crucial instrument for maintaining the welfare state and, thus, coming full circle, being able to offer equal education for all.

Is it possible to achieve high-quality equality at the same time? Or, do we face an educational paradox? Could it be that in the means designed for attaining competitive quality, more inequality will, unavoidably, be created in the content and structure of Scandinavian education? Educational consequences of the new global market economy ideology seem to be that more people shall learn traditional school subjects more effectively and more efficiently than before through management by objectives, evaluation, and accountability.

Even though the general impression of the Scandinavian education scene at the beginning of the 1990s is an attempt at "quality of equality," there are some interesting variations between the countries. The most clear expression of a rather complete change to a market-economy based educational policy is found in Sweden (Miron 1993). In the past few years, the conservative educational policy leadership carried out extensive changes with the concepts of quality and competition as main guidelines. This policy seems to be accepted and followed by the recently appointed social democratic government. What the conservatives found previously to be social democratic equality rhetoric in legal and curriculum documents now has been more or less removed in favor of a pure quality-inspired vocabulary. When the social democrats have chosen to maintain these new educational principles, the most obvious reason seems to be the difficult financial situation of the country as a whole. Sweden needs competitive quality of education as a strategy in order to retain its economic force.

While Sweden is moving towards the introduction of market-forces in education, Denmark, which was the first Scandinavian country to implement the new ideological signals, also seems to be the first one emitting signals towards some shifts, i.e., a return to more humanistic and process-oriented principles in pedagogy. In Denmark these alternatives came after a change of government in 1993: a social democratic-led coalition has a minister of education from the radical-center party. He has already given several signals of educational shifts, indicating an extended concept of quality of education, where quality is to include more than high achievements in traditional academic subjects. A good learning environment is again seen as important in relation to quality. The teacher trade unions have expressed satisfaction with this change. At the same time, it remains to be seen if these announced changes are much more than temporary tributes in order to highlight the radical and professional groups' indignation about ten years of tough market orientation in Danish education. It remains to be seen also whether the Danish development is a strategical adaptation to mainstream or a signal of a more profound reaction against continental academic traditions and market economy-based quality.

The other Scandinavian countries—Finland, Iceland, and Norway—have experienced less dramatically expressed influence from market economy ideology within education. All three are small, traditionally very egalitarian and with a longer distance to mainland Europe than their two bigger brothers. Common for them are considerable efforts to make the education policy efficient in their international competition. Finland and Iceland have governments based on center coalitions, while Norway has a pure social democratic government based on a minority support in Parliament. Norway seems to be the country most clearly sticking to the social democratic aims and values of the past. At the same time the back-to-basics movement is clearly present, as is the principle of education as an instrument to make the country internationally competitive. Like Denmark, Norway has also had an exceptional educational policy entrepreneur as minister of education. During his term (until the end of 1995), he had considerable success in rapidly reforming all three levels of the education system. The minister, Mr. Hernes, is by training a professor of sociology, with a particular interest in the sociology and economics of education (Hernes 1975).

CONCLUSIONS

Summing up what has been presented and discussed about Scandinavian educational policies of the 1990s, it seems reasonable to state that a clear change towards a neo-liberalist market economy has occurred. Moreover, the aim of keeping up welfare state educational traditions and values is clearly stated. The content of the curricula is to a considerable degree turning back to basics and international, mostly western-European, academic standards of quality. The change is motivated by a desire to increase the competitive power of the country through academic achievement. Enrollment is being increased at both secondary and tertiary levels, a phenomenon motivated both by a need to utilize the total intelligence of the country and by referring to traditional equality aims for education. There is nothing particularly new in the understanding and practice of the pedagogy challenges of more academic subjects for all and of retention of the whole youth cohort for more years within the education system. Responsibility for the implementation of the curricula has been decentralized and, at the same time, an intensified central control has emerged through streamlining a system of management by objectives, external evaluation, and accountability. There are no significant signs of efforts to professionalize the teachers and school leaders to achieve "quality of equality." The teaching profession is, in general, reluctant or negative about the market-oriented reforms. The members of the profession seem not to be particularly preoccupied with the pedagogical challenges; instead, they are worried about their salaries, working conditions and classroom autonomy.

Scandinavian education should see more differentiation, more privatization and a return to more traditional pedagogy. A rational curriculum code of the 1990s is expected to emerge. Education may be seen as the optimal competence-producing strategy for the nation's trade and industry. The Marxist-based analysis from the 1960s and 1970s of the qualification needs of modern capitalism may prove to be more relevant than one might have expected a few years ago (Masuch 1972).

At the same time as the traditional social democratic aims and values are restated, the actual development of Scandinavian schooling should resemble that of the United States. There may be a deterioration of some public schools, as an "inner-city problem," and an emerging market for private schooling. In private schooling, quality will most likely have as criteria high achievements in, first, the subjects of value for business and technology sectors of society, and, second, the traditional liberal education subjects. For both the public and private schooling's pedagogy, there may be a return to more instrumental or, to use the Freirian term, "bank-pedagogy." The courageous progressivist attempt of Scandinavia and North America to develop a concept of schooling—different from the classical Greek heritage and aimed at making the school a meaningful place for all, independent of the students' socio-cultural and academic background—may have now lost its impulse in relation to what modern economic development and markets are demanding.

At this point one should not be tempted to make assertions but restrain comments to mere suppositions. The first is that functional schooling in modern capitalism seems destined to be unequal. The second is that what most people conceive as functional and attractive schooling may not be cognitively attainable by the majority. The third is that Scandinavian education is being pushed by opposite forces and is oscillating like a pendulum between quality and equality.

NOTES

1. This is a revised version of a chapter in W.K. Cummings and N. McGinn, eds., *Handbook of Education and Development: Preparing Schools, Students and Nations for the Twenty-First Century* (Oxford: Pergamon, 1997).

2. By November 30, 1994, referendums in Finland and Sweden voted "yes" to joining the EU, while Norway voted "no."

REFERENCES

Arnove, R.F., Altbach, P.G., and Kelly, G.P., eds. 1992. *Emergent Issues in Education. Comparative Perspectives.* Albany: State University of New York Press.

Aubert, V. 1956. "Lærernes holdning till sin yrkesrolle og oppdragelsesspørsmål" (The Teachers' Attitude Towards Their Professional Role and Education Topics), in *Norsk Pedagogisk Tidsskrift* nr. 3, Oslo.

Chinapah, V., ed. 1992. *Evaluation of Higher Education in a Changing Europe.* Stockholm: The Swedish UNESCO series no. 2.

Danish Ministry of Education. 1994. *Development of Education 1992- 1994. National Report of Denmark to the 44th UNESCO International Conference of Education,* Copenhagen.

Finnish Ministry of Education. 1994. *Development of Education 1992-1994. National Report of Finland to the 44th UNESCO International Conference of Education*, Helsinki, 1994.

Hernes, G. 1975. *Om ulikhetens reproduksjon* (About the Reproduction of Inequality). Copenhagen: Christian Ejlers Forlag.

Holmesland, I. da Silva. 1994. *Private and Public Schools: A Comparison Between Norway and Brazil.* Oslo: The ELI-Group, University of Oslo.

Icelandic Ministry of Education. 1994. *EURODICE Report 1994.* Reykjavik.

Illeris, K. 1981. *Modkvalifiseringens pædagogik* (Resistance Education). Copenhagen: Unge Paedagoger.

Kozma, T. 1992. "The Neo-Conservative Paradigm: Recent Changes in Eastern Europe" In *Emergent Issues in Education. Comparative Perspectives*, eds. R.F. Arnove, P.G. Altbach, and G.P. Kelly.Albany: State University of New York Press.

Lauglo, J. 1995. "Populism and Education in Norway." *Comparative Education Review*, 39, no. 3.

Lauvdal, T. 1994. *Pedagogikk, politikk og byråkrati* (Education, Politics and Bureaucracy). Doctoral thesis. Trondheim: University of Trondheim.

Masuch, M. 1972. *The Political Economy of Education.* Hamburg: Rowohlt (Politische Oekonomie der Aussbildung).

Miron, G., ed. 1992. *Towards Free Choice and Market-Oriented Schools. Problems and Promises.* Stockholm: Institute of International Education, Stockholm University and the National Agency for Education.

Miron, G. 1993. *Choice and the Use of Market Forces in Schooling: Swedish Education Reforms for the 1990s.* Stockholm: Institute of International Education, Stockholm University.

Norwegian Ministry of Education. 1987. *Mønsterplan for grunnskolen* (National Curriculum for the Primary and Lower Secondary School). Oslo.

Norwegian Ministry of Education. 1993. *Laereplan for grunn- og videregaaende skole* (National Curriculum for the Primary and Secondary School). Oslo.

Norwegian Ministry of Education. 1994. *The Development of Education 1992– 94. National Report to UNESCO's 44th International Conference on Education.* Oslo.

Nytell, U. 1994. *Govern or To Be Governed? A Study of School Leaders' Work and Working Conditions* (Doctoral thesis). Uppsala Studies in Education 58. Uppsala: Uppsala University.

Rydin, S.A. 1991. *Det amerikanske utdanningssystem. Et desentralisert system i kontinuerlig krise* (The American Education System. A Decentralized

System in Continuous Crisis). Advanced Degree Thesis/Cand.Polit. ELI Report. Oslo: Faculty of Social Science, University of Oslo.

Slagstad, R. 1994. "Arbeiderpartistaten som skolestat," in *Nytt Norsk Tidsskrift* nr. 3-4 (The Labor Party State as Education State). Oslo: University Press.

Swedish Ministry of Education. 1994. *The Development of Education. National Report from Sweden, to UNESCO's 44th International Conference on Education, 1994.* Stockholm.

Telhaug, A.O., and Tønnessen R.Th. 1992. *Dansk utdanningspolitikk under Bertel Haarder 1982-92. Nyliberalistisk og nykonservativ skoletenkning* (Danish Education Policies under Bertel Haarder 1982-92. Neo-Liberal and Neo-Conservative Education Thinking). Oslo: University Press.

Tjeldvoll, A. 1992. "Attempts to Introduce Evaluation of Higher Education and Research in Norway." In *Evaluation of Higher Education in a Changing Europe,* ed. V. Chinapah. Stockholm: The Swedish UNESCO series no. 2.

Tjeldvoll, A., ed. 1992. *Education in East/Central Europe: Report from the Oslo Conference.* Buffalo: Comparative Education Center, SUNY, Buffalo.

Todd, E.M. 1991. *England's Education Policy.* Advanced Degree Thesis/Cand.Polit. Oslo: Faculty of Social Science, University of Oslo.

Wilenski, H. 1964-65. "The Professionalization of Everyone?" *American Journal of Sociology* 70.

CHAPTER 2

Populism and Education in Norway[1]
Jon Lauglo

INTRODUCTION

This article argues that the Norwegian variety of populism has had an enduring influence on the evolution of education in that country. Attempts in comparative education to explore the educational implications of populism have been scant, one reason being that populism often takes the form of short-term protest movements, which rarely have left any enduring stamp on education. In addition, populist ideas have been notably weak in shaping the major "metropolitan" systems of education that have exerted great international influence (although some populist influence is evident in the United States). Populism's conceptual difficulties and its diverse expressions are other reasons for its neglect in comparative analysis. That populist movements themselves often do not acknowledge the label of populism, reflects this diversity.

Although there is a risk of exaggerating the force of tradition, Margaret Scotford Archer reminds us that examining the early formative period of a national system of education is crucial for understanding its evolution.[2] Education shows great inertia once it has become established as a system, with a distribution of authority and with staff trained to follow in the footsteps of those already in place.

THE CONCEPT OF POPULISM

"Populism" is used in comparative analysis to reveal similarities among political and cultural movements, although many "populists" are reluctant to be labeled as such because of a pejorative connotation often associated with the term.[3] Populists in North America are an exception. Here, the term is a valued attribute and acknowledged by many of those—on both the political left and right—to whom it is applied.[4]

In negative terms, populism—often taking the form of protest movements in the name of the cultural, economic, and political values and beliefs of ordinary people—is a reaction against elites. In "positive" terms, populism represents a direct and local democracy that seeks to empower ordinary people. Edward Shils defines populism as subscribing to the principle that the "will of the people" should be supreme and that there should be a "direct" relationship between people and leadership.[5] Moreover, since the mid-nineteenth century, populist movements have commonly been a defensive reaction against the adverse effects of modernization. When populist movements do offer a vision of the future, they seek to give new value and meaning to the culture and community identities of ordinary people.[6] The specific goals of populist movements vary widely, however, depending on the circumstances in which these movements emerge.

Do populist movements seek to clip the wings of a moneyed oligarchy (the banks or railroads) in order to safeguard the interests of an entrepreneurial and "individualistic" farming class, as in the historical case of North American populism?[7] Do they take the form of a pilgrimage "to the people" among intellectuals who propose an anticapitalist and local "communalist" form of economic development, as in the case of the *narodnichestvo* movement in Russia during the 1870s?[8] Do they react against large-scale landed estates and seek to create a freeholding yeomanry, as in the case of Eastern European "peasantist" movements early in this century?[9] Do they turn on foreign capital and its compradors, as in the case of Latin America? Do they acquire a fascist character and turn against minorities at home and against neighbors abroad?[10] Do they promote a democratic form of "folk nationalism" at peace with a world perceived as "a community of nations"? Or do they seek to cut down to size and call to more direct account the establishment of professionals and bureaucrats in a democratically constituted welfare state, as in the current case of rightist populist politics in some countries? Given these varied expressions, one's sympathy for or antipathy toward populism will be contingent on the ingredients of any particular case.

Detractors argue that populist politics offers simplistic solutions to complex issues, at the expense of careful and responsible consideration of what can be achieved when cost is taken into account. Those who today use "populism" pejoratively act in the tradition of those ancient Greek critics of direct democracy who changed the interpretation of "demagogue" from a teacher of the people to someone who misguides the people by manipulating their emotions. Plato thought that direct democracy—votes in the assembly of all citizens within a small city-state—was a flawed governmental form because the populace would too easily be manipulated by demagogues and turn against a Socrates. Then, as now, critics feared how easily charismatic leaders could misguide the populace.

Deeply embedded in European languages are classical terms, laden with positive value, whose etymology reveals a world view that identifies political and cultural achievements with an urban elite. From the Latin city—*civitas*—we have the terms "civilization," "citizen," "civil," and "civic." From the Greek *polis* come "politics," "policy," and "police." In English, even the terms for local government ("municipality" and "township") have an urban etymology. In addition, Europe's main ideologies of modernization—rationalism, liberalism, and socialism—also viewed the cities from which they emerged as the most progressive part of society and in contrast to a sleepy and less developed hinterland. Angus Stewart argues that since populism is a response to the problems posed by modernization and its consequences, it represents the tension between metropolis and the province.[11] Thus, populism would spring from both the tension between more modernized countries and less modernized ones and the tension between more and less modernized parts of the same country. In this sense, populism tends to be a political response of the rural periphery to adverse effects of social change emanating from the center.[12]

In a populist view, ordinary people are considered the main carriers of society's cultural values and national identity. This is implied in the double meaning of the Latin *populus*, from which the word "populism" is derived. On the one hand, the word refers to an organic national group united by a shared language, belief system, and historical experience. On the other hand, it also denotes a distinction between the common people and a small patrician elite or upper class, with each group aware of its separateness. "Common" also has a double meaning: "ordinary" as well as "shared." Thus, *populus* has connotations of the populace being the carrier of nationhood, with a strong sense of *gemeinschaft*, and being set apart from a narrow elite. This dichotomous model may fit a simple division of labor, as in those agrarian societies where the people derive their livelihood from manual labor and large differences based on property ownership and formal education are absent.

The classical concept of direct democracy is echoed in modern populist ideas of government, such as Jean-Jacques Rousseau's argument that all citizens should meet to decide what is best for the community and then enact appropriate laws, or Abraham Lincoln's much-celebrated phrase "government of the people, by the people, for the people."[13] The historical importance of populism as a democratic political force probably peaked during struggles to replace leaders who inherited power or only acquired the consent of an elite electorate—before democratic representative government became securely institutionalized on the basis of a franchise that included all adults.

Contemporary industrialized societies have become so economically differentiated that a simple dichotomy between the people and an elite no longer suffices, however, and politics have been based on a universal franchise for generations. Nevertheless, populism has not disappeared as a political force. What one sees in such societies is a distinctly conservative form of populism that combines the reassertion of traditional values and identities (e.g., antiabortion movements, religious revivalism, and anti-immigration sentiment) with general disillusionment about the welfare state. This kind of populism has important consequences for education because it attacks the twin buffers that have sheltered the autonomy of educational professionals from local intrusion: deference to their professional expertise and their bureaucratic accountability to a centralist state.

Donald MacRae argues that populist movements share an implied theory of personality that suggests that "the division of labor in society fragments the human character."[14] This view, which incorporates elements from the works of Rousseau and J.G. Herder, also influenced Karl Marx's theory of alienation and his utopian vision of a communist society. Populism, however, views the assembly line and modern bureaucratic organization with equal hostility. Populist ideas of economic advancement stress the rural community, craft workshops, cooperative forms, production for local markets, and national self-sufficiency rather than urban industry producing for international markets.[15] But even while populism and socialism may differ in their attitudes toward bureaucracy, both attack unregulated capitalism and "unearned" income from speculation or absentee landownership.[16]

"Folk " is not tantamount to social class, however. Herein lies a key distinction between populism and socialism. Social class is international and transcends different folks. Conversely, within a given state, "folk" is a more inclusive concept than that of class. Populism stresses the shared particularistic cultural identity of a folk, while socialism is more universalistic, having been shaped by Christianity, egalitarian ideas from the French Enlightenment, and Marxism. Populism reacts radically against the cultural and political hegemony of an upper class, but it is also conservative in how it values the way of life among ordinary folk and their beliefs and values. Socialism is rationalistic, with faith that science and specialized expertise can promote social reconstruction. Populism, on the other hand, has historically been legitimated by the Romantic movement—especially national Romanticism—rather than rationalism. It stresses the personalism of *gemeinschaft* rather than impersonal *gesellschaft*— emotions and identity rather than universalistic reason.[17] Socialism is cosmopolitan and internationalist. Conversely, populism implies a folk-based concept of nationalism—but not a nationalism based on the exploits of an upper class. Characteristically, the United States exhibits historical and regional links between populism and isolationist foreign policy.

A populist view, with its emphasis on *gemeinschaft,* necessarily implies a strong awareness of boundaries between outsiders and insiders. In this sense the identity of a tribe is a primordial form of populism. Tribal leaders are within the folk group, but an elite imposed by conquest would be outside the boundary of the people.[18] In such a dichotomized model of society, nonelite minority groups considered cultural outsiders to the common people are easily marginalized and vulnerable to discrimination, especially if they are perceived as handmaidens of a resented elite. The history of decolonialization is replete with examples of minorities marginalized in this manner, such as those of Asian origin in East Africa. Alternatively, if minorities pose no threat and if the prevailing belief system so ordains, they may be seen as other peoples—to be tolerated but still cultural outsiders. Thus, while populism celebrates the importance of ordinary folk and their rights and culture, it is hardly a view of society that eases acceptance of immigrants. To be accepted, immigrants need to become assimilated into the culture they are joining, but this is no easy task when folk identity is rooted in shared history. The United States presents an exception to this general rule, as the nation's moving frontier and the myth of shared identity itself stressed the theme of leaving old identities behind—of "settling" and being assimilated.

Another noteworthy aspect of populism involves leadership. Despite an idealization of the right of ordinary people directly to rule themselves, tension exists between this localist, decentralist tendency and the role that charismatic leadership typically has in populist movements.[19] Charismatic leadership is legitimated by loyalty to an individual—a condition that can greatly concentrate power in a leader's hands, rather than genuinely empower ordinary people. Modern history offers many examples in which the cult of personality has combined with populist rhetoric—caudilloism, fascism, Maoism, and the Kim Il Sungs and the Ayatollah Khomeinis of the world.

It remains a task for political theory to differentiate among different forms of populism and to identify conditions that lead to them.[20] One might hypothesize that for populism to be democratic localism, its leadership must be rooted in a local civil society marked by popular civic participation. Conversely, when the people can be mobilized as a "disposable mass," populism can slide into an oppressive form of centralism in which leaders manipulate people's emotions and create a "tyranny of the majority"—a common fear among both liberal and conservative critics of populism.[21]

Local social structure also plays a key role in shaping the nature of populist movements. In a comparative study of agrarian structure and the emergence of rural politics in Scandinavia, Øyvind Østerud concludes that agrarian politics during the mid-nineteenth century in Norway—unlike Denmark and Sweden—became a communalist defense of peasanthood against intrusion from the outside.[22] He argues that this reflected the distinctly Norwegian situation of a relatively independent yeomanry confronted by a bourgeois-bureaucratic elite outside their local community rather than a local landholding aristocracy.

The kinds of philosophy that have most often been associated with populism are ones that celebrate folk identity (Herder) or direct democracy (Rousseau) or that blur the Platonist distinction between theory and practice (Dewey's Pragmatist epistemology). But since a populist view of the world denies claims to superior judgment or refinement by an intelligentsia, it is not especially hospitable to philosophy and can even fan anti-intellectualism.[23] Nevertheless, intellectuals often play leadership roles in populist movements, especially cultural ones, or they try to create popular movements without achieving any significant following from ordinary folk, as in the case of the Russian *narodniki* in the 1870s. Typically, cultural populism attempts in part to uplift the people to higher valuations, with intellectuals frequently involved in such efforts to reconstruct a high culture that is close to the people and dignifies their condition. But such movements that seek to uplift—including language revivals, religious revivals and temperance movements—contrast with the high culture of an aloof elite. Among the strains of Christianity, the more radical forms of Protestantism have most clearly prepared the ground for egalitarianism by stressing an emotionally charged direct relation of man to God and seeking to extend the political rights of ordinary people. In England, for example, both the Liberal and Labor parties can trace their roots to the Non-conformist chapels and the seventeenth-century Puritan rebellion against the king and established Church.[24] It is important to note, however, that cultural populism militates not only against the high culture of an establishment but also against the remoteness of avant-garde cultural radicalism.

The educational implications of cultural populism reflect these tendencies, as neither classical languages nor modern abstract art have any place among its educational ideals. Instead, native language, literature, and historiography that celebrate pupils' own cultural roots are stressed. Frequently, religion also has been important to a populist concept of valued culture as well as practical craft skills. Populism views the home, the community, and civic or cultural institutions as important educational arenas for passing on fundamental values, with schools playing a supplementary role.

POPULIST TRAITS IN NORWEGIAN SOCIETY

In the late 1960s and early 1970s, intellectuals from the Socialist Left Party and the left wing of the agrarian party *Senterpartiet* attempted to inject *populisme* into Norwegian political debate, a term introduced in a 1966 book by Ottar Brox on the development of Northern Norway.[25] At that time, *populisme* meant defense of small communities and their way of life, participatory democracy, rejection of the market forces of urban industrial capitalism, opposition to Norwegian membership in the European Common Market, and general opposition to technocratic expertise. Today, however, this term is used more often in the mass media as a pejorative term by those who consider it the irresponsible politics of playing to the gallery. The Norwegian mass media now use the term mostly to describe attacks on the welfare state and illiberal strains that appeal to folk nationalism in formerly Communist countries.

Yet the national myth of Norway is profoundly populist. The national anthem by the poet Bjørnstjerne Bjørnson, for example, is replete with populist imagery—the rugged coast rising above the sea, the scattered homesteads of ordinary people, love of forebears, dreams inspired by ancient sagas. Another Bjørnson song declares: "Norway, Norway—homesteads and cottages but no castles." Such songs that celebrate sturdy self-sufficiency were staple fare in the primary schools a generation ago. The resistance to the German occupiers during World War II deepened this "folk-in-rugged-nature" nationalism, cleansed it of fascist-like tendencies, and led the labor movement to embrace nationalist symbolism rather more firmly than before.

In this same vein, the history of Norwegian sports has a distinct orientation toward the wilderness, although the pioneers of sport came from the urban bourgeoisie. The exploits of F. Nansen in the Arctic and R. Amundsen in the Antarctic became fused with the political project of achieving complete national independence, and the athletic ideal that they propagated centered on the conquest of rugged winter nature. Cross-country skiing, for example, became important to the Norwegian national identity as both athletic achievement and mass leisure.[26] The simple lumberjack coming in from the backwoods to win glory on the ski tracks represents a national cultural hero. In fact, Gunnar Skirbekk has argued that the valuation of "life in nature" has become an existential value rather than a mere preference in sports or leisure.[27] Østerud suggests that while urbanization and cultural internationalization have now eroded much of this distinctly Norwegian cultural identity, the "existence in nature" may help to explain the strength of the environmental movement in Norway—which has retained more territory unspoiled by pollution than any other European country.[28] During holidays Norwegians trek in great numbers to cabins in the mountains, the valleys, and along the coast, with the ideal location not in some quaint village (as in France or England) but out of eyesight from other dwellings as most people are few generations removed from the farm or fishing boat.

Norway is itself a country on the European periphery. As S. Rokkan has observed, the Norwegian political system has focused on the cultural and economic interests of the country's rural districts and more remote parts to a degree that greatly exceeds their population base.[29] It is no accident that scepticism is so strong in Norway of joining the European Union because this opposition feeds both on populist traditions and on socialist anticapitalism. One would infer that populist sentiments similarly were important determinants of the recent vote in the German-speaking parts of Switzerland against closer economic cooperation with the European Union.[30]

Populist politics stresses the right of ordinary people to exert power over public institutions, including schools. Such influence can be achieved through plebiscites by direct election of local public servants, or, as in the case of Norway, by the use of small units of local government that are close to the community. Norwegian units of elective local government used to coincide with parishes, and even with a major amalgamation of *kommuner* during the 1960s, their median population today is only 4,352.

Nineteenth-century Norwegian populism, which sought to reduce the power and cultural authority of the country's upper class and civil service, had two cultural strains: a more secular variety that promoted "national awakening" based on folk culture and local self government, and a low-church religious revival of Pietist Lutheranism.

The former—like the Russian *narodnichestvo* movement—was in many respects a creation of populist radicalism among intellectuals. From the long list of authors and poets in this tradition, the most prominent include Henrik Wergeland, Ivaar Aasen, Aasmund Olavsson Vinje, Arne Garborg, and Bjørnson. Yet even though this cultural populism upheld rural folk and their way of life as carriers of Norwegian national identity, it still looked abroad for ideas—especially to N.F.S. Grundtvig in Denmark (who was influenced by Herder) and J.G. Fichte in Germany. Grundtvig did much to introduce *folkelig* as a valued concept into Nordic political and cultural terminology.[31] In this process, the earlier notion of *almue* (commoners) came to be replaced by the concept of *folk*, which had precisely the double connotation of "people" noted earlier: both ordinary people and nation.[32] These became the acknowledged labels in Norway and the other Scandinavian countries of phenomena described here as populist.[33]

Ironically, these populist intellectuals drew inspiration from literature and social thought in the very countries whose historical influence on Norwegian high culture they sought to reduce—a parallel to the more recent independence movements in developing countries. Populism and a movement for national independence also were entwined in Norway, and their combination led in 1905 to separation from a monarchical union with Sweden that had been imposed in 1814.

Pietism, which had been originally imported from Germany by 1700, resurfaced in the early nineteenth century as a folk movement led by the lay preacher Hans Nielsen Hauge against the rationalist ideas of the Enlightenment prevailing in the established church. Although the movement was repressed, Pietism later became the main stream within the Lutheran state church and a consistent force for local lay influence. This strain of Pietism fed into agrarian politics, in competition with the national Romanticism and the more humanist Pietism of the Grundtvigian folk high schools. Religious anti-establishmentarianism is less evident in the rise of the Norwegian labor movement during the twentieth century, but here too there are little-studied connections with dissent outside the state church, especially the Methodist chapels in some towns.

When Denmark was forced to cede Norway to Sweden as part of the settlement after the Napoleonic wars, an 1814 constitutional assembly in Norway attempted to preempt incorporation into the kingdom of Sweden by declaring independence. Although Norway had to submit to a monarchical union with Sweden, independence was largely achieved in other respects. The 1814 constitution extended the franchise to all adult male owners of land, creating a framework that enabled even small-scale yeoman farmers to transform themselves from subjects to citizens later in the nineteenth century. The history taught in schools has stressed that an elite who could frame such a constitution must have been unusually people-oriented in their patriotism to begin with.[34]

The demand by yeomen for autonomy in their local community was the impetus behind the 1837 act that introduced elected local government. The main task for local government initially was to assume from the clergy the responsibility for establishing and operating local elementary schools. Eventually, agrarian politicians joined urban and more liberal allies to form Venstre, the party of the Left that gained power in 1884 and forced the Swedish-Norwegian king to institute a parliamentary form of government. While the agrarian parliamentarians were loath to use state finance for academic schools, with their classical subjects and upper-class clientele, they favored support to adult education (the folk high schools) catering to youth from popular backgrounds.[35]

Venstre extended the franchise, strengthened local government, increased local lay influence in church affairs, and promoted language reconstruction (New Norse) along the lines of rural dialects. It was also the party of a rising folk nationalism which culminated in separation from the dual monarchy with Sweden in 1905. Its political heartland was in the rural areas, in contrast to the more urban bourgeois radical-liberal parties that took the early lead in extending the franchise in England, France, and Germany. The coming together of folk nationalism, the politics of rural interest groups, and advancement of democratic political rights gave Norwegian nationalism a distinctly rural and "democratic" orientation.

It is interesting to note that the Labor Party, which has dominated Norwegian politics since the 1930s, also has been strong among smallholders and fishermen in the rural periphery. The party's strength has owed much to the coalition of these groups and industrial workers, and its first parliamentary representatives came from fisherman-smallholder constituencies in the north rather than industrial towns. Although educational policies in the twentieth century have been shaped mainly by the Labor Party, support from rural-based centrist parties that can be traced back to Venstre also has been very important. The system's distinctive features can be traced to the foundation laid in earlier years by Venstre, to continued support from Venstre's successor parties, and to the considerable infusion into the Labor Party's own policies. Compared to social democratic parties in the main Western European countries, the Norwegian Labor Party has been a more determined advocate of the common school, more sceptical of purely "academic" secondary education, and more attuned to rural interests. Admittedly, the Labor Party has been more statist than the country's centrist parties, but they all have shared a trend of looking for ways to reduce the cultural gap between school knowledge and ordinary people and also to organize schools so as to make them more accessible socially and geographically.

Compared to Venstre and its centrist successors, Norwegian social democracy has been more concerned with urban conditions and has shown greater receptivity to industrial development while according a key role to the state in efforts to make society more modern and egalitarian. The role of intellectuals typically differs between populist and social democratic movements. In the former their role in cultural revival is more visible, while in the latter their function as technocratic experts—tools in the service of society—is more evident.[36]

In both France and Prussia during the nineteenth century, rural teachers seem to have gained local social standing by being part of the central government's civil service, but they were modernizing agents of the state, rather than spokesmen of any rural populist culture. Conversely, strong control of education by local school boards in the United States placed teachers in a dependent position, especially in small towns and rural areas as late as the early 1960s. Although rural populist politics never developed in England during the nineteenth century, schools emerged by local and voluntary initiatives, and it was in village England that teachers found themselves most subservient to the vicar and squire.

In Norway, however, many of those who made their mark in rural politics were school teachers cum deacons/cantors (*kirkesanger, klokker*) in the churches of their home parishes. They were also frequently farmers on the side.[37] The stereotype of teachers, after they became trained, is of men playing an active role in local public life, and many of the dominant personalities in agrarian populist politics were farmers cum teachers or simply teachers. Farms were too small throughout most of Norway to sustain any gentry class so wealthy that it would not respect the teacher's greater learning. It is probably in such areas that teachers played their most important role as local activists for the Venstre party. In the 1950s, when Venstre had been reduced to one of several centrist parties, school teachers remained greatly overrepresented in its ranks.[38]

The period from 1880 to 1920 was the golden age of the teacher cum Venstre politician, whose knowledge gave him/her scarce, politically important skills in a society where cultural issues were significant: nationalism, the New Norse language revival, political rights, lay control of churches, and the temperance movement. In many areas teachers stood out as the most educated persons of popular origins, having advanced through the limited educational avenues available to gifted farm youth—the folk high schools and the teachers' seminaries. A number of well-known authors have been primary school teachers, many of whom became involved in writing local history. These rural teachers were usually males, and although female teachers were gradually added, this occurred without driving males from primary school teaching. Women teachers came from more urban and higher social backgrounds, and unlike the United Kingdom and the United States, females did not dominate primary school teaching in Norway until the 1970s.

During World War II the reputation of teachers was again boosted by their early organized stand against Nazi indoctrination in the schools. It could be that the respect and autonomy that Norwegian teachers have enjoyed owe more to their historical role in public life than any public recognition of their professional expertise. Although their reputation of high idealism is now gone, their historical role undoubtedly helped to prepare the ground for extending their school—the primary school—at the expense of academic secondary schooling. It is also likely that their strong record of public involvement strengthened union advocacy efforts on their behalf.

POPULIST FEATURES IN NORWEGIAN EDUCATION

A key feature that distinguishes Norwegian educational enrollment patterns and expenditures from those of other industrialized countries is the emphasis given to primary and lower secondary schools. A 1987 report by Kjell Eide (the Norwegian Ministry of Education's scientific adviser) showed that among countries that belong to the Organization for Economic Cooperation and Development (OECD), Norway and Sweden devote a higher proportion of expenditures to these levels of education than other countries.[39] As a result, costs per pupil in basic education are distinctly high in Norway. At the same time, public expenditures per student in higher education were lower in Norway than in nearly all other OECD countries studied by Eide during the late 1980s. The high-priority basic schooling starts at a late age, however, as Norway lags behind other OECD countries in enrollment rates for children age six and below.[40] As for higher education, Norwegian enrollment rates are low compared to other OECD countries.

Thus, Norway is above all the country of the basic school, where students start at age seven and receive a fairly uniform education up to

age sixteen.[41] State policies have long sought to compensate for
geographical inequalities in the local resource base available for
financing education. Expenditures per pupil for primary and lower
secondary education are much higher in thinly settled areas than in
larger towns, and there are many small schools at this level. One in six
primary schools (ages seven to twelve) has fewer than 20 pupils, with a
mode size interval of 50-199 pupils. At the lower secondary level (ages
thirteen to sixteen), one in three schools has fewer than 200 pupils, with
a mode of 200-299 pupils.[42] The small classes in such schools meant
that each full-time-equivalent teacher in the basic schools averaged
only 10 pupils in 1989. Keeping schools within reach of all children
and adolescents in thinly settled areas is expensive, as the unit recurrent
cost in remote schools (most of it teachers' pay) is often three times that
of larger schools. Not all sparsely populated countries choose to expend
so many resources in order to provide schools close to homes in the
rural periphery.

A Strong Common School and a Weak Academic School Tradition

Like other Lutheran countries, Norway introduced mass schooling
early. Influenced by the Pietist movement within Lutheranism, an
educational ordinance was issued in 1739. It required a modicum of
schooling, in that confirmation was made compulsory and children
were required to have attended school before they could be
confirmed.[43] It also ordained that the school be a common school that
gathered all children without regard to their parents' status. During the
first half of the nineteenth century, secular ideas about the need for
educating the masses added their weight to the cause of schooling for
all. The Education Act of 1827 was a legislative milestone that sought
more firmly to establish both compulsory provisions and attendance.[44]
It is noteworthy that this legislation applied only to rural areas. Similar
provisions for children in towns were not enacted until 1848.

By the late nineteenth century, elementary schools had become
recognized as preparatory for further schooling, even if only a minute
proportion of youth entered secondary schools. By 1920, completing
primary school (ages seven to fourteen) became the only route into
state-subsidized secondary schools. Thus, the extension of common
education from age fourteen to age sixteen during the late 1950s built
on a long tradition. This contrasts with policies in other European

countries, where selection to academic secondary school at age ten or eleven prevailed at least into the 1950s. It is also likely that the early development of a common school in Norway softened political and professional resistance in the 1960s to mixed-ability teaching in the new upper stage (ages thirteen to sixteen) of basic education.

A common school and curriculum for all local children agree with the populist concept of a culturally unified community of ordinary people. Populist sentiments oppose the early creaming off of outstanding pupils into elite schools that would educate a few select children of popular origins away from their home and community. It is characteristic of Norwegian education that the *Nordahl Rolfsens lesebok*—the reader used for generations as the main textbook in primary schools—was culturally oriented toward rural communities through its selections of poetry and fiction by nationally known authors and from folk tales.

The teaching of Latin and Greek represents another area in which Norwegian education is distinct. Elsewhere in Europe, these remained key subjects in academic secondary education even after World War II, but in Norway they had lost ground to modern subjects much sooner. As early as 1869 science and modern languages became alternatives to classics in Norwegian academic secondary schools, and at the high tide of populist politics, after 1884, classical languages were nearly banished because they were considered antithetical to Norwegian culture. Classical subjects survived only in one line of specialization in the upper secondary schools, with science and modern languages replacing them as the dominant specialties among students preparing for the university. In 1914 a Norse line was also introduced as an alternative to Latin and Greek, stressing national history and literature and the old Norse of medieval times.

Norwegian secondary schools have long been less exclusively geared to university entry than their European counterparts. Even in the 1960s, before the massive expansion in upper secondary schooling, Norway stood out because so many upper secondary school drop-outs chose forms of further education other than universities. Teachers' colleges and engineering schools were more select in their entry requirements than university arts and science faculties, for example. Since the 1960s, secondary schools have moved even further away from the academic type, with all compulsory subjects counting equally when students compete at age sixteen for access to upper secondary school. Mathematics is given no more weight than home economics or crafts, and optional academic subjects such as a second foreign language confer no extra selection points. In fact, vocational courses in the upper secondary school often have higher minimum entrance requirements than the general education track. In addition to school performance, work experience counts in selection to many post-secondary institutions.

The Superior Authenticity of the Vernacular

In the nineteenth century, the gap between Norway's standard written "cultivated speech" and the vernacular forms was far narrower than the distance that separated the official language and local or regional dialects in Germany, Italy, France, or Britain. But because the standard form had Danish origins, it was resented by nationalists. Thus, in 1885—when schoolchildren in Britain and France risked physical punishment for using their vernacular dialect—Norwegian teachers were instructed to adapt *their* speech to *pupils'* dialects, which they were not supposed to correct.[45] At the same time, political support grew to replace the Danish-based standard language with a Norse rooted in rural dialectics. New laws allowed each local council to decide whether New Norse or the previously standard language, which was eventually redesignated *bokmål* (book language) would be used in schools. In towns and rural areas influenced by urban culture, the *bokmål* successfully withstood the onslaught of the rural cultural populists. Although New Norse never touched the towns, it conquered much of the countryside for a time. At its peak in 1943, 42 percent of rural primary students and 34 percent of all children nationwide were instructed in New Norse. Since New Norse was more common in small schools, the percentage of schools using it was even higher—55 percent. By the late 1970s, however, usage of New Norse had steadily declined to 16 percent of primary schoolchildren, with only minor gains in recent years. However, the *bokmål* standard has assimilated much syntax and vocabulary from the vernacular over the past century.

Teachers were among the strongest supporters of New Norse. Although only 31 percent of primary students were being taught in New Norse by 1949, current research shows that 45 percent of teachers preferred New Norse themselves at that time, with a marked difference evident between older and younger teachers.[46] The New Norse advocates were in a clear majority (53 percent) among older teachers, most of whom were trained before World War II, while 69 percent of younger teachers (up to age thirty-one) preferred the *bokmål* mode. Most teachers still came from farms in 1949, and individuals from this background were the strongest (56 percent) New Norse supporters. Unlike Venstre, the Labor Party with its large urban working-class constituency did not promote New Norse. But it did actively seek to adapt the *bokmål* mode toward greater vernacular forms until the late 1960s. In fact, a number of ministers of education from Labor have themselves used New Norse, which likely received more official use in the Ministry of Church and Education than in other government departments as New Norse was gaining in popularity (up to World War II) and during the early postwar decades. More recently (1976-1990), such a pattern is documented with regard to government circulars.[47]

At present, the language issue evokes less passion because it is no longer a struggle in which one mode seeks to replace the other. New Norse has failed to realize its ambition, and government attempts to further bend *bokmål* toward vernacular forms have ceased. Nevertheless, vernacular dialects have become more frequent in pop music, on the radio, and in television programs since the 1970s. An important earlier role model for the use of dialects in popular music was Alf Prøysen, a farmworker turned poet and radio troubadour, noted for his lightheartedness and irreverent irony on rural social inequality. His main theme was everyday life among poor farmworkers on rich farms—a form of rural popular culture that the labor movement would embrace much more warmly than New Norse. The use of dialects in pop music received a major boost in the wake of the successful 1972 mobilization resisting Norwegian entrance into the European Union.

For the Majority Folk: Few Historical Signs of "Education for Social Control"

The educational ideas of Grundtvig, which influenced Norwegian educators considerably in the nineteenth century, stressed the need to educate ordinary folk for responsible citizenship. At mid-century, there was also some upper-class concern about educating Norway's rural poor so as to better prepare them to withstand "radical agitation" after the Thrane movement among the rural proletariat.[48] In addition, efforts were made to strengthen schooling to safeguard the Lutheran orthodoxy of the state church after 1845, when religious dissent became officially allowed. But apart from this brief period at mid-century, there is little empirical support in Norway for the thesis that European mass education policies were driven by the desire to defuse political and religious restiveness.

Until the 1960s, however, schools were deliberately used to Norwegianize linguistic minorities—the *Same* people (Lapps) and the Finnish speaking minorities in the country's northern outskirts. Such measures were especially strong during the nationalist buildup to complete independence at the beginning of the century. Thus, Norway, too, has exhibited the historical populist impulse to impose the national culture of the majority on minorities—not to accord to them equal rights to develop their own culture.

Norwegians may be conditioned by their own struggle for independence to value the rights of other peoples to have their own states. Support for liberation movements in the Third World reflects this tradition, as does sympathy for political leaders in those newly independent countries whose policies are perceived to be democratic populist. But it is noteworthy that internationalism on behalf of subject peoples abroad is currently combined with unusually tight immigration policies at home. Attempts to devise appropriate policies for educating immigrant children have produced a particularly large amount of soul-searching. On the one hand, in an effort to avoid ghettos and promote assimilation on Norwegian terms, refugee immigrants are deliberately scattered throughout the country and there is much public concern to ensure that immigrants learn Norwegian. On the other hand, it is equally likely that the vernacular's importance in Norway's own cultural history has helped to create a receptivity among Norwegian educational theorists to the argument that immigrant children also need to master their mother tongue as a stepping stone to integration into Norwegian society. Thus, immigration has brought close to home populism's inherent educational dilemma concerning cultural pluralism, with its emphasis on cultural roots and authenticity, when one is not solely concerned with asserting the rights of one's own group.

Beware of Too Much Schooling: The Importance of Upbringing in Home and Community

The informal learning that occurs in the home, the workplace, and in the community is highly valued by populism.[49] Arguably, the most original contribution to educational theory reflecting this view is that of Erling Kristvik, who for many years was director of Volda Teachers College, right at the cradle of the New Norse movement. He also became the first professor of education at the College of Advanced Teacher Education in Trondheim, an institution that gave in-service courses to primary school teachers, especially in rural areas. Kristvik was an unusually learned and internationally well-connected scholar whose writings stand firmly in a populist tradition. Critical of both Marxist materialism and capitalist industrialization, he was skeptical of the rationalist optimism that industry, science, and urbanization would bring progress. Instead, he looked for educational ideals in the altruistic values of family life—in keeping with the folk culture of rural communities. Above all, his writings stress parenthood and education as moral upbringing.[50] Such concerns are consistent with Grundtvigian views and Lutheran educational tradition more generally, and Norwegian curriculum policy since the 1970s has shown revived interest in increasing parental involvement in education and fostering links between home and community.

A suspicion exists in a populist view of culture that too much schooling entails risks of "trained incapacity." It is no accident that a Norwegian American added this wry concept to the social science vocabulary—Thorstein Veblen.[51] As recently as the 1950s, for example, children in rural Norway attended school only every other day for "lack of resources" or because of geographical conditions. But such a policy was also consistent with the notion that school is not the only important learning arena, especially under conditions of unmechanized agriculture in which the household serves as the basic unit of production. Attendance every other day gave room for socialization in practical skills related to such production in the household. This concern to avoid too much schooling at the expense of other learning spheres still has some political force in Norway. Today, although students attend schools five days a week, compulsory education does not begin until age seven. Furthermore, the school day remains shorter during the early grades than it is in other industrialized countries, with only 23 weekly periods of 45 minutes in grade 1. One Norwegian researcher estimated in 1984 that an eleven-year-old British student would have received close to three times as much instructional time with a teacher as a Norwegian child of the same age.[52] A comparison with Japan, whose students are among the most intensively schooled in the world, would show an even more dramatic gap.[53] This late and gentle start—in a country that stands out internationally for its high unit expenditures on primary and lower secondary education—shows the enduring influence of a populist, rural tradition in education. Attempts are now being made to catch up with other industrialized countries by starting students at age six and increasing the hours in early schooling.

Decentralization of Control and Provisions

In Norway, schools nearly always carry the name of their locality, or a constructed place name with connotations of home and community. This is no mere coincidence. Although the Lutheran state church played a key early role in education, the firmer establishment of schools was tied to the beginnings of local government.[54] The creation of local school committees in 1827 was a precursor of the 1837 act that established elected local government, and those responsible for operating local schools had their own children in them. The supervisory authority exercised by the local Lutheran parson (backed up by the dean and the bishop) receded gradually, to be replaced by a single state director of schools in each county.

The Leftist (*Venstre*) alliance of agrarians and liberals wanted decentralized control, with the primary school act of 1889 representing the high tide of such populist efforts. Local councils were given the right to introduce New Norse as the language of instruction, to appoint teachers, and to determine their own "education plan" (though national guidelines were provided[55] and syllabuses were undoubtedly shaped by the few available textbooks). Each school was to have a supervisory committee with representatives of parents in the majority, and in rural *kommuner*, this committee had the right to be consulted on the short listing of teacher applicants. The municipal school committee (on which the parson was no longer the chairman ex officio) could also delegate some budgetary decisions to these supervisory committees. In practice, however, the committees turned out to be rather sleepy bodies. In the 1920s and 1930s, the Ministry of Education gradually asserted more regulatory power over the curriculum. The apparatus of central government had by then come under the control of those who earlier had rallied against the upper-class hold on the state and the civil service. Such greater central regulation suited the teachers, who may have felt that the extreme localism in the 1889 Education Act entailed risks of too much inequality among *kommuner* and too much lay direction of their own work.

The Labor Party came to pursue more centralist educational policies, as part of a wider strategy for building a welfare state and a more egalitarian society. These broader policies stressed redressing inequalities between richer (often urban) communities and poorer (often remote) ones, which was reflected in the centrally led transformation of school structure and contents. As a party that supported common schools freed from early selection to academic education, even more strongly than its agrarian-liberal predecessors, the Labor Party came to be a natural ally of the union for primary school teachers union after World War II. By the 1970s, however, having completed its agenda of egalitarian structural changes in the schools, the Labor Party was ready to decrease this central control. It was also losing electoral support and increasingly found it necessary to compete for votes from the political middle ground.

Since the late 1960s, several decentralization policies have been carried out with broad political support. Various advisory councils were established at each school to ensure that all groups involved should have a defined right to be consulted in the decision-making process. New curricula for the basic school (1974 and 1987) gave greater autonomy to both schools and local government, with the latter gaining more budgetary power over its schools since 1986. A major change is that the *kommuner* now receive state budgetary support in a block grant rather than funds earmarked for education—a switch resisted by teachers' unions.

In short, the preference in Norway for small schools with a simple division of labor among staff reflects the country's strong populist tradition, with little thought apparently given to the possible advantages provided by the choice and variety larger schools can offer. In towns, too, staffing ratios in preschool education are strikingly high (about 1:5). By a decision of Parliament, junior secondary schools with more than 450 pupils are judged too large on educational grounds and should be avoided, even when a larger school could be sustained financially and may offer economies of scale.

Thus, both local political control and sensitivity to the educational needs of communities in the periphery conform to a populist tradition in culture and politics. Populist values are also expressed in the more generalized preference for small schools and the low regard for the possible economies of scale or gains from specialization that larger schools may facilitate. There is in the populist tradition much skepticism of the large-scale, impersonal institution—and the Romantic suspicion that division of labor all too easily can lead to fragmentation of the human character.

CONCLUSION

Norway is no longer a country of farming and fishing folk, in which most people live in rural communities and children leave school at age fourteen to find work. Only about 6 percent of the labor force now work in farming, forestry, or fisheries. In fact, there are now more teachers than farmers. Most people live in towns (about half the population is concentrated in the counties adjoining the Oslo fjord), and some 85-90 percent of students stay in school until at least age eighteen.

Nevertheless, clear traces of populist influences on Norwegian education remain, such as the operation of schools by elected local government and the value placed on small schools—even in urban settings. This localist orientation in education was reasserted in government policy, which mandated that curriculum should emphasize the local community and increased the power of local government over educational budgets. The selection mechanisms and curriculum elements that have characterized academic secondary schooling elsewhere have been far less evident in Norway.

Furthermore, while the rural populist movements previously discussed abated long ago, their enduring influence on culture may help to explain why resistance to joining the European Union is so strong in Norway. The party that gained most new voters in the 1993 parliamentary election was the Center Party, which firmly opposed Norwegian membership in the European Union. In spite of this century's dramatic reduction in the farming population, this historically agrarian party became the second largest party in Parliament for the first time. The November 1994 referendum on whether Norway should join the European Union yielded the same result as a 1972 vote on the same issue: the measure was defeated. Only in the capital and in some nearby counties did the majority of voters favor membership. This outcome suggests that a populist and democratic form of nationalism—stressing the interests of the periphery and exhibiting little enthusiasm for modernization—remains politically potent in Norway.

In spite of the amalgamations into larger units of local government necessary for more complex administrative tasks, a countervailing ideal emphasizing the importance of small local government and "community" remains. Local voluntary organizations and newspapers receive considerable subsidies, for example, to reinforce the strength and diversity of local civic life at a time when there is some political anxiety that modern society has in its train the threat of eroded civic participation. Some of the larger *kommuner* are experimenting with government at the submunicipal level such as the possible move by the local council of Oslo toward giving responsibility for operating schools to the *bydel* (subdivision or precinct) and instituting elective councils at that level.

At present the dominant national policies are tight public finances and the need to improve industry's international competitiveness. In Norway, as elsewhere, officials have attempted to restrain public sector growth and to make public services more cost effective by introducing measures such as management by objectives. Efficiency concerns are the manifest motive behind such accountability measures, but making professionals more externally accountable also can be interpreted as a rightist populist reaction against the welfare state bureaucracy—sentiments that are most evident in *Fremskrittspartiet*, or the Progress Party.

Skeptics of decentralization suspect that local control of education—whether in the hands of teachers or local government officials—has gone too far and that the system needs tightening up to ensure better overall quality (i.e., in this case cognitive achievement and habits of hard work) and more efficient use of resources. Such views are expressed by the members of the Conservative Party, which historically has opposed populist movements and the Norwegian Association of Employers. There also appears to be a sense in the present Labor government that localism has gone too far. Although Labor has had a strong base among small landholders and fishermen in the periphery, it—like the Conservatives—has nonetheless been a modernizing party, more identified with urban and industrial interests than the centrist descendants of Venstre. Since the 1980s, the policy gap has narrowed between the Labor Party and Conservative parties, and the fact that they are the main advocates of Norwegian membership in the European Union reflects their shared identification with the values of urban modernization.

The present Labor government is seeking ways to better monitor learning outcomes and resource utilization in the educational system, both nationally and locally. In 1992, the Ministry of Education issued draft proposals of a new comprehensive curriculum for primary and secondary schools that suggest a movement away from the emphasis during the 1970s and 1980s on "soft" process goals of learning. There is a reassertion of cognitive knowledge within school subjects and tangibly defined skill objectives. Such harder achievement values seem congruent with wider policies that seek to make public services more cost effective and to increase the accountability of public officials, including teachers. Although those educators who see competition as an educational evil have reacted with hostility to this reorientation, teachers' unions are losing ground as they (like trade unions generally) have become more detached from the policy formulation process in the Labor government. Furthermore, even as teachers' unions clash with centralists who favor a leaner, more accountable public sector, they are also coming into conflict with localists who favor stronger local management of schools. This tension—between the professional insiders and their external political taskmasters—could be an important feature of Norwegian educational politics for some years.

In comparative education, the historical evolution of mass schooling has typically been perceived as an aspect of modernization— the interlinked processes of urbanization, division of labor ("bureaucratic" organization in the wide sense), modern technology, secularization, and the development of science. Scholars have debated whether mass schooling has served mainly to promote social integration and preparation for economic roles and active citizenship, the creation of a modern basis for legitimating social inequality, or more generally "the modern reconstruction of the individual and the expanded linkages between the individual and newly emerging, more inclusive social units—the rationalized society and the rational state."[56] But in all these approaches, scant attention has been given to the influence on education of movements that have sought to preserve premodern values of roots and community in the face of modernity. The case of Norway shows that it is possible for such populist responses to modernity to strongly influence politics, culture, and education. During such evolution, populist educational policies that seek to preserve premodern values of roots and community can bridge the gap between the culture of the home and that of the schools and also help to reinforce local civic life. Firm cross-national generalizations about the educational expressions of populism seem unwarranted, however, because the contents of populist causes are so varied. When based on an infrastructure of local civic life as in the Norwegian case, for example, populism may lead to distinctly *local* control of education—to community control and power for parents. But populist ideas also have been invoked by charismatic leaders who have concentrated power in their own hands, and there have been other cases in which populist movements of majority groups led to oppression of minorities. Thus, populism remains a concept that needs to be disaggregated so that its types may serve as sharper tools for comparative analysis.

NOTES

1. This article has been published in *Comparative Education Review*, vol. 39, no. 3, 1995.

2. Margaret Scotford Archer, *The Social Origin of Education Systems* (London: Sage, 1979).

3. Peter Worsley, "The Concept of Populism," in *Populism: Its Meanings and National Characteristics*, ed. Ghita Ionescu and Ernest Gellner (London:Weidenfeld and Nicolson, 1969), pp. 212-50, see esp. p. 218.

4. Harry C. Boyte and Frank Riessman, eds., *New Populism: The Politics of Empowerment* (Philadelphia: Temple University Press, 1986).

5. Edward Shils, *The Torment of Secrecy: The Background and Consequences of American Security Policies* (London: Heinemann, 1956), pp. 98-104. Worsley has further elaborated the implications of that definition in "The Concept of Populism."

6. Gianna Pomata, "A Common Heritage: The Historical Memory of Populism in Europe and the United States, " In Boyte and Riessman, eds., pp. 30-50, quote on p. 35.

7. See Richard Hofstadter, "North America," in Ionescu and Gellner, eds., pp. 9-27; and S.M. Lipset, *Agrarian Socialism* (Berkeley: University of California Press, 1950).

8. Andrzej Walicki, "Russia," in Ionescu and Gellner, eds., pp. 62-96. Walicki also cited Franceo Ventury, *Roots of Revolution: A History of the Populist and Socialist Movements in Nineteenth Century Russia* (London: 1960).

9. Ghita Ionescu, "Eastern Europe," in Ionescu and Gellner, eds., pp. 97-121.

10. Wiles writes: "There is much populism in fascism. . . . The main things that differentiate it from true populism are elitism, the cult of violence, the rejection of religion, and the demand for obedience to the leader" (Peter Wiles, "A Syndrome, Not a Doctrine: Some Elementary Theses on Populism," in Ionescu and Gellner, eds., pp. 166-79, quote on p. 176).

11. Angus Stewart, "The Social Roots," in Ionescu and Gellner, eds., pp. 180-96. Stewart elaborates on earlier observations by Edward Shils in "The Intellectuals in the Political Development of The New States," *World Politics* 12, no. 3 (1968).

12. As an extension of his earlier writing on populism, Gellner has argued that modern nationalism is a political response to unequal modernization—that it may be understood as a reaction of the periphery against the center from which social change emanates (Ernest Gellner, *Nations and Nationalism* [Oxford: Blackwell, 1983]). One exception to this pattern may be found in Argentina, where the main base for Peronism has been urban. This mass support has largely come from recently arrived rural migrants who have been marginalized in the industrial labor market and who, like populists elsewhere, have been nationalist and hostile to foreign capital and its local compradors. In that sense, Peronism too was a movement of a peripheral country against the influence of international metropolitan centers located abroad. Other variants of Latin American populism have also been more explicitly oriented toward the peasantry and their struggle for land reform. See Alistair Hennessey, "Latin America," in Gellner and Ionescu, eds., pp. 28-61. Latin American populism has undoubtedly been an important historical cradle of both dependency theories of economic development and Castroism.

13. In the history of the democratic idea in political philosophy lies a recurring tension: "a struggle to determine whether democracy will mean some kind of popular power (a form of life in which citizens are engaged in *self*-government and *self*-regulation) or an aid to decision-making (a means to legitimate the decisions of those voted into power—'representatives' from time

to time)" (David Held, *Models of Democracy* [Cambridge: Blackwell, 1987], p. 3). Populist concepts stress self-government, not only government by the consent of the governed.

14. Donald MacRae, "Populism as an Ideology," in Ionescu and Gellner, eds., pp. 153-65, quote on p. 159.

15. Gavin Kitching, *Development and Underdevelopment in Historical Perspective: Populism, Nationalism and Industrialisation* (London: Methuen, 1982).

16. A major theme in Norwegian agrarian politics has been to subject market forces to political control. During the period of breakthrough from subsistence agriculture to production for markets (1870-1920), agrarian politicians first strove to discourage industrialization. Later they sought in diverse ways to subject the establishment of new industry to public control. They also achieved state support in favor of their interest as producers, buyers, and employers, subjecting the market forces that impinged on agriculture to much public regulation. See Trond Nordby, *Det moderne gjennombruddet in bondesamfunnet: Norge 1870-1920* (Oslo: Universitetsforlaget, 1991).

17. MacRae sees the wish to restore an agrarian *gemeinschaft*—the peasant community or the village of sturdy yeomen——as the key defining element in populist ideology. In keeping with Herder's ideas, populism militates against "rootlessness," and it values "belonging" and "fraternity" more than the "liberty" of individualistic self-assertion (see MacRae).

18. Wiles writes: "Populism shows a strong tendency to mild racialism: the good common people are of different ancestry from the bad Establishment. Sometimes this belief is mythical or nearly so. Thus the Levellers and the Diggers propounded the theory of the Norman yoke: the seventeenth-century Englishman, whose traditions were democratic, was being exploited by a Norman aristocracy with a feudal ideology. Sometimes the racial distinction emphasized is . . . correct. . . .Sinn Fein attacked the English 'garrison'; Cárdenas, Haya de la Torre, Belaúnde were all spokesmen of the Aztecs or Incas vis-á-vis the Creoles" (Wiles, pp. 170-171).

19. "Decentralization" is a cloak of many colors, even more than "populism." Its various forms have quite different rationales and give pride of place in decision making to rather different local groups. Thus, in addition to the local-community orientation associated with populism, one may point to these other forms: federalism, participatory democracy (as focused on each institution), liberalism, pedagogic professionalism, the market mechanism, deconcentration, and arguably also management by objectives. A discussion of

these forms is given in: J. Lauglo, "Forms of Decentralization and their Implications for Education," *Comparative Education* 31, no. 1 (1955).

20. See the chapters by MacRae, Wiles, Stewart, Kenneth Minogue ("Populism as a Political Movement," in Ionescu and Gellner, eds. [n. 2 above], pp. 197-211), and Worsley in pt. 2 of Ionescu and Gellner, eds.

21. William H. Riker, *Liberalism against Populism* (San Francisco: W.H. Freeman, 1982).

22. Øyvind Østerud, *Agrarian Structure and Peasant Politics in Scandinavia* (Oslo: Universitetsforlaget, 1978).

23. See, e.g., Richard Hofstadter, *Anti-intellectualism in American Life* (New York: Knopf, 1963).

24. Radical Protestantism may have been no direct impulse for secular free thought. But when they have been faced with repression, the struggle of Protestant groups to secure religious freedom for themselves has had latitudinarianism in its train. The diverse "modernizing" social consequences of Protestantism have attracted much scholarly interest. There is, e.g., the well-known thesis by Max Weber on the connection between Protestantism and the rise of Capitalism, and there is Robert Merton's work on "Science, Technology and Society in Seventeenth-Century England," *Osiris* 4, no. 2 (1938).

25. Ottar Brox, *Hva skjer i Nord-Norge? En studie i norsk utkantpolitikk* (Oslo: Pax, 1966).

26. Tor Boman Larsen, *Den evige sne: En skihistorie om Norge* (Oslo: Cappelen, 1993). The historical identification that Boman Larsen notes between nationalism and winter sports may be a major reason why Norway embarked on the project of hosting the 1994 Winter Olympics, in spite of its staggering costs and the present tight squeeze on public expenditures.

27. Gunnar Skirbekk, "Nasjon og natur. Eit essay om den norske væremåten," in *Ord* (Oslo: Det Norske Samlaget, 1984).

28. Øyvind Østerud, "Nasjonalstaten Norge: En karakteriserende skisse," in *Det Norske Samfunn*, 3rd ed., eds. L. Alldén, N. Rogoff Ramsøy, and M. Vaa (Oslo: Gyldendal, 1986, pp. 7-32.

29. Among his numerous publications on this theme, see S. Rokkan, "Norway: Numerical Democracy and Corporate Pluralism," in *Political Oppositions in Western Democracies*, ed. R.A. Dahl (New Haven, Conn.: Yale University Press, 1966), and "Geography, Religion and Social Class: Crosscutting Cleavages in Norwegian Politics," in *Party Systems and Voter Alignments: Cross-National Perspectives*, ed. S.M. Lipset and S. Rokkan (New York: Free Press, 1967).

30. The national myth of Switzerland is similarly populist: the history of a yeomanry rebellion against foreign oppression and of establishing cantonal self-government.

31. It is hard to translate this term into English—perhaps "popular" in the sense of popular movements, pertaining to "the people" viewed as a valued collectivity, "demotic" in a positive sense.

32. For a major source in English on the philosophical and educational ideas connected with the folk high schools in the Nordic countries and on the connection between these schools and popular movements see Rolland G. Paulston (with contributions from E.F. Pain and others), *Other Dreams, Other Schools: Folk Colleges in Social and Ethnic Movements* (Pittsburgh: University of Pittsburgh, University Center for International Studies, 1980).

33. Scandinavian political culture has embraced these terms. The labor movements too have their *folkets hus*—the assembly houses of the folk. Numerous political parties have made the term a part of their name—even the Danish conservatives, who historically were the opponents of the *folkelig* movements in that country. The amalgamated Norwegian system of social security insurance schemes is characteristically called *folketrygd* (*trygd* means social security).

34. It was also expedient to make appeals to the sovereignty of the people when the framers of the 1814 constitution, who were largely civil servants of the Danish state, sought to preempt Swedish rule by declaring independence.

35. Before Venstre gained power, its parliamentary leaders had on several occasions argued that the state should have no responsibility for academic secondary schools: such education should be left to private initiative.

36. Ron Eyermann, "Intellectuals: A Framework for Analysis, with Special Reference to the United States and Sweden," *Acta Sociologica* 35 (1992): 33-46.

37. A discussion of the historical role of rural school teachers in civic life in Norway, France, England and the United States is given in Jon Lauglo, "Rural Primary School Teachers as Potential Community Leaders? Contrasting Historical Cases in Western Countries," *Comparative Education* 18, no. 3 (1982): 232-55.

38. S. Rokkan, "Party Preferences and Opinion Patterns in Western Europe: A Comparative Analysis," *International Social Science Bulletin*, vol. 7 (1975).

39. Kjell Eide, *Norsk utdanning i internasjonal sammenheng*, Report 23.10.1987 from the scientific adviser, Ministry of Education, Oslo.

40. Norway still seems to listen to Martin Luther, who reportedly once suggested that age seven was appropriate for starting school. Right from the

beginning of compulsory education (1739), school has started at age seven; however, the school entry age is likely to be lowered to six in the near future.

41. Decentralization policies since the early 1980s have opened for somewhat greater variety, but there is still much emphasis on a curriculum that should be common to all pupils.

42. Rune Kvalsund, Petter Løvik, and Jon Olav Myklebust, *The Location of Rural Schools* (Volda: Møre & Romsdal Research Foundation, 1992), pp. 2-3.

43. The early beginnings of mass schooling and the dissemination of literacy in all the Nordic countries are examined in Knut Tveit, "The Development of Popular Literacy in the Nordic Countries: A Comparative Historical Study," *Scandinavian Journal of Educational Research* 35, no. 4 (1991): 241-52.

44. However, the first decrees that sought to establish a modicum of schooling, as preparation for Confirmation in the Lutheran Church, are 250 years old.

45. In neighboring Sweden, by way of contrast, it was only from 1972 that teachers were no longer supposed to correct children's dialects.

46. The data on New Norse usage among teachers have very kindly been made available by Professor Strømnes. His material is based on a 10 percent random sample from a population of 14,000 teachers who took part in a membership survey conducted by the primary school teachers' and folk high school teachers' interest organizations in 1949. The population included in that survey is estimated at roughly 90 percent of all teachers then employed in the schools.

47. Stortingmelding, nr. 53 (1191-92), *Målbruk i offentlig tjeneste*, p. 23.

48. Hans-Jørgen Dokka, *Fra allmueskole til folkeskole* (Oslo: Universitetsforlaget, 1967), pp. 131-39.

49. There exists in imported strains of populism a concern to ensure close connections between education and the local community. This is well known in the case of Grundtvigianism and American Progressivism. Pietism stressed schooling as an extension of religion at the parish level. In the German *Arbeitsschule*, there is emphasis on parental involvement, e.g., the concept of *die Schulgemeinde* in the Jena plan for Thüringen—a plan that was well known to prominent Norwegian educators in the interwar years through their connections with Professor Peter Petersen at the University of Jena. Research on these German-Norwegian personal links is being conducted at present by Ola Stafseng of the Programme Research on Youth, Norwegian Research Council.

50. Martin Strømnes, "Bokmannen og idéane," in *Festskrift til Rektor Erling Kristvik på syttiårsdagen,* eds. Astrid Vatne, Martin Strømnes and Per Myklebust (Oslo: Olaf Norli, 1952), pp. 59-83.

51. Thorstein Veblen, *The Theory of the Leisure Class* (1899; reprint, New York: Mentor, 1953). His disdain for "conspicuous consumption", his distinction between an "upper class" and the "common man," and his appreciation of "workmanship" all agree with a populist perspective.

52. Karl Jan Solstad, *Ein skole for samfunnet* (Oslo: Cappelen, 1984), p. 26.

53. A Japanese twelve-year-old has received about as many hours of instruction as a British fourteen-year-old.

54. By contrast, in France and Prussia public schools for the populace were established as extensions of central authority, and they were operated by the state, with teachers as state employees. In England, private venture "dame schools" were among the first that catered to common children, and schooling on a large scale emerged with the establishment of religious charitable foundations to promote education for poor children. The state later moved in to fill the gaps in these private provisions, which had been set up by middle class charity for "other people's children."

55. Annually, the minimum number of weeks of school was only 12, but 6 more weeks could be added (with voluntary attendance).

56. John Boli, Francisco O. Ramirez, and John W. Meyer, "Explaining the Origins and Expansion of Mass Education," *Comparative Education Review* 29 (May 1985): 145-70.

CHAPTER 3

Parents' Participation in Danish Schools: Genuine Influence or Pseudo-Legitimation?

Jens Hoff

INTRODUCTION

The last decade has been a very turbulent period in Danish educational policy. Thus, at all levels of the educational system more reforms and changes have been undertaken than in any other decade since World War II. This is especially true for the comprehensive school system (primary and lower secondary education; K-10th grade), which is the focus of this chapter. Here three major reforms have been implemented within the last seven years. These reforms are of a quite different nature, but together they aim at fundamentally reforming the governance, form, and content of education at this level.

The first of these reforms was a new law on the governance of public schools which came into force on January 1, 1990. The main purpose of the law was to significantly increase user influence on school policies and to convert to a model of the "management by objectives" type by simultaneously: a) strengthening the economic supervision of schools (by the municipal councils), and b) increasing the autonomy of the individual school. The law divides authority on school matters between school boards consisting of 7-11 members with a majority of parents (5-7), and the school leader (headmaster). The school board has the authority to make decisions on principal matters like the allocation of the school budget (but not its total volume), the organization of teaching (number of lessons given, number of special subjects, etc., but not questions of hiring and firing of teachers and school leaders), school-parent cooperation, evaluation principles, rules of conduct for the school, etc. The school leader is in charge of the detailed daily decisions and management of the school.

The second reform took place in 1992/93 when the municipalities took the right from the Ministry of Finance to negotiate collective agreements with the teachers union. This was meant to give the municipalities a greater freedom in negotiating wages, work time, etc. Following the reform new collective agreements were negotiated between the National Association of Municipalities and the teachers union, which created a novel basis for the calculation of teachers working hours, the number of teachers at each school, etc.

The third reform was the 1993/94 major revision of the general law on comprehensive public schools. The foundation for this reform was laid in 1991/92 with the launching of extensive developmental activities. Thus around 400 million Danish crowns were used to finance more than 8,000 projects at different comprehensive schools all over the country. The experiences from these projects were summarized in 26 evaluation reports, which constituted an important source of background material for the reform. All involved parties have seen this material as very future oriented and ambitious, and the reform has been called the best-ever reform of primary and lower secondary education in Denmark. The law has four fundamental features: First, the last traces of two-level teaching are removed, as it is no longer possible to teach subjects in 8-10th grade at, respectively, a "high" and a "low" level (and thereby implicitly sorting the pupils). Instead teaching is supposed to be individualized on the basis of "plans of action" for the individual pupil. Second, teaching is supposed to be cross-disciplinary to a much greater extent, and pupils are expected to work more on projects, especially in 8-10th grade. Third, evaluation of each pupil is to be a permanent process, which will take place through dialogue, tests, etc., and form the basis for the "plan of action." Fourth, the minimum number of weekly lessons taught is increased, and especially linguistic skills in Danish are given a higher priority.[1] At one level, this development can, as mentioned in chapter one in this volume, be seen as a change in Danish educational policy in a neo-liberal direction and as an adaptation to educational policies in the European Union (EU).

This interpretation is strengthened by the fact that all of the above mentioned reforms were passed or initiated by the different center-right coalition governments in power between 1982 and 1993. Also, it is quite clear that central foci in the reforms are individual choice, competition, quality, effectiveness, and efficiency.

However, the reforms are surely more than that, and it might be a limitation of the perspective to interpret the changes solely along the "old" left-right continuum. Thus, it is telling that even though there was a shift in government to a center-left coalition in 1993, educational policies have not been changed in any significant ways since. Also, there is a tradition for very broad agreements involving most parties in Parliament concerning educational reforms. This tradition has been kept up by both the center-right and the center-left governments since 1982. Thus, there has been a broad consensus behind the reforms mentioned.

An alternative to the "political" explanation might be an "institutional" explanation emphasizing the importance of endogenous developments within the educational sector itself. Such endogenous development is quite clear in relation to, for example, the 1993/94 revision of the general law on comprehensive schools, which was based on significant development activities within the school system as well as on the reform concerning school boards, which was inspired by the type of governance of some successful private schools.

However, it is not the aim of this chapter to test the validity of these explanations. Also, it is probably more correct to see the two explanations as complementary rather than as competing.

Instead, what we shall do in this chapter is to focus on one important aspect of the reforms; namely on the question of (increased) user participation in the management and daily activities of comprehensive public schools.[2] Thus, apart from the detailed aims concerning teaching methods, evaluation, and curriculum in the reform of the general law on comprehensive schools, the overarching goals of the reforms can be said to be improved political possibilities of steering, and improved user influence. Both of these goals are contained within the law on user boards, while the first goal is clear in the collective agreements reform. Thus, both of these reforms aim at strengthening the power of politicians and users, and thereby implicitly limiting the power of the teachers. It is thus symptomatic that the teachers union and most teachers were strongly opposed to the law on school boards. Only when it became clear that the reform had broad political support did the teachers back down and demand representation in the new school boards (in which they succeeded).[3]

One major discussion in relation to the law on school boards (which is now a part of the general law on comprehensive schools) is whether the boards represent a real democratic innovation or whether they are just a new cog in the traditional political steering of the schools, allowing a better fine tuning of means and goals? In other words, do the user boards give users genuine influence on school matters, or should they rather be seen as a sophisticated attempt at improving the faltering legitimation of the traditional political steering—a kind of pseudo-legitimation? This is the question that this chapter will try to answer. However, we will not limit our analysis of user influence only to the influence exercised through the users boards (formal influence) but will locate this in a broader investigation of other types of user influence (informal influence).

DATA ON USER PARTICIPATION

The primary source on which the following analysis is based is the Danish Citizenship Survey conducted in October/November 1990. The sample consisted of 3,000 randomly selected persons aged sixteen and over. The sampling and personal interviewing was done by the Danish Gallup Institute according to its normal standards: 2,080 responses were obtained—a response rate of 69 percent—which is considered satisfactory in these kinds of surveys.[4] These data are supplemented by a 1995 nationwide Citizen Survey conducted by the Municipal Software House (*Kommunedata*). The sample size in this survey was 2,016 persons aged eighteen and over. Here 1,722 responses were obtained—a response rate of 85 percent. Furthermore, these data are supplemented by secondary analysis/reference to a number of case studies done within the last 2-3 years concerning the functioning of the new school boards in Denmark (Cranil 1994; Sørensen 1995a, 1995b; Pedersen and Thomsen 1994).

The Citizenship Survey was part of a project on democracy and citizenship in Denmark carried out by a team of researchers from several universities in Denmark, of which the current author was a member. The purpose of the project was to analyze political participation and political culture in various institutional arenas and at various institutional levels. The project thus involved an analysis of "traditional" forms of political participation (voting, party membership, and activity in voluntary associations, etc.). As something novel in surveys on political participation, user participation was explicitly dealt with and regarded as a third democratic channel.[5] Thus, in the design of the questionnaire pains were taken to cover both different kinds of user participation, as well as areas in which possibilities of "voice" and/or "exit" exist (see below), as well as areas in which such possibilities are small or nonexistent. Thus, attempts were made to analyze the role of the citizen as not only a "user," but also a "consumer," and a "client." Also, the idea behind the choice of areas for analysis was that both areas with a "service character" as well as areas with an "authoritative" or "controlling character" should be analyzed.

Concretely, this resulted in the choice of seven areas for analysis: the health sector, local tax authorities, day care centers (from birth to age six), public schools (K-10th grade), local social welfare institutions, labor exchange offices, and the "local community" (in practice contact with local technical administrations concerning roads, environmental matters, etc.). Within each of these areas a set of similar questions was asked regarding contact with institutions, satisfaction with services, use of "voice" (and its possible success), considerations on "exit" (if a possibility), and perceived influence. In the areas where any kind of formal user representation exists (schools and day care centers), respondents were asked about their participation in the bodies established for user representation.[6]

DEMOCRACY IN PUBLIC SCHOOLS

There are many ways in which it is possible to discuss democracy and evaluate democratic performance. Here we have chosen to use the three ÒclassicalÓ elements of democracy as our point of departure, namely: *freedom, equality, and solidarity* (brotherhood) (Young 1986).

In the liberal, Anglo-Saxon conception of democracy, freedom is normally equated with personal autonomy, to have the freedom to choose one's course in life. The fundamental prerequisites to do this are normally considered to be the constitutional rights to think, speak, publish, and meet without hindrances, and the right to possess and trade private property. Here we have chosen to operationalize the way in which this freedom is exercised vis-à-vis public schools through the concepts of "voice" and "exit" (Hirschmann 1970). The citizen uses "voice" when he/she tries to speak up, complain, or take other initiatives to influence or change the service delivered to him/her.

"Exit" is when a citizen leaves an organization to obtain a wanted service elsewhere or expresses a wish to do so.

Equality can be measured in different ways. However, what is important here is whether user participation tends to create (new) socio-demographic inequalities and, thus, possible inequalities in policy outcomes. What we will look at here is, therefore, the socio-demographic differences between the group of users as such, the group of users who use "voice" and the elected user representatives. We shall look at whether the possible social inequalities accumulate through the three groups. Also, we shall comment on differences in political outlook among the three groups, as well as differences between this form of participation and other forms of political participation.

The extent of this chapter, as well as our data, makes it impossible for us to analyze the question of solidarity. However, our data show that user satisfaction with public schools in Denmark is high (89 percent of users say that they are "very" or "rather satisfied" with services (Hoff 1995:41). If one combines this knowledge with data from other surveys showing a high degree of willingness to finance public schools (as well as most other public expenditures within the educational, health, and social assistance areas; see Goul Andersen 1988, 1995), the conclusion must be that there is a reasonably high degree of solidarity with the services delivered by the public schools.

Voice

Table 1 shows different aspects of "voice" or formal and informal user participation in public schools in Denmark. Formal user participation is defined as aspects concerning elected user representatives and interest in this kind of elections. Informal user participation is defined as aspects concerning all other channels by which users might try to exert influence on the service in question.[7]

As can be seen from table 1, most aspects of informal participation involve considerably more users than formal participation. In Denmark interest in the elections for the new user boards in public schools, and in the work going on in these boards was quite high (51 percent and 74 percent). However, this interest was only to some degree reflected in actual participation in terms of voting (29 percent in 1990; 17 percent in 1994).

Also the number of elected representatives in public schools in Denmark is quite impressive and has increased from 1990 to 1995 (from 23 percent in 1990 to 36 percent in 1995). However, this figure includes both representatives elected to the school boards as well as elected (parent) representatives of the single classes.[8] Our data make it impossible to separate the two groups. However, we must assume that the elected class representatives constitute the vast majority of the group of elected representatives.

Table 1. Formal and informal user participation in public schools in Denmark. Percentage of users.

	Denmark 1990	Denmark 1995
Formal: Interest in user board (very/somewhat interested)*	51	74
Participated in elections	29	17
Elected representative**	23	36
Informal: Attended parent meeting	95	98
Other contact with teachers	55	—
Contact with principal, school board, or parent association	29	—
Talked with other parents about school matters	60	—
Participated in other school activities	57	48
Attempted changing conditions at school	44	—
N (no. of users)	458	347

* In 1995 the question concerned interest in the topics on the school board agenda.** In 1990 the category "elected representative" included persons who, within the last year, represented the old school committees.

This relatively high level of especially informal user participation has a correlate in users' evaluation of the possibility of their influencing conditions in their child/children's school. Thus 71 percent of users say that they have "good" or "very good" possibilities to do so. However, if we change the focus to municipal school politics the efficacy decreases considerably. Here, only 29 percent of users say that the possibility of their influencing conditions are "good" or "very good."

In the following we shall scrutinize one aspect of voice, namely, the question about "attempted changing conditions at school" (the highlighted item in Table 1). We have chosen this item because in the different analyses of the Scandinavian citizenship surveys, this question has been used to illustrate "user power." A follow-up question was thus whether the user had been successful or not in his/her attempt at changing conditions.

As can be seen from Table 1, 44 percent of Danish users (parents) had taken an initiative within the last year in order to influence school services. Out of these 44 percent, 33 percent were successful. Thus around one-third of the users in this field exert some amount of influence or "power."[9] Also, this means that the rate of success (percent successful/percent initiative) is around .75, or that around 3 out of 4 who use voice are successful.

In a "power" perspective, it is also of importance to look at the group of users who have not taken an initiative. Is this inaction caused by satisfaction with services, or because these users perceive their possibilities to change existing conditions as remote? The answer to this question is very simple. Out of the 56 percent of the users (parents) of public schools who had not taken an initiative to change existing conditions, 53 percent were satisfied ("very" or "rather" satisfied). Only 3 percent had not taken an initiative and were simultaneously dissatisfied with services (were "apathetic," according to Petersson et al. 1989).

Furthermore, our analysis shows a correlation between users' perception of their own influence (efficacy) and their experiences with voice. If a user has used voice, and been successful, he/she has considerably more faith in the possibilities of exerting influence than if he/she has not used voice or has used voice unsuccessfully.

This result might sound trivial, but it indicates that concrete experiences as a user can become resources in their own right. Thus, it seems logical to assume that if someone has positive experiences with attempts to influence services, this will stimulate further attempts. This can start a "good circle" wherein (successful) participation stimulates further participation. The creation of such "good circles" is, of course, most likely in areas where the probability of success is high.

Exit

The Danish Citizenship Survey questionnaire contained two questions meant to tap the exit dimension. First, all respondents were asked whether they thought that private alternatives to the dominant public services in the areas of hospitals, schools, and day-care institutions were important. Second, we asked (only) users of public schools more concretely about whether they had seriously considered exit within the last year. The answers yield some interesting results, as shown in Table 2:

Table 2. Users' evaluation of the importance of exit, and users actually considering exit. Percentages.

	"Do you think the existence of private alternatives is important?"	"Have you seriously considered private school for your child?"*)
Important/yes	80	19
Indifferent/don't know	14	8
Am against/no	6	73
N=	458	458

*within the last year

As we can see, as many as 80 percent of the users of public school services think that the existence of private alternatives is important. In a welfare state such as the Danish, based heavily on universalism and publicly organized services in the areas of education, health, and social affairs, such figures are quite surprising. However, the high figure here is probably due to the fact that as far as schools are concerned, private alternatives are very visible and have a long tradition. This also means a long tradition for competition and a sort of balance between public and private services—a competition and balance that users seem to find important. This explanation finds support in the fact that the figure is considerably higher than that pertaining to hospitals, where private alternatives (on a large scale) are of a relatively recent origin.[10]

When the question about exit becomes more personal and concrete 19 percent, or almost 1 out of 5 users, have seriously considered exit. Furthermore, we know that about 2.9 percent of pupils in public schools will switch to private schools during their first 7 years in school (Ministry of Finance et al. 1995:25-26) and that 14 percent of all children from kindergarten class through 10th grade attend private schools (1994 figures; Kommunedata/Lars Torpe 1995). This strengthens our conclusion about the visibility of the exit option and shows that users are ready to use the option in the event of concrete dissatisfaction.

A final and important question about voice and exit is whether users consider them as mutually exclusive or as complementary. One could, for example, be led to believe that users of voice are less inclined to consider exit possibilities than those who have not used voice. This is not the case. The correlation between voice and exit is .27 (Pearsons r). Thus, a more likely conclusion is that voice and exit are perceived as complementary and that users wish to use both possibilities in their attempts at obtaining the desired "service package" (the right quantity and quality of the service).

Inequality

One of the most debated topics in relation to user participation is whether this type of political participation tends to deepen existing socio-demographic differences in political participation or even create new cleavages among the citizenry with possible consequences for policy outcomes.

In an attempt to analyze this question, we have looked at differences in socio-demographic "profile" between the user group as such, participants (the 44 percent of the users who have used "voice"), and elected user representatives (Table 3). Table 3 shows, first, that the differences between the user group and participants (2-1) are not significant regarding gender, age, or employment status. However, looking at differences relating to education and occupation, the figures seem to confirm popular assumptions about user participation: that persons with education and in (higher) non-manual positions are overrepresented among participants.

Table 3. Socio-demographic differences between users, participants and elected user representatives. Percentages.

	(1) Users	(2) Partici-pants	(3) Elected user representatives	Differ--ence (2-1)	Differ-ence (3-1)
Gender				*	
Female	55	56	68	+1	+13
Male	45	44	32	-1	-13
Age				*	*
18-29	5	5	4	0	-1
30-39	48	49	52	+1	+4
40-49	42	42	39	0	-3
50-59	6	5	5	-1	-1
60-69	0	1	0	+1	0
Education					*
7-9 years	36	31	37	-5	+1
10 years	44	43	43	-1	-1
11+ years	20	26	20	+6	0
Occupation					*
Self-empl.	12	7	13	5	+1
non-manual,high	14	17	16	+3	+2
non-manual medium	13	20	15	+7	+2
non-manual, low	31	29	33	-2	+2
manual, skilled	11	10	9	-1	-2
manual, unskilled	19	17	14	-2	-5
Employment					*
status	88	88	93	0	+5
employed	7	6	6	-1	-1
unemployed	2	3	0	+1	-2
pension<60	0	1	0	+1	0
pens. 60-66	2	3	1	+1	-1
housewife					
MCA-analysis		beta-coeff.	beta-coeff.		
gender		.03*	.18		
age		.07*	.06*		
education		.15	.05*		
occupation		.14	.02*		
R2		5.2 percent	3.6 percent		
N=	458	199	87		

+) In 1990, the category "elected representatives" included persons who had, within the last year, been representatives in the old school committees and the new school boards, and had been class representatives.

* = not significant at the .05 level

The differences between the user group as such and the elected user representatives (3-1) confirm this picture but only to some extent. Thus, surprisingly, the group of elected user representatives is seen to deviate less from the user group as such than the participants. Thus, no accumulation of social differences seems to occur as we move from users to elected representatives. Only concerning gender do we see that women are significantly overrepresented among elected user representatives. This is probably due to the fact that elected class representatives are included in this category. If one looks only at the group of elected members of the school boards, the proportion of women will decline and educational and occupational bias increase. However, no systematic (nationwide) investigations have been made into this question.

In order to penetrate deeper into the question of social inequalities in user participation, we have done some regression analyses (MCA type),[11] where the different socio-demographic variables (gender, age, education, and occupation) are used as independent variables and the two types of user participation (use of voice and being an elected representative) as dependent variables. The analyses show how much of the variation in participation each socio-demographic variable explains (the beta coefficients) and how much of the variation the regression model (all the independent variables together) explains (the R2 value).

The results basically confirm what has been said above. Concerning participants, we see that both education and occupation contribute significantly to explain the variation. However, the explanatory value of the variables is limited, as they explain only around 2-3 percent of the variation. Also the regression model as such has limited explanatory value as it explains only 5.2 percent of the variation.

Regarding elected representatives we see that here the socio-demographic variables explain even less of the variation in user representation. Actually only gender has significant explanatory power, and the regression model as such explains only 3.6 percent of the variation in user representation.

In conclusion, we can say that some social inequalities seem to exist concerning different types of user participation in public schools. However, inequalities are smaller than could be expected. Neither in isolation nor together do the socio-demographic variables explain very much of the variation in the different types of participation. It is therefore likely that other factors are more crucial for user participation. These factors could be the users' own motivation or "institutional factors" such as, for example, the willingness or ability of teachers and pedagogues to encourage participation, something which is again related to the organizational culture and institutional heritage of the institutions.

Finally, we will take a look at differences in the political profile of users, participants, and representatives because it has been claimed in the public debate that groups with certain (school-) political ideas and attitudes are able to dominate the user boards, thereby creating a systematic bias in policy outcomes. As our data do not include any information on school political attitudes, we have instead—as a rather crude approximation to the problem—tried to look at the party preference of the three groups at the latest national election (in this case the 1988 parliamentary election). The results are shown in Table 4:

Table 4. Political profile of users, participants, and elected representatives. Percentages.

	(1) Users	(2) Participants	(3) Representatives	(3 - 1)
Voted socialist	55	58	51	-4
Voted non-socialist	45	42	49	+4

As we can see from the table, participants deviate a little from the user group as such as they seem to be leaning somewhat more towards the socialist parties.[12] However, for representatives it is the other way around—they seem to be leaning a little more towards the non-socialist parties. The picture is therefore unclear, and deviations from the user group as such and from the population average) are so small that it is hard to believe that participants or representatives are able to systematically bias policy outcomes.[13]

Above we have demonstrated that even though there are some social inequalities in user participation in public schools in Denmark, these inequalities are small, and in general socio-demographic variables are not very important in explaining differences in user participation. However, these conclusions are based on comparisons between representatives, participants, and users, or intra-sector comparisons. So even though differences might seem small, they might be bigger than those related to other types of political participation. Below, we have therefore compared the social bias in user participation with the social bias in other forms of political participation. In order to focus on inequality, we have included only those groups that are often found to be politically underrepresented in the table.

Table 5. User participation in schools compared with other forms of political participation. Selected social groups. Percentages.

	Women	7-9 yrs. edu-cation	Un-skilled workers	Workers (skilled + un-skilled)	Unempl oyed
Total popul. (survey)	52	46	22	34	6
Voters	50	47	20	32	5
Grassroot	51	35	19	30	6
Member of vol. assoc.	49	39	18	28	5
Elected repr. in vol. assoc.	36	35	17	25	5
Member of pol. party	36	55	13	18	2
Elected repr. in pol. party	23	43	7	12	0
User participation (7 areas)	52	34	15	25	7
User participation in schools	56	31	15	24	6

The figures in the table are weighted. Thus, what is counted is the number of positions and not the number of cases. Therefore, if a user participates in two areas, he/she is weighted with a factor 2, etc. The table includes both an index of user participation in the 7 areas mentioned above as well as the distribution of participation (use of "voice") in public schools among the relevant groups.

The table shows, first, that along socio-demographic lines, participation in schools does not deviate very much from user participation in general. Only as it concerns gender do the schools seem to be somewhat different, which confirms our findings above. More interesting, however, is the fact that user participation—both in general (the 7 areas) and in schools—compares favorably with other types of political participation. If one uses a simple statistical measure as the sum of squares of the deviations of the different forms of political participation from the distribution of the total population, we see that the most socially equal form of participation is voting (which is an obvious conclusion given the high turnout at national elections in Denmark). In second, third, and fourth place come "grassroots" activities, membership of voluntary associations, and user participation. The most socially unequal forms of participation are clearly membership and representation in political parties, as well as the level of representatives in voluntary associations. This is very surprising given the fact that political parties and voluntary associations have normally been considered to be institutions serving as vehicles for a broad popular involvement in politics. Today in Denmark they do not serve that purpose very well. Rather, the institutions guaranteeing a broad popular involvement in politics today seem to be "grassroots" movements/initiatives and different kinds of user participation. This is a result with potentially wide-reaching implications for the discussions about the future of our political system, a discussion which is, however, outside the scope of this chapter.

CONCLUSION

Concerning our original research question about whether or not user boards (formal participation) give users genuine influence on schools matters, we must admit that we are not able to answer this question directly, as we have not entered into an analysis of the internal workings and decision-making processes of the school boards. However, our general attempt at evaluating the democratic content of user participation in comprehensive schools (K-10th grade) in Denmark has given us some clues to the answer.

Thus, user boards seem to represent a democratic paradox. Interest in the topics on the agenda of the school boards is quite high and has risen from 1990 to 1995 (from 51 percent to 74 percent), while voting turnout for the boards is low and has declined further (from 29 percent in 1990 to 17 percent in 1994). One possible way to interpret this paradox is that in general users are quite interested in school matters, an assumption that is confirmed by the high level of user participation in other types of school-related activities (parent meetings, etc.). However, they do not seem to perceive the school boards as a relevant channel for expressing their interests. The most likely explanation for this is probably, as pointed out by several authors (Sørensen 1995a, 1995b; Cranil 1994; Pedersen and Thomsen 1994), the unclear and quite limited authority of the boards.

This seems to point to the user boards as a democratic failure and as institutions basically meant to improve the legitimation of the traditional political-bureaucratic type of governance. The logical conclusion could thus be to close them down and start thinking about other types of democratic governance institutions. However, this might be jumping at conclusions. Thus, our analysis showed that different more informal types of participation are widely used, that users perceive themselves as quite influential, and that the social bias in user participation is quite small. Therefore, the user boards are, so to speak, embedded in a participatory culture and in institutions which are, by the users, seen as quite receptive to their demand. Therefore, it seems more advisable to revitalize the user boards instead of closing them down. Such revitalization could take place along the lines recommended by, for example, Sørensen (1995b), who suggests—among other things— that the user boards be based on functional representation, meaning that they should be composed of class representatives instead of being directly elected. This would ensure a better dialogue between parents and representatives as well as a better representation of all user interests.

NOTES

1. This is a clear reaction to many years of public criticism of the declining linguistic abilities of graduates from comprehensive school.

2. It is of course basically the parents who—on behalf of their child/children—participate in the management of the schools. Strictly speaking

the parents are not users but rather a kind of semi-users. For a treatment of the importance of this distinction, see Sørensen 1995b.

3. However, it is up to the municipal council whether or not they will grant the teacher representatives the right to vote in the school board elections. As far as we know teachers have been granted this right in almost all municipalities.

4. For a more detailed account of sampling, questions, frequencies, etc., see Asbjørnsen, Hoff & Andersen 1995 or Andersen et al. 1993.

5. The major publications from the project include Andersen et al. 1993 and Andersen and Torpe 1995.

6. For a comprehensive analysis and comparison of these data with Swedish and Norwegian data (in English); see Hoff 1995.

7. It is questionable whether the phrase "talked with other parents about school/day care matters" represents any kind of user participation. However, as the question was included in the questionnaire, we have decided to report it here as an illustration of users' general concerns about the offered service.

8. The system of electing class representatives among the parents of the pupils is common in Scandinavia. The class representatives act as spokesmen for the parents and typically help the teachers in arranging parties, excursions, etc.

9. Petersson et al. (1989) use the term "power" about this type of influence. We define power in this context more broadly, and see it as the combined effect of voice and exit.

10. Concerning private hospitals, 52 percent of the population deem their existence important. For child care institutions, the similar figure is 63 percent.

11. The analyses are so-called multiple classification analyses done with the statistical package SPSS.

12. Socialist parties include the Social Democracy.

13. An interesting curiosity is that users considering exit are more socialist oriented than any of the groups above. One would expect it to be the other way around given the ideological connotations of the "privatization" debate.

REFERENCES

Andersen, J., et al. 1993. *Medborgerskab. Demokrati og politisk deltagelse.* Herning: Systime.

Andersen, J., and Torpe, L., eds. 1995. *Demokrati og politisk kultur.* Herning: Systime.

Asbjørnsen, N., Hoff, J., and Goul Andersen, J. 1995. *Nordiske medborgerundersøkelser* (The Democratic Citizenship in the Nordic

Countries). Project paper no. 3. Institute of Political Science. University of Copenhagen.

Cranil, M. 1994. *Decentralizering og selvforvaltning i folkeskolen.* Copenhagen: Ministry of Education.

Goul Andersen, J. 1988. "Vælgernes holdninger til den offentlige udgiftspolitik." In *Fra vækst til omstilling,* ed. K-H. Bentzon. København: Nyt fra Samfundsvidenskaberne.

Goul Andersen, J. 1995. "Velfærdsstatens folkelige opbakning." *Social Forskning,* August.

Goul Andersen, J., and Hoff, J. 1995. "Lighed i den politiske deltagelse." In *Demokratiets mangfoldighed: Tendenser i dansk politik,* eds. M. Madsen, H-J. Nielsen, and G. Sjöblom. København: Politiske Studier.

Hirschmann, A.O. 1970. *Exit, Voice and Loyalty: Responses to Decline in Firms, Organizations and States.* Oxford: Oxford University Press.

Hoff, J. 1995. *Micropower: The Politics of Welfare State Roles - User Participation in Scandinavia. The Democratic Citizenship in the Nordic Countries.* Project paper no. 6. Institute of Political Science. University of Copenhagen.

Kommunedata/Lars Torpe. 1995. *Landsdækkende borgeranalyse 1995.* København.

Ministry of Finance, et al. 1995. *Folkeskolens økonomi.* København: Schultz.

Pedersen, A.R., and Thomsen, K. 1994. Brugerindflydelse i skolebestyrelsen. Unpublished M.A. Thesis. University of Roskilde.

Petersson, O., et al. 1989. *Medborgernas makt.* Stockholm: Carlsson.

Sørensen, E. 1995a. Democracy and Regulation in Public Governance Institutions. Unpublished Ph.D Thesis. Licentiatserien. Institute of Political Science. University of Copenhagen.

Sørensen, E. 1995b. "Brugerindflydelse og demokrati: Brugerindflydelsens rolle i udviklingen af det danske demokrati." *Politica,* vol. 27, no.1, pp. 24-37.

Young, R. 1986. *Personal Autonomy: Beyond Negative and Positive Liberty.* London: Croom Helm.

CHAPTER 4

The Impact of Research on Norwegian Educational Policy

Kjell Eide

INTRODUCTION

Does research have an impact on political decisions? For many researchers this is a crucial question, as their livelihood may depend on it—for politicians, too, as it may influence their political success. Many researchers have tried to assess the impact of research on policy making. They have mostly come up with rather pessimistic conclusions or at least pointed to the many obstacles to a successful interplay between research and policy making. The traditional idea of a linear relationship between quantitative research, reform planning, and improved practice was challenged twenty-five years ago (Eide 1971) and has now gradually been abandoned.

Huberman still argues in terms of this positivist tradition and specifies the conditions under which such a model could function (Huberman 1995). He underlines, however, the importance of sustained mutual interaction between policy makers and researchers, thus discarding the idea of a linear model as a one-way flow of information. Weiss finds few examples of direct use of research findings for political problem solving but emphasizes the "enlightenment" function of research, which gradually will also influence political decisions (Weiss and Bucuvalas 1980). From a post-modernistic point of view, Watkins argues that all knowledge is socially or individually constructed and that the dominance of some ideas is largely a result of the power that groups may exert in promoting their perspectives. Knowledge that is generalizable, objective and/or theoretical does not constitute valid knowledge in specific contexts (Watkins 1995). Powell and DiMaggio (1991), in the tradition of institutionalism, point to the tendency of institutions to mimic others of their kind as a manifestation of their institutional identity. Louis tries to find a middle ground, accepting in a modified form the post-modernist idea that truth is normally local in time and space and the tendency of institutions to mimic other institutions but maintains that some generalizable knowledge does exist. The utilization process is, however, complex and difficult to predict. There will be no production function based on dissemination and knowledge utilization models (Louis 1995).

In this maze of theories and empirical findings, could there be a contribution from a small country, such as Norway, with its fairly transparent system of governance and its system of informal contact networks relatively intact? The Research Council of Norway, pointing towards educational policy as a suitable field for this kind of analysis, has convinced the Ministry of Education, Research and Church Affairs that a preparatory project might be worth financing. A full-scale project would have to include approaches from different disciplinary angles: history, political science, sociology, education, economics, and organization theory. The impact of specific disciplines over a long period of time would have to be studied. Case studies of specific reform efforts could be undertaken. The theory that extensive follow-up research and evaluation could lead to significant corrections in the implementation of reforms should be tested. As research findings with potential political impact do not necessarily emerge from Norwegian research, what role is played by dissemination through international organizations, such as bodies for international governmental collaboration? Would it be possible to compare the Norwegian experience in such fields with those of other countries? What has been the educational research policy of the Ministry of Education, and how is it organized in order to facilitate its relations to the research community?

The preliminary studies reported here aim at testing out some of the possible approaches. The first study focuses on ideology development in Norway during the last fifty years, the second on political argumentation based on economic theory during the same period, and the third on international exchange of research-based ideas, using the Organization for Economic Cooperation and Development (OECD) as an example. The common theme of the studies is the impact of research on educational policy making through different channels. In the following essay some of the major findings of those studies will be presented.

THE BELIEF IN SCIENTIFICATION OF POLITICS

In Norway, as in many other countries, the experiences of World War II created a strong belief in the potential of science to solve fundamental societal problems. Such beliefs were common among natural scientists and technologists and especially among the young Norwegian scientists returning from war efforts in British research laboratories. More important for our theme, however, are the attitudes of young researchers in the emerging Norwegian social sciences (Eide 1995a).

While the Norwegian universities were closed by the authorities during the German occupation, a young professor of philosophy at the University of Oslo, Arne Næss, brought together a group of youngsters interested in philosophy and its relationship to the social sciences (mixed with their interest in resistance activities, as Næss was one of the heads of the allied intelligence service in Oslo). This group wanted the social sciences to make politics more "rational." The philosophical school to which Næss belonged at that time, logical positivism, was marked by a strong belief in such possibilities. Næss had, however, certain reservations towards the more extreme positivistic views of that school, and this also applied to many of his collaborators. In the postwar years, this group came to have a strong influence on the development of social sciences in Norway, based on the new, private Institute for Social Research in Oslo.

Somewhat similar attitudes could be found in the strong econometric milieu at the University of Oslo, headed by the future Nobel Prize winners Ragnar Frisch and Trygve Haavelmo. Frisch saw no limits to the possibilities of econometrics to solve the essential problems of economic policy, but Haavelmo was somewhat more skeptical, examining carefully the limits to the validity of economic theories.

Another group of young students, centered in the Norwegian Socialist Student Union, developed somewhat different ideas about the role of social science. They had no faith in the possibility of social research to find the "right" answers to essential societal problems. They believed, however, that it might be possible through social research to develop a commonly agreed-upon knowledge base relating to the essential problems of society and also a more profound understanding of the societal inter-relationships underlying such problems. On this basis, political debate and political negotiations could be focused on the genuinely political problems and conflicts of interest in society. Such a common understanding would facilitate political governance in a society with strongly organized corporative interest groups and permit temporary compromises as a basis for continuous societal reform. Eventually many individuals from this group came to obtain key positions in politics, public administration and professional life.

Norwegian politicians were more skeptical of an essential role of science in a political context. A few key politicians in the Labor Government that took over in 1945 became, however, firm believers in the political importance of research. Our young Minister of Defense, who had been the head of military resistance in occupied Norway, pushed hard for the development of Norwegian technological research. The Minister of Finance, on the other hand, saw great possibilities in econometrics as a basis for economic planning. Research councils were established in the late 1940s, and they were gradually provided with substantial governmental funds. The emergence of planning departments in most ministries allowed more frequent contacts between research and public administration at the central level. In the 1960s, Harold Wilson's enthusiasm for the combination of science and socialism was even to some extent picked up by our Prime Minister.

The rapidly growing Norwegian social sciences came, in fact, to a great extent to follow such directions in the first twenty years after World War II. There were elements of critical research, but the main efforts went into the building of a broadly accepted knowledge base constituting a framework for the political negotiations between the government and different interest groups. Social research, often located in new, government-run institutes, became an essential element of, and condition for, the development of the so-called "Nordic model of governance." This model was marked by extensive reform initiatives, based on thorough enquiries by Royal Commissions through several years, formal and informal negotiations with all interested parties toward workable compromises, extensive pilot experiments, and slow implementation in order to obtain a certain feeling of ownership towards the reforms among those who should put them into practice.

During the 1960s, more critical voices were heard, also among researchers, towards the form of interplay that had developed between research, knowledge, and politics. In the "youth revolt" around 1970, this criticism took extreme forms. Many activists rejected completely the idea that social research could develop a common understanding of the conditions of society. Social conflicts were based on fundamentally different conceptions of society, and a search for a common knowledge base just served to camouflage conflicts that could not be reconciled. This attitude amounted to a complete rejection of the social democratic model of governance with carefully negotiated, gradual reforms.

The revolt left a strong influence on both Norwegian research and Norwegian politics. It weakened the authority of the central government, with "decentralization" and "participation" in institutional and local decisions as a result. It also weakened the authority of social research in its attempt to provide answers to political questions and "objective" descriptions of the conditions of society. It was clearly demonstrated that research functions politically, its results not being neutral.

The reaction in the late 1970s against the youth revolt and the wave of rightist politics in the 1980s were probably more moderate in Norway than in many other countries. But even in our case, there was no restoration of the research-based authority of knowledge or of the political authority of position. As in many other countries, there gradually emerged among politicians a feeling of disempowerment: Can modern society be governed at all? They felt that the media to a great extent had taken over the "problem formulation privilege," and internationalization had led to loss of control over most parameters of political action. The loss of political legitimacy was probably also influenced by the transition from an industrial to a postindustrial society, with the power structure of the industrial society still largely intact.

The faith in the potential of research to find solutions to urgent problems in society had disappeared. Furthermore, political authority had also been weakened and was in need of legitimation for political actions, and then research could be useful. Increasingly, political initiatives were bolstered by more or less selective research findings, chosen in order to prove that the proposed political answers were the "right" ones. This hardly reflected a regained trust in research, but the failing respect for research made it easier to misuse its findings.

Science, and particularly social science, came under stricter control, and many researchers soon registered the signals from the government.

In the 1990s, the break with the traditional "Nordic model" of governance has been more clearly marked. Political reforms are not so often prepared by extensive commission work and exploration of the possibilities for compromises. Reforms are decided upon and implemented in rapid tempo, in order to demonstrate efficiency and ability to act. Follow-up research and evaluation are supposed to serve as a basis for possible corrections of the course of the reforms as they develop. This is a form of policy making likely to increase the conflict level in society. It also raises the question of the political costs involved in correcting the course of a reform fought against heavy opposition. A politician does not go unpunished when experimenting with a whole population, if the experiment fails.

One feature of Norwegian social research, which deviates from what is found in many other countries, is the absence of partisan "think tanks." The role of Norwegian social research as an important underpinning of the Nordic model of governance has made all research institutions, public or private, extremely keen on maintaining their "academic respectability," and their image of neutrality in societal conflicts. Over the years, some attempts have been made to establish partisan research-based think tanks but with limited success. The developments in recent years, however, as clearly demonstrated in the debate about Norwegian membership in the European Union (EU), may indicate that even here, we are heading towards a watershed, with an increasing number of research institutions openly fighting for a center of excellence.

The developments in Norwegian research and politics, as sketched above, have their parallels in other countries and may be seen as a reflection of international trends. But there are also clear differences, such as the form of interplay between social research and the mode of governance which developed after World War II and the somewhat different impact of the youth revolt in Norway. However, it may seem as if the developments in the 1990s imply a closer adaptation of Norwegian policies to international trends. In a way, we have experienced, especially in the first twenty years after the war, a certain form of scientification of politics. Currently, we seem to move more towards a politicization of research.

The main purpose of this sketchy analysis of certain aspects of Norwegian history during the past fifty years has been to generate questions. Can the variations over time in the interplay between research and educational policy making be found when the focus is on individual research disciplines? What are the implications of the changes in the Nordic model of governance for the social sciences and their impact on policy making? To what extent is it really possible to identify specific influences of research on political decisions, and through what channels have research findings become premises for such decisions? Are Norwegian experiences in this field comparable to those of other countries? Could the current emphasis on evaluation as a basis for political decisions be seen as a form of "scientification" of politics even if the scientific legitimacy of evaluation procedures is doubtful? To what extent is the impact of research dependent upon individuals, usually civil servants at the higher level, serving as brokers between researchers and decision makers, and how does the organization of central government administration influence its ability to relate to research?

ECONOMICS AND EDUCATIONAL POLICY

Economic concerns are often claimed to be the prime determinant in educational policy, and a study of the impact of economic research and economic theories was a logical follow-up of the reflections above. The idea that economic welfare is desirable, and that tasks should be solved with the least possible use of resources is, however, thousands of years older than economics, and its impact on politics is not our theme. But efforts by economists to examine how economic welfare and effective activities can be achieved fall within the limits of this study. The effects of economic research on politics in general are, however, only taken into consideration when educational policy is especially affected (Eide 1995b).

The study is mainly concerned with political argumentation, as it appears in documents from the Norwegian government. The main sources are the government's eleven four-year plans from 1950 through today, and the White Papers and Royal Commission reports from the Ministry of Education in the same period. Added to this is the author's experience as a General Director in that Ministry for more than thirty years, twenty of which were spent as the head of its Planning

Department. The documents offer us a picture of the government's thinking on educational policy during nearly fifty years. They also demonstrate what kind of arguments the government has found appropriate in order to gain support for its policy. Their aim is to explain government policy and to sell it to the national public.

The emphasis on economic arguments in the presentation of the government's educational policy has varied significantly over time, by and large with corresponding variations in the general long-term plans and in the documents from the ministry responsible for educational policy. But the emphasis on economic arguments is somewhat stronger in the long-term plans. This difference may be due to the fact that the long-term plans are the responsibility of the Ministry of Finance. But it appears that the Ministry of Education has had a fairly close control over the presentation of educational policy in the long-term plans, and the explanation may be of a different kind. Through the long-term plans, the Minister of Education addresses primarily the public interested in politics in general, while the Ministry's own documents may be more targeted towards its own constituency in the education sector, those who will eventually have to implement the policy. The last few years have deviated somewhat from the general picture, as the emphasis on economic arguments for educational policy seems stronger in the documents from the Ministry of Education than in the long-term plans. This may reflect the specific relationship between the political leadership of that Ministry and the education sector in general in recent years.

The government's long-term plans also deviate in another sense from the documents of the Ministry of Education, mainly because the political functions of the long-term plans have changed over the years. In the 1950s, the long-term plans specified quantitative objectives to be achieved through government policy in different sectors of society, and the plans had a strong steering effect upon decision in all ministries. The plans from the 1960s were more focused on public activities, due to the abolishment of many public regulations. The plans from the 1970s concentrated on the interplay between politics in the different public sectors, emphasizing cross-sectoral problems. This implied that they lost some of their steering effect on the policies of the individual ministries. The plans prepared in the 1980s—a period of coalition governments—were marked by the attempt of the coalition partners to formulate political consensus between themselves and the avoidance of problems on which no such consensus had been achieved. The two plans from the 1990s again emphasize policy integration between different sectors but without the discussion of underlying principles of the plans from the 1970s or of the specification of policy objectives of the 1950s.

The documents from the Ministry of Education reflect to some extent the same variations, but the main trend here is that the Ministry tends to regard the long-term plans as a less suitable forum for essential political decisions and for the presentation of its policy.

The emphasis upon economic arguments for educational policy during those fifty years has been fairly modest compared to other types of arguments, such as the personal development and growth of an individual and the equalization of social, geographic, sexual, and other personal differences. The driving force behind the enormous expansion of the educational system in this period has, however, clearly, been the steadily increasing demand for education in the population. The idea that Norwegian educational policy has been dominated by concerns for the country's economic performance is not confirmed by the material examined in this study. There are, however, significant variations in the relative emphasis on the different rationales for political initiatives in the education sector. The 1950s and the early 1960s are clearly marked by the "discovery" (or rediscovery) of education as an essential factor of a country's economic performance. For that period, one might speak of a "push" from research findings upon policy. But it occurred in a situation in which politicians in Norway as well as in other countries despaired at the fact that traditional investments in physical capital yielded so little in terms of increased productivity in the economy. Thus, there also existed a "pull" upon economic research, and this combined "push" and "pull" had undoubtedly a real impact on the political will to favor educational expansion.

In the 1960s this type of economic argument played a less important role, and in the 1970s it practically disappeared. Probably this had less to do with reduced trust in the economic importance of education than with the diminished effect of such reasoning as a political sales argument. In the 1980s, it also became a political objective to reduce public spending, and governments then found it opportune to underscore the importance of such a resource-requiring public sector as education.

The interest in education as a factor in economic growth and for a country's economic competitiveness reemerged towards the end of the 1980s. Contrary to the 1950s, this was not due to any "push" effect; nor was it based on any research findings. But Norway was influenced by the international political wave, dominated by unwillingness to change the fundamental features of the economy causing unemployment. Educational expansion was politically less dangerous and had at least as important a political symbol function, in addition to its immediate effect on employment through the removal of individuals from the labor market. The legitimation function of research was clearly visible in this context.

In the Norwegian case, the relative emphasis on the importance of education as an instrument for economic growth is not strongly dependent upon the political color of the government. More important seems to be the "spirit of the times"—the dominant philosophies and attitudes in the Western countries. Actual Norwegian politics, however, showed more continuity and seemed less influenced by international ideas.

Another factor may, however, have contributed to the variations in the argumentation for educational policy in Norway. When great reforms are planned and have to be sold to the broad public, general political objectives of concern to everybody are strongly emphasized. In periods of implementation of politically decided reforms, the arguments focus more on the norms and values of the education sector. The variations during the past fifty years correspond with such a theory.

During the past ten to fifteen years, ideas from business economics about how activities can be conducted in an efficient way also appear in the debate on educational policy. This does not seem to be the result of new research findings of political interest; it seems more to be a question of legitimizing lower budgetary priorities for a popular public sector. In addition, problems of political governance and the legitimation of political authority created a need for symbols demonstrating the government's efficiency and ability to act.

There may also have been other rationales behind this. The previous silent acceptance that the education sector's own experts knew best how resources could be utilized was partly replaced by the belief that external experts know best how to run affairs effectively, even if they have little substantive knowledge of those affairs. Behind this lies a more general skepticism towards what is seen as an increasing power of professionals in different fields, which is blamed for causing problems of governance.

This renewed trust in economic expertise implied that one form of professional power is substituted by another. It is a well-known political tactic to confront one profession with another, in order to give the politicians some leeway for action in the no-man's land between the professional trenches but such a policy can only succeed if a proper balance between the professions is maintained, and in reasonable proportion to the relevant expertise held by the different professions. Norwegian politics of the 1980s can hardly be regarded as a success in this respect.

The prime reason for this is that economic theories have been developed in relation to activities fundamentally different from service processes of long duration, in which process qualities are often more important than any measure of the final outcome. The objectives of such processes are multi-dimensional, and "optimizing" such activities in relation to a few of the objectives offers little guidance for politics. In the case of education, the measured outcome of the process is also more determined by factors outside school than the school's own efforts, and the "value added" by the school cannot be measured. The "efficiency policy" in the education sector of the 1980s and 1990s must at least partially be categorized as an attempt to strengthen the politicians' image of efficiency.

The identification by economists of a connection between the educational level of a country and its economic performance offered no answer to the question of what causes this connection. The observed relationships also proved highly dependent upon external factors and offered few indications for a sensible educational policy in a specific country at a specific time. Suggestions that the economic importance of education should argue for special emphasis on specific fields of education, such as technology, natural sciences, and economics, got no confirmation in further studies. The same applies to suggestions that specific school subjects, or teaching styles, are particularly important in an economic context. Probably, there may be connections here, but they can only be identified through research in other disciplines, and their findings point to other conclusions than politicians have tried to deduct from economic research.

New ideas about governance, inspired by economics, have put their mark on public administration in recent years. This has happened with no careful examination of the relevance of such ideas for public services in such a field as education. The widespread skepticism that existed in research milieus concerned with organization theory, in Norway as well as in other countries, was disregarded. The apparent value of the new ideas as symbols of efficiency was tempting for the politicians, and they could also be a useful weapon for special professional groups in the internal struggles about competence in public administration.

The need for similar symbolic effects may underlie the attempts to include elements of market operations, such as institutional and personal competition and positive or negative economic sanctions, in public administration. In this case neither available research nor practical experience offer a valid basis for trust in the postulated effects of such policy instruments. In this case, as in the above-mentioned cases, ideological motives have probably played the most dominant role. What existed of research-based knowledge had to yield to the political will.

The research-based economic premises for educational policy in this period have to a great extent been produced in Norway, mostly in connection with the activities of the Ministry of Education. Research evidence of the impact of education on economic performance was presented very early in Norway. Already in 1951, research findings similar to those presented by scholars working with human capital theory a decade later were presented and extensively used in the first government long-term plan, covering the period 1954-57. The contact with international research in this area has been very close, and Norwegian contributions have played a role in the international professional development. An essential advantage in this context was the early development of Norwegian expertise in the economics of education, capable of critical evaluation of the international fads which occasionally spread over the Western world in this field. It sometimes functioned as a counter-expertise based on the education sectors' own premises, even in relation to our national economic milieu.

Those conditions were weakened in the 1980s. For the fifty-year period as a whole, however, it is probably correct to conclude that research-based economic premises for educational policy have played a more limited role in Norway than in many other Western countries (not to speak of Eastern Europe and many developing countries). Maybe the most important contribution of economics to Norwegian educational policy has been that it has sheltered our policies from the exaggerated and professionally unfounded use of economic arguments. The situation today, however, may raise doubts about the possibility of maintaining this position.

OECD AND NORWEGIAN EDUCATIONAL POLICY

The most important political impulses for Norwegian educational policy from other countries have probably come from Nordic collaboration, especially connected to the work of the Nordic Council of Ministers. Professional impulses of potential political impact have reached our research milieus and practitioners through more or less formalized international professional collaboration and may have found their way to political decision makers through our professional milieus. International organizations for governmental collaboration have, however, also played a role, and among such organizations, the Organization for Economic Cooperation and Development (OECD) has definitely been the most important during the past four decades. An extensive study of the interplay between Norway and the OECD in the education field examines the activities of this organization and the extensive contacts which gradually developed between the organization and Norwegian political and professional milieus.

This international governmental collaboration had its origin in the European Organization for Economic Cooperation (OEEC) whose prime task was to coordinate the economic policy of Western Europe within the framework of the Marshall Plan. The aim was the recovery of the Western economies and the dismantling of obstacles to international trade. Behind this lay the Cold War, and the idea that restoring economic balance in the Western European economies and creating more welfare for all would be an efficient way of containing Communist influence in those countries. The economic crisis of the interwar period would have to be avoided, and experiences from World War II seemed to indicate that economic planning might be an important instrument for this purpose.

In the course of a decade, the Western European countries succeeded largely in stabilizing their economies, but the development of productivity in their economies was slow, and there was a substantial gap between the Western European and the American technological level and economic productivity, which created imbalances in international trade. The question how productivity could be increased emerged as a key problem in international economic collaboration, and the OEEC established a network of productivity institutes in its member countries.

The Sputnik shock in 1957 raised fears in the Western world of being bypassed by the Russians in technological research and education. The former Soviet Union seemed to be able to develop far greater resources in terms of technical and scientific manpower than the West. Encouraged by the United States, the OEEC, therefore, established in 1958 a separate subcommittee for scientific and technical personnel (CSTP). This Committee organized an extensive survey of scientific and technical personnel resources and educational capacity in the Western countries.

In Norway, the Joint Committee of the Research Councils had already in 1955 conducted a major study of the supply of and demand for academically trained manpower. In collaboration with the three Norwegian research councils, the Joint Committee established a subcommittee, the Committee for Specialized Manpower, which through several years followed the development in this field, and established contacts with similar work in the Netherlands and Sweden. The Committee also followed the studies by OEEC with interest.

In 1961, the OEEC was converted into an organization with wider membership, the Organization for Economic Cooperation and Development (OECD). The United States, Canada, Australia, and New Zealand became members, to be followed by Japan somewhat later. The mandate of the organization became broader, and its tasks extended from economic stabilization and the regulation of international trade to general economic growth in the member countries. This also opened wider perspectives for the work of the STP Committee.

OECD's scientific and technical personnel committee did, however, also approach the problems from another angle, through attempts to clarify the interrelationships between education and economic performance. As mentioned, Norwegian studies of such interrelationships had already in 1951 had a strong impact on the long-term plans of the Norwegian government. Through the Nordic Cultural Commission—the governmental agency for collaboration in the cultural fields—such ideas were spread to central economic/political circles in the other Nordic countries. One of those who was engaged in this, was the Dane Hennig Friis, who became the first chairman of

OECD's STP Committee. He initiated the establishment of a special subgroup under the committee, the Study Group in the Economics of Education, which brought together key economic experts in the member countries interested in the interplay between education and the economy. The driving force among those was the leader of economic long-term planning in Sweden, Professor Ingvar Svennilsson, whose interest in such problems had also been inspired by the Nordic collaboration under the Nordic Cultural Commission. In 1961, when heading the secretariat of the Joint Committee of the Norwegian Research Councils, I was called to Paris to head a major part of the work under the STP Committee. I had undertaken the Norwegian studies on education and the economy in 1951 and had headed the studies on academic manpower in addition to holding the post of secretary of the Nordic Cultural Commission (Eide 1990).

The famous OECD conference in Washington, D.C., in the autumn of 1961 offered an opportunity for the presentation of the work of the Study Group in the Economics of Education on the interrelationship between education and the economy to a large number of leading politicians in the OECD countries. The main message of the conference was that the economic growth planned by the member countries would require a substantial expansion of their educational systems. Such an expansion was a decisive condition for the realization of such daring economic targets. The message was received, and contributed to a major political breakthrough for education.

In the OECD secretariat Kjell Eide was in charge of three major research programs. The first was a comprehensive mapping of the resources of academically trained manpower in the OECD countries, and their capacity for the training of such personnel. The study was the first of its kind, and formed the basis for the later work in the OECD on comparative educational statistics. The Study Group in the Economics of Education was turned into a "think tank," examining such central issues as the residual factor in economic growth, the national organization of educational planning, the financing of education, and the social objectives for educational policy. Its conferences on such themes attracted top-level international experts.

The most ambitious program, however, consisted of the establishment of agencies for educational planning in the member countries. In the course of a few years, such agencies were established in a majority of the OECD countries. The leaders of those agencies were brought together for frequent meetings under the auspices of the OECD, for examination and discussion of the national educational plans which eventually were produced, and planning methodology and professional work of importance for educational planning. A major fellowship program for educational planners, with practical training located in national planning agencies, was operated for a number of years. The national plans gave a new dimension to the "reviews" of educational policy in the member countries, which the STP Committee had initiated and gave the review reports more political clout. They also constituted an important contribution to comparative education.

The group of educational planners, with their central positions in national administrations, became an important political instrument and could be seen as a competitor to the STP Committee. Initially, the OECD secretariat had developed contacts with economic authorities in the member countries, even when dealing with educational policy. The educational planning program demonstrated, however, that collaboration in this field in the OECD would have to be based on direct contact with national educational authorities. This provided a more solid basis for the further development of collaboration, but it also created tensions in relation to the rest of the OECD, with its prime orientation towards economic/political problems. Such tensions have been a constant feature in the OECD to this date.

Norwegian authorities were rather passive towards the educational collaboration in the OECD in the early 1960s. In 1964, Eide was, however, called home to head a new department for research and planning in the Ministry of Education. The department prepared the long-term plans for the education sector in Norway to be integrated in the government's long-term plans. The department also conducted a series of studies, forming the basic material for a series of Royal Commissions working on radical reforms in primary, secondary, and higher education in Norway in the late 1960s.

The themes of those studies were closely connected to the themes that were taken up by the OECD. But Norwegian educational policy in those years was in many ways in the forefront of the political issues raised by the OECD, and, in Norway, the OECD studies functioned primarily as a legitimation of the main directions of Norwegian policy more than as an inspiration for such policies.

The strong increase in Norwegian expenditures for education in the 1960s needed, however, legitimation in relation to other urgent demands, and arguments could be found in the OECD's work. The radical reorganization of the structure of Norwegian higher education could be shown to be in line with the international trends of the times. The same applied to the extension of compulsory education in a comprehensive mode and the strong expansion in secondary education with the gradual removal of the distinction between general and vocational education. After a while, even our radical legislation on adult education got confirmation in the international emphasis on this part of the educational system. The political climate in the OECD at that time was influenced by the strongly divergent political attitudes of the member countries, which made it possible for the OECD to operate as a kind of international think tank for critical examination and the eventual testing out of new political ideas. The OECD secretariat and the national experts, brought in through the planning program and the country reviews, were usually oriented towards educational reforms. The Nordic countries experienced a period of radical reforms in this field, and were often seen as forerunners by the OECD. The Nordic delegates to the OECD played well together, and, until well into the 1970s, the political agenda of the OECD's educational collaboration was strongly influenced by the Nordic countries.

Towards the end of the 1960s, the main issues in the educational collaboration in the OECD had partly outplayed their role. The research on the economic importance of education had ended in a blind alley, and the faith in manpower forecasting as a basis for educational planning was largely gone. Planning was still important, but would clearly have to be much more concerned with the internal problems of the education sector, drawing upon research from such fields as sociology and pedagogy. And most important was the "youth revolt," creating a new agenda for educational policy and pushing many of the traditional issues into the background.

The response of the OECD was to change the STP Committee into an Education Committee, which meant adapting to the development that had already taken place in the education collaboration in the organization. Furthermore, a Centre for Educational Research and Innovation (CERI) was established. This Centre, which had its own governing board appointed by the OECD, had a somewhat greater autonomy in relation to the member governments than the Education Committee, and it was supposed to work in a more research-like manner than the Committee. The secretariats of the two bodies had, however, a common leadership.

Of great importance to the education collaboration in the OECD in the 1970s was the attitude of the organization to the youth revolt. Contrary to the situation in many member countries, where political polarization was strong, the OECD secretariat made contact with some of the leading activists. The new ideas that were put forward—the claim for "relevance" in education, democratization and participation in the leadership of educational institutions, inter-disciplinary collaboration, and closer contacts between the institutions and the surrounding society—were all taken up and examined by the OECD. This also applied to the new types of institutions and forms of governance which were tried out in a series of countries. Such phenomena were treated by the OECD in a sober way, marked by a general interest in what could be of value in such political innovations.

In Norway, as in many other countries, the attitude of the OECD in this context made the organization an important mediator. It legitimated the need for reform and contributed to a certain acceptance in governmental circles of some of the new ideas as well worth consideration and even realization. Norwegian educational authorities may have felt that they tackled the youth revolt in a better way than their counterparts in many other countries, but the international interest in the new ideas also made them more acceptable in our political milieu. The economic backlash in the latter part of the 1970s, and the wave of rightist politics that both created and thrived on the "economic crisis," manifested itself in the educational field primarily through a lower budgetary priority for the education sector. The interplay between education and working life came in the foreground, also because of the rapidly growing youth unemployment. The claim that education should be more relevant for the problems of society was reformulated to a claim for more relevance for the economy.

Through its anti-depression policies, Norway avoided the more drastic consequences of the economic backlash. Yet, expansion in the education sector flattened out, and the time of major educational reforms was past. The interplay between education and working life became a major political theme even with us, although with a main emphasis on the possibilities of economic enterprises to support the achievement of educational goals.

The work on educational issues in the OECD was still for a long time marked by attitudes corresponding fairly well to those found in Norway. Its bodies for educational collaboration kept up a consequent resistance against the downgrading of the political priority for education which could be found in a majority of the member countries.

In the course of the 1980s, however, especially the U.S. representatives in those bodies became more aggressive in their insistence that the key topics of conservative educational policy should be included in the OECD's agenda, and they were supported by several other countries.

The new slogans—quality in education, free choice of schools, new sources of financing, close contact with industry, accountability, effective use of resources, and financial incentives—entered in turn the agenda of OECD's educational bodies. Largely, however, the OECD was capable of handling such questions in a balanced manner.

The special political constellations in Norway, with frequent coalition governments spanning a major part of the political spectrum, made the impact of such international fashion waves fairly moderate. Our rejection of the more extreme conservative varieties of educational policy may have found a certain support in the sober analyses by the OECD.

The interest in close contact between education and industry, in efficiency measures and in more effective forms of governance in the OECD, had broad support from the member countries. A close contact between education and working life coincided fairly well with Norwegian traditions, and the OECD studies of structural changes in working life and their educational consequences were also closely connected to our traditional educational practice.

The work in the OECD on the development of information systems and evaluation as instruments for educational policy seems to have had a significant impact on Norwegian initiatives in this field, especially after the country review of Norway in 1987. OECD projects on teacher training, the situation of teachers, teaching methods and school curriculum were followed with interest in Norway, also because of our intensive involvement in curriculum development in the 1980s and 1990s.

The Planning Department of the Ministry of Education was the central contact point for the connection between the Ministry and the OECD. Already in the 1960s, however, other departments within the

Ministry and its advisory councils were brought in contact with individual OECD projects, and those contacts gradually widened. As in the 1970s, the Ministry became responsible for the funding of a significant part of Norwegian educational research, a considerable number of Norwegian researchers became engaged in OECD's professional work and meetings. In some areas this may have given impulses to our professional milieus, as in the case of the OECD work on the integration of the handicapped in regular schools, and on environmental education.

OECD activities in the field of comparative educational statistics were greatly expanded around 1990. A major program of experimental development of new statistical indicators was initiated, including measures of educational outcome in terms of pupil performance in different subjects. If the ambitions of the OECD in this field are carried forward, we may end up with a push towards international standardization of the subject requirements in the schools which may strongly influence the national aims of educational policy.

The educational work of the OECD today may be somewhat weakened by the retirement of their most experienced secretariat members. The organization work on education has also been more integrated in its general orientation towards economic problems, and the educational thinking within the secretariat may appear more conventional than previously. The pressure from dominant member countries for OECD work to legitimate its own policies also seems to have reached its educational work to a greater extent than previously.

At the same time, membership in the OECD will apparently be widened to include countries in Southeast Asia, South America, and Eastern Europe. This may lead to a stretching of the limited research resources of the OECD, and a redirection of its agenda away from typical Western European concerns. The European Union has also become a powerful competitor, possibly found by most Western European countries to be a more appropriate forum for collaboration. It may be that we see the end of the epoch in which the OECD was our most important international forum for educational collaboration.

The responsibility within the Norwegian government administration for contacts with the educational work of the OECD has also changed, as the responsibility for this contact has been spread out between different departments within the Ministry of Education. Political changes in the Nordic countries have also brought to an end the close Nordic cooperation in relation to the OECD, and the Nordic countries are not any more a dominant element influencing the agenda for its educational work. On the Norwegian side, it may seem that we have lost some of the ability to pursue a consistent policy towards the OECD. Our professional contacts with the OECD are still quite broad, but the choice of issues and the way of handling problems within the organization seem to be more remote from the problems of Norwegian education.

In the nearly forty years which have been sketched here, the collaboration with the OECD has in certain periods had a significant impact on Norwegian educational policy, and we have also occasionally been able to influence the agenda of the organization in this field. Of the different activities of the OECD, some projects seem mainly to have been used to legitimate a policy already pursued in Norway. Other projects may have reinforced ideas that already existed in our political and administrative circles and perhaps contributed to their realization through political decisions. Finally, the tendency of institutions to mimic features of comparable institutions in other countries may also have a certain validity for ministries of education. When a problem is regarded as essential in the educational policy in a number of other countries, there may be reasons why we should also take such problems seriously. An international organization, such as the OECD, without supranational authority, camouflages the political aspects of the topics dealt with and argues in terms of selected research results. Indirectly, the OECD may thus have contributed to the scientification of politics.

All those conditions for an impact of international collaboration upon national policy have been present in the context of a series of OECD projects. What made our situation in relation to the OECD somewhat special was our ability to influence the activities of the organization, which made the collaboration a form of interplay, and made it possible for us to a considerable extent to influence the impulses reaching us from the organization.

SOME TENTATIVE CONCLUSIONS

There are many theoretical models of the interplay between research and policy making. Politics may be "knowledge driven," when new research findings provide the basis for political initiatives ("push effect"). The interplay may be characterized as "problem solving," when political problems initiate new research problems ("pull effect"). The interplay may follow an "interactive" model, when researchers and decision-makers are in regular lasting communication. Policy decisions may be based upon "enlightenment," when research gradually forms attitudes in broad circles, eventually also influencing political decisions. Finally, policy making may follow a "garbage can model," when research findings in a political context are used for political legitimation or as an excuse for the postponement of decisions.

The studies undertaken in the preliminary project indicate that all those forms of interplay have occurred in Norwegian educational policy in the period examined. No single explanatory model, however, is capable of grasping the kind of interaction that has taken place. Each case of interaction has to be examined in detail in order to identify the forms of interplay at work.

A striking feature is the combined "push-pull" effect related to the economics of education in the 1950s and early 1960s. Equally striking is the use of economic arguments in the 1980s and 1990s, which seems unrelated to any new research findings in this field. The relatively modest place of economic arguments in key documents on educational policy during the past fifty years calls, however, for closer studies on the impact of research in other fields. The extensive use of presumably research-based ideas disseminated by the OECD as legitimation of already established or intended national policies and the possibility of influencing the agenda of such an international organization are important elements in this kind of interplay. Perhaps the most essential finding is the indication that an increasing distrust in political circles towards research as a basis for political decisions is accompanied by an increased tendency to use research findings as arguments for such decisions. This may reflect a shift away from the "Nordic model of governance" based on extensive studies and political negotiations preceding major reforms. This increasingly seems to be replaced by rapid, "effective" policy decisions, followed by evaluations and follow-up studies during the implementation period of reforms. Such feedback should then serve as a basis for corrections of policy directions during the implementation phase. This may imply a major shift in the traditional Nordic style of governance with very substantial consequences for the role of research.

The preliminary studies demonstrate that an historical approach based on extensive documentation and personal experience can offer new insights into the interplay between research and educational policy making, not only through the mapping of actual cases of interaction, but also regarding the conditions under which such interactions can function in a fruitful way. The studies have examined a specific research discipline and a central international body for dissemination of research findings. Yet they are only partial approaches to the main theme of the project. Primarily, they provide a clear indication that a more general approach, based on different disciplines and problem formulations, may highlight central problems in Norwegian educational policy and politics in general, in a fruitful way. They make a strong case for a much broader follow-up in this field.

The experience from a lifetime of work in the grey zone between policy making, administration and research has convinced me that an effective interplay between those three areas of activity is an important prerequisite for well-conceived policies. The forms of this interplay are, however, quite decisive for the outcome. We need a much deeper understanding of the conditions under which such an interplay can function in a fruitful way, both in terms of the organization of relevant research, the organization and competence of government machinery, and the development of consistent policies based on a more profound understanding of the complexities of the problem.

REFERENCES

Eide, K. 1971. *Educational Research Policy.* OECD, Paris.

Eide, K. 1990. *Thirty Years of Educational Collaboration in the OECD.* UNESCO, Paris.

Eide, K. 1995a. *Vitenskapeliggjøring av politikk. Et essay om bakgrunnen for prosjektet.* Institute for Studies in Research and Higher Education, Oslo.

Eide, K. 1995b. *Økonomi og utdanningspolitikk. Økonomisk forskning om premiss for utdanningspolitikken.* Institute for Studies in Research and Higher Education, Oslo.

Eide, K. 1995c. *OECD og norsk utdanningspolitikk. En studie av internasjonalt samspill.* Institute for Studies in Research and Higher Education, Oslo.

Huberman, M. 1995. "Research Utilisation: The State of the Art." *Knowledge and Policy* 7, no. 4.

Louis, K.S. 1995. *Two Steps Forward, One Step Back: Do We Need a New Theory of Dissemination and Knowledge Utilization?* Unpublished manuscript.

Powell, W., and P. DiMaggio, eds. 1991. *The New Institutionalism in Organizational Analysis*. Chicago: University of Chicago Press.

Watkins, J. 1995. A Postmodern Critical Theory of Research Use. *Knowledge and Policy* 7, no. 4.

Weiss, C., and N. Bucuvalas. 1980. *Social Science Research and Decision Making*. New York: Columbia University Press.

CHAPTER 5

The Swedish School Reforms: Trends and Issues

Torsten Husén

BACKGROUND

From the early 1950s to the late 1960s, I was closely involved in the Swedish school reforms as an expert and as an advisor to so-called Royal Commissions and in conducting studies to extend the knowledge base for these commissions. Since then one major task of mine, along with the conduct of international comparative investigations, has been to study critically the school as an institution in Western industrialized societies, including, of course, the Swedish society. One of the outcomes of these studies was my book *The School in Question* (London: Oxford University Press, 1979), which is now available in seven languages, including Japanese.

Recently I had a particular reason to take a retrospective, critical look at the Swedish school reforms from the mid-1940s to the late 1960s. I had been invited to prepare a contribution to a seminar organized in honor of Dr. Ragnar Edenman, expert in the Ministry of Education from 1946, Swedish Minister of Education 1957-1967, and political architect of the nine-year comprehensive school which was legislated for the entire country in 1962 (Husén, in press). The focus, in particular, had to be on "what went wrong," since the theme of the seminar was how political decisions often lead to consequences which, even though they are imaginable, are unwanted.

I shall here try to view the Swedish experiences under the time perspective of the quarter of a century that has elapsed since the major legislation on comprehensive schooling was passed. A closer look at problems of school reforms has been taken in my 1985 book *The Learning Society Revisited* (Oxford: Pergamon Press).

SOME GENERAL OBSERVATIONS

Before trying to identify and briefly comment upon the major issues, particularly upon "what went wrong" in the Swedish reforms, I shall make some overriding observations about the reforms in general.

First, the issues are very much the same as those in other industrialized countries in Western Europe and North America, and having read some summary reports from the governmental Ad Hoc Council on Education appointed by the Prime Minister in 1984, I would dare to say, in Japan. These countries have gone through a period of rapid increase in student enrollment, first at the lower secondary, then at the higher secondary, and finally at the tertiary level to the extent that the phrase "enrollment explosion" has been coined to characterize the process. In Western Europe in 1945, on the average, only some 20 percent of the students proceeded from primary to secondary school. By now lower secondary schooling is almost universal in these countries. The great majority, in some countries more than 80 percent, go on to upper secondary school.

The broadening of extended education has been concomitant with structural changes in a comprehensive direction with all the students and all the programs under the same roof instead of in separate schools at different levels of prestige and social compositions. Behind these spectacular changes are social and economic changes which have inspired a school policy guided by egalitarian and pragmatic principles and ideas.

Of course, the common denominator among industrialized countries should not be exaggerated. It is limited by different historical, cultural, and social traditions. But it is striking to an observer of what has happened in the OECD countries over the last few decades how big this common denominator is after all. The egalitarian element has been stronger in some countries than others. Likewise the structural changes have occurred at a rather different pace. By and large, the change has been more rapid in the United States than in Western Europe. In addition, the more or less unforeseen and unwanted consequences of the changes have occurred earlier in the United States than in Europe.

Second, the reforms affecting the structure of the basic school, its curriculum as well as access to ongoing education, have to be viewed in the larger framework of the Swedish welfare state. After, or concomitantly with provisions for social security, full employment, and decent medical care, education gained priority in public policy. Looking at the experience from Sweden, one is tempted to talk about a policy-making sequence in the reform process affecting the society. After a certain minimum of social security and welfare has been achieved, it is time to provide universal secondary education on an egalitarian basis beyond basic literacy and numeracy. On the horizon one begins to see provision for tertiary education or at least lifelong education for all.

Thus, educational reforms are in the last analysis social reforms and should be analyzed as such. They cannot be limited to changes in pedagogic or didactic principles. Educational reforms are part and parcel of overriding social changes. In order to succeed they have to be integral parts of reforms pertaining to the larger societal context. They cannot be a substitute for social and/or economic reforms.

Looking back on the debate on educational reform in Sweden as well as in other European countries, one is struck by the observation that professional educators, teachers, often reason as if schools are operating in a social vacuum. Therefore, political decisions that are at cross purposes with strongly held opinions among educators were often seen as improper "interference" on the part of the politicians into affairs that are none of their business. Reforms were regarded as the proper domain of the "experts," in this case the professional pedagogues, including some professors who sometimes like to play the role of "Platonic philosopher-kings" (Husén and Kogan 1984).

One reason why educational problems tend to be conceived in isolation from their social and economic context is, I assume, because social interventions in the educational domain are less controversial and politically less dangerous than attempts to change the overall social and economic order.

To be sure, changes in the structure of the national school system in Sweden, as in other countries, tended to stir up an intensive political debate. But among educators they were discussed as didactic problems. However, broadening of educational opportunities is often perceived by the privileged as threatening to their prerogatives.

The blueprint of making the first nine years of public education in Sweden comprehensive in a unified system was tested in an extensive pilot program from 1950 to 1962 with an increasing number of school districts participating (Marklund 1985; Orring 1962). The program was continuously evaluated with regard to learning outcomes. Well into the early 1960s educators dealt with the structural changes as if they were entirely pedagogical problems. How far up in the grades would it be possible to teach all the children with diverse backgrounds and ability in the same program or even in the same classroom?

Third, Sweden has discovered that reforms in the educational system do not take place overnight once the requisite legislation has been passed. Institutional changes cannot be forced to occur, even though some pushing and incentives are necessary. The comprehensive school reform needed at least three decades for its planning, tryout, and full implementation. In an interview with the former British Minister of Education, Sir Edward Boyle, my colleague Maurice Kogan (1973) asked about the role of educational research in preparing the comprehensive reform in Britain. Boyle referred to the Swedish social democratic planning which had covered "a cycle of twenty years over which a major piece of social engineering was achieved," then "five years of research by Husén, etc." The same government and even the same Prime Minister was in office during the entire reform period in Sweden. Certainly, political stability (as well as a remarkable political consensus on matters of schooling) meant a consistency in planning and implementation that is not possible when frequent changes in government and central administration take place. The labor market had over a long period been relatively peaceful with strong central federations of unions and employers and an efficient system of wage negotiations. The social welfare reforms starting in the 1930s and completed after the war laid the ground for an enhanced standard of living, which, in its turn, gave rise to enhanced aspirations for education. A policy of full employment and a system of basic and income-related pensions for all workers provided a framework of social security. A system of health insurance was another pillar in the social safety system. The educational reforms were concomitant with the introduction of child allowances, school health programs, free school lunches, free teaching materials, study grants for upper secondary school, and study loans at the tertiary level.

Once the political decision had been made, carefully planned long-range implementation had to be put in motion against quite a lot of resistance, especially among those who perceived that their working conditions had deteriorated. Strongly imbued traditions and practices tended to prevail in spite of legislative changes along progressive guidelines. New preservice teacher training had to be instituted as well as inservice training of teachers already in the field. Around 1960, after ten years of pilot program, the information and the attitudes teachers held about the school reform, which, for a long time, had been intensively discussed and about which hosts of information material had been distributed, were assessed (Marklund 1985). It was found that secondary school teachers whose working conditions and status would be, as they perceived it, adversely affected held more negative attitudes towards the reform than did elementary school teachers whose status would be enhanced by serving in the same schools as secondary school teachers. But more interestingly, secondary school teachers knew less about the reform than did elementary school teachers in spite of the fact that both categories had been subjected to the same amount of information. Not surprisingly attitude scores and scores on the information test were correlated so that those with negative attitudes knew less about the reform than those who held positive attitudes. Thus negative attitudes in a way served as a screening device against factual information, a phenomenon well known in perceptual psychology.

ISSUES DURING THE REFORM PERIOD

So far, we have outlined some of the more general observations about the reforms. I shall now take a look at issues and problems, first as they appeared when the reform was planned and when the blueprint was a political issue. I shall then take up some of the issues and problems—some of them unforeseen—which we have encountered in the wake of the reform. Sweden shares several of these problems with other systems of education in which reforms on a national scale have more recently been legislated, particularly in countries where the reforms mandate universal secondary schooling.

Comprehensive education (*école unique, Gesamtschule*), at least as it applies to the European scene, has two main features: 1) All types of schools covering mandatory school age, say from six to sixteen, are integrated into a common school which caters to *all* pupils in a given catchment area. Thus, traditional parallelism at the lower secondary level between schools with different purposes and serving pupils from different social class backgrounds is abolished; 2) Various programs at the lower and upper secondary level, both the "general" and "vocational" ones, are brought together into one unified system. This makes flexibility in transfer between programs possible. Choice of program does not imply definitive choice of a particular vocational path.

Educators in Europe, including Sweden, for a long time did not realize that the parallelism between schools serving the ten- to fifteen-year-olds to a certain extent also meant social segregation. Problems of school structure were discussed as pedagogical ones in terms of "differentiation" and "inherited ability" (Husén and Henrysson 1959; Husén 1962; Husén and Boalt 1968). This meant sorting the students with regard to capacity to cope with academic subjects. Scholastic aptitude was assessed in terms of verbal ability, which, apart from differences in inherited potential, was more developed among students coming from more educated homes. The problem of differentiation was defined as that of separating the academic goats from the non-academic, "practical" sheep (Husén 1962). It would take me too long to spell out in detail the arguments pro and con an early separation of "theoretically" and "practically" oriented students. Suffice it to point out here that all sorting criteria, such as school marks, examinations, and standardized tests, are not independent of social background. We now have, not the least of which come from studies conducted in connection with the Swedish school reforms, a massive body of evidence that shows that social handicaps are involved both in the selection for entry into upper secondary or university and in the screening process that occurs during these stages (Svensson 1980; Marklund 1985). Social handicaps stem from the fact that all criteria used in selection procedures are correlated with social background, particularly with parental education. This explains the finding from the so-called Stockholm study, in which an age cohort was followed up from grade 4, when structural differentiation took place, through grade 9, that students at a given level of ability with lower class background were more often rejected than students with upper and middle class background (Svensson 1980).

The Swedish school reforms—both the one on comprehensive school legislated in 1962 and the so-called gymnasium in 1964—that thoroughly affected the school both at the lower and upper secondary level and provided universal secondary education, were launched under the dual banner of equality of opportunity and the formation of a citizen for modern pluralistic and democratic society (Marklund and Bergendal 1979). The first goal was conceived within the framework of the classical liberal philosophy of equality: everybody should be put on the same starting line and begin the race for a life career. Differences in school attainments would thereby reflect who "by nature" was better or worse than the others. From the policy point of view everybody should be given the opportunity to go ahead in the formal (selective) system according to his or her ability (and motivation) independently of place of residence and parental background. The principle of equality in education for a long time appeared to be very simple and straightforward until surveys in the late 1960s and early 1970s began to reveal that the reforms did not bring about the equalization anticipated (OECD 1971). It was not just a matter of removing geographic and economic barriers. Social stratification according to home background prevailed. Not even in highly centralized systems, where strong policy actions were taken to increase participation in higher education among students with lower class background, did one succeed in breaking the pattern.

ISSUES IN THE WAKE OF THE REFORM

The 1946 School Commission in Sweden in its main report at some length spelled out how the "new" type of school recommended by the Commission by means of its curriculum and, in particular, methods of teaching and school work would form democratically oriented and responsible citizens with independent and critical personalities. Individualized teaching, independent study, group work, and activity methods of work would constitute a progressive pedagogy by means of which individuals with allegiance to democratic values would be formed. The "new" school was expected to get away from the authoritarian pedagogy of the "old" school and educate harmonious and creative students.

How Did These Grandiose Visions Turn out in Reality?

Given the subsequently obvious discrepancy between high expectations and bland rhetoric on the one hand and gray reality on the other, it would be hasty to characterize the outcomes of the reforms as failures and to put the label of "crisis" on the present situation. I once heard a U.S. Assistant Commissioner of Education at an OECD hearing calling the American high school a "disaster area." But disenchantment and disappointment have to be assessed not only with regard to aspirations and expectations. A proper standard of comparison would be the school system as it was before reforms subjected to sweeping evaluation were launched. Such comparisons cannot but tell us that spectacular progress has been made. Prior to the changes taking place over the last few decades, only a small select social, and not always intellectual, elite had access to postsecondary education, which prepared them for more qualified and elevated positions in society. The great masses had access only to low quality primary education of the kind we find today in many developing countries. The methods of instruction are now less authoritarian and give more freedom and scope to the individual student for developing his or her potentialities. In a way, the school has become a victim of its own successes, which have raised the level of aspirations considerably.

Typically, a major policy issue in Sweden since the late 1960s has been the role of school grades, whether they should be given at all, in what grades they should be given, and what weight should be given to them in selection to upper secondary and higher education. Behind this discussion is a pervasive feature of modern industrial and technological societies with increasing international trade competition and increasing dependence on technology which depends heavily on a labor force with a high level of formal education. We increasingly find symptoms of a growing meritocracy (Husén 1974). One of these symptoms has been called the "diploma disease." In the highly industrial societies, irrespective of social and economic order, there is a mounting tendency on the part of the employment system to leave it to the educational system to do the sorting and sifting of prospective workers. Job seekers are lined up according to the amount of formal education they have been able to absorb, and formal education increasingly has become the first criterion of selection. Young people at an early age become aware of this, and the increased competition for formal credentials has serious repercussions by distorting genuine educative values and school motivation. It fosters a tendency in school to work for external and not for internal rewards. The "examination hell" is part and parcel of a meritocratic society.

Those who cannot meet the demands and are unwilling to "stick it out" by staying as long as possible in school in order to secure a good position in the line of job seekers tend to give up at an early age. Absenteeism, classroom discipline, violence, and vandalism are part of the problem created by such conditions by "the new educational underclass." It consists of what in Sweden euphemistically has been referred to as the "booktired," those who come from underprivileged or deprived homes. It is "new" in that it is a small minority of some 5-15 percent without articulate spokesmen and therefore without significant political clout. The problems of this minority cannot be solved by the school alone, because they are inherent in a highly complex, technological, and growth-oriented society where social status increasingly has become dependent on the level of formal schooling.

I would submit that Sweden, as well as most other industrial societies with or without major structural and/or curricular reforms is beset with a series of goal conflicts, which the proponents of reforms are, of course, not willing to acknowledge. The spectacular expansion of secondary and tertiary education took place in the years preceding the oil crisis, when national economies were growing steadily and could accommodate the costs of their growing educational systems and, therefore, meet the rising popular aspirations. Enrollment in Sweden, as in other countries, grew rapidly over a period of some 15 years. During the same period, the per-pupil expenditure increased in constant prices in Sweden some 70 percent without causing any particular concern. But the growing expectations cannot be met any longer. Constant, or even reduced, resources call for a "management of decline."

Have we really asked ourselves why the school should be in a position to be able to equalize life chances? It is after all an institution like others in a meritocratic era, which exists in order to impart competencies, convey distinctions, and reinforce individual differences, which to a certain extent are determined by social background. Irrespective of the kind of society we are dealing with, some children come from more education-conscious homes than others and, therefore, to paraphrase Orwell, are "more equal than others."

Another area of conflict has to do with the fact that schooling increasingly has become a major determinant of social status and social mobility. This has led to an increased competition in school—a scrambling for good marks. The reward in the long run for good school achievement is employment, advancement, and higher status.

Competition and cooperation are competing goals that cannot easily be accommodated. Achievements are evaluated individually and not collectively. But group work is a collective enterprise. Tests and examinations abound in spite of quite a lot of rhetoric in some quarters about the futility of grades and the need for character-building by means of group work.

Finally, as resources have begun to become scarce, equality comes into conflict with quality. This applies particularly to the extension of upper secondary and higher education to all. It has been signaled by falling standards in subject areas where high quality teaching is of crucial importance, such as in mathematics and science (Husén et al. 1973; Liljefors and Murray 1983).

CONCLUDING REMARKS

What, specifically, are the lessons that can be learned from the Swedish experience? Let me conclude by venturing some generalizations.

1. Reforms have to be conceived in a wider socio-economic context.

2. Reforms do not occur overnight. Institutional changes need a lot of time, political stability, and a certain amount of consensus in order to occur in an orderly way and not be limited to paper.

3. Reforms have to consider the stake that educators have in the status quo. Proper incentives have to be administered as well as reform programs of pre- and inservice teacher training.

4. Reforms have to take into consideration the entire ecology of interdependent educative influences. Schooling is only one of these. Changes in school practices have to be coordinated with changes in other institutions.

I have tried here to come up with a diagnosis of the present problems in many of the OECD countries. Needless to say, a diagnosis, I hope of a relevant nature, has to precede any attempts to indicate what could be done to rectify what "went wrong." To be sure, it is easy to issue recipes and prescriptions for improvement. But the social scientist who takes time and goes through some pains in his/her diagnosis runs up against formidable problems in conveying the results to the key people in the educational establishment: policy makers, administrators, teachers, and, last but not least, parents. He or she meets, as I have pointed out, institutional inertia and attitudes of defence against any change. Some contend that there are no problems. Others are unwilling to accept the facts constituting the problems. My present task, however, is not to even indicate a framework, nor to speak of concrete proposals for policy actions that would have to be taken. I have done this where more time and space has been available (see, e.g., Husén 1979 and 1985a, 1985b).

My experiences over many years in the field of international and comparative education have convinced me of the utility of cross-national comparisons of the "anatomy" of educational reforms. Why is a particular kind of reform successful in one country, and why is it that what seems to be a similar reform fails in another country? Why are teachers and/or school administrators willing to back reform plans and support their implementation in one country but not in another? Of course, constellations of cultural, social, and economic conditions, not to speak of vested interests, vary from country to country. Socio-cultural influences, historical traditions, political winds, and the inner dynamics of the social order are important determinants of how the formal system of education operates. But in spite of all these differences there is a common core of determinants that we can identify in the highly industrialized and highly scholarized countries today in various parts of the world. They have, to a large extent, the same institutional problems in their school systems. They are groping for reforms in very much the same directions. And, more important, they have all run up against unexpected problems of a social nature which they must try to solve in order to prevent school from becoming a disaster.

REFERENCES

Boucher, Leon. 1982. *Tradition and Change in Swedish Education*. Oxford: Pergamon Press.

Coleman, James S., and Torsten Husén. 1985. *Becoming Adult in a Changing Society*. Paris: OECD (also in French).

Dahllöf, Urban, et al. 1966. *Secondary Education in Sweden*. Stockholm: National Board of Education.

Hoerner, Horst. 1970. *Demokratisierung der Schule in Schweden. Genese, Deskription und Explikation*. Weinheim: Beltz.

Husén, Torsten. 1962. *Problems of Differentiation in Swedish Compulsory Schooling*. Stockholm: Scandinavian University (Svenska Bokförlaget).

Husén, Torsten. 1963/64. "Social-Determinants of the Comprehensive School." *International Review of Education* 4, no. 2: 158-174.

Husén, Torsten. 1974. *Talent, Equality and Meritocracy.* The Hague: Martinus Nijhoff.

Husén, Torsten. 1975. *Social Influences on Educational Attainment.* Paris: OECD (also in French, German, and Spanish).

Husén, Torsten. 1979. *The School in Question: A Comparative Study of the School and Its Future in Western Societies.* London and New York: Oxford University Press (also in Japanese).

Husén, Torsten. 1980. "Egalitarian Policies in Swedish Education—Rhetoric and Reality." *Skandinaviska Banken Quarterly Review* No.3-4:56-62.

Husén, Torsten. 1985a. "The School in the Achievement-Oriented Society." *Phi Delta Kappan,* February 1985: 398-402.

Husén, Torsten. 1985b. *The Learning Society Revisited.* Oxford: Pergamon Press.

Husén, Torsten. "Skolreformerna: Vad som gätt rätt respektive 'snett'" (The School Reforms: What Has Gone 'Right' and 'Wrong,' Respectively). *Statsvetenskaplig Tidskrift* (Political Science Journal). Forthcoming.

Husén, Torsten, and Gunnar Boalt. 1968. *Educational Research and Educational Change: The Case of Sweden.* Stockholm and New York: Almqvist & Wiksell International and John Wiley & Sons.

Husén, Torsten, and Sten Henrysson, eds. 1959. *Differentiation and Guidance in the Comprehensive School.* Stockholm: Almqvist & Wiksell International.

Husén, Torsten, and Maurice Kogan, eds. 1984. *Educational Research and Policy: How Do They Relate?* Oxford: Pergamon Press.

Husén, Torsten, et al. 1973. *Svensk skola i internationell belysning: Naturorienterande ämnen* (The Swedish School in International Comparisons: Science). Stockholm: Almqvist & Wiksell International.

Jüttner, Egon, and Detlef Glowka. 1975. "Schulreform und Gesellschaft in Schweden 1940-1970." In *Schulreform in gesellschaftlichen Prozess, Vol. 2,* eds. Saul Robinsohn et al. Stuttgart: Klett, 431-598.

Kogan, Maurice. 1973. *The Politics of Education.* London: Penguin.

Liljefors, Robert, and Åsa Murray. 1983. *Matematik i svensk skola* (Mathematics in the Swedish Schools). Report from the Second International Mathematics Survey. Stockholm: National Board of Education, Research Report No. 46.

Marklund, Sixten. 1963. "The Attitudes of Intending Teachers to School Reform in Sweden." *World Year Book of Education*, eds. Eric Houle and Jacquette Megarry. London: Kegan Paul.

Marklund, Sixten. 1980a. *The Democratization of Education in Sweden: A UNESCO Case Study*. Stockholm: Institute of International Education, University of Stockholm.

Marklund, Sixten. 1980b. "The Role of Central Government in Educational Development in Sweden." *World Yearbook of Education*, eds. Eric Houle and Jacquette Megarry. London: Kegan Paul.

Marklund, Sixten. 1980c. "New Stages in Education: A Swedish Viewpoint." *Comparative Education*, 16:3

Marklund, Sixten. 1981. "Sweden: Setting up the Comprehensive School." *Prospect* 11, no. 2.

Marklund, Sixten. 1984. "Sweden." In *Educational Policy: An International Survey*, ed. J.R. Hough. London and New York: Croom Helm and St. Martin's Press.

Marklund, Sixten. 1985. *Skolsverige 1950-1975, Vol. 4: Differentieringsfrågan* (The Swedish School 1950-1975: The Problem of Differentiation). Stockholm: Liber Utbildningsförlaget.

Marklund, Sixten, and Gunnar Bergendal. 1979. *Trends in Swedish Educational Policy*. Stockholm: The Swedish Institute.

Marklund, Sixten, and Pår Söderberg. 1967. *The Swedish Comprehensive School*. London: Longmans.

OECD. 1971. Group Disparities in Educational Participation and Achievement. Background Papers Nrs. 4 and 10, Conference on Policies for Educational Growth. Paris: Organization for Economic Cooperation and Development.

Orring, Jonas. 1962. *Comprehensive School and Continuation Schools in Sweden*. Stockholm: Ministry of Education.

Paulston, G. Rolland. 1968. *Educational Change in Sweden: Planning and Accepting the Comprehensive School Reform*. New York: Teachers College Press, Columbia University.

Stenholm, Britta. 1970. *Education in Sweden*. Stockholm: Swedish Institute.

Svensson, Allan. 1980. "On Equality and University Education in Sweden." *Scandinavian Journal of Educational Research* 24, No. 2: 79-92.

CHAPTER 6

School Fatigue and "Too Many Bad Excuses": Swedish Teenage Girls Talk about Truancy

Mina O'Dowd

INTRODUCTION

During the past few decades the problem of truancy has reached major proportions in Europe, especially so far as metropolitan secondary school pupils are concerned.[1] The Scandinavian countries have also experienced an increase in truancy among secondary school pupils. School fatigue is a concept that is used in Sweden to describe both the phenomenon of truancy and the causes of truancy, implying perhaps that there is a causal relationship between school fatigue as a state of being and as the act of truancy.

School fatigue is a nebulous problem. Some sources attribute the school fatigue pupils experience to the increasing rate of female participation in the labor market. Other sources cite the increasing number of single parent households and the high rate of divorce. It is true that all of these factors taken together constitute a changing demographic context, but their effect on the so-called "school fatigue" is not known.

Social attitudes to single mothers, divorcées, and mothers with careers are not easily discerned. Nor is the purpose of this chapter to investigate these social attitudes. An attempt is made here to account for the reasons individual teenage girls give for school fatigue within the framework of an exploratory study. In this context it is necessary to mention that the highest rates of female participation in the labor market are to be found in Sweden,[2] that nearly 40 percent of all households in Sweden are single parent households, the majority of which are single female households,[3] and that the divorce rate is high.[4] Such factors as the extremely low public confidence in Sweden in regard to the capacity of schools to teach subjects and to develop qualities in students[5] and the surprisingly low rate of Swedish pupils who like school are less cited factors[6] that may be as important as the aforementioned ones in determining the sources of the widespread problem of school fatigue.

THE PROBLEM AND THE METHOD OF RESEARCH

The underlying question is: Is school fatigue an educational problem that has social repercussions or a social problem that has educational repercussions? Or is it both? An attempt is made herein to address this question by asking students to define school fatigue.

The assumption upon which this study is based is that students' subjective experience of schooling is essential in a discussion concerning school fatigue. An understanding that students can provide valuable information as to which aspects of schooling contribute substantially to the relationship students have to schooling is the starting point for this exercise. Questions such as: How important are teachers, peers, the structure of schooling, and the students as far as school fatigue is concerned? What do students think of their teachers? and How do students perceive themselves? are best answered by students.

For this purpose, semi-structured interviews were conducted with three female ninth grade students in a school in the greater Stockholm area. The interviews were approximately 90 minutes long, and participation was voluntary. These students: 1) were all in the same class; 2) all have parents who have an academic education; 3) all have divorced parents; 4) all live in single parent households; 5) all have different levels of achievement, i.e., Marie is a high achiever, Ellen is above average, and Sofia is below average, in relation to their classmates. These students do not constitute a representative sample. The purpose of this study is to acquire information from a small group of students who have personal experience of having divorced parents and of living in single parent households on the topic of the sources of school fatigue as they see it. This study is undertaken in order to investigate what may or may not be factors that influence school fatigue from the perspective of students.

THE STRUCTURE OF THE CHAPTER

An introduction and a brief presentation of the problem and the research method used herein have been given. A description of the students who were interviewed will be presented in the next section as well as a brief description of their school. In the main section of the chapter the students voice their thoughts about school fatigue and about their lives. A short analysis will then be presented, and reflections will follow the analysis. Finally, some concluding remarks will be made.

DESCRIPTION OF THE PARTICIPANTS

The three girls who have been interviewed have a lot in common as has been mentioned above. There are several dissimilarities as well that will be touched upon below.[7]

Marie

Marie has a high grade point average. She is a so-called well-rounded student. In other words, she is equally proficient in many areas. She has been selected by teachers and staff to participate in a formal student group that functions as a support group for other students who have problems. She is outspoken and has taken an active stance against student manifestations of racism and neo-Nazism. She does not want to go to high school in the municipality. She is going to apply for admission to the English-speaking high school in Stockholm.

Marie lives with her mother and her little sister in a large apartment near both of their schools. Marie's father has moved to a Stockholm suburb located 70 kilometers away from the suburb in which Marie lives. She is the fourth child in her family. She takes a great deal of responsibility for her little sister, who is six years younger. Marie's older brother and sisters no longer live at home. Marie's parents divorced when she was eleven years old. Even though it was a difficult period in her life, she thinks that the divorce was for the best.

Marie's father is Swedish, while her mother has a non-Swedish ethnic parent as well as a Swedish parent. Marie's mother has an academic education. Her father was educated in an academy of fine arts.

Marie's mother is single. Marie's father is remarried. He has little or no contact with his five children. As Marie puts it, "He considers it to be his children's responsibility to maintain a relationship with him and not vice versa."

Marie is sixteen years old and is the oldest of the three teenage girls who were interviewed. (Marie is older than her classmates.)

Ellen

Ellen has an above average grade point average. She is a conscientious student. Despite the fact that her father is a teacher at the high school in the municipality, Ellen wants to apply for admission to the English-speaking high school in Stockholm. It is uncertain if she will be able to raise her grades high enough this year in order to gain admission.

Ellen and her older brother live two weeks of every month with their mother and the other two weeks with their father. Their parents both live near their schools. She lives in her mother's condominium and in her father's apartment. Ellen's parents divorced when she was eight years old. According to Ellen, "It hasn't influenced me negatively. I understand why they decided to divorce."

Ellen's parents are both Swedes. Her mother and her father have an academic education. Ellen's father is single. Ellen's mother has a partner. Ellen's parents both take an active part in their children's lives, education, and upbringing.

Ellen is fifteen years old. She is the same age as the majority of her classmates.

Sofia

Sofia's grade point average is below average. She is worried that she will not be able to raise her grades enough so that she can gain admission to the hotel and restaurant school to which she aspires.

Sofia lives with her mother in an apartment, while her older brother lives with their father in his house. Sofia's parents divorced when she was four years old. Her parents' homes are located approximately 100 kilometers from each other. Sofia has had little or no contact with her father during long periods of time. She has a good relationship with her brother, however.

Both of Sofia's parents are Swedish, and they both have an academic education. Sofia's father has had several relationships. The present relationship is very problematic for his children. Sofia's mother is single.

Sofia is fourteen years old, and the youngest of the three girls interviewed for this study. (Sofia is younger than her classmates.)

DESCRIPTION OF THE SCHOOL

The three students who have been interviewed for this article are classmates. They all attend a public school in a Stockholm suburb. The majority of students who attend this school come from working-class homes. There is a significant number of pupils in the school with non-Swedish ethnic backgrounds. The school in question has been considered a so-called "problem school." It has recently undergone total reconstruction, a project that has taken over a year and involved a remodeling and reorganization of the entire school. Reconstruction work has taken place during the whole school day for over a year. The final product is a combined secondary and elementary school, housed in the same building, with the secondary school pupils on the second-story level and the primary school pupils being housed on the ground floor. Despite these efforts and other efforts to change the image of the school by means of the creation of a "profile," "nothing has changed at school, except the buildings," according to Marie.

The principal of the school is a woman, and there are twice as many female teachers as male teachers in this school. The total number of teachers is 31. There are separate classes for pupils with special needs at both the primary and the secondary levels. The total number of pupils in elementary school, including pupils with special needs, is 260. The total number of students in secondary school, including pupils with special needs, is 375. The total number of pupils with special needs is 17.

The population in the community in which this school is located is composed of predominantly working-class and middle-class homes. During the last five years, the number of well-educated and well-situated households has decreased in the community, while the number of less well-educated and less well-situated households has increased, posing large problems for the economic solvency of the community due to reduced tax income. There is a relatively large group of inhabitants with non-Swedish background in the community. A majority of these people are so-called "first generation" immigrants, the largest ethnic group being composed of Assyrian refugees, coming mainly from Turkey.

During the past few years, the municipality in which this school is located has implemented substantial cutbacks in schooling, day care, leisure time care, and leisure time activities for children and youths as well as elderly care and services. Similar cutbacks in these areas have occurred in municipalities throughout Sweden during the same period. Criticism has been voiced throughout Sweden by parents and educators in regard to what many consider to be drastic cutbacks in areas that should have been spared. At the same time, reforms have been introduced to improve schooling.[8] A new curriculum has been introduced, and new methods have been suggested.

STUDENTS DISCUSS SCHOOL FATIGUE

Marie

Definition of school fatigue. "School fatigue is when you grow tired of school and don't want to go to school. Everything that has to do with school starts to feel meaningless, and you completely lose your motivation to go to school and to do good school work." It is like "a depression that influences both your life in school and out of school and your relationship to your friends." School fatigue is "a problem that pupils have to solve. Pupils need the help of teachers and the school to solve the problem of school fatigue . . . school fatigue is a more complicated issue than whether or not one's parents are divorced. It has to do with a lack of confidence and a lack of feeling that one belongs. School fatigue has to do with the atmosphere in school. . . . School isn't as safe as it was before. There are pupils in school who have weapons. Pupils are physically abused daily in school. There are teachers who are physically abused in school daily. School should be a safe place to go to—to learn, to develop, to mature and learn to know others and oneself. . . . But school isn't like that any more. It is a place that one is forced to go to . . . many pupils consider school to be like a jail . . . they have to go to school, they wish that they were somewhere else, and they can't wait until they can quit school. . . . It is possible to overcome school fatigue."

Factors influencing school fatigue. In answer to the question, "To what extent is school fatigue dependent upon the following factors: teachers, other students, the school itself, oneself?" Marie says that school fatigue depends primarily upon the pupil inasmuch as the pupil "always has a choice if she/he wants to make school a priority or if she/he wants to just forget about school completely." In other words, pupils influence their own attitudes to school and thus their own school fatigue by 40 percent. School fatigue is influenced by schoolmates by 30 percent. Teachers and schooling itself both influence school fatigue by 15 percent.

Teacher characteristics. Marie thinks that about 75 percent of her teachers are good teachers, while 25 percent are not good. "A good teacher is strict enough and has humor. She/he does not slavishly follow the curriculum or text books, but has her/his own ideas. A good teacher shouldn't be predictable. She/he should be able to surprise her/his pupils and to take risks. Often it is the experienced teachers who dare to take risks, while inexperienced teachers are afraid to try new things. Good teachers respect students, but they are strict enough to make students respect them. Good teachers should be nice, but they should also be strict so that they can keep things under control in the classroom. They should be competent. . . . But *how* they teach is extra important. . . . Teachers who are not good teachers are often not strict as far as discipline is concerned. They want students to think that they are very nice, and they want to have a good relationship with their students. At first they are too nice, and students don't learn to have respect for them. Their intentions are good, but often the result isn't good . . . students don't take them seriously. They are often knowledgeable, but they are boring teachers . . . they stand in front of the class and talk and talk and talk about the same things for forty minutes, . . . you tire of them. They do the same thing during every class, with the exception of the classes when they show a boring educational movie. Their teaching is very monotonous."

Pupil characteristics. "What is important is how one feels about oneself. You have to have self-confidence. You have to have a goal, and you have to work in order to reach your goal, and not just have excuses for yourself. There are a lot of people who have excuses for themselves. There are a lot of teachers who have excuses for pupils who do not do well. We have too many excuses for everything. Individuals should be responsible for what they do. There are too many bad excuses used all the time for why pupils get in trouble and become school fatigued."

Future plans. Marie does not know what she wants to do "when she grows up," but she does want to get an academic education.

Self-perception. Marie considers herself to be a good student. She says, however, that she doesn't always work up to her capacity. "This is due to motivation. There are some subjects that are more interesting than others, and I work harder in those subjects. Of course, there are other subjects that are less interesting. And I believe that whether or not a pupil works hard has to do with the teacher. It depends on the pupils as well, but a lot depends on the teachers, too." Marie says that she likes all of her teachers, and she thinks all of her teachers like her. She is not happy with the division of "gangs" at the school, however. "I consider myself to be 100 percent Swedish. Some of my friends, who know my mother and know that she comes from another country, consider me to be an immigrant. This is a little confusing for me. If my mother came from Turkey, then everyone would consider me to be an immigrant because I would have dark hair and dark skin, while I still considered myself to be Swedish. But because I have light skin and I don't have dark hair, most people think of me as being Swedish, too."

Suggestions for change. "The atmosphere in school should be friendly . . . Organized activities between classes like Ping-Pong, basketball and a cafe that is open for students make the atmosphere more friendly. Teachers should encourage students who feel school fatigue . . . they should talk to them and cheer them on. Teachers should talk about students' qualities and not just discuss their shortcomings . . . Teachers should encourage students to work harder by giving them the chance to choose how and what they want to work with."

Comments. "We *have* to go to school in order to get a job, any job. And it may not even be a good job at that. If you don't go to school, you know that your whole future will go to the dogs. This contributes to school fatigue. It is hard to live with all of the demands. There is so much at stake, and so much depends on how one does in school. I think that this is very difficult for some pupils who lack self-confidence. When all of these demands are made on them, they may experience that they are feeling pressured by the support their parents give them. And teachers' constant talk about grades and the future can make school very difficult to cope with . . . there's so much at stake."

"I don't personally feel that my parents' support is difficult to cope with. I consider it to be supportive. Their demands help me to advance and to want to succeed . . . I know that one of my friends thinks that her mother's support is hard to cope with. That which the mother considers to be supportive, the daughter feels is too demanding."

"My parents' divorce has affected me personally, but it hasn't affected my school work. I have more parental support now that my parents are divorced than I had when they were married. My mother knows that, for all intents and purposes, I only have one parent, and she wants to help me because she knows that I don't get any help from my father. . . . All of my friends whose parents are divorced are very different. I think that it is a generalization if one assumes that there is a stereotype for single mothers and their children, because there are so many different kinds of people involved, and none of them are alike, at least none of them that I know."

Ellen

Definition of school fatigue. School fatigue is a state "when one is tired of everything . . . the teachers and all of the homework and the school and one's classmates and problem pupils . . . well, nearly everything about school. Boring teachers and boring classes. The feeling that there are things to be done constantly. A lot of homework and a constant feeling that there are things one has to do. Three or four different assignments to be done every day. You feel pressured . . . to accomplish everything. It feels very difficult sometimes. . . . A part of school fatigue is the feeling one has at the end of the school year before summer vacation when school is difficult and one thinks, 'I want to quit school now.'"

Factors influencing school fatigue. In answer to the question: "To what extent is school fatigue dependent upon the following factors: teachers, other students, the school itself, oneself?" Ellen said that school fatigue is primarily dependent upon oneself. Sixty percent of school fatigue is dependent upon oneself. "Other people can't do anything to help if one doesn't help oneself. Of course, if one believes in oneself, everything will be fine."

"I believe that teachers influence a lot. If they are boring and stand in front of the class and talk sort of over one's head . . . right out into the empty space, then one doesn't learn anything. You get tired. You just can't cope with listening any longer. You turn yourself off. Tune out. Approximately 20 percent of school fatigue depends on what kind of teachers one has."

According to Ellen, 10 percent of school fatigue is influenced by other students. The final 10 percent of school fatigue is dependent upon the school itself and school-related factors.

Teacher characteristics. Ellen thinks that all of her teachers are good, but some of them are boring. Eighty percent of her teachers are good, while 20 percent are boring. "Some of them just stand there and babble and babble, and the students don't understand . . . They don't care about their students. Sometimes it feels as if they think that they are on a higher level than we are. . . .When I feel that that is the case, I just can't concentrate on what they are saying. It doesn't happen very often. Most of the teachers are very good, and they talk *to* us. Only a few teachers talk down to us. . . . We have modern teachers in our school who communicate with their students. Teachers should be on the same level as students. They should talk *to* students, and not over their heads, so that all of the students understand. They should enjoy teaching . . . they shouldn't just sit there and think that everything is boring. Of course, one can't expect teachers to be happy every class, because they are only human. But they should take a deep breath before each new class. If they have a difficult class, then they should take a deep breath before the next class starts. They should think, 'a new group is coming now and I need to work with them. If they are difficult, then I will just have to get angry again.' But they should start the new class at a normal level. They should be open for new impulses as well."

Pupil characteristics. "You have to have a positive attitude. If you are negative and think, 'everything is shit and nothing is good' then nothing is going to be good either. If you are positive and try, then almost everything turns out right. If you think school is boring, then you have to try to change your own attitudes. You have to try to listen and learn and do your homework. Even if it is boring, you have to try to do it. You have to do a lot of work with yourself. . . . In general, students should be nice. . . . You have to believe in yourself and in your capability."

Future plans. Ellen wants to combine her interests in foreign languages, people, and travel. She doesn't want to be a teacher. She can't see herself having the same job her whole life, as her parents have done. "I don't feel that I can have the same job all of my life. I don't want to be a teacher and work as a teacher all of my life. I want to work as a group leader for a travel agency. I want to work for an international firm for awhile or something like that. I like computer science. I want to do a lot of different things. . . . I don't want to specialize in something."

Self-perception. Ellen describes herself as "trustworthy, quite ambitious, and nice, most of the time." She likes most of her teachers, and she thinks that they like her. "My classmates think that I am nice, most of the time—but not all of the time." Ellen defines what she means by "nice" as "a personality trait that is a combination of being trustworthy and pleasant."

Suggestions for change. In response to the question "If you had a chance to change something in school to make it better, what would it be?" Ellen said "I would change teachers, first of all. They should ask pupils what they want to do and how they want to work. In our English class, for instance, we can work on our own. If you feel that your teacher trusts you, then you take more responsibility. Then school work becomes more interesting. More independent work. Writing things on one's own. Classes that give you something. When you leave a class, you should feel that you have learned something and not that you've just been sitting and listening."

Comments. "When there is a large group of students who are negative in a class, they ruin classes for the other students. Some of them just sit there and don't care at all about their classes. Other students talk a lot . . . they talk to one another and they get all of the teacher's attention. The students who sit in class every day and do their work and listen don't get any attention because teachers give the students who cut classes all of their attention."

"I think that my parents are supportive. I don't feel pressured by their support."

Sofia

Definition of school fatigue. "School fatigue is when you don't want to go to school. My brother had a bad case of school fatigue. He started to get into fights, and he started smoking. He became a 'problem child' in lower secondary school. He treated Mother badly.... You have to go to school because you have to achieve. Staying at home only causes a lot of problems. School fatigue is no fun.... I think that it is one of the worst things that can happen to you. You don't achieve well, and you are tired. You take everything out on your parents ... or, in my case, parent.... It's difficult, very difficult ... it's a depression ... you feel depressed and tired. You can't cope, and you don't want to cope.... You convince yourself that you can't cope, and it becomes true.... It hurts sometimes ... when you have to do something and you don't want to do it."

Factors influencing school fatigue. According to Sofia 25 percent of school fatigue depends upon one's peers. Twenty percent is influenced by the school itself. Fifty percent is influenced by teachers. Five percent of school fatigue is influenced by oneself.

Teacher characteristics. "I think that I have a great many good teachers. Eighty percent of my teachers are good teachers. I don't have very many bad teachers. A good teacher is strict but at the same time fair. A good teacher would rather give several small tests than one large test to ascertain how much students have learned from a 50-page assignment." A good teacher is "a nice and a pleasant person who makes you feel at ease and who makes you feel comfortable, who takes care of students and who cares. If he/she sees that someone is unhappy, he/she asks what the matter is and so on. A bad teacher shouts and complains all the time. A teacher is bad when she/he is unpleasant and gives a lot of tests and homework simultaneously."

Pupil characteristics. Sofia says that "students should have patience and a nice disposition. They should not be rude." She stresses that students should "try to show interest, even if they are not interested. Finally, students should be respectful towards teachers."

Future plans. Sofia hopes to be able to raise her grade point average so that she will be admitted to a hotel and restaurant upper secondary school. She wants to be a chef.

Self-perception. "Many people think that younger people make problems a lot bigger than they really are . . . but I don't know . . . I've gone through so many things that I have become 'older and wiser'. . . . I consider myself to be devoid of intelligence. . . . I feel so 'little' because I am only fourteen years old, and I am in the ninth grade."

Suggestions for change. "Teachers should help students who have problems with school fatigue. If a student skips classes a lot, they [the teachers] should try to talk to her/him. [Teachers should] help them [students] to get help from the school advisors. [Teachers should] help them [students] get help with courses/subjects that they are having problems with . . . individual instruction in subjects they are having trouble with. . . . [They should] give students a chance to get help during the daytime—not after school. Even if that which one says to the school advisor is confidential, the school advisor usually talks to the school nurse. The school nurse talks to the school doctor, and the doctor talks to the class teacher."

Comments. "I have felt the most school fatigue this year in the ninth grade. There is a lot of stress now. I don't enjoy my class, because my classmates are so difficult and noisy. And I have problems at home. Not my mother, but my father . . . the class has calmed down a bit since the seventh grade. The boys have calmed down but the girls have gotten worse . . . the 'cool broads' who brag about the number of boys they've had sex with. . . . I look forward to upper secondary school, because then I will have had a chance to choose the course I am taking. . . . In upper secondary school you are given more responsibility for yourself. There is more pressure to achieve good grades. You have to get good grades in order to get a good job after school. . . . You know that if you don't do a good job there, then you're going to go to the dogs after school. There are new problems all the time with my father, and they get bigger and bigger all the time. . . . Sometimes I think that I should just forget about my father, but it is very difficult because I need him. When he lets me down all the time, I take it out on Mother. . . . I fight with her then, and I think that everything is terribly wrong. . . . My mother supports me 100 percent. . . . My parents pressure me to get an academic education. I don't like the pressure I'm under. I want to be a chef."

A BRIEF ANALYSIS OF THE INTERVIEW MATERIAL

All of the teenagers are in agreement so far as a definition of school fatigue is concerned. They do not, however, agree on the extent to which the four factors, i.e., teachers, the school itself and school-related factors, peers, and the students themselves, influence school fatigue in their own lives. They each gave an estimate of the degree to which they consider these four variables to contribute to school fatigue. In the school world Marie has depicted, school legislation and educational reform can directly influence only 30 percent of the factors that Marie feels contribute to school fatigue. Seventy percent of the factors that contribute to Marie's school fatigue lie outside of the realm of traditional school reform. Such is the case for Ellen as well. In Sofia's school world, however, 75 percent of the factors that influence school fatigue lie within the realm of traditional school reform.

Both Marie and Ellen propose that students are individually responsible for their own school fatigue, while Sofia deems that teachers are responsible for the school fatigue that can plague her from time to time. Indeed, she says that "school fatigue is just about the worst thing that can happen to you." The girls were asked to evaluate their teachers to determine whether they have good teachers in accordance to their own definitions of what constitutes a good teacher. Marie said that 75 percent of her teachers are good, while 25 percent are not good. Ellen said that all of her teachers are good, but 20 percent of them are boring. Sofia is in agreement with her classmates: she says that 80 percent of her teachers are good teachers, while 20 are not good. It is interesting that these girls have quite similar opinions so far as their teachers are concerned.

The girls were asked to specify the characteristics of a good student. They were also asked to describe themselves in relation to those characteristics. Both Marie and Ellen consider themselves to be good students. Self-confidence is an attribute that both of these girls consider necessary for a good student. Sofia is more hesitant in her description of a good student and in the manner she describes herself in relation to good pupil characteristics.

During the discussions, none of the students mentioned academic qualities with reference to teacher characteristics. All of the students, on the other hand, discussed the manner in which teachers relate to students, implying that for these students teachers' social competence is of primary importance.

Although the girls were not asked to directly discuss their own self-images, the results of the interviews indicate that Marie and Ellen have positive self-images, while Sofia's self-image is more negative. It is apparent that she does not have the self-confidence that both Marie and Ellen have, nor does she include self-confidence among the characteristics that she considers important for a student.

All of the students feel that the situation in Sweden with unemployment, cutbacks in nearly all sectors of society, economic stagnation, and the uncertainty these factors cause influence their attitudes toward education.

REFLECTIONS

School fatigue, as described by the three Swedish teenage girls interviewed for this study, is a personal problem that has consequences for one's relation to oneself, to one's friends, and family and, in extension, to one's future. School fatigue is influenced by factors that are intrinsic to the schooling arena as well as factors that are extrinsic. Whether or not school is safe, whether or not there are jobs to be had in the labor market, whether or not students can cope with other students, homework, tests, and teachers are all factors that enter the picture in regard to school fatigue.

School fatigue is exactly what it sounds like. It is a feeling that one is tired, tired of school, and everything that has to do with it. All kinds of students experience school fatigue. Good students as well as students who are not as high achievers experience school fatigue.

All of the students in this study agree that teachers are important. They feel that teachers should help and encourage the students who feel school fatigue. Marie says, "they should talk to them and cheer them on. . . . Teachers should talk about students' good qualities and not just discuss their shortcomings." All of the girls agree that students should be given a greater chance to decide on what and how they want to work. They want a friendly atmosphere in school, and they want to feel that their teachers trust them. "If you feel that your teacher trusts you, then you take more responsibility. Then school work becomes more interesting."

Despite the fact that both Marie and Ellen consider school fatigue to be a personal problem, they think that students need help to solve the problem of school fatigue. Student advisors who can listen to students' problems, individual instruction in school subjects and courses during the school day, and organized activities between classes are suggestions these girls have for helping students with school fatigue.

All of the students are confident that school fatigue can be "overcome," as one of them expresses it. Sofia and her situation raises the question as to when parents' support stops being supportive and begins to become a burden for students. Indeed, it is Sofia's situation that Marie is referring to when she says, "I know that one of my friends thinks that her mother's support is hard to cope with. That which the mother considers to be supportive, the daughter feels is too demanding."

The results of the interviews suggest that there may be a relationship between students' self-perceptions, achievement, and school fatigue. Self-confidence seems to be a mediating factor.

There is an anti-academic climate among some of the students in the school upon which all of the girls comment. It seems to present a problem for Marie, Ellen, and Sofia. As Marie puts it, "There are two gangs in school: those who think that they are tough and cool–they stand outside on their side of the school yard and smoke between classes–and the others who are a little more . . . common; they don't think that they are superior to everyone else and they don't look down upon students who get good grades and who don't spend their weekends out on the town, smoking and drinking." How good students resolve the problem inherent in being looked down upon by the "tough and cool" gang is a topic worthy of further discussion.

None of the girls feel that their parents' divorces have affected their school work nor do they consider their parents' divorces to be a cause of school fatigue. All of the girls think that living in a single parent household has not had a detrimental influence on their schooling. Indeed, they all agree that their mothers support them, and Sofia and Marie say that their mothers even try to compensate for the fact that they do not receive any help from their fathers. Sofia says that "it is better to have one's parents in two different households than to have them living under the same roof fighting with one another." What becomes apparent in this study is the fact that two of the girls' fathers are fathers who take little or no responsibility for their children. These fathers are absent fathers in the physical sense of the term. The manner in which they have emotionally distanced themselves from their children leads one to conclude that they are dysfunctional fathers as well. Not only does their inability to function in their parenting role deprive their daughters of the support that teenagers need, but it would seem that they constitute an emotional problem for these two girls: one of the fathers is involved in a relationship that is problematic for both of his children and the other father refuses to assume responsibility for his children, maintaining that it is his children who should assume responsibility for his relationship to them. To what extent these dysfunctional fathers constitute a burden for their children is not an easy matter to investigate. It is clear, however, that this situation constitutes a disadvantage for the students in question. As one of the girls puts it, "school fatigue is a more complicated issue than whether or not one's parents are divorced. It has to do with a lack of confidence and a lack of feeling that one belongs." Another one of the girls stresses, "I think that it is a generalization if one assumes that there is a stereotype for single mothers and their children, because there are so many different kinds of people involved and none of them are alike, at least none of them that I know. . . . All of my friends whose parents are divorced are very different."

CONCLUDING REMARKS

A realistic fear is that school fatigue will increase in the future, resulting in higher dropout rates and a greater disenchantment in regard to the power of schooling to meet the needs of the young and the needs of the nation. Perhaps the future will also see a growing discrepancy between the needs of the nation and the needs of youths. Educational indicators often mirror the needs of policy-making bodies and decision-makers. Whether or not these indicators mirror the realities of youths or they disguise those and other realities is an interesting question.

One would hope that the crisis facing schooling in the form of economic uncertainty, cutbacks, and vague reforms will give rise to individual and group initiatives in the schooling arena and a greater receptivity for change. The climate of crisis can lead, in extension, to a climate conducive to change. If that is the case, schools in the future may well become safe and democratic places in which teachers and students meet, as one of the girls suggests, "to learn, to develop, to mature, and to learn to know others and oneself."

NOTES

1. T. Husén, A.C. Tuijnman, and W.D. Halls, *Schooling in Modern European Society. A Report of the Academia Europaea* (Oxford: Pergamon Press, 1992).

2. OECD, *Education at a Glance. OECD Indicators* (Paris: OECD, 1995).

3. Statistics Sweden, "Fakta om den svenska familjen" (Facts about Swedish Families) *Demografiska Reporter.* 1994:2 (Stockholm: Statistiska Centralbyrån, 1994).

4. Statistics Sweden, "Fakta om den svenska familjen" (Facts about Swedish Families) *Demografiska Reporter.* 1994:2 (Stockholm: Statistiska Centralbyrån, 1994).

5. OECD, *Education at a Glance. OECD Indicators.* (Paris: OECD, 1995).

6. T.H. Postlethwaite and D.E. Wiley eds. *Science Achievement in Twenty-three Countries* (Oxford: Pergamon Press, 1992).

7. All of the girls' fathers have the same first name, a fact that the girls found to be amusing.

8. G. Miron, *Choice and the Use of Market Forces in Schooling. Swedish Education Reforms for the 1990s* (Stockholm: The Institute of International Education, 1993).

REFERENCES

Husén, T., A.C. Tuijnman, and W.D. Halls. 1992. *Schooling in Modern European Society. A Report of the Academia Europaea.* Oxford: Pergamon Press.

Miron, G. 1993. *Choice and the Use of Market Forces in Schooling. Swedish Education Reforms for the 1990s.* Stockholm: The Institute of International Education.

Organization for Economic Cooperation and Development (OECD). 1995. *Education at a Glance. OECD Indicators.* Paris: Organization for Economic Cooperation and Development.

Postlethwaite, T.H., and D.E. Wiley, eds. 1992. *Science Achievement in Twenty-three Countries*. Oxford: Pergamon Press.

Statistics Sweden 1994. "Fakta om den svenska familjen" (Facts about Swedish Families). *Demografiska Reporter*. 1994:2 Statistiska Centralbyrån.

CHAPTER 7

Comparative Perspectives on Professionalism among American, British, German, and Finnish Teachers

Reijo Raivola

INTRODUCTION

This chapter deals with the conclusion of a research report on the history of teaching. The development of teacher education in four countries—the United States, England, Germany, and Finland—is pursued in order to see if the proletarianization hypothesis can be corroborated (Raivola 1989). In ancient times teaching was a respected profession, in authority next to the priesthood or, in fact, intertwined and embedded in it. However, as soon as teaching was separated from sacred ceremonies and became, instead, adopted for livelihood, the deterioration of the profession began.

First, the four countries are compared using the Hansian idea of *tertium comparationis*. In fact five different dimensions are utilized (Judge 1988). Then the deprofessionalized status of teachers is discussed on a more general level.

THE FIVE CHARACTERISTICS OF A UNIFIED PROFESSION

National, Regional, or Local Control

In the United States, the school and, accordingly, the teacher as part of the institution have traditionally been controlled by the neighborhood society (*gemeinschaft*). At the other end of the continuum lay Prussia, whose compulsory school had a clear political and national function. Finland adopted the German model. The school seemed to be controlled by local laymen, but in essence the teachers were civil servants and state functionaries, and the school educated the young for state citizenship. In England the chaotical conglomerate of schools was articulated into local systems towards the end of the nineteenth century.

National systems have quite early produced uniform contracts of service for teachers (salary, pension, and qualification requirements), national curricula, and final examinations. Teacher training is harmonized, especially for public institutions. Application for an office and conditions of employment are regulated in detail.

From a historical point of view, it is quite understandable that after the Reformation in Prussia and in Finland, the secular power and the clerical power shared an interest in educating a model citizen and an obedient member of the state church. Extreme examples are the oath of allegiance demanded from teachers and the banning of leftist teachers.

In England, on the other hand, the Catholics, the Anglicans and the Dissenters fought each other for the right to teach children. This rivalry was an obstacle in the birth of a widely accepted educational ideology. The parties opposed any interference by the state; it would have been interpreted as a pro-Anglican act. So, in a way, the establishment of a local administration of education was a compromise.

The construction of American states "out of nothing," individual settler attitudes and the vastness of territories compressed education into a local activity of the neighborhood. The teacher was made a trustee of society. This educational and training ideology of the early stage of the Industrial Revolution has been handed down until the post-industrial era. This is one of the reasons for the present mismatch between education and the wider society (cf. Ringer 1979).

Despite the differences, each nation had to guarantee the political reliability of teachers, i.e., their capability to preserve social order. That is why their training programs were very strictly regimented. Thus awakening of political and economic consciousness was hindered. By applying strict norms the maladjusted were screened out of the system. The curriculum consisted of moralizing and socializing content rather than of psychological and pedagogical skills. The final unprofessional subjugation was carried out by inspectors who mainly came from outside the teaching ranks, especially in England. The working conditions and the teacher-proof material made up the technical imperative that maximized discipline and order as a necessary condition, and even as an ultimate end, of teaching. In England, for example, the Revised Code was a reaction to the fear of a class upheaval. The school in Europe should mirror and support class society (Grace 1985).

Stratification of the Profession

The United States did not inherit the European division of the educational system into common and academic schools. The medieval Latin school did not gain a footing in America. The democratic high school evolved from the elementary school. That is why the teaching profession shares approximately the same status irrespective of the stage of teaching. But the stratification of teachers in England, and even to a greater extent in Finland and Germany, was very clear until recently. The European secondary school teacher originated from the middle class, went to elite schools, and studied "subjects" in a university. Then he started teaching the same subject without any or with very limited formal teacher training. He was a member of a "learned profession." Hegel, for example, wrote some of his major works when working as a headmaster of a Nuremberg school.

The primary school teacher, on the other hand, originated from the common people. He, or increasingly often she, had to remain poor, diligent and faithful. Part of the teacher's authority has always come from the status of the parents whose children he or she has been teaching. So it is no wonder that differentiated training and different pupils produced separate teacher categories.

Müller (Müller et al. 1987) interestingly describes the sociologics that works up the structures of the education system and differentiates the teachers to correspond to the differing demands of a hierarchical society. He compresses his examination into the concept of systematization. A number of independent schools with relatively free admission and heterogeneous student body evolves into an articulated system of institutions. Each type of school has its own curriculum, recruitment population, and teacher body with specific qualifications. The system of education is a model example of a Weberian rationalization process. It differentiates into finer and finer subclasses along with the developing class or status society, thus legitimizing the hierarchical division of labor. The teaching profession also becomes hierarchical as an integral part of the process. The explanation seems to correspond to reality. The parallel school forms (the common school and the academic school) developed a third type in between them: Realschulen in Prussia, "technical" schools in England, and middle schools in Finland. Later on even the gymnasium differentiated into parallel forms in Prussia.

Müller's theory does not, however, explain development in England very well. Only one type of upper secondary school evolved (grammar school). Traditional public schools were not much affected by the new social divisions. In Prussia the centralized administration of education guaranteed the qualifications given by schools. In England the free competitive market did the same. But in both countries social hierarchies were converted into educational hierarchies—and back again. Although the curriculum in England did not symbolize the school's status as clearly as that in Prussia, in both countries the educational structure and the economic structure, present in emerging industries, were converging.

It is even more difficult to apply Müller's theory to the situation in the United States. Education had a democratic meaning in the construction of the new nation, not only in public speeches but also in reality. Since the days of the first presidents, a shared suspicion arose of those who tried to give birth to any kind of a new aristocracy. Andrew Jackson said that college was "a haunt of dandies" and "a protector of well-born and stupid" (Orr 1987). Unlike the European situation, the public school had to assimilate diverse ethnic and cultural groups into an integrated nation. Education had to bring forth both enculturation and acculturation. Three basic principles have moulded the American educational policy from the beginning: education must be universal (right to education); it must be independent of the political regime (decentralization); it must guarantee a common core of civilization to everyone (comprehensiveness). It was the number of years in formal education, not the type of an institution, that stratified people.

The universalistic interpretation of functionalism can be disputed on other grounds, too. In America the school did not earn the right to act as a gatekeeper to working life for a long time. It was not the only elector of people to status positions. In England there was a remarkable overlap between descending grammar schools and ascending primary schools. Grace (1985) shows that as opposed to functionalistic and deterministic reproduction theory, "the representatives of the employers' interests," the inspectors, acted openly and strongly against the Revised Code and for the rights of the teachers. Usually they were products of "Oxbridge" and famous public schools, which openly resisted the values of the competitive meritocratic society. Through their supervisory activities, these values were bound to reflect on the teaching profession, too. The teacher was not a servile follower of the will of his superiors, although Henry Bérenger at the turn of the century said that the souls of the intellectual proletariat were fatally inclined either to slavery or to rebellion. The trade union movement in England chose to rebel quite early.

One has to remember "the veto of the powerless." Even if the teachers in their hierarchical positions are objects and means of the use of power, they can always water down the will of their suppressors. Their pedagogical autonomy makes it possible.

The conflict theories of education come from the branch of social sciences that aims, besides producing new knowledge, at a pointed social criticism. The lack of equity and democracy is the target of criticism in education. But Jürgen Schriewer (Müller et al. 1987) shows us that the analogy of reproduction comes from biology. The opposite of reproduction among organisms is not equity but extinction.

Autonomy of the Profession

Secondary school teachers, in particular, have enjoyed great autonomy in England. Curricula were born (often undocumented) at the level of a school or even in the mind of an individual teacher. The choice of teaching material was limited only by resources. The teacher as a state official in Germany was more strictly tied by numerous norms whereas the American teacher was the object of the parents' arbitrary will. However, through their right to collective bargaining, teachers have fought themselves, step by step, for more space and air to act independently. In many European countries, the democratic development has culminated in a kind of a paradox: an individual teacher's power of decision is restricted by the union rules! Teachers have never achieved the highest stage of professional decision making, i.e., collegialism.

In the United States, the school has always been managed by "neighborhood managers." Industrial and managerial ideas of efficiency have restricted teachers' autonomy. Efficiency is seen mostly as pedagogical, and it is measured by standardized achievement tests. Now, when resources allocated to education are decreasing, demands for accountability are intensified, not only in the United States but in England, too. It is not enough for a teacher to have graduated from an accredited college. She must be licensed, too. Sometimes she has to pass competency tests. She is paid by merit. Classroom responsibilities are identified in detail, and activities must be reported regularly. In England central government has taken on responsibilities for curriculum planning, resource allocation, etc. In countries such as Finland, where administration has traditionally been centralized, the opposite is occurring. Disentangling the norms and cutting down bureaucracy (deregulation) have delegated the right of decision downwards. Autonomy of Finnish teachers, or should we say Finnish schools, has increased.

Unity of the Profession

Unity of the profession is one of the central characteristics of professionalism. This does not mean that a profession cannot differentiate into specialties. After all, a physician is a physician whatever his special field is, be it surgery or pediatrics, for example. There have always been two categories in teacher corps: the teacher of the academic school and the teacher of the common school. The former has been the transmitter of codified knowledge and has selected his clients on a competitive basis. Teaching imparts thorough knowledge of the subject matter. Therefore teachers have been university graduates with no need for pedagogical qualities. The common school teacher, on the other hand, has been a substitute parent for young children. Custodial care and supervision have been the school's main functions. There was no need for its teachers to demonstrate their knowledge. What they needed was pedagogical and psychological control skills, because they made education in the proper sense possible (Lundgren 1987, 21-22).

The educational system has assigned teachers to status groups according to the level and track of education. The most essential divider was the question of whether the teacher was teaching a child or a subject. The higher level he/she taught, the less pedagogical training was needed. The more pedagogical qualifications were included in the training, the less highly the occupation was regarded. Even in the academic school, the teacher was valued according to the subject he/she taught.

Except in the United States, teacher unions are split according to the stage of the educational system. As for the United States, one of the main unions has included employers' representatives as members. In England, headmasters, women teachers, etc., have their own organizations. Subject teachers usually have their own pedagogical associations. In Finland, for example, legislation has prevented administrators from using a teacher, appointed to a particular office, on different levels or in different school forms. On both continents, the principal is no longer *primus inter pares*. He is a full-fledged administrator and the employer's representative.

The heterogeneity of the occupation has been an obstacle to the establishment of an official teacher register. The register, which includes every certified and licensed teacher, and only such teachers, constitutes a guarantee of skills and proficiency. The register is an assurance for clients and customers that the profession bears the full responsibility for its members' behavior and craftsmanship. Among teachers there have always been unqualified and untrained members. In many countries, for example England, these unqualified teachers have been appointed permanently in remote areas. They have formed a floating *underclass*, which is not supposed to honor the professional code of ethics or whose interests were not taken care of by unions. In England such teachers were excluded from union membership.

Teachers have always been a miscellaneous lot, differing by education, capabilities, and personal traits. Teacher training has been in a state of continuous change, thus producing wide intergenerational differences in qualifications and dividing teachers into different salary grades.

Various trends in professional, political, and union development have, however, brought different teacher categories closer to each other. The extension of compulsory schooling from 7 to 9 years has also contributed to the harmonization of primary and secondary teacher training and lowered the barriers between different school forms and categories of teachers. But now, the zeal for accountability and the concern for the quality of education have turned the wheel back towards differentiation. In the United States (and Japan), for example, there are plans to divide teachers into professional categories according to their training, experience, and demonstrated efficiency.

Unionism

In all four countries, it was clearly understood that especially the common school teachers on primary and elementary levels did not deserve full recognition or, by social contract, did not obtain the essential elements of a professional status. They had to resort to the labor movements, i.e., unionism. The first to radicalize was the English teacher at the end of the nineteenth century. The German teacher followed in the days of the Weimar Republic, the Finnish and the American teacher not until the end of World War II. From the point of view of professional ethics, unionistic radicalization can be, and in fact has been, detrimental to professional aspirations. Whether professionalism and unionism are incompatible by nature remains to be seen in a future research project. There is no doubt, however, that in addition to the continuous rise of the social import of schooling, teacher unions have tremendously improved teachers' economic position and their contracts of service. Allies have been sought sometimes among the political Left, as in England, sometimes among the state bureaucracies.

THE PROLETARIANIZATION HYPOTHESIS

One of the leading themes in this research project has been the proletarianization hypothesis. The project has dealt with the reasons, in classical antiquity and the Middle Ages, for the deterioration of teachers' original highly regarded status (Raivola 1989). In the following section, those factors are discussed which are connected with the birth and development of modern educational systems. Metzger (1987) writes in his brilliant essay:

> that as the amount of knowledge increases, so too does the relative amount of ignorance, for each person can know only a decreasing fraction of what can be known; that knowledge, as it becomes more specialized, also tends to become more potent, more capable of being used for good or ill; that the growth and specialization of knowledge produce not a mass society but a lay society, a society in which everyone is at the mercy of someone more thoroughly in the know, that this state of mutual dependency grows more dangerous as knowledge, which has once been in the hands of holy men, kin and neighbors, passes into the hands of strangers. . . .

We are living in a world of specialists. If our television set breaks down, we need a specialist to repair it. We can also live without it or buy a new one. TV mechanics are not vital to our well-being. They are not professionals. If we break our bones, we again consult a specialist. Only a medical doctor is able to and allowed to heal us, but he is not only a specialist but an expert and a professional. Teachers are neither! Many sociologists claim that teachers lack both special know-how and an expert's authority. Silberman (1970, 436) says: "No one ever died of a split infinitive." Teachers have no monopoly on any knowledge area. Although they are university educated, they have no clear, undisputed scientific basis for their practical work. Educational sciences already had a bad reputation before they were incorporated in university curricula. Other fields of science had centuries-old traditions and established boundaries. Education and psychology tore up the institution, its distribution of power and the mechanisms of resource allocation. When the rise of social sciences began, education wanted to be part of it. It claimed scientific independence. It wanted to be both a science and a provider of professional knowledge, both within the scope of one degree. Older sciences recognized neither of these claims. Education was placed as and remained the lowest discipline in the academic order.

The determinants of successful teaching are mastery of content, knowledge of children, and familiarity with methods. The subject teacher's mastery of content is only a necessary, not a sufficient condition for good teaching. All the prerequisite knowledge of teaching cannot be covered by one discipline. The scientific basis for teaching must be broad. If we consider upbringing instead of instruction, many philosophers see that as a normative activity it cannot be the object of science—indoctrination could be that. Good teaching is an art! A professional can be an intermediary between knowledge, service, and the client, but in education, science cannot generate direct instructions or directives for practice.

An expert uses knowledge in his work without sharing it with the client. Even a psychiatrist does not form a close and direct personal relationship with his patient. Expert authority maintains a knowledge gap between the layman and the professional. Pedagogical (anthropological) authority is used to narrow the gap. Whereas continuity of professions supposes that clients are dependent on experts, teachers should encourage pupils towards independence. In the classroom the teacher's main tool is his/her personality; the professional has his/her monopoly on knowledge (Dove 1986, 110-11; Schwebel 1985; Silberman 1970, 426-427.) To put it more bluntly: the expert is not interested in the client but in his problems.

The problem of legitimized knowledge must be seen in the historical context. An ever-lasting war prevails between the world of work and the world of education, between the promoters of science and the practitioners. No final solution is in sight, because the differences in opinion are caused by different epistemological understandings. But it is possible to adapt to each other. It takes several decades, however, before opponents are sufficiently adapted. For example, it was not until the 1930s that a university education was demanded for lawyers in court in the United States, and in the 1950s formal training finally displaced the apprenticeship system. Likewise, it took 40 years before the Johns Hopkins model of medicine was adopted by the profession. On a global scale, university education of teachers has not been required yet. The state of ferment is mirrored, among other things, by the unusually common discontent of teachers with their initial training (Spring 1980).

Teaching in the compulsory school has always been a constitutive mass occupation (Groothoff 1982, 12-16), which has had nothing to do with the training of a nation's political or economic elite. The common school teacher directed the young to factories, fields, and offices. Social qualifications were more important than technical ones. For that reason the teacher was to serve as a model for her pupils. Especially in the countryside, she lived like a fish in an aquarium. This pressure for conformity and living under strict moral surveillance made the teacher a second-class citizen, at least as far as his/her personal liberties were concerned. On the other hand, severe school discipline together with other structural characteristics of the school made the teacher a very authoritative figure for his/her pupils. Only the reform pedagogy took the school ". . . away from the authoritarian . . . and theoretically-oriented school to a more child-centered education . . ." (Wigger 1986).

Appealing to caretaking and custodial obligations of the teacher, society saddled the school not only with moral education and instruction but also with an ever-increasing number of often-contradictory tasks of well-being and surveillance. The job description of teaching was blurred. The teacher became a jack of all trades.

In a profession, marginal tasks are delegated to assisting personnel. In classrooms the work has differentiated in the opposite way. Beside and, more often, above the teacher work different types of specialists: psychologists, curriculum experts, welfare officers, nurses, etc. Didactics made the teacher an applier of different techniques, when he/she tried to meet the efficiency demand by trying to achieve the objectives set by outsiders with minimum resources. Curriculum studies during initial training emphasized the development of technical self-understanding. Teaching strategy was modeled after the concept of technical work, and classroom tactics were chosen to solve the problems with contextual knowledge. However well the teacher did his/her work, it was never finished. The medical doctor heals the victim of an accident; the lawyer solves a legal problem; the priest promises the sinner an absolution. The teacher, year after year, has new raw material to shape, but he/she never sees his/her product as ready. The teacher is very much an institutional role figure, a representative of a power organization rather than the solver of acute human problems.

Conflicting hopes and expectations have always been directed to the school. The most essential question for the elite and academic school was whether it should be a producer or a reproducer of knowledge. Because the university started to change into a research institution as late as the nineteenth century, it is natural that its graduates delivered only the knowledge they themselves had acquired. Pieces of this knowledge, separated from the whole, were transferred into the curriculum, but they were blurred into rudiments and relics, which had very little to do with the everyday life of the students.

Even today the education of teachers and that of researchers are different. One reason for this can be that the teacher trainers' backgrounds, careers, identifications, and intellectual orientations differ from those of other university teachers. In the United States their salary and status are lower than those of the other faculty. The culture of teacher training differs from cultures of other programs, often in an unintellectual direction (Schwebel 1985).

The first thesis in the Metzger quote on page 169 is also illuminating. Although our relative ignorance in the flood of information and in the world of specialists increases continuously, that does not apply to school. Knowledge of teaching has experienced no information explosion. At least it does not show in the organization of schooling. Functioning principles and even part of the curriculum are much the same as they were at the birth of the modern educational system. If new knowledge should happen to show in school activities (and of course it does), very soon it would be in "public domain delivery." Pupils and students have a wider experience of different teachers and teaching styles than teachers themselves, who very seldom know what is happening in other classrooms. Parents have often had more education than teachers. Everyone seems to be an expert on school and education. Teaching is difficult to mystify.

Whether a professional really knows more than lay people, whether he/she has expert knowledge or not, is not essential according to the symbolic interpretation of professionalism.What is essential is that those whose services are in demand believe and, what is important, want to believe in the superior knowledge of the professionals. Parents will not believe in teachers in this way, because they do not want to give up their rights over their children to the school. In many medical, legal or technical problems they feel they are at the mercy of experts, but in education they feel they are as expert as anyone else. They want to maintain their integrity in relation to the school.

Longer and more effective teacher education has undoubtedly produced teachers who are more skillful technicians, but a kind of one-sided contract cannot make them into professionals. If the structure and conditions of the job do not change, no training can make teachers into professionals. Teachers think that they are already at the professional level; the problem is that the general public does not see it. However, procuring objective, distinctive characteristics of professionalism is not the objective of education. They do not even exist. It is a question of a symbolic relationship between the suppliers of services and the clients. Laymen give professionals the power of attorney for taking care of their complicated problems, and professionals guarantee that the problems will be taken care of in a discreet and professional way. A professional status is given as much as it is taken.

The history, status, and working conditions of primary and elementary school teachers work against achieving a professional status (Spring 1980). Working conditions have traditionally been wretched. Classes have been big. The teacher's energy has been depleted by keeping order rather than by teaching. Sykes (1984) mentions "the deal" American teachers make with difficult students in high schools: if you do not disturb me and my class, I won't disturb you either; if everything goes peacefully, I will give you a D in my subject. The salary has always been low. The social status of the common school teacher has been vague. She originates from among the common people, but does not belong to them any more; the middle class and the intelligentsia are suspicious and do not accept her as a member.

The marginal conditions of teaching and its low social and economic compensation have frightened the most capable individuals away from the field, especially in times of general prosperity, when the economy has offered more dynamic alternatives for earning one's livelihood and for self-fulfillment. When the school, because of its internal mechanisms and inevitable functions, has not been able to keep up with social development, teachers have been blamed. Public criticism has caused many teachers to leave the field. The high turnover of teachers is even a bigger problem than their quality. The school has always been controlled by others rather than teachers: by the church until the first half of the nineteenth century, by the social structure for the next hundred years, and by the economy for the past forty years. Servants are not highly respected.

Teaching offers very few career prospects. To advance is to leave teaching: to move up is to move out. A tension prevails between career consciousness and role commitment. In the segmented school, the teacher is obliged to instruct syllabi in forms and levels of school for which she does not feel qualified. Good work is seldom rewarded. The automatically increasing salary (seniority bonuses) provokes routines. The concept of merit pay, as it is understood in the United States, is no solution, because its criteria are not agreed upon.

CONCLUDING REMARKS

Modern professions were born with the rise of the capitalistic form of production and with the scientification of universities. At the same time the need to create a state citizen and the change in living patterns brought about by the Industrial Revolution, formalized education into school systems. New professions close their ranks from minorities and women. Professions were occupational cartels controlled by the elite of the mainstream culture. The teacher served without discriminating against anyone. The quantitative demand for teachers was greater than the concern for the quality. First in England, then in the United States and finally in Finland and Germany, the occupation became dominated by a female majority. In present-day Europe, only Greece and the

Netherlands have a male majority at the primary level. In 24 countries surveyed in 1983, the average percentage of women was 71 percent. In the former GDR, the proportion was the highest—87 percent. In general, 80 percent seems to be the ceiling; then men start to return to teaching (Braster 1988).

As higher education has become more general among women, the number of women teachers in secondary and tertiary education has increased. However, the lower the stage of education, the greater the proportion of women among teachers (Braster 1988), because pre-primary education as a care occupation almost without exception was in the hands of women. Educative tasks attached to the gender became the women's responsibilities in school. As an indicator of wealth, GNP correlates negatively with the proportion of women as teachers. Further, it is an international fact that the number of women as teachers and the salary level as well as the length of training and the number of female teachers correlate negatively. During economic booms men enter more respected occupations, which leaves more room in the teaching profession for women. When the recession comes, there are no more vacancies in teaching left for men. The conclusion is that in patriarchal societies the female majority in the occupation has been an obstacle to social and professional status.

Organizationally it is easy to return to teaching after many years' absence, as if no break existed. Those who return are usually women. Teaching is often the first college-based job for racial or ethnic minorities or for those who yearn for social mobility. A medical doctor or a lawyer is perceived as an individual, while a teacher is seen as a representative of his/her occupation. Thus, the label of lower strata is linked to the occupational group.

The professional knows, when offering his/her services, what knowledge must be applied and in what way, whom he/she may consult for advice, what measures and how many operations are needed and what their costs will be, when and in what order operations must be executed and why. The teacher lacks collegial support. He/she is seldom cost conscious. His/her sociological and political understanding of the school's functions is limited. He/she teaches her pupils at the time and for as many years as some formal rule tells his/her to. The prefixed curriculum answers mainly "what" and "how" questions and only occasionally "why" questions. In all four countries the university education of teachers is justified by scientification of teaching. Theories are taught deductively: novices are acquainted with different theoretical approaches to teaching and then they try to apply some of them. If the basis of the teacher's work is practical, as it seems to be, theories should be built inductively as experiences accumulate. The vaccination theory has dominated teacher education until the 1970s: once vaccinated, always safe. If teaching is an inductive and practical activity, teachers are in need of continuing education.

My final question is, thus, whether teaching can be considered more art than science. If so, is there any reason for the vocation to strive for a professional pressure group ideology and status?

REFERENCES

Braster, J. 1988. "The Feminization of Teaching." In *The Social Role and Evolution of the Teaching Profession in Historical Context*, ed. S. Seppo. Jyvuskylu: Joensuu.

Dove, L. 1986. *Teachers and Teacher Education in Developing Countries*. London: Croom Helm.

Grace, G. 1985. "Judging Teachers: The Social and Political Contexts of Teacher Education." *British Journal of Sociology of Education* 6, no. 1, 3-16.

Groothoff, H.H. 1982. *Funktion und Rolle des Erziehers*. München: Juventa Verlag.

Judge, H. 1988. "Cross-National Perception of Teachers." *Comparative Education Review* 32, no. 2, 143-158.

Lundgren, U. 1987. "New Challenges for Teachers and Education." Standing Conference of European Ministers of Education. 15th Session, Helsinki.

Metzger, W. 1987. "The Spectre of Professionalism." *Educational Researcher* 16, no. 6, 10-19.

Müller, D., Ringer, F., and Simon, B. 1987. *The Rise of the Modern Educational System*. Cambridge: Cambridge University Press.

Orr, J. 1987. "The American System of Education." In *Making America*, ed. L. Luedtke. Washington: USIA.

Raivola, R. 1989. *Opettajan ammatin historia*. (The History of Teaching). Kasvatustieteen laitos A 44. Tampereen: Yliopisto.

Ringer, F. 1979. *Education and Society in Modern Europe*. Bloomington: Indiana University Press.

Schwebel, M. 1985. "The Clash of Cultures in Academe: The University and the Education Faculty." *Journal of Teacher Education* 36, no. 4, 2-7.

Silberman, C. 1970. *Crisis in the Classroom.* New York: Vintage Books.
Spring, J. 1980. *Educating the Worker-Citizen.* New York: Longman.
Sykes, G. 1984. "The Deal." *The Wilson Quarterly* 7, no.1, 59-77.
Wigger, L. 1986. "Bericht vom XXII." Salzburger Symposion-Pädagogisches Rundschau 40, 615-623.

PART II

Reforms of the 1990s

CHAPTER 8

Restructuring Education in Sweden

Gary Miron

INTRODUCTION

In recent years, reforms in the Swedish education system have gained considerable international attention. While Sweden was far behind other countries in restructuring educational services, one can now say that–in many respects–it has taken the lead. While school voucher schemes have been tested in other countries, they have typically existed on a small scale since the education systems are rather decentralized. Only in highly centralized Sweden could a central authority mandate such a nationwide reform. These restructuring reforms in Sweden have also gained attention since they occurred so rapidly and since they marked a clear break with the past.

Sweden has been renowned for its careful planning and implementing of school reforms. The extensive reforms which brought to an end the parallel school system and led to the comprehensive nine-year compulsory school in Sweden are often brought as an illustration of how a good education reform should be conducted. One can only wonder if Sweden will soon serve as an example of how not to conduct school reforms.

While reforms have affected all levels of the Swedish education system, from pre-schools to universities, the focus of this article will be upon the compulsory level of the education system.

RECENT REFORMS CONCERNING RESTRUCTURING

During the 1980s more and more flexibility was allowed for schools to create their own profiles, and further steps were taken to allow schools to operate outside of the municipal school system.[1] Deregulation and decentralization were important themes during the late 1980s. The municipal governments were given more and more of the responsibility for planning and administering social services, including education. Likewise, the municipalities have received more responsibility for financial matters and the decisions concerning how the resources are to be distributed. In 1989, central regulations concerning positions and salaries of school employees were abolished, and in 1991 the municipalities received the state's share of funding for formal schooling in one lump sum, rather than several smaller sums earmarked for each level or type of schooling.

In 1991, the Parliament approved of legislation (*Government Bill* 1990/1991:115)[2] requiring the municipalities to distribute resources to both public and independent schools in the same way as was done for all municipal schools (i.e., based upon the specific needs of each school). Approved independent schools would be given the economic resources in order to conduct their instruction. This new system of distributing resources, however, never went into effect.

After the national election in 1991, the Social Democratic-led government was replaced by a coalition of four center/right political parties. The new government set off a wave of reforms in many sectors concerning privatization, choice, and the use of market forces. By March 1992 a new proposition was made (*Government Bill* 1991/92:95)[3] concerning the introduction of school vouchers for approved compulsory-level independent schools. This bill was approved in June 1992 and went into effect the following month, thus superseding the previous reform. With this reform, municipalities were required to distribute at least 85 percent of the average cost per student in the municipal schools for each student in the independent schools. Besides differences in the relative size of resources to independent schools and the actual mechanism for distributing funds, these two proposals also varied in the role that municipalities would have in the supervision and evaluation of independent schools. The latter proposal required municipalities to distribute funding to independent schools even though they would have no legal right to access their relevant needs or to monitor or evaluate their activities.

In 1993, similar reforms were made in upper-secondary schools and schools for children with mental retardation. Reforms in the administration and financing of higher education were also introduced which gave the universities and other higher education bodies more autonomy and linked parts of their funding to output indicators. In fact, since the pre-school services were already applying choice and market forces, one can say that the entire formal education system of Sweden has been touched by the reforms dealing with decentralization, choice and the use of market forces.

In 1994, the Social Democrats won sufficient support in the national elections to retake control of the government. During the election campaign, one of the promises of the Social Democrats was to remove school vouchers and to return to the arrangements established in the 1991 reform proposal. After the election, however, the Social Democrats have hesitated in removing the voucher system, although they have reduced the school voucher that previously paid 85 percent of the average municipal costs for pupils to 75 percent. A commission has also been appointed to examine the current voucher system and the regulations surrounding independent schools. Among the issues being taken up by the commission are those dealing with how to increase the role and influence of municipalities in the approval and supervision of independent schools. It is anticipated that the commission may recommend ending the use of school vouchers, or forbid independent schools who receive school vouchers to collect fees. Another likely recommendation is that a lower number of students be established in order for an independent school to be approved (e.g., 15 students). The final report and recommendations of the commission are expected to be presented at the end of 1995.

The reforms taking place in recent years have dealt with 1) decentralization, 2) choice, 3) use of market forces, and 4) privatization. As a result of these reforms, most of the administration, planning, and the responsibility for resource distribution for compulsory and upper-secondary schooling has been decentralized and left to the municipalities or to the schools themselves. A new national curriculum was approved in 1994, placing more emphasis on centrally-defined goals. In this way the role of the central government has shifted from planning the imputs to evaluating outputs.

Choice has been augmented by the reforms as well as by the new national curriculum. Students now have more chances than before to choose which subjects they wish to participate in or study in depth. The number of choices increases over the years. Schools now have more choice in the instruction they offer. The national curriculum specifies the goals in each subject, and the schools have more choice in deciding how they are going to attain that goal. Schools can also make choices in how they wish to distribute the specified number of hours of instruction per subject. Schools can also choose to create a specific profile, for example, within a specific subject area, through the arts, or they might even choose to adapt an environmental profile.

The use of market forces in controlling the supply and distribution of educational services is best exemplified by the school vouchers which municipalities are required to pay to independent schools based upon the number of students they have enrolled. In many municipalities, competition for students is also encouraged among the municipal schools by using a similar voucher mechanism. The demand for educational services and the relative productivity of institutes and departments in the higher education system are now important factors in determining how government resources are distributed.

The reforms have led to greater possibilities for private individuals or groups to receive public funding for the instruction they offer or wish to sell. The reforms have even increased the possibilities for municipalities to contract out educational services to private persons, organizations or companies. Higher education bodies have been given more autonomy, and two university/colleges have been put under non-state ownership (i.e., foundations).

FORCES BEHIND THE REFORMS

The issue of free choice and market-oriented schools is being widely discussed in many countries of the world. It is interesting to consider why this issue has come up in so many different countries during this particular period of time. One of the main impetuses seems to be economic. There are, of course, other factors that have influenced this issue, such as political and social factors.

To a large extent, this trend is linked to pressure put on education systems by economic problems. This pressure is related to the reconstruction of world economies over the past few decades and the predominantly dismal economic situation that persists in much of the world. As a result, demands are being made for more efficiency in educational systems. Similar pressures and responses are apparent in other social sectors in Sweden.

The economic competitiveness among various countries has given further emphasis to the importance of the education system in providing a given country with the competitive edge to develop its economic base and to compete for markets. In a few of the traditionally leading industrial countries, such as the United Kingdom and the United States, a perplexing situation seems to have arisen as educational results have fallen behind other countries. Along with this decline, the quality of teachers as well as the educational infrastructure and curriculum have come into question. In some respects, education has become a scapegoat for general economic failures.

Political factors can also be said to influence reforms towards free choice and market-oriented schools. The Cold War era has ended, and many saw the result as a victory for "democracy" and "freedom." Furthermore, the disintegration of the former Soviet Union and the Eastern European Block was interpreted in practice as a victory for market forces over centralized planning and steering. The shift to market forces in order to control the production and consumption of goods and services can be seen today in a whole array of countries from those that tolerate little democracy to those whose political and social framework is very democratic. A large number of political parties—not only the traditionally right-wing parties—seem to be affected by the conservative and neo-liberal winds that are blowing through the political arena. Along with these various changes, belief in the welfare state has also declined.

The social and cultural factors specific to individual countries have also influenced this trend. Besides the public's general discontent with ineffective schools, it seems that in some countries discontent has also arisen because public schools cannot be easily altered or influenced by parents and local politicians. In the case of Sweden, some felt that public schools were too uniform and narrow and regulated by the state in minute detail.

Some claim that due to these and other factors, the general public confidence in state-run schools has receded. This "legitimacy crisis" is not limited to the realm of education but is also part of the decline in confidence in the welfare state. One response to this "legitimacy crisis" has been decentralization and devolution; another is the trend toward privatization.[4] The shift in overall policy objectives (i.e., from "equality," "democracy," and "solidarity" to "efficiency," "quality," and "individual liberty") in Sweden is also explicit in many other countries.

ARGUMENTS *FOR* AND *AGAINST* THE NEW REFORMS

Proponents of the reforms believe that more choice and the introduction of market forces in the schools can lead to a more efficient school system, can give parents and students more influence in the schools, and can lead to an overall improvement of the Swedish education system.

Opponents, on the other hand, believe that the reforms can increase the overall costs of schooling, lead to further segregation by socio-economic class and benefit some groups at the expense of others, and, in the end, lead to reduced output in the national school system. While many of the opponents of the reforms criticize the use of market forces in the school sector and see the reforms as a means to privatize or make cuts in the education system, others simply are concerned that there are not enough precautions taken to avoid negative consequences. In many instances, the focus of criticism seems to be the manner in which the reforms were implemented and the means through which choice is being augmented.

Three general aims of the reforms are to increase choice, further decentralize the school system, and provide equivalent conditions for municipal and independent schools. The proponents claim that this reform will lead to improvements in the performance and well-being of students, teachers, and schools.

Students, it is thought, are likely to perform better and accomplish more within the learning environments they have chosen. There is no single best school for everyone. Thus the diversification of school options will give more opportunities for students to participate in the school form that is most suitable to their needs. Some proponents also feel that independent schools can better adapt the content and methods to individual needs. We must also consider that government subsidies to independent schools may put these schools within reach of those families who otherwise might not have had the economic resources to enroll their children in an independent school.

Teachers, it is proposed, can also benefit from more flexibility and the opportunity to try new methods, or even relocate to another school that has a program in which they are better suited. This can enable educators to be more engaged and interested, and it can raise the status of the teaching profession by making teachers more responsible and autonomous. As some proponents believe, more choice for both teachers and students can create communities of shared values, which foster effective schooling.

Greater choice for parents and students can be a useful stimulus for improving schools, especially by making them more accountable. By making public and private schools more or less equal in terms of competition, schools that are not performing well will get a clear message that something must be done. The reform can be an impetus in reorganizing the education system, which is difficult to do otherwise, because of the extensive and lethargic bureaucracy and the vested interests of many actors. It is expected that the reform will lead to greater participation and interest by parents, which will positively effect the performance of children and the overall operation of the school.

Furthermore, the proponents believe that competition will lead to a more cost-efficient school system. One of the underlying aims, as mentioned by the government, is to improve overall educational output. Furthermore, the reform can lead to better opportunities for gifted children to excel and to lift the school system as a whole.

The opponents of the reforms have pointed out a number of potential shortcomings. In this section, the more general issues will be discussed relating to the influence of increasing choice in the schools. These include, for the most part, issues related to economic questions, segregation and the steering and control of schools.

According to the critics, the education system is being economically assaulted from two sides. On the one hand, they believe that the reforms will lead to higher overall costs for the education system because a number of small schools that are less cost-efficient than larger school units will be supported. On the other hand, due to the difficult economic climate just now, a number of cuts are being made. First of all, sector grants from the national government to municipalities have been drastically cut. On top of this, many municipalities are making further cuts in the education sector. While the Ministry of Education and Science in 1992 acknowledges that extensive cutbacks were being made, it did believe that this would lead to a decline in quality.[5]

Opponents point out that, even with the economic and human resources available today, it is difficult to provide for a single line of schools; a parallel structure would be far too expensive. One of the anticipated results is that many public schools will have fewer students, and the per-student costs will either go way up or else the classes will become overcrowded, and the quality is most likely to decline. Some of the opponents see this reform simply as a means to make cuts in the education sector that could not be carried out easily within the former structure. Others interpret the new reforms as a way of taking resources from the public schools and giving them to the private schools.

Another potential problem is that segregation will take place, and disparities in educational access will increase. This may involve segregation by social class and ability, besides the more obvious segregation by ethnic and religious groups. Due to the higher costs and greater resource needs, schools may simply refuse to accept children with special learning needs or disabilities. Some questions have also arisen regarding the new grading system and the role that it will play in the government's reform. While the implications are still unclear, we must remember that grading can be an important means of streaming children and in ranking schools.

Some opponents fear that independent schools can establish rules for entry so that they can get precisely the number and type of children they want. This can be seen in the few independent schools that use entrance tests and rather high fees as a means to maintain a rather homogeneous group in the school. The public schools cannot do this; they have the obligation to accept all children, and they must provide schools or arrange access to schools for sparsely populated and remote areas. As some opponents have pointed out, while it can be seen as positive that there is an increase in choice for consumers, it is important to distinguish this from an increase in the choice of consumers by the producers of education.

Critics also believe that greater disparities in choice will arise. They feel that as an end result the schools in more socially disadvantaged and difficult areas will lose resources, while schools in well-established areas will gain resources. New private schools are more likely to spring up in the socially well-established and more affluent areas. Thus, children in these areas will have more choice, and more resources will be diverted to their neighborhoods. Regarding urban/rural disparities, we see today that it is largely students in urban areas who benefit from the reform, since it is not feasible to provide a diversity of options in rural and remote areas of the country. Opponents also fear that this reform will lead to increased polarization of student groups according to social background and an increased hostility towards immigrants. As pointed out by some critics, in this game there are always winners and losers, and the game is conducted so that those who are already advantaged win more and those who are less advantaged lose more.

The reform has a number of implications regarding the organization and control of the school. While the proponents feel that parents will have more influence, opponents fear the opposite. The democratically elected officials will have less control of the schools. The market is not necessarily a means of democratic steering. On top of this, the municipalities will lose much of their control over schools. Economic planning and school mapping will be more difficult. In fact, some opponents note that the government is intruding upon the autonomy of the municipalities and assuming some of the municipality's responsibility in deciding upon school matters. A large number of responsibilities is placed on the National Agency for Education, including the approval and monitoring of independent schools. Some opponents feel that this is too big a task for the National Agency for Education, given their resources, and they prefer the former arrangements when the municipalities also had a role in supervising and monitoring the activities of the independent schools.

IMPACT OF THE REFORMS

Now that we have traced the general arguments for and against the education reform, some of the initial impacts of the reforms will be highlighted. In an earlier report,[6] I have traced the changes in the independent schools during the period encompassing the two years prior to and following the introduction of the reforms in terms of the nature and types of independent schools as well as their enrollments and average fees. While many of the trends were not clearly distinguishable then, we can now—after more than three years—see a number of trends emerging, and we can begin to start assessing the impact of the reforms. Nonetheless, many of the outcomes will be difficult to attribute to specific causes, since there are so many changes occurring simultaneously in the Swedish education system.

Changes in Enrollments

A large shift in enrollments from municipal to independent schools was expected to be one of the most immediate impacts of the reforms. Nonetheless, the enrollments in compulsory level independent schools have increased from only around 1 percent during the 1991/92 school year to 1.9 percent during the 1994/95 school year. Increased enrollments in independent schools are visible only in larger cities.

During the 1994/95 school year, there were 217 independent schools operating at the compulsory school level (4.4 percent of all compulsory-level schools in the country). There were 17,273 students enrolled in them. The independent schools are still quite small: an average of 80 students per school as compared to an average of 192 students in municipal schools.[7]

The majority of independent schools (34 percent) have a special pedagogical approach (i.e., they are either Montessori or Waldorf schools). Enrollments in Montessori schools have increased most rapidly among the various independent school types. The next largest group of independent schools includes those that have a curricular and pedagogical approach similar to that of municipal schools–although they are owned and operated by private individuals or organizations. These schools comprised 22.4 percent of independent school enrollments in 1994. Schools with religious profiles have not increased as rapidly as they did just after the introduction of the reforms. In 1994, they comprised 16.9 percent of the independent school enrollments. During the past few years a number of Islamic schools has also been added to this category of religious schools, which is still largely dominated by Christian schools. These schools are typically very small, and none of them are sponsored by the State Lutheran Church. Schools with a language or ethnic profile comprised 9.3 percent of enrollments, and international schools comprised 7.8 percent of the enrollments in independent schools. Schools with a special subject profile comprised 8.3 percent, and residential schools accounted for 0.9 percent of the total enrollments in independent schools.

Reduction of School Fees

Many independent schools still require school fees. The National School Agency is concerned that the fees are unreasonably high in more than a dozen cases. Among the newly established independent schools, however, school fees are not very common at all. Overall average school fees in the independent schools have decreased since school vouchers were introduced.

Increasing Segregation

Another impact of the reforms is growing segregation and increasing disparities among schools. This is becoming increasingly apparent in the three larger urban areas of the country, where independent schools are most common and where many families are often choosing a municipal school other than the one to which they were assigned.

In Stockholm and its surrounding municipalities, a number of reports have come out about the ethnic sorting of students. Children of Swedish origin are being removed from schools that have a large number of immigrant students. This can have more widespread effects than were initially perceived. While in practice such a change affects the movement of one student; in real terms, it can result in a negative valuation placed upon all the students left behind.

Similar reforms in other countries have awoken the old issue of selectivity vs. a common comprehensive school; yet, in Sweden, it is difficult—or too early—to say whether this will become a disputed issue related to the new reforms.

Disparities in choice can also be said to be increasing in Sweden, since very few independent schools are being established in rural or remote areas of the country. Thus, the "free choice revolution" remains largely an urban phenomenon.

Reductions in Costs or Just Plain Budget Cuts?

There have been extensive reductions in costs for compulsory-level schooling during the past four years. These reductions, however, are largely due to cuts from the state and municipal governments and are not necessarily the result of increased efficiency. Between 1991 and 1994, there was a 17-percent reduction in spending on instruction in the schools. On the other hand, the costs for other areas has increased; for example, the costs for school facilities increased by almost 8 percent. Altogether, total costs for compulsory-level schooling in Sweden has decreased by 7.5 percent between 1991 and 1994 (in fixed prices).[8]

In Stockholm, the additional cost based on the number of independent schools in 1991 was estimated to be 31 million Swedish crowns.[9] One study found that the additional costs for the municipalities during the 1993/94 school year was estimated to be 200 million Swedish crowns.[10]

Some of the effects of cuts made in the education sector can be seen in increasing class sizes. The cuts can also be seen in the decreasing number of teachers over the past five years, especially teachers for children with special learning needs, and home-language teachers.

Children with Special Learning Needs

While cuts are being made in all areas, the support for children with difficulties and special learning needs seems to be the most affected. A report from Stockholm School Administration[11] noted that in Stockholm alone, 80 special teacher positions (which is nearly a quarter of all special teachers in the municipality of Stockholm) had been eliminated, half class sessions were cut back and the number of hours devoted to speech therapy was cut in half. This report also expressed concern for increased segregation by ability.

Increased Accountability

Perhaps the greatest impact of the reforms has been the pressure put on the municipal schools by the existence of independent schools. Many municipal schools are making improvements to win back students, etc. Today school choice is being exercised mostly with reference to municipal schools. Greater responsibility and autonomy for school leaders, combined with the increasing pressure from independent schools, has induced many municipal schools to innovate and initiate dynamic changes in their schools.

CHANGES TO MAKE, PRECAUTIONS TO BE CONSIDERED

Avoid Extreme Characterizations

Much of the literature available concerning choice and the use of market forces is emotionally and ideologically charged. This seems to be in regard to an issue that touches upon such sensitive yet fundamental issues as equality, individual freedom, efficiency, and democracy. Thus, it happens that the "facts" and details brought forth are easily and often distorted by the opponents and proponents. There are strongly conflicting values and conflicting goals among the proponents and the opponents of this reform. We should be aware of this and attempt to dislodge or at least distance the debate from political/ideological domains and deal with it in pedagogical terms.

Consider Both Quality and Equality

The Swedish education system has largely served to maintain unity and guarantee equality in opportunity during the past several decades. As in other countries, the present trend is moving the educational system in the direction of providing for a plurality, but with an emphasis on efficiency. The aim should be to improve the quality of schooling, but not at the cost of equality. Thus, it is important to recognize when checks and safeguards in the present system will need to be added and to act upon them quickly. Unregulated choice plans are likely to result in extensive inequalities in the provision of educational services.

It will be necessary for the state or the municipality to intervene when schools are performing poorly (even if this goes against the principles of the market). This is an important measure to safeguard equity, and it is a necessary measure to maintain or raise the national achievement levels. While Sweden has been able to boast of relatively high standings in international comparisons of achievement and with remarkably small differences between regions, between schools, and between genders, one can only wonder if this will change with the new system. Efforts should be taken to safeguard such important achievements in the Swedish education system, not allowing them to disappear in the marketplace.

Safeguard Against Segregation and Increasing Disparities

A general concern is that the public schools may become a dumping ground for disadvantaged and underachieving students. One can imagine that after the segregating begins, it could accelerate quickly (i.e., as the quality of public schools goes down, more and more parents will try to remove their children, with the most capable students succeeding in leaving the public schools). This tendency can be found, to a varying extent, in other countries. Of course, the notion that schools serve the purpose of reproducing class and legitimizing the leading elite is not new. What does seem to be new is that in more and more cases, public—rather than private—funds are being utilized to support the private schools—a measure that expedites this process.

Examples of some safeguards are 1) fair and equal admission procedures, 2) effective outreach and counseling to foster informed choices, 3) opportunities for all children to benefit, rather than creating winners and losers, and 4) measures to improve public schools and ensure that real educational choices are available.

Balance Collective and Individual Interests

While the trend is moving toward an emphasis on greater diversity, some feel that overall public mistrust of the schools could grow, if the pendulum swings too far in favor of private schooling. The school is one of the most important institutions in society, mediating the diverse interests of the collective and the individual. During the 1980s, a shift from looking at education as a social, collective right to looking at it as an individual civil right took place.[12] As a result of this shift, the political policy objectives have changed, and a number of steps have been taken to reform the education system accordingly. Yet it is important to realize that there are many implications of changes which affect the balance between the collective and the individual. Schools can be a means to manage social tensions between ethnic and religious groups. However, we cannot forget that schools can also be a means to promote these differences and bring about further social tension.

Do Not Overlook the Implications for Students with Special Needs

Internationally, Sweden has been considered to be a leader when it comes to educating children with disabilities and/or special learning needs. Yet increasing competition and demands on efficiency are likely to encroach upon the position of these children in the schools. With the further decentralization of financial matters, school leaders and municipal authorities are induced to make cuts in the services for children with special needs in light of the high costs involved. The reforms concern not merely choice but also efficiency. While the government suggests that there should also be more freedom of choice for children with disabilities, schools can now refuse a child with a disability, if the placement of such a child is associated with significant economic or organizational difficulties. Nevertheless, the School Act states that students with difficulties should come first, before resources are used for other purposes.

Focus Attention on Both Municipal and Independent Schools

While parents should have the right to establish and choose independent schools, they must also have the opportunity of enrolling their children in public schools of high quality. In order to assure this, the rules of the game have to be carefully made up; they should be well thought out, and they should be piloted. While the privilege and opportunity to choose is important, it should not be secured at the expense of families who wish to have local municipal schools of good quality.

The emphasis on improving the school system has been focused largely on independent schools. Attention should also be given to the public schools and their staff in school improvements, especially in places where the municipal schools are not faced with competition from independent schools or even from other municipal schools. One example of this could be to encourage greater diversity among, and flexibility for, classroom teachers and the municipal schools. At present a number of municipal schools have Montessori or Waldorf classes within their schools. This could be a way to increase choice in the rural and remote areas of the country.

Address the Existing Restrictions on Choice

There are a number of factors that currently hinder choice and the use of market forces and that are likely to limit the implementation of the reform in the coming years. Currently, there is very little variety in school options throughout the country. This is particularly acute in rural and remote areas. It may be a long time before there will be a sufficient diversity of options in Sweden to satisfy the demands.

The reform is dependent on educators who will develop real choices for families, either in independent schools or in municipal schools with specific profiles. Some question whether there is a sufficient number of educators who are interested and willing to assume greater responsibility. Parents and students may not be interested in choosing other schools. This can be due to a lack of information or due to the long-standing dominance and tradition of public schooling in Sweden. Even when surveys conducted in other countries indicated the desire for choice among parents, few parents choose—in practice—a school other than the one nearest to home.

Student fees required by many independent schools prevent some families from choosing them, especially when they have more than one child. While there were apparent decreases in student fees as a result of the reform, one would expect that there would be substantially greater decreases.[13]

While there are some efforts to begin spreading information at the national and municipal level, the information is still insufficient. There is also a danger that the information will not be fair and accurate and that schools will revert to misleading advertising in order to attract consumers. Thus, there will be a need for controlling the nature and content of the information. In other countries, the costs of informing parents and students about available choices was found to be much greater than expected.

Give the Municipalities a Larger Role in the Steering and Monitoring of the Independent Schools

The municipal authorities should have more responsibility to follow up on all the schools in the municipality. In the government's plan, the municipality has no legal mandate to follow up and evaluate the independent schools, even though they finance nearly half their budgets from their own resources. The municipalities should also have the opportunity to adjust grants to the independent schools, when their fees are judged to be excessive. More flexibility should be given to the municipalities in order to adapt the reform to their own characteristics. This may be a means of establishing an appropriate balance between the steering of the schools through democratically-elected local officials and the steering of the schools through the market. Currently a number of municipal schools, which are small in size, are being closed because of the economic pressure on the municipalities. At the same time, independent schools cannot be rationalized by the municipality, because they are too inefficient. This pressure will increase with the growing number of small independent schools that the municipalities are forced to finance.

Do Not Overestimate the Role of the Market or Exaggerate Its Ability to Mediate Collective and Individual Needs

Here are three arguments which suggest the need for government involvement in the provision and financing of education: 1) imperfection of the market in which education is traded; 2) imperfections of the information available to those making the decisions; and 3) the possible divergence between the benefits to individuals and the benefits to society.[14]

The market operates on motives that conflict with the traditional values and motives of the Swedish educational system. The market does not distinguish group or societal needs. It does not account for the special needs of some. In fact, the inability of the market to consider the needs of the weakest groups and individuals is perhaps its greatest fault. The market pursues individual interests before national interests, and short-sightedness is inherent in the market.

Many of the concepts and models that apply to market economics are difficult to apply to schooling. Furthermore, educational choices do not necessarily follow the logic of the market. For example, experience from other countries indicates that children flee to better areas, not necessarily to better schools. Additionally, schools with a high demand do not always expand, rather they often become more selective. It is not the intention of many of the independent schools to expand and obtain more school vouchers; rather they will establish and select the number of students that is most economically favorable.

While the market can be an effective tool for promoting choice and improving schools through competition and increased accountability, there is a danger that we overestimate exactly what it can accomplish. We are still lacking substantial evidence from studies on the use of market forces in education. We do know, however, that in a number of countries privatized social services can be more expensive than government controlled services. The proponents of the use of market forces believe that "the market" can control, among other things, class size, teacher competency, and the quality of schooling. But is the market really so reliable? Can we risk handing over an institution that is so important for society and that constitutes such a valuable asset for the future to something so unpredictable as "the market"? In the end it is the people in the schools who will make schools better and not the market. The question is whether the market can improve the performance of the nation's educators.

Even in countries such as the United States and the United Kingdom, where market forces have played a much bigger role in controlling the production and distribution of social services, problems have arisen with the introduction and use of market forces in schooling.

Thus, it is reasonable to imagine that such a reform will be more difficult to introduce in Sweden, where the State has traditionally played a larger role in controlling the production and distribution of social services. It is an especially valid concern since the reform is being implemented on a larger scope and more quickly in Sweden than in the other two countries.

Conduct Research about This Reform and Give Further Attention to the Existing Studies

There is a growing amount of literature being produced on this topic, which ought to be consulted, and more research needs to be conducted in Sweden. The speed at which the reform was implemented left no time to evaluate or even to test the new methods of distributing financial resources. Therefore, both formative and summative evaluations will be needed.

Nonetheless, even with the many limitations in the existing research, policy-makers should not overlook the research that has been done. This material should be brought into the debate and used to ground new research in Sweden. The experiences in Britain are of great relevance to Sweden, due to the many similarities between the reforms and manner in which they were implemented in Sweden and Britain.[15] Thus, further attention should be given to the studies being carried out there. Nevertheless, in the end, it will not be the research findings that count but rather the willingness of the decision-makers to listen to them and to utilize them.

CONCLUSION

There are a number of general rules and guidelines that should be followed when planning and implementing educational reforms. Husén[16] summed up five general strategy rules regarding educational reforms: 1) educational reforms should be part and parcel of social reforms; 2) reforms cannot be implemented overnight; 3) resources are needed; 4) central government and grassroots participation are key factors; and (5) educational research and development are necessary. Breaking or overlooking these rules can lead to a number of problems in the implementation of a given reform and may lead to outcomes that are quite different than planned.

In an earlier work,[17] I considered the ongoing reforms concerning choice and the use of market forces in the Swedish educational system in light of these five rules. As should be apparent, all the rules have been broken, except for the first one. According to this first rule, one can claim that the reforms taking place today coincide with general economic reforms of the current government (i.e., these reforms are being planned and implemented within the larger framework of socio-economic change). Privatization and cuts in social spending are prevalent in many sectors, not only in education.

Another rule which perhaps should be considered when planning and implementing successful educational reforms is the need for political stability and consensus. The reform process which led to the nine-year comprehensive school in Sweden took nearly twenty years to complete, when the planning, testing, and implementation phases are included. It is important to note that this occurred with the same government in power; stability, in this sense, is also very important for successful reforms. An apparent weakness of the current reforms is that they are not likely to survive a political election intact.

Freer choice of educational options and the introduction of market forces in the production and consumption of education *may* improve the effectiveness and efficiency of schooling. However, there are many precautions that need to be taken. It is important to remind ourselves that the pursuance of such reforms involves risks: 1) a risk that educational costs will rise further; 2) a risk that disparities rise and segregation increases; and 3) a risk that more social tension will arise with its negative implications.

The debate and the decisions made concerning this issue have been dominated by politicians. The reforms proposed in 1992 have occurred so quickly that, in fact, other than politicians, few have had the chance to play an active role. The general media has largely judged and recorded the implementation and initial outcomes of the reform. Educators and educational researchers should be more involved in both of these processes. Likewise, it is extremely important that the issues involved with these reforms be discussed in pedagogical, not political, terms.

At this point in time, it seems important that educationalists can at least take part in the actual "fine-tuning" of the reform (i.e., determining what kind of choice plans are feasible and what safeguards can be made to ensure that the changes do not lead to increasing segregation by race or ability, to increasing overall costs, or a decline in the overall educational output). As we have seen in some small-scale attempts in other countries, responsible choice plans can counteract segregation rather than promote it, and responsible choice plans can increase the accountability of schools and facilitate greater influence from parents and students without necessarily leading to additional costs or increasing disparities among schools.

The barriers and obstacles facing the reform plan are many. Presently, there is relatively little diversity of school options in Sweden, particularly outside of the large cities. Further, there are indications of insufficient support from teachers, parents, and other grassroots actors. Finally, while the reform is likely to initially require more resources in order to maintain the present services, extensive cuts are being made in education, both by the central government and by the municipalities. Thus, one can speculate that the outcome of this reform may turn out differently than expected, possibly leading to both a decline in quality and equality. Nevertheless, it is still much too early to predict the outcome of the reform. It is important that one does not underestimate the dynamic effect that such changes can have if they gain wider support among educators and parents.

NOTES

1. Sixten Marklund "Fristående skolor och alternative pedagogik," *Skolöverstyrelsen Rapport* 86:23 (Stockholm: The National Board of Education, 1986).

2. *Government Bill* 1990/91:115. "Vissa skollagsfrågor m.m." (Certain School Law Questions, etc.), Regeringens proposition.

3. *Government Bill* 1991/92:95. "Valfrihet och fristående skolor." (Freedom of Choice and Independent Schools), Regeringens proposition.

4. Jane Hanniway and Martin Carnoy, eds., *Decentralization and School Improvement: Can We Fulfill the Promise?* (San Francisco: Jossey-Bass Publishers, 1993).

5. Ministry of Education and Science. "The Development of Education: National Report from Sweden." Report for the International Conference on Education in Geneva (Stockholm: Utbildningsministeriet, 1992).

6. Gary Miron. *Choice and the Use of Market Forces: Swedish Education Reforms for the 1990s.* Studies in Comparative and International Education No. 25 (Stockholm: Institute of International Education, 1993).

7. National School Agency, *Jämföreslsetal för skolhuvudmän* (Comparative Figures for Schools). (Stockholm: Skolverket, 1995).

8. These figures are from the National School Agency, reported in Dagens Nyheter, "Kommuner spara på undervisning" (Municipalities Save on Instruction). September 9, 1995 (Stockholm: Dagens Nyheter, 1995).

9. SOU 1992:38. *Fristående skolor. Bidrag och elevavgifter* (Independent Schools. Grants and Student Fees). Statens offentliga utredningar (Stockholm: Allmänna Förlaget, 1992).

10. Social Democratic Parliamentary Group, *Spara och slösa – kommunal och privat skola idag.* (Save and Waste – Municipal and Private School Today). Stockholm: Socialdemokratiska riksdagsgruppen, 1993).

11. Stockholm School Administration, *De Stora små förlorarna. Situationen för elever med svarigheter och särskilda behov* (The Big Little Losers: The Situation of Students with Difficulties and Special Needs). (Stockholm: Stockholms Skolor, 1992).

12. Tomas Englund, "Education for Public or Private Good" In: Gary Miron (ed.) *Free Choice and Market-Oriented Schools: Problems and Promises.* (Stockholm: The National School Agency, 1993).

13. Of the 86 schools that reported information on student fees in September 1992, only 38 percent had no fees, and 16 percent had voluntary fees (Miron 1993). Since then, school fees have decreased further or disappeared in most of the independent schools, however, there remains a number of schools whose fees have gone largely unchanged.

14. J. Wiseman, "Finance in Education." In: T. Husén and T.N. Postlethwaite (eds.) *The International Encyclopedia of Education* (Oxford: Pergamon, 1985).

15. Gary Miron. *Choice and the Use of Market Forces: Swedish Education Reforms for the 1990s.* Studies in Comparative and International Education No. 25 (Stockholm: Institute of International Education, 1993).

16. Torsten Husén, "Strategy Rules for Educational Reform: An International Perspective on the Spanish Situation." In T. Husén (ed.) *Education and the Global Concern* (Oxford: Pergamon, 1990).

17. Gary Miron. *Choice and the Use of Market Forces: Swedish Education Reforms for the 1990s.* Studies in Comparative and International Education No. 25 (Stockholm: Institute of International Education, 1993).

REFERENCES

Englund, T. 1993. ÒEducation for Public or Private GoodÓ In *Free Choice and Market-Oriented Schools: Problems and Promises,* ed. G. Miron. Stockholm: The National School Agency.

Government Bill 1990/91:115. "Vissa skollagsfrågor m.m." (Certain School Law Questions, etc.), Regeringens proposition.

Government Bill 1991/92:95. "Valfrihet och fristående skolor." (Freedom of Choice and Independent Schools), Regeringens proposition.

Hanniway, J., and M. Carnoy, eds. 1993. *Decentralization and School Improvement: Can We Fulfill the Promise?* San Francisco: Jossey-Bass Publishers.

Husén, T. 1990. "Strategy Rules for Educational Reform: An International Perspective on the Spanish Situation." In *Education and the Global Concern,* ed. T. Husén. Oxford: Pergamon.

Marklund, S. 1986. "Fristående skolor och alternative pedagogik." *Skolöverstyrelsen Rapport* 86:23. Stockholm: The National Board of Education.

Ministry of Education and Science. 1992. "The Development of Education: National Report from Sweden." Report for the International Conference on Education in Geneva. Stockholm: Utbildningsministeriet.

Miron, G. 1993. *Choice and the Use of Market Forces: Swedish Education Reforms for the 1990s.* Studies in Comparative and International Education No. 25. Stockholm: Institute of International Education.

National School Agency. 1995. *Jämföreslsetal för skolhuvudmän* (Comparative Figures for Schools). Stockholm: Skolverket.

Social Democratic Parliamentary Group. 1993. *Spara och slösa—kommunal och privat skola idag* (Save and Waste—Municipal and Private School Today). Stockholm: Socialdemokratiska riksdagsgruppen.

SOU. 1992:38. *Fristående skolor. Bidrag och elevavgifter* (Independent Schools. Grants and Student Fees). Statens offentliga utredningar (SOU) 1992:38. Stockholm: Allmänna Förlaget.

Stockholm School Administration. 1992. *De Stora små förlorarna. Situationen för elever med svarigheter och särskilda behov* (The Big Little Losers: The Situation of Students with Difficulties and Special Needs). Stockholm: Stockholms Skolor.

Wiseman, J. 1985. "Finance in Education." In *The International Encyclopedia of Education,* eds. T. Husén and T.N. Postlethwaite. Oxford: Pergamon.

CHAPTER 9

Political Ideals and Pedagogical Dilemma: On Beginning School for Six-Year-Olds in Norway

Peder Haug

ELEMENTARY SCHOOL REFORM 1997

This chapter presents several aspects of a recent Norwegian educational reform and discusses more closely some of the consequences of a significant change of strategy in contemporary Norwegian developmental and decision-making processes in educational policy. The reform in question is the Elementary School Reform '97. It was finally approved in the Norwegian Parliament in 1995 after a process of several years. The reform is to take effect in all Norwegian municipalities beginning August 1997. Typical for Norwegian thinking, the educational reform includes initiatives which exceed by far the isolated concerns of the school. It is presented as four partial reforms, only one of which is directly related to schools in the narrow sense.

- A children's reform, inasmuch as schools will now have to assume responsibility for the "whole" child through a combination of school and after-school activities.
- A family reform, inasmuch as the school will now help families by supervising children during necessary time before and after school hours.
- A cultural reform inasmuch as the school will assume greater responsibility for the content of children's free time.
- An educational reform inasmuch as schools will be expanded so that children begin at the age of six, primary education thus lasting

ten years. (Previously, school began at the age of seven and the obligatory school period was nine years.)

Pedagogical and political debates over these reforms have taken place simultaneously, and to some extent it has been difficult to distinguish between them. An understanding of what has taken place in the one has presupposed an understanding of the other. For this reason it is necessary to consider politics and pedagogy in a common context. In this chapter I will thus present some of the main points both from the political development and from the pedagogical debate, which arose in connection with the reform. My primary interest is the relation between the political processes that created the reform, and the pedagogical practice through which its intentions are to be realized. What sort of political processes and ideas form the basis for the reform? What kind of pedagogy is desired and what are the chances for producing results? This presentation builds primarily upon my own research work through the ten years that frame these questions (Haug 1992; Haug 1994).

REFORM STRATEGIES

In a manner of speaking, politics always takes place in an arena of formulations, and presents itself in the form of texts which, nonetheless, most often have change as their objective. The processes of formulation and of realization take place in two essentially different arenas with completely different actors and under widely different conditions. It is thus particularly difficult to establish a complete correspondence between them. In order to illustrate this, Brunsson (1989) defines four relations between a political formulation and subsequent action:

- the formulation leads to a particular action;
- the action leads to a particular formulation;
- there is no connection between action and formulation;
- the formulation conceals the fact that the action does not correspond with the formulation in a particular usage.

It is likely that the process leading to policy formulation also plays a role with respect to realization. Rolf et al. (1993), distinguishes between pragmatic and idealistic models for the development of new reforms. Inspired by Brunsson (1989), I would add a third model, the model of political development. These models or strategies have differing strengths and weaknesses.

According to the pragmatic model, the interested parties participate in negotiations in order to resolve a problem. The different parties reach reciprocal agreement on how they will act in order to engage particular solutions. The central concern is to create consensual action. The strength of the pragmatic model is the ability to act, since it unites those involved around a common definition of goal, need to act, field of action, and action. On the other hand, knowledge about the case is subordinated to what those concerned with the case are in agreement on, which is decided through negotiations. In principle, it is not a matter of what is true, right, or sensible but rather of that on which agreement can be reached.

Idealism as a model of change is characterized by an intellectually rational and knowledge-based process of change. Central political actors formulate a diagnosis, define different alternatives for action, and prioritize them according to a conception of what is most profitable. The challenge is to reach solutions through imaginative vision and facts. Idealism's strength lies on the intellectual level. It concerns the comprehensive collection and analysis of data. It is the model of action which gives the most room to research results as a basis for decision. This model also has the strength of being much more independent of interest groups than the pragmatic model. The weakness of idealism as a reform strategy is its belief in the possibility of understanding and explaining a social system. Considerations easily become rhetorical and symbolic. Visions can be false or based on an unfounded insight. The main question is still to what extent the idealistic point of departure manages to create support and motivation for change.

The political model for change has to do with developing the case in question through processes in which the purely political interests determine the results. In such strategies for change a great deal of political consensual activity is necessary in order to reach a decision in the matter. On the one hand, the reward is that the school is given a clearer profile in terms of educational policy. The school is thus placed under more political and formal control than before and should in this way secure, more than ever before, the ensemble of its interests. There is less chance that ponderous social and professional groups will have the opportunity to define the school according to their own needs. In this article, I will illustrate some of the difficulties that result from the political model of change. This model has the same epistemological problems as the pragmatic model, without having the practical insight, which is the strength of the pragmatic model. In addition, it has the rhetorical difficulties and the participation problems from the idealistic model.

THE POLITICIZATION OF EDUCATION

The pragmatic analysis was for a long time the usual model for new educational reforms and curricula in Norway. When the handling of the reforms and questions of curriculum were given to the political organs, they were already to a great extent settled and had already received large support both politically and from professional experts (cf. Hagemann 1992; Telhaug 1992a). According to Telhaug the large majority of educational reforms in Norway until the 1980s developed according to this pragmatic model in order to, among other things, achieve rapid change in the educational system (Telhaug 1990). The development of today's reforms and curriculum in Norway has deviated from that model. This happened in part through structural changes, that is, through discontinuing all professional counsels connected to school operation, both through a transformation to a large degree of goal-oriented management, through an extended decentralized centralization (the responsibility is decentralized, the power is centralized) and by making use of professional groups other than pedagogues as experts. The reforms in higher education, for example, are to large extent prepared in agreement with the ideological model, through rational and intellectually challenging visions (Rolf et al. 1993). Elementary School Reform '97, which is our theme, is quite precisely a political product, appearing in response to a directive from the political leadership in the department. It is based on processes proper, in particular, to the Labor Party and to the Norwegian Parliament. The main question itself—whether or not six-year-olds should begin in school—has never been the object of a comprehensive public evaluation. Some research work and other professional activity have taken place, but this has had, as far as we know today, little or no effect on the development of the policy around the reform (Haug 1992).

It is not inappropriate to see this development as, among other things, a consequence of the power structure in Norway, which recommends an increasing managerial collusion between state and society and a strong corporate social power (NOU 1982: 3).[1]

THE STRATEGY

The strategy that the government chose in order to push through the reform was to begin the practical execution before the Parliament had approved it and then to work toward the formal decisions underway. It is my conviction that without this strategy, the reform would not have been approved today. It is hardly conceivable that Parliament would have approved this comprehensive reform voluntarily if the pressure from the municipalities had not been strong.

The phase of action is two-part, the first part guaranteeing that six-year-olds in school be offered supervision (up to 40 hours a week) so long as children are in kindergarten. It was an important precondition for lowering the starting age for school. After-school activities required that building and health codes be respected and that there be pedagogical supervision. Otherwise it was mostly up to local officials. Combined with generous subsidies and a forceful political marketing this resulted in the number of vacancies in after-school activities climbing from 10,000 in 1990 to around 50,000 in 1995.

The other part involved "tricking" six-year-olds into school through the back door. This was done by changing the kindergarten law in such a way that kindergarten groups could be created for six-year-olds in the schools but with the headmaster as the kindergarten director. In reality elements of the kindergarten are moved over to the school and set under the school's administration but on the basis of the kindergarten law. This was seen to be a particularly successful operation: in 1995 about 40 percent of six-year-olds enrolled in such a program.

Both of these practical changes were made by presenting the question as a comprehensive educational reform. The after-school activities were introduced by revising the budget, the six-year-olds' program being the result of a debate about the kindergarten. The discussions about these questions were not particularly long or set in a common perspective.

What is typical about the reform is that it developed simultaneously in two domains—the political and the practical. The details are established in the practical domain before the corresponding elements emerge in the political domain. These two domains have not had a particularly good relationship with each other. Both domains have developed quite freely and independently without reciprocal regulations or considerations. In the end, however, the strategy secures a political majority. The contradiction lies in the fact that the way in which this strategy was deployed results in policy and practice developing independently of one another. It is possible that an administrative problem will be created at a later time when the state begins to regulate activity and make more decisions concerning content and work methods.

THE BACKGROUND FOR THE RESOLUTION CONCERNING SCHOOL FOR THE SIX-YEAR-OLDS

The government's official argument for the reform may be divided into three parts: first, it is heavily concerned with the need for a better qualified work force in a more and more knowledge-based society where, in particular, international competition is growing. Productive life is ever more dependent upon the capacity for creative thinking, production, and sorting and applying knowledge. These are the preconditions for further economic development and growth. This aspect is strengthened by contemporary periods of economic decline and growing unemployment. A nearly worn-out citation from the commission in which the Cabinet Minister was the leader (before becoming Cabinet Minister) illustrates this point: "The challenge for Norwegian educational policy is that the country does not sufficiently harvest competence from the population's talent" (NOU 1988, p. 7).

Part two of the government's argument is based on conceptions of changes in the environment in which the child grows up and the challenges that these create. Increased urbanization, looser family ties, more single mothers, more families with two working parents, fewer children per family, more troubled and violent neighborhoods, increased negative effect of the media, etc., are elements that persist in discussions of this development. It is important to keep these changes from affecting children negatively. Lowering the age for beginning school is a partial strategy.

A third part of the argument is that, given an increasing demand for knowledge and ability in developing areas and the fact that conditions in which children grow up vary considerably, it is important that all children in Norway receive an equivalent pedagogical program. In contrast to a voluntary kindergarten program, school reaches all, independent of status, residence, and family finances. It will thus be possible to counter occurrences of differing learning abilities and wish to learn which are attributed to unequal upbringing conditions and social background. This reform will especially improve conditions for children with immigrant backgrounds. At the same time, continuity and coherence will be created in content from the age of six and through the rest of the school career.

THE PROBLEM OF KNOWLEDGE

With respect to research-based knowledge in this area, all these basic assumptions are, technically speaking, debatable. Nonetheless, they have neither been tested nor submitted to debate among professionals in connection with this reform. This problem of knowledge may be illustrated by indicating several central themes: it is debatable just what the relationship is between the problem of growing competition, managerial marketing, economic difficulties, and education. The theory of human capital is often employed to explain these relations (Schultz 1961). Parts of the assumptions listed above may be regarded as a rehabilitation of that theory. Many have gradually put this theory into question and, among other things, underscored that it is indeed the market which influences education and not the reverse (Broady 1978; House 1991). There is little disagreement about the notion that the conditions in which children grow up have changed with time, but it is extremely unclear whether these changes as a whole are for the better or for the worse (Gullestad 1994). The answer to that question depends in particular on the basis of comparison, especially on the criterion of quality. The confusion, which can certainly be documented, is in any case greater in some parts of the country than in others. In the end, the question of dignity and equality in education is extremely problematic. That human beings in society are offered the same or an equivalent educational program is in no way a guarantee that increased equivalence in results will be produced. The only thing that is assured by an expanded unified school is that all children will receive a more or less formally equivalent school program. That does not guarantee that results of that schooling will be equal (Coleman 1990; Hernes 1974).

In a more rigorous analysis, I conclude by saying that the main arguments that are used are traditional social-democratic views. The arguments have been used in educational policy before, for example, in the 1950s when the real expansion in education began in this country (Haug 1996). In this sense these views are much more ritualistic than they may appear, and they reflect, at the same time, the fact that the different reforms with which they have been associated previously have not reached the rather ambitious goals that are woven into them.

RESISTANCE

The Cabinet Minister met strong resistance from within his own government, his own party, and the opposition parties. The conflict revolved around the school reform, there being strong agreement on the three other partial reforms. That resistance led to a comprehensive strategic policy effort which lasted several years and was implemented while the field of practice simultaneously developed the content of the program on a free basis, independent of the political activity. The protests were of all varieties: economic, symbolic, and those associated with principled educational policy. They reflect an unclear and confused parliamentary situation for a minority government.

ECONOMICS

The economics around the reform have presented a considerable problem. One consideration is the question of 9- or 10-year obligatory education. By lowering the age for beginning school while maintaining the 9-year education, one would earn 11 billion crowns yearly based on the supplementary income which a one-year increase in working life activity would lead to (Førsund et al. 1991). That corresponds to around 47 percent of the disbursements attributable to the Norwegian educational budget for 1995.[2] The other problem was the disbursements to the reform itself. These are expenses the municipalities do not budget for. While there was agreement that the reform would not lead to additional disbursements for the municipalities, there has been a lot of debate about the amount of these expenses and their source of finance.

PEDAGOGY

Simply speaking, three points of view regarding an adequate pedagogy for six-year-olds have been evoked. The first supposes that the same pedagogy used with today's first graders should be applied to the six-year-olds. This position is supported by the right side of the political landscape. The second stresses that these children should continue learning with play—a concept emphasized by the kindergarten pedagogy and supported by the bourgeois center parties and the socialist party. The third recommends that children be exposed to a combined form of pedagogy that includes elements from the school and the kindergarten pedagogies. It took some time to reach agreement on this problem even within the governing party. This must be regarded against the background of Norwegian pedagogy understood as progressive and anti-intellectual. This point of view also reflects the particularly forceful resistance from pre-school teachers to the notion that six-year-olds should be moved from the kindergarten to the school. Their protest had in part to do with securing their own institutions. It also represents a fear that children will be placed in too strongly structured and managed learning situations, a debate found in many countries (cf., for example, Kagan and Ziegler 1987). The Norwegian kindergarten is based on a principle of free education and differs from the school in that regard.

POLITICAL MANIFESTATION

Another reason why this process took considerable time was the political manifestation directed against Cabinet Minister Gudmund Hernes. He is the most dynamic and effective Minister of Education that Norway has ever had. He has reformed the entire Norwegian educational system in the course of five years. Throughout these changes, he has provoked many people and created a growing need among the opposition to manifest itself. He therefore met unexpectedly hard resistance when the matter came up for consideration in Parliament and thereby required political solutions.

INSTITUTIONALIZATION

The resistance to the institutionalization of pre-school children in Norway has traditionally been great and reflects a bias in family policy connected to primary sustenance and traditional men's and women's roles. This is in opposition to the image of Norway as a place of emancipation and equality. Lowering the age for beginning school while at the same time expanding the obligatory school day represents a rather strong rupture with previous arrangements and traditions even though the reform would only put Norway on a level with other European countries (Telhaug 1992b, p. 185).

THE BEST OF THE KINDERGARTEN AND SCHOOL TRADITIONS

Resistance to school and school pedagogy for six-year-olds was great, not the least in the governing party. In order to obtain a majority vote, political compromises had to be worked out. Formulations acceptable to other political parties had to be negotiated. The governing party obtained approval from several of the parties in Parliament, both to the right and in the center. Gradually a political majority was developed for the notion that six-year-olds would be offered a different program than that which the school ordinarily offers to first graders. The idea was that six-year-olds are too young to go through a traditional first grade. They require much more play and much more free activity than school ordinarily offers. Two rather central objectives grew out of this basic concept, and they persist wherever the program for six-year-olds is being considered:

- The content of this program should be influenced by the best of both kindergarten and school tradition.
- The presence of six-year-olds in school represents an important initiative for modifying work on the other grade levels in the direction of the kindergarten tradition.

In other words, pedagogy in the elementary school is being changed in a radical way. And that is sensational. First of all, it is a child-centered, activity-oriented pedagogy that contains a rather direct critique of the established school. It is based on the notion that the school is too "school-ish," that it is too structured, stiff, programmed, fact-oriented and, at the same time, not challenging and development-oriented enough in the creative areas, taking children, their qualities and needs too little into consideration. Second, it represents a political orientation in an innovative direction which struggles against contemporary restorational rhetoric in educational policy and pedagogy. In this regard it is much more a matter of effectiveness, exploitation of teaching, knowledge, and performance in subject and theme. This is the expression of a victory for the progressive counter-movement in Norway.

The question is what these formulations actually mean—what purpose and function they serve. My understanding is that they form the basis for a political compromise and are, thus, a part of a political rhetoric and must be understood from the point of view of a purely political rationality. They are ideals which are formulated on the basis of political needs in order to obtain a majority for the proposal. Therefore they idealize and harmonize the circumstances both in school and kindergarten pedagogy. They reflect, to a smaller degree, a pragmatic interest, an understanding of what is necessary in order to realize such a pedagogy in the school or what is possible to do in practice (and I will come back to this later). The assertions also give the impression of being idealistic and visionary but are in reality superficial and built upon faulty knowledge bases. They fail to take into consideration or even measure the relevant research which has been done in this field. At the same time, the assertions are deceiving. They promise quite a bit. A good number of failures must happen before anyone opposes what is considered "the good and the best," no matter how unrealistic the formulations might be. That is why these central assertions of political compromise also constitute a minor rhetorical *chef d'œuvre*, just as political texts "should" be when the case is difficult.

The question is to what extent the formulations are appropriate both as the basis for developing curriculum and for practical work. The dilemma is that the political solution is supposed to guide the development of further content in the curriculum. What functions positively and constructively on the formulation level in one arena (Parliament) can be particularly problematic to concretize and realize in other arenas. Formulations aimed at creating political compromise are not always so appropriate as a basis for developing concrete curriculum and pedagogical practice. A consequence of this compromise can be— and this is my forecast for development—that forces in the school itself assure that the content in the new school remains the same. Another consequence can be that those who further develop the curriculum fail to seize upon the more essential political formulations, instead creating their own definitions for them. I will take up this matter and argue for it below.

WHAT IS THE BEST?

So what is, respectively, the best of the kindergarten and the school? In the political documents, a general answer is given to this question. The best of the kindergarten has to do with free-form work and, in particular, with free play. The best of the school has to do with the structured and systematic subject-oriented teaching. How are we to understand this? I limit my presentation to three main points in order to illustrate problems, challenges, and possible consequences.

UNDERSTANDING KINDERGARTEN PEDAGOGY

The first question is exactly what lies in the notion of kindergarten pedagogy. How should this concept be understood?[3] For me it looks as though the idea of play and the notion of kindergarten pedagogy are, so to speak, used as synonyms. That is a simplification. The kindergarten markets itself as a unified pedagogical alternative in which free activity, work with themes, and, in particular, the use of those daily routines associated with meals, clothing, etc. together constitute the pedagogical program and pedagogical effect. It is the context and the association between these three elements which define and constitute the particularity of kindergarten pedagogy. What is remarkable in the political discussion is that one element of kindergarten pedagogy's tradition is drawn out and emphasized. How this element is supposed to function without the others, I can't say. It seems to me that the combination of the kindergarten's free activity and the schools' teaching will have to be something other than what we have previously seen both in kindergarten and school.

The notion of play is, on the other hand, understood according to the manner in which the kindergarten defines and practices it. This provides one perspective on activity and development, though not the only one. Both play research and many basic theories of play make it possible to analyze, for example, subject-oriented activity in the school in terms of play to a far greater extent than we have been accustomed to (see, for example, Eik 1995). That precisely this one understanding is chosen instead of another is not the result of a rational evaluation of all the other alternatives. It is more likely that insight has been limited and, especially, that the influence of professional groups and institutions have been strong.

Interestingly enough, Cabinet Minister Hernes is almost the only one who has taken an interest in a notion of play different from the one established in the kindergarten tradition. He has done this by continuously emphasizing that there is no opposition between play and learning, that they belong together regardless of what is taught or of the age of the student. In the Parliamentary debate in 1994, he underscored in part the seriousness of play which he claimed was a part of all subjects, "in fact right up to the university level." The Cabinet Minister believes that the concept of play is much more cognitive than some people will admit. Perhaps we can profit from this idea in order to reevaluate a claim that still persists—that the elementary school and the elementary school teachers don't know anything about play. Perhaps they know it in another way and for other reasons than the pre-school teachers in kindergarten.

In a slightly superficial way we can say that this policy aims to guarantee six-year-olds development and learning through play and teaching without clarifying this connection. It is a long way from assertions stating that six-year-olds must play and learn subjects to realize them in practice. It is not obvious what is meant by the notion of play here, even though the kindergarten concept is taken as a point of departure. It is not self-evident how the systematic learning of subjects is to be comprehended. Seen in this way the political statements veil the difficult theoretical and practical challenges that are implicit in the assertions but which do not appear before a proper analysis is undertaken.

CAN A PEDAGOGY BE CONSTRUCTED?

Is it possible to unite two pedagogical traditions? Can a pedagogy be made like bread, where it is simply a matter of having the ingredients and proceeding. Take a bit of the one and a little of the other, stir together and voilà! done in one, two, three? Or is developing a pedagogy something we can manage and control only to a limited degree? In such cases, which forces influence and create the pedagogical field and the pedagogical praxis and what can we do about it? This is a basic question which in itself demands comprehensive working through and discussion (see, for example, Durkheim 1977).

This is not the place for such fundamental analysis. In lieu of that, I will present some different analyses which may be well worth pursuing and which together indicate the challenges which lie ahead for Norwegian educational development.

We cannot really say whether it is possible to create new pedagogy in the school for six-year-olds. The project is in any case rather daring and constitutes a formidable developmental task which is both composite and complex.

THE TECHNICAL-RATIONAL PERSPECTIVE

The technical-rational or instrumental understanding apparently sees no problem in such a situation. Taking elements pell-mell and mixing them together into a totality is primarily a matter of forming the right conditions and developing insight, will, and ability in the personnel who are to carry out the pedagogy. In other words, the matter is essentially seen as a practical question. It is my understanding that those participating in the debate in Parliament represent to a large degree such an understanding of the expression "the best of the two traditions." This point of view is in any case indirectly supported because it is an indication that thinking and praxis in the kindergarten and the school have drawn close to one another in the past few years. The main tendency both in Norwegian and international kindergarten development is characterized by academicization and institutionalization (Kjørholt, Korsvold, and Telhaug 1990). In addition, it has been claimed (without any scientific support) that work in the first grade is more and more influenced by the kindergarten. The central question is whether that is a guided action of will, a functional adaptation to new demands and expectations, or a contingent variation within a tight margin of action.

The rational definition of the relation between policy and pedagogy is, in part, the basis for much of the dominant understanding of curriculum. In Norway, curriculum is regarded as a state-ideological instrument of management determined by state politicians which the schools and teachers are required to implement and realize. The obvious difficulties with such a perspective are well documented. Curricula are seldom (maybe never?) carried out according to intentions. In the comprehensive Norwegian experiment with six-year-olds, they had, for example, more significance as legitimation than as inspiration (Haug 1990). The claim that the more things change, the more they stay the same is a deduction from this point (Cohen 1988). Klette (1994) modifies a similar, rather general assertion. She considers that knowledge content is the most resistant to change. The regulation format, she believes, has been changed from a strong authoritarian administration and control on the part of the teachers to a large degree of negotiation and collaborative strategies. The instruction format, on the other hand, points in both directions. She finds both the classical teacher domination and what she calls the modernized recitation. It is impossible to answer the interesting questions about what meaning the curriculum has in these changes and what the consequences of pressure from other fields are.

THE INSTITUTIONAL PERSPECTIVE

The institutionally oriented person will argue that pedagogical action is to a large extent connected to the institutional and contextual traditions and conditions (March and Olsen 1989). This implies that to each of these two traditions belong not only particular values, conceptions, ideas, and actions but that preconditions such as buildings, rules for behavior, norms, etc. are developed to an equally large extent. Both the ideological and the concrete physical norms in the institutions are adapted to the pedagogical tradition they belong to, and they have also been decisive for how the tradition has developed itself. The school's physical point of departure is, for example, a church building, whereas the kindergarten's is a home. This produces dissimilar conditions for action. The question is whether the traditions can be carried out independently of the contexts that have developed them. What happens when a particular pedagogical tradition is placed within institutions and contexts other than those in which it "belongs"? What happens if one tries to realize kindergarten pedagogy in a school setting, being thus required to submit to other regulations and norms? Is the result a kindergarten pedagogy or will an adaptation to the school take place?

Experience from the Norwegian six-year-olds experiment (1986-90) showed that the institutional influence was particularly large (Haug 1992) and that institutions in which the activity took place had a significant influence independent of whether grade-school teachers or pre-school teachers worked with children. The analyses of teaching were built upon observations made on six-year-olds throughout whole days, and registered on standardized forms. In addition, I analyzed TV recordings of this teaching using the Bellack system for classroom interaction. Both of these methods of investigating pedagogical work indicated that when the program was situated in the school, the set-up was far more school oriented than when it was situated in the kindergarten. These results are confirmed in a reproduction carried out in 1995 (Haug, 1996). There was more free activity when the six-year-old program was localized in the kindergarten than when it was placed in the school, even though the curriculum was the same, and this happened no matter what teacher groups were teaching. The pre-school teachers were, in fact, more dominating and directive than the grade-school teachers when they worked in the school despite the fact that the educational ideology and the rhetoric of the pre-school teachers aim for the opposite. In other words, the institution for which the program is designed possesses a form of definitional power over praxis. Thus the content of teaching is not only an individual competence problem but also an institutional problem.

CURRICULUM CODES

Another method of analysis consists of examining and studying the curriculum codes in the two institutions (Lundgren 1983). It is then possible to develop an understanding of whether these two pedagogical traditions build upon completely opposed ideologies or nuclei. The analyses of these two traditions which have been carried out in connection with the six-year-olds experiment conclude dissimilarly on many levels:

- The curriculum code in the kindergarten is primarily child centered in the sense that the choice of content generally builds upon the child's personality development. The curriculum code in the school is primarily subject centered in the sense that the basis for activity is connected to acquisition of the subject and knowledge of the topic.
- The curriculum code in the kindergarten is child centered in the sense that the child has the freedom to undertake his or her own activities and self-development, where play in particular is a central element. The curriculum code in the school is child centered in the sense that both the subject and the teaching are

adapted to the child's level and development, though others have determined the activities.

- The curriculum code is use-oriented in both institutions (rational curriculum code) in the sense that children should be engaged in activities that interest children and that the child will find useful and rewarding.
- The curriculum code in the kindergarten is contextual in the sense that the pedagogue usually works with articulating situations in frameworks within which children will function. In the school the curriculum code is far more case-oriented in the sense that pupils must work with concrete assignments and questions.

The question is whether it is possible to gather together very different curriculum codes into one, while maintaining the capacity to identify the elements. Is it possible to unify freedom and obligation which can in many ways be the basis for work in the two institutional levels? Or is it equally as problematic as mixing fire and water, when the two different elements are each other's greatest enemies?

WILL SIX-YEAR-OLDS HAVE AN EFFECT ON THE SCHOOL?

Moving the kindergarten tradition up one grade in order to make the school less "school-ish" is a great challenge for the development of the new Norwegian elementary school. The question is whether it is realistic to suppose that a new school class will be able to have an effect on work done by the nine others which have been in the school for hundreds of years.

Students of social processes will, among other things, be interested in whether there is something here comparable to earlier education reforms. The closest we can come is the situation when different educational courses were made into one. That happened, for example, in Norway in the 1960s, when "continuation school" and "middle school" were combined to form a common elementary school which constituted the last three years of the obligatory common elementary school. "Continuation school" was practical. Pupils who completed it usually went directly out into professional life. "Middle school" was academic and was meant, among other things, to qualify pupils for acceptance into the high school. According to the plan, the new elementary school took the best from both of these two levels of schools. Subsequent experience, however, shows that it is the "middle school" tradition that was maintained to the greatest extent (Telhaug 1990). The education and the institution with the greatest social and academic prestige dominates in the new school. There are examples of this from England as well (Goodson 1988). Supposing analogous social forces will dominate in our field, this indicates that it is most likely that "new" pedagogy will be dominated by the conceptions and praxis which are the basis for work in the school. Consequently, a well-established school will guide work with six-year-olds, not the inverse.

POLITICAL IDEALS AND PEDAGOGICAL DILEMMAS

This chapter has presented some aspects of the development of one of the most comprehensive Norwegian educational reforms in this century. Its primary characteristic is the purely political developmental pattern that has been employed. Directly formulated, it is more concerned with how a political majority in Parliament may be achieved than with consideration of both knowledge in the field and what is conceivably realizable in praxis. A cloud of political rhetoric hangs about the reform. Its sole objective is to conceal the problems, difficulties, contradictions, oppositions, etc., thereby creating the basis which will enable realization of the reform. For me it is perfectly clear that the assertions have primarily been ideal. They have had clear political functions and worked toward lowering the school age. That is completely legitimate in a political institution such as the Parliament and corresponds to the task appointed to elected officials, namely, to solve problems.

Thus far, three considerations have been decisive for evaluating this reform to lower the school age. The first is the question of what kind of problem it solves. I must honestly admit that I can find neither imposing problems nor great difficulties which the lowering of the school age can solve with any degree of probability. On the other hand, I can see that behind the rhetoric lies the basic argument for that portion of the reform which directly concerns education, characterized by traditional social-democratic values where the notion of education as investment, equality, equal worth, and compensation still persists. Interestingly enough, that situation produces a more progressive pedagogy than that at the point of departure. Whether that, too, is only idle talk, we will soon see.

The second understanding I have reached is that the most central assertions for the reform have other functions than pedagogical. They have been advanced on the basis of political consideration.

- They are intended to legitimize political points of view and processes with respect to voter groups.
- They have a high level of generality because the political milieu neither has the time nor the competence to be more concrete and practical.
- They are full of contradictions. Partly because they are the result of compromise but also because at that level of generality, it is possible to be in favor of a case which in practice is the opposite of what was intended.
- They promise a lot, among other things because the content is to be sold both to other politicians and to voters. Reforms which promise the most receive the most support.
- They obfuscate and harmonize the case. A reform which is problematic has difficulty finding support.

The third element in my understanding concerns whether the Department's and Parliament's insight into the question of education is great enough for them to evaluate and to work out reforms in a defensible manner and whether the political parliamentary processes and the political use of language alone are appropriate as a basis for developing both reforms and curriculum. Can it be that by excluding the corporate and other public elements, reforms and curriculum can be accomplished for which there is a political majority but which are not in practice realizable? Elements of the analysis presented here may indicate that. In this way the reforms serve exclusively political interests, giving political rewards to those able to participate in decisions about the reforms and compromises. The reform function thus acquires more the character of a legitimation of political parties and political systems than of real change within education for the benefit of the majority of people. This is the most important problem for the reform to try to solve. Still, legitimizing a more or less lame state is an insoluble matter.

The danger and the contradiction is that a "politicization" like that of an educational policy can give other and more occult forces the occasion to dominate over content in the school. It can be difficult to know what these may be, but as a rule those who already have power will continue to hold it. And in that case, political resolution is no guarantee of accomplishing change.

NOTES

1. That the Minister of Education in his previous position as professor of sociology was responsible for this account only strengthens such a conclusion.
2. Disbursements are 23.5 billion krone (Kirke-, utdannings- og forskningsdepartmentet. 1994-95. *For budsjetterminen 1995.* Oslo: Stortingsproposisjon nr. 1 (Parliamentary Report, no. 1), p. 317.
3. I could just as well have asked the question about understanding of content and work methods in the school. By discussing one of the institutions, the main point is illustrated sufficiently.

REFERENCES

Broady, D. 1978. *Utbildning och politisk økonomi* (Education and Political Economy). Forskningsgruppen för läroplansteori och kulturreproduktion. Stockholm: Högskolan för Lärarutbildning.

Brunsson, N. 1989. *The Organization of Hypocrisy.* Chichester: John Wiley & Sons.

Cohen, D.K. 1988. "Teaching Practice. Plus Que Ça Change." In *Contributing to Educational Change*, ed. P.W. Jackson Chicago: McCutchan Publishing Corporation.

Coleman, J.S. 1990. *Equality and Achievement in Education.* Boulder: Westview Press.

Durkheim, E. 1977. *The Evolution of Educational Thought.* London: Routledge & Kegan Paul.

Eik, L.T. 1995. *På sin plass med lek? Lekens plass i det pedagogiske tilbudet til 6-åringer i skolen* (A Place for Play? The Role of Play in the Education of Six-Year-Olds). Hovedoppgave i barnehagepedagogikk. Høgskolen i Oslo: Avdeling for lærerutdanning.

Førsund, F., et al. 1991. *Mot bedre vitende? Effektiviseringsmuligheter i offentlig virksomhet* (Against Better Knowledge. Possibilities for Making the Public Sector More Efficient). Stiftelsen for samfunns- og næringslivsforskning. Bergen: Norges Handelshøyskole.

Goodson, I. 1988. *The Making of the Curriculum.* London: The Falmer Press.

Gullestad, M. 1994. "Om å studere 'barns egen kultur'" (To Study Children's Own Culture). In *Bærekraftig pedagogikk* (Sustainable Pedagogy), eds. P. Aasen and O.K. Haugaløkken. Oslo: Ad Notam.

Hagemann, G. 1992. *Skolefolk. Lærernes historie i Norge* (School People. The History of Norwegian Teachers). Oslo: ad Notam Gyldendal.

Haug, P. 1990. "Does Educational Planning Lead to Planned Education?" *Nordisk Pedagogikk,* 4.

Haug, P. 1992. *Educational Reform by Experiment.* Stockholm: HLS Förlag.

Haug, P. 1994. *Formulering og realisering av utdanningspolitikk. Om det politiske arbeidet med å innføre skulefritidsordningar og skule for 6-åringar* (Formulation and Realization of Educational Policy. The Political Struggle to Introduce After School Child Care and School for Six-Year-Olds). Møreforsking Volda/Volda lærarhøgskole (Møre og Romsdal Research Foundation/Volda College of Education).

Haug, P. 1996. *Barnehage på skule. Evaluering av kjerntilbod og organisering og skulefritidsordningar for 6-åringar* (Kindergarten at School. An Evaluation of School and After School Child Care for Six-Year-Olds). Trondheim: Norwegian Centre for Child Research.

Haug, P. 1996. *The Norwegian Discussion on the Age for Starting School.* Trondheim: Norsk Senter for Barneforskning (Norwegian Centre for Child Research).

Hernes, G. 1974. Om ulikhetenes reproduksjon (On the Reproduction of Difference). In *I forskningens lys. NAVF 25 år* (In Light of Research. The Norwegian Research Council 25 Years), ed. M. Sundt-Mortensen. Oslo: Lyches Forlag.

House, E.R. 1974. *The Publics of Educational Innovation.* Berkeley: McCutchan Publishing Corporation.

House, E.R. 1991. "Big Policy, Little Policy." *Educational Researcher* 20, no. 5.

Kagan, S.L., and E.F. Ziegler. 1987. *Early Schooling. The National Debate.* New Haven/London: Yale University Press.

Kirke-, utdannings- og forskningsdepartmentet. (Ministry of Education and Church Affairs) 1992-93. *Vi smaa, en Alen lange* (We Small, an Inch Long). Oslo: Stortingsmelding. nr. 40.

Kirke-, utdannings- og forskningsdepartmentet. (Ministry of Education and Church Affairs) 1994-95. *For budsjetterminen 1995* (The Budget of 1995). Oslo: Stortingsproposisjon nr.1.

Kjørholt, A.T., T. Korsvold, and A.O. Telhaug. 1990. *Pedagogisk tilbud til 4-7-åringer i internasjonalt perspektiv. En studie av England, Frankrike, Japan og USA* (An International Perspective on Education for Children 4-7 Years of Age. A Study of England, France, Japan, and the United

States). Rapport nr 18. Trondheim: Norsk Senter for Barneforskning (Norwegian Centre for Child Research).

Klette, K. 1994. "Skolekultur og endringsstrategier" (School Culture and Strategies for Change). Doctoral dissertation, University of Oslo.

Lundgren, U.P. 1983. *Att organisera omvärlden* (To Organize the World). Stockholm: Liber.

March, J.G., and J.P. Olsen. 1989. *Rediscovering the Institutions.* New York: Collier Macmillan Publishers.

NOU. 1982 (3). *Maktutredningen* (The Analysis of Power). Sluttrapport (Final Report). Oslo, NOU.

NOU. 1988 (28). *Med viten og vilje* (With Knowledge and Purpose). Oslo: NOU.

Rolf, B., E. Ekstedt, and R. Barnett. 1993. *Kvalitet och kunskapsprocess i högre utbildning* (Quality and Processes of Knowledge in Higher Education). Nora: Nya Doxa.

Schultz, T.W. 1961. "Investment in Human Capital." *American Economic Review,* 51 (March).

Telhaug, A.O. 1990. *Forsøksrådet for skoleverket 1954-1984. En studie i norsk skoleutvikling* (The Research Council of Education. A Study of Norwegian School Development). Oslo: RSF-NAVF / Universitetforlaget.

Telhaug, A.O. 1992a. "Tekst og kontekst. Høringsutkast til Læreplan for grunnskole og videregående opplæring. Generell del. KUF 1992. En historisk analyse" (Text and Context. A New Curriculum for Primary and Secondary School. A Historical Analysis). *Grunnskolenytt 2.*

Telhaug, A.O. 1992b. *Norsk og internasjonal skoleutvikling. Studier i 1980-årenes restaurative bevegelse* (Norwegian and International Educational Development. Study on the Restorative Movements in the 1980s). Oslo: Ad Notam Gyldendal.

CHAPTER 10

Upper Secondary School Reform in Norway
Anne-Lise Th. Iván

INTRODUCTION

This chapter describes the frame of reference of Reform 94 in Upper Secondary School, its background, aims, and principles, and focuses on the means of steering and implementation used by central authorities. The chapter questions whether Management by Objectives (MBO) as a steering principle, coupled with leadership training, is an adequate tool in furthering innovations and keeping up the national educational aims.

The first section introduces the context of the upper secondary school and the way it is managed, giving a rather comprehensive picture of the innovations and changes brought about by the reform.

The school's situation between central governance and decentralized freedom ruled by MBO as a principle regarding steering aspects and curricular practice is described. Tensions and conflicts are reflected upon. The article describes the Leadership Training Program initiated by central authorities as a mechanism for steering and implementing change.

The second part presents experiences and empirical research related to the implementation of Reform 94 thus far, illustrating some tendencies.

In view of the lessons learned, this article finally sums up some essential conditions for a successful implementation of change.

REFORM 94 AND ITS FRAME OF REFERENCE

The Context of the Norwegian Education System

Education is given high priority within public activities in Norway. Out of the total population of 4.2 million, nearly 900,000 people are predominantly occupied with education. In addition, around 700,000 annually participate in adult education courses.

Innovations and important changes are taking place in Norway in the 1990s. Education has become an area of focal political interest, and various reforms, mainly structural, have been launched, aiming at the consolidation of the system and reform of the content of education, from the primary stage up to higher education. Although the reform has focused mainly on upper secondary education, the whole structure of the management of education has also been reviewed.

These reforms have also implications for the legislation. Therefore, different educational acts are being re-examined in order to improve their correlation and consistency.

A New Direction for Education Policy: Main Social and Political Priorities

In terms of educational service, the principle of equality has a long tradition in Norway. The overall aim of its government has been to ensure all people equal rights to education, regardless of sex and social, geographical, and cultural background.

Education policy is also based on the recognition that people's ability to receive and be motivated for new knowledge depends, to a large extent, on the quality of the educational provision. Therefore, the current focus is on the content and quality of education. The guiding principle for the 1990s is to improve educational standards for the whole population by consolidating and improving the system. Thus, the objective of the present education policy is defined as "quality of equality."

These are rather ambitious aims, which lead to the formulation of questions such as:

* Will factors such as decentralization and delegation from central to local levels and the passing of a new municipal law—which allows more local freedom—create uneven economic prerequisites among

municipalities and, perhaps, make it impossible to fulfill the ambitious national aims?

- Are the principles of management and the means used by central authorities adequate to carry out the national educational objectives?
- Will the reform program for upper secondary schools, in the long run, turn out a success or a failure ?

WHAT IS REFORM 94?

Before looking further into the questions raised, a short introduction to Reform 94 is given here by presenting the background, problems, and challenges associated with it, and the solutions proposed for upper secondary education.

Background

Since the beginning of the 1970s, upper secondary education in Norway has undergone several changes and developments. The most important was the change associated with Reform 74 that made upper secondary education comprehensive by extinguishing the traditional separation between vocational training and academic education. Today, the large majority of Norway's upper secondary schools (ca. 750) offer both vocational and academic courses. Whereas 20 years ago upper secondary education was limited to a relatively small part of the age cohort, the last two decades have witnessed an influx of large numbers of young people and adults. There have been gradual changes in the dual system of vocational training over the past 15 years. A parallel system of vocational education, either in the schools or in the industry, has slowly developed into a combined system where basic vocational training is supplied by the schools while specialized training is obtained through apprenticeships in industry.

Problems

During the 1980s, it became evident that the system of upper secondary education, particularly in the field of vocational training, faced many difficulties:

- declining status of vocational education relative to college preparatory schooling;

- increasing number of drop-outs that left the system without the necessary qualifications either for an occupation or for further education, in other words, basically trained for unemployment;
- inefficiency of the dual system of vocational training due to low availability of apprenticeships and weak interaction between the schools and the industry;
- geographical and social inequalities;
- premature decisions concerning specialization, leading many toward wrong choices;
- unsuitability of educational contents and methods to future requirements in the job market.

Challenges

As the education system was confronted with demands from society and a labor market characterized by factors such as structural change, mobility, rapid technological innovations, increasing internationalization, and serious ethical challenges, the need for rapid change became evident. It was necessary:

- to raise the status of vocational training and make it attractive to a larger part of the age cohort;
- to create a diverse educational structure which could encompass all young people and adults and give them formal competence;
- to find solutions for the dropout problem;
- to prepare those who enter secondary education as sixteen-year-olds in 1994 for participating in the labor force until about 2040;
- to educate pupils and apprentices for today's labor market as well as for jobs not yet envisioned;
- to train pupils and apprentices for devising new jobs and becoming, in effect, entrepreneurs.

Solutions

Based on the identified needs, several changes have taken place in upper secondary education. Some of the consequences of Reform 94 are:

- All sixteen to nineteen year olds are given the right to three full years of secondary education, which the regional authorities are obliged to provide.

- All pupils have the right to be admitted to one of their top three choices when applying to upper secondary education.
- At the end of their training, pupils shall have either a diploma qualifying for college or university education, or a certificate as a skilled worker.
- General education has to be an integral part of vocational training.
- A statutory "follow-up-service" is established for dropouts;
- A broad concept of knowledge is introduced where knowledge, manual skills, ethical values, and development of personal qualities (e.g., social abilities, communicative capabilities, creativity) are all given weight.
- All curricula are redesigned to meet future challenges in society and in the labor market.

The reform represents a rather radical and comprehensive transformation of the whole system. A description of the approaches and the procedures of the planning process behind the reform is given by Briseid (1995).

A NEW COMMON CORE CURRICULUM

The changes in society and the structural changes in education made it necessary to review the different guidelines governing the purpose and content of education. The aims, as stated in the Acts governing education, were carefully re-read and their interpretation reviewed. In view of the fact that large-scale reforms are introduced in primary, secondary, and higher education simultaneously, it seemed natural and appropriate to provide a common formulation of the common core for the curriculum, emphasizing how the stages of education are linked together, including adult education. The central ideas in former guidelines for primary and secondary education in Norway were examined and employed. The work also builds on principles set out in central policy documents debated and given parliamentary approval during the last few years. A draft of the document was widely circulated and discussed and the text subsequently revised before being presented in its final version to Parliament, which gave its full consent without further alteration to the text.

The curriculum, which was drawn up in 1993, states the goals and principles, i.e., the basic values for primary, secondary (general and vocational), and adult education, and provides an ideological basis for curriculum development within all these educational sectors. The document constitutes a binding foundation for the development of separate curricula and subject syllabuses at the different levels of education—the common core for the Norwegian Educational system. All 400 curricula are being redesigned. A single set of syllabuses is being produced to be used by all groups. Choice and adaptation of methods are the responsibility of the professional teacher, assisted by the teaching guides which accompany the syllabuses. The syllabuses are so designed as to facilitate teaching in modules.

The Reform, which started in August 1994, is being subjected to ongoing assessment. The pedagogical and methodological implications are considerable. One of the major challenges is to find suitable teaching methods for the whole cohort, in both academic and vocational education. The Core Curriculum puts the human being and human values in focus.

Previous official guidelines—as stated in § 2 Principal Aims of the former law—governing the upper secondary school have hitherto existed more on a formal basis, whereas the new Core Curriculum is supposed to permeate all the educational activities. It is expected that the individuals responsible for its implementation, on all levels of the system, will act in accordance with this document. The aims, however, are broad and based on a political consensus and agreement between parties. They will have to be interpreted, and their operationalization defined precisely before put into action. This is a difficult task and a new burden on the school principal who will be responsible for carrying out this process.

ROLES AND RESPONSIBILITIES IN THE GOVERNANCE OF THE EDUCATIONAL SYSTEM

Vital questions to be naturally raised here are: How are the innovations implemented into the system? How do the national authorities push this process further? How is the work followed up? How is Reform 94 proceeding?

These questions are further examined. However, before discussing the problems associated with the reform's implementation and assessing the first tendencies for success or failure, it is necessary to make a short presentation about the way the education sector is managed.

Ownership and Maintenance of the School

Norway is divided into 19 counties, which are the administrative units of the regions, and 454 municipalities. Primary and lower secondary schools are administered at the municipal level and upper secondary schools are the responsibility of county authorities. This means that the municipalities run compulsory education and are responsible for the administration of school buildings and appointment of teachers, while the county is responsible for the administration of upper secondary schools, including the intake of students and the appointment of teachers. For the apprenticeship system, each county has its own committee.

Reorganization of the Structure of the Education System

To meet the challenges facing upper secondary education, a number of reports and documents relevant for the content and management of education have been published.

As far as the central administration of education is concerned, it was viewed as needing rationalization and consolidation of authority. A White Paper (Nr. 37, 1990–1991) concerning the organization and management of the education sector was unanimously approved by the Parliament in June 1991. It emphasized the importance of considering the various levels of management coherently, since changes at one level will have consequences on other levels. Therefore, the national, regional, and municipal levels and the level of the individual institution or school were taken into account. The objective was to attain the highest possible degree of coordination and consistency between the various management levels and educational spheres. The system of organization was analyzed and many weaknesses found, which indicated a lack of coordination between the educational spheres and a lack of clarity in the division of tasks and responsibility among the large number of councils and agencies. The main conclusion was that the entire system had to be revised and new management tools to be defined.

As to the tasks and the distribution of responsibility, among other suggestions, the Ministry of Education proposed that:

1. The responsibility for the performance of the national education policy be deeply rooted in the Ministry; and

2. The division of responsibility and tasks between the different authorities involved in public education be made explicit.

Which Are the New Principles of Organization and Management?

The following principles are the basis for how the education sector is to be organized and managed.

- The central administration is to help to ensure equal educational opportunities, a common background of knowledge and culture for the whole population, and the teaching of basic ethical values, aesthetic awareness and a high standard of relevant knowledge.
- Management by objectives (MBO) is the management approach to be adopted, but it must be applied with due consideration of the special needs of the education sector.
- Clear and consistent central government management must be ensured in areas of national interest.
- National tasks that can be more appropriately implemented at regional levels are to be delegated to centrally coordinated regional links. This means that tasks considered not relevant to the national education policy are to be decentralized and performed by county or municipal administrators or by the schools and institutions.
- A better coordination of education policy cutting across the separate educational spheres is needed.
- Arrangements must be made for ensuring an optimal utilization of resources.
- The education system must be organized in a simple and user-friendly way.

On the basis of these principles, Parliament has decided that the Ministry of Education shall be responsible for the national application of tasks issued by the central government. Such tasks include the definition of educational objectives and principles, establishment of general educational content that can ensure a common national level of knowledge and culture, adjustment of the capacity of schools and other educational institutions to current needs, establishment of general guidelines for the level of competence that the various types of education are supposed to provide, and training of teachers and development of general teaching aids. The tasks are to be Organized in such a way that it might be possible to coordinate them across educational spheres whenever necessary. Most of the former national councils and committees have been dissolved, except for the National Council for Vocational Training, the National Parents' Committee, and the Saami Education Council. As a replacement, National Education Offices, one per county, were established in August 1992. They are responsible for carrying out central government tasks delegated to them within the educational sector, as, for instance, ensuring that decisions made by county and municipality bodies be in accordance with relevant statutory provisions. The schools, thus, will be given greater autonomy. Summing up, the governance of the national education policy is to take place at the central level, while the responsibility for the execution is given to the local level.

How Is the System Controlled?

In accordance with these principles, heavy emphasis is now being put on the follow-up process. A data-gathering system has been developed for upper secondary education, and it is being constantly updated. Recently, a national plan for evaluation of the whole school system has been instituted. Situation reports, analyses, and area evaluations informing the Ministry and the Parliament about the education sector have now become common. Documented results are demanded in return for the funds granted. Systematic school-based evaluations are now one of the new great challenges facing schools.

Through its steering, the central authority will control how the counties and their municipalities carry out the national education policy. The official education policy is to be reflected at the school level. In the White Paper Nr. 37, the role of the school principal is emphasized. Within the principle of managing by objectives, i.e., local allocation of funds and greater freedom for the individual school, the principal has a more distinct professional role than ever before. His/her ability to attain the national aims is of vital importance.

Furthermore, it is also stated that the function of management and leadership is not just the principal's responsibility because modern leadership is characterized by teamwork. As a consequence, a new Employment Agreement was signed in 1993. This agreement entails flexibility within a wide framework, making it possible to strengthen the common teamwork and planning process.

Seen in the light of the New Municipal Law of 1992, the system of education administration at county, municipal, and institution level must be reviewed. It is important to establish an organization that contributes to good relations between the various educational spheres as well as makes a clear division of responsibility between the labor market training schemes and educational authorities. The new municipal law draws up new perspectives for administrative systems in municipalities and counties and for the state administration/control of municipal management. An important aim of the law is to give the municipalities more freedom to organize their activities on the basis of local requirements and wishes. The new municipal law paves the way for the regulation of objectives and frameworks that represent a decisive break with the state's more detailed governed administration of the school system.

It is, therefore, a challenge for the state to give its administrative signals new forms which give the municipalities greater freedom of action, while, at the same time, the municipalities must put the administrative signals from the state into practice within the framework of municipal administration.

Comprehensiveness, coordination, and cooperation are concepts being stressed in official papers constituting the new system, and these aspects seem to be taken into account in various ways. The latest example is the attempt to revise and coordinate school legislation (the present legislation is not homogeneous and is badly coordinated). A draft proposal is now being considered by the appropriate bodies.

According to the previous municipal law, the county administration had to appoint a head to the county municipality's school administration. The new law, however, neither imposes such a directive nor gives instructions as to the role performance. It is now left to the county administration itself to choose where to place the educational tasks among their different departments.

DECENTRALIZATION

Decentralization of decision making has been a general trend of Norwegian education since the late 1980s. The professional autonomy of the individual schools and institutions of higher education has gradually increased. A major step in the direction of decentralization was made by the introduction of a new sector grant system in 1986. The former earmarking of grants to primary and secondary education from central to local/regional authorities has been replaced by a system where local and regional authorities receive a lump sum covering all central government subsidies for school education and culture as well as the health service. As a consequence, the municipalities and counties now enjoy greater autonomy regarding educational provisions.

Tensions and Conflicts

There are, however, problems connected to the concept of decentralization. County and municipal authorities and the individual institutions operate in a force field between governmental control and the mandate of the local population. Central administration is based on the need for equality and national unity, and local democracy is built on values such as freedom and democratic participation in addition to efficiency and effectivity. It is a difficult task to find the right balance between government control and the user's autonomy. Indistinct boundaries between the state's general responsibility and that of the municipality regarding planning and execution of specific enterprises can result in tensions at the point of intersection between local and central control. Thus, conflicts might arise when there is an imbalance between the funds allocated by the state and the tasks the municipalities are expected to execute.

A good professional contact between schools and authorities, as part of the national governance system, seems vital under the prevailing circumstances. Certain premises must be present, for instance, a clear communication of the official national education policy (its principles and regulations) and establishment of management and leadership strategies that create favorable conditions for an effective coordination between central and local administrations.

A problem can be expected to emerge here due to the counties' desire for freedom opposed to the state's need to control. It may look as if the counties are asking for a greater degree of freedom but at the same time sending out signals that the Ministry ought to give more general directives. As the counties are responsible for the management and administration of decisions, they must define their own role and its content. The Ministry sets the frames, whereas the county is responsible for the practice. However, an absolute loyalty towards the national principles set for the school is expected.

It may be seen as a dilemma for the state to ensure national control and, at the same time, delegate authority to lower levels. Depending on the economy, different county authorities may give education different priorities. This may result in local differences in the quality of education. Under present circumstances, since the state has relinquished control, it will not be able to intervene immediately. In this way, decentralized management of the school may be a threat to the principle of equality.

THE MINISTRY'S STEERING TOOLS

The Ministry has no budgetary steering and only a small set of regulations. The practice of management by objectives and the assumption of loyalty toward the agreements made are the means the Ministry has for securing the implementation of the national objectives for upper secondary education.

Management by Objectives: A Feasible Approach to Be Followed?

The main management practice which is intended to permeate the administration of all sectors, both in public and private spheres, is management by objectives (MBO). In recent years, various central documents have established that management by objectives is to be the main girder of public administration. This principle also applies to the state sector. A relatively precise definition of the term, is given in White Paper Nr. 4 (1988–89):

> Using management by objectives, a higher authority (e.g., a government department or Ministry) steers its institutions by issuing objectives and priorities for each of them. Within the framework of their resources the institutions can decide for themselves how the objectives are to be reached. The institutions are, however, to report their results to their higher authority. In this connection, it is important to develop specific demands. On the basis of these reports the departments will investigate the degree of success and contribute towards carrying out any necessary corrections.

The Advantages of Management by Objectives

Compared to more traditional models, MBO can be described as being an overall system of performance appraisal which has certain advantages, such as less need to spend time on rules and regulations and more freedom to carry out professional tasks. No intersubjective agreement seems to exist on the classification of MBO as a type of decentralization. However, the principle is often launched as an alternative way of steering opposed to management by rules and regulations, leading to a greater degree of freedom on the lower levels of an organization regarding choices of means and methods. But governance through objectives, entailing demands for planning of work activities and information about results, is probably stronger than management by rules. On these grounds, MBO is expected to increase organizational efficiency and effectiveness. The single institution or organization is given more freedom to choose its own ways to follow up the objectives, which must be put in concrete terms so as to make it possible to measure their realization by means of performance indicators. Planning at the micro-level is regarded as a device to gain stronger commitment from the individual toward overall aims of the organization.

Is the MBO Approach Suitable for Schools?

Opponents to MBO claim that since the school is quite different from other organizations, especially those occupied with producing goods, this approach is not appropriate for managing schools. The external frame for the school's pedagogic activities rests on a foundation of both legal, economic/administrative and ideological elements. In addition to the aims, rules, and regulations written down in laws, agreements, and curricula, the school is ruled by certain principles, expressed in public documents. One such principle is MBO, which was approved by the Parliament for the whole public administration, including the educational sector.

The introduction of Reform 94 has led to role changes for all those directly involved with school activities—students, teachers, and principals—and has made an impact upon all of them. As the processes of information, decision making, and aims clarification have received more attention, the communication has increased. The consequences of the Reform on the daily practice of the school underline a need for interplay, cooperation, and a shared responsibility. The students are expected to take a more active part in the learning process and assume more responsibility for their own learning.

Concerning the teachers, they are expected to enter into a more obligatory type of cooperation with both colleagues and students, in the planning, execution, and evaluative phases of the work. The teacher has, by virtue of his/her professional skill, an extended responsibility to organize the learning conditions in the best possible way in the classroom. Therefore, new teaching methodologies that emphasize project work, learning by experience, learning through responsibility, student autonomy, and self-confidence building, challenge the proficiency of the teacher. The demand that students be taken out of their traditional role as observers and given a role as responsible participants leads to more student-involvement in the daily work. The new role of the teacher implies a change from being merely a teacher to becoming also a trainer, coach, and guide for the students.

In cooperation with the rest of the staff, the school leaders will be responsible for formulating the goals and objectives in accordance with what is pre-established and for executing the objectives. Follow-up and result evaluation at every stage are considered an important part of the management practice.

The role of the principal is very important in processes of change. The main responsibility of the principal is to facilitate the learning process within the organization, making sure that it includes both the students and the staff. Analytical skills and competency in didactic seem to be necessary prerequisites for the principal if he/she shall be able to deal with the whys, whats, and hows of the school's organizational life. The challenge awaiting the principal is to turn resistance of the staff toward the Reform into a feeling of ownership and motivation to carry it through. Besides, the principal should remember to continue thinking of him/herself as representative of the employers. The question to be asked here is whether the school as an organization will be able to meet the new situation. Do the students, staff, and principal have enough proficiency? A new way of looking at curricula, both in theory and practice, for adapting Management by Objectives, seems to require training.

MBO challenges the educational system to find appropriate tools that will secure the special value system and mission of the school. The perception of MBO as a rational, linear process may be problematic.

Some teachers may be unfamiliar with the terminology and philosophy. The critics fear that priority might be given to what can easily be measured in concrete terms, which can result in short-term gains.

The separate curricula and subject syllabuses are all based on the agreed principles of Management by Objectives. In the process of implementing Reform 94, a goal-oriented learning process is focused. It is presupposed that there exists a straight line toward and an open channel for information and communication about the aims. Shared responsibility and cooperation between the central and local levels seems necessary in this respect. Thus achievement of the educational goals will depend upon the coordination and dialogue between all parties involved in their administration, both at the central as well as at the school level.

The Different Tools of Governance and Steering in the Educational System

In addition to the principles laid down, the central authorities make use of different means. The management of the school rests on two types of steering—political and professional. The school may be described as balancing between political and professional steering. Political steering comprises setting the overall goals, the basic legal principles, and the use of economic resources. Professional steering implies interpreting and operationalizing aims, choosing methods and content in the process of planning, carrying out, and evaluating learning activities. The aim of the Ministry is to institutionalize the Reform in the classroom. The challenge is to formulate the aims and signals of governance attached to educational practice. Management by Objectives based on the ethics and values of the school makes it necessary that the values and the ethic perspective be expressed in the activities of the school and made visible in the stated aims.

Before looking at the steering means used by the Ministry, the question "What is steering?" may be asked here. Steering may be simply defined as using those mechanisms which the authorities have at their disposal to reach the accepted objectives. Besides laws, regulations, and budgets, these mechanisms might also include:

- Curricula
- Evaluations and reports
- Centrally initiated projects and research

- Information, guidance, support
- Basic and upgraded training for teachers
- Leadership and leadership training

The central authorities regard leadership as one important area of development and, in line with international educational research, emphasize the important impact of the school leader in reform implementation. The school leader has a vital role to play as a change agent, both in the process of initiation as well as implementation and institutionalization of the reform.

In an information brochure published in 1993 by the Ministry, it is stated that using the Leadership Training Program, school leadership will be able to put national and local educational objectives into practice.

LUIS—A LEADERSHIP TRAINING PROGRAM

An important premise for successfully carrying out the national education policy is that the municipalities have a sufficient number of qualified school leaders capable of realizing locally the stated aims regarding knowledge, skills, and attitudes. A vital initiative taken by the central authorities is the effort made so far for building a leadership program for those involved in learning and development. The LUIS program, launched in 1993, is among the different development programs initiated by the central authorities in recent years. This program is built upon previous experiences and its content is intended to meet new challenges. A clear division of responsibilities and cooperation between the state and the counties and municipalities has been decisive for successful outcomes.

In line with the adopted principle of considering the education sector as a whole, LUIS is a joint program for development of leadership for primary, lower secondary, and upper secondary education and is regarded as a means for accomplishing educational reforms in these school sectors. The Ministry is responsible for leading and coordinating the LUIS program on a nationwide basis and allocates funding for its implementation. This requires that the Ministry establishes its own plans of action for arranging the development of the necessary skills for implementing the program.

The Ministry is responsible for facilitating contact and cooperation between various organizations such as the National Education Offices, the Norwegian Association of Local Authorities, colleges, and universities and, also, for building up contacts with academic and research bodies both nationally and internationally. The National Education Offices have responsibility for arranging and coordinating leadership development in their regions. In cooperation with the local and regional authorities, colleges, universities, and other relevant bodies, the National Education Offices are responsible for establishing the actual planning of the training initiatives for the leaders at school level. Local and regional authorities are responsible for the implementation of training programs for their school leaders. This must be seen in connection with the other local and regional authority leader training initiatives.

Tasks and Division of Responsibility

The county has the responsibility to operationalize the national goals and is at the same time responsible for fulfilling the objectives at the regional level. As the employers, the regional authorities are also responsible for the implementation of training for their school leaders. This must be seen in connection with the other local and regional authority leader training initiatives. As to the content of the LUIS program, the state is responsible for pedagogical and leadership/management issues, while the municipalities provide a general training of management skills. Today, the municipalities have a greater autonomy to organize their own tasks, therefore there is:

- An increased awareness of the municipality's responsibility for its schools;
- An increased delegation of authority to the operative level;
- A change of planning systems;
- An increased awareness about principles and systems for leadership training.

In most municipalities, increased emphasis is given to leadership/management training across sectors as a means to build up an identity within the municipality, which is regarded as an organization in which the school represents one of the central elements in the total environment of the child/youth.

According to the LUIS program, the state, represented by National Education Offices at the regional level, is responsible for training school leaders for primary and secondary schools. This is, for several reasons, a difficult plan to carry out in practice and represents a dilemma when, for instance, the leaders at the county level do not find such training to be of any interest. The division of tasks and responsibilities connected to the LUIS program, thus, presents a multicolored picture. Even though the pitfalls are many, coordination of activities seems absolutely necessary,

What Are the Experiences of LUIS ?

A rather substantial amount of money has been put forth by the state and even more from the regional authorities over past years. Strategic plans have been developed and structures of cooperation networks have been built. No external evaluation has been initiated so far; the yearly reports from the National Education Offices outline the priorities and resources spent. The activities show signs of variation both as to content and frequency. A committee has been recently appointed to look at the program and find ways of maintaining closer connections to the general work of reform implementation going on in the Ministry of Education.

In a report to the Ministry of Education, Kvist (1995), among other aspects, points toward the fact that pedagogical issues in the content of the LUIS program might be reduced or even disappear during the process of implementation of the training by regional authorities. Although the municipalities act loyally when planning and prioritize the requests received from the central authorities, greater weight might be placed on the administrative tasks of the school leader that agree with the needs of the municipality.

In its report, the committee mentioned above concludes that leadership training through the LUIS program is an adequate means of steering, both for the state and the municipalities. Based on experiences from the previous leadership programs, research, and individual experiences, the committee finds that the development within leader training over the past few years has been positive.

A further concentration on development of leadership is recommended. The committee considers leader training through LUIS a suitable steering tool to be used by the central as well as regional or local authorities. The committee regards the leaders working at school level as key persons and the most important target group for the training. It is recommended, though, that the whole group of school leaders be trained together. Concerning the content of the training, it should be specific for the school and reform oriented, emphasizing competency in didactic and curriculum analysis.

THE IMPLEMENTATION OF REFORM 94

In the previous section, the intended reform and its premises were dealt with rather comprehensively in order to give the necessary background for this section, in which the realities concerning the operationalization of the reform will be discussed.

Reform 94: A Success or a Failure?

One year has passed since the introduction of the reform. This is of course too short a period for making judgmental statements about the outcome of the reform. However, thus far, some trends and tendencies are showing up, making it possible to sketch the present situation.

In addition to the system prevailing in the public sector (including the educational sector) which requires the institutions to report their results to their higher authorities, the Ministry of Education initiated a research-based evaluation of the reform EVA-94 along with the launching of the reform in August 1994.

In a paper outlining the purpose and structure of the evaluation, competent bodies were invited by the Ministry of Education to present their proposals and bids for the evaluation process. The evaluation:

1. determine to what extent the most important goals of the reform have been attained and
2. provide information and insight while the evaluation itself is in progress. This should be in a form that would enable quick decisions about necessary adjustments and corrections to be made, keeping in mind the changes and improvements necessary for reaching the goals of the reform.

Seven research institutions were chosen to take part in this evaluation program. The starting points for the evaluation are the principles and aims of the reform. Central areas and issues, formulated as key questions, have been stated by the Ministry of Education.

In spite of leadership and leadership training being regarded by the Ministry of Education as vital areas for the outcome of the reform and as a means for steering the implementation process, this dimension should not be evaluated as a separate issue. Evaluation of the leadership function in the school will be made in connection with issues associated with the curriculum and its implementation by the teachers, under the area of organization and cooperation.

Based on the existing data collected and published up to this point, it is not possible to answer all the questions formulated throughout this paper and make final statements about the successes and failures of Reform 94. The reports published thus far give some indications about developments and proceedings and give, also, a general impression about the reform's present state of affairs. There is good reason to believe that as to the structural aspects, the reform has been successful. The difficulties observed seem to be attached more to the content or the pedagogical aspects of the reform.

Data taken from the half-year reports presented by three of the research institutions in the spring of 1995 give relevant information about the implementation of Reform 94, which is further discussed:

First, the answers given to the key question "How is the Core Curriculum interpreted/understood and used by teachers?" as reported by Monsen (1995), show that the teachers find the Core Curriculum too wordy and do not believe it will have any special importance in their jobs as teachers. Everything seems to indicate that the Core Curriculum is not included in the teachers' work with the syllabus. The Core might perhaps form part of the argumentation and reflections connected to the school's curriculum work, but the researchers find few traces of such practice.

Second, in connection with the question "How is the principle of Management by Objectives understood and how does this approach function when working with curricula and syllabuses?" the teachers' answers indicate that the principle is interpreted in different ways, according to the views of the principals. Furthermore, it also seems that the county administration has an impact on how the principal looks at his/her own role and responsibility in connection with the principles of MBO.

The researchers found two significant differences of opinion. Some look at MBO as the managerial responsibility of the principal and think that it can best be described as a general steering principle. Others are more concerned with the notion that the curricula are based on a principle that can be used to formulate learning objectives for the students. However, few teachers seem to be actually using MBO actively to formulate learning objectives for their students. Those who have tried have been met with little enthusiasm by the students.

Third, the questions "How is the work with the objectives and main factors carried out?" and "What are the implications in practice?" brought out the following facts:

Most teachers do not take the objectives of the curriculum as a starting point. They rely on textbooks that deal with stated objectives. Many of them compare the contents of textbooks with the curriculum, though, as a means of control. The curricula are used when working plans are developed but in such a way that the textbook is the basis for the work and serves as a point of reference in comparison with the curriculum. Many teachers report that the objectives are too vague and do not give sufficient indications as to how thoroughly every single item should be treated, thus creating uncertainty.

Even though the researchers themselves point to the fact that the evaluation data used thus far in the process give insufficient information for drawing reliable conclusions, they supply the basis for answering questions such as:

1. How will unequal budget situations at the local level affect the national aim of equal education for all?
2. Is Management by Objectives a suitable practice for managing schools? and
3. Is leadership training an adequate means for steering?

The data collected suggest that the communication process and process of transforming the national overall educational goals take place within certain limits in the schools. Some tentative statements drawn from the data are:

1. The teachers lack the necessary knowledge and competence to put the MBO principles into practice in their teaching.
2. The students have not learned what is meant by MBO and do not see the relevance for their own learning process.
3. The principal of the school does not take full responsibility as the leader for the total learning processes.
4. The curricula are constructed in such a way that make it difficult to operationalize the objectives.

The above-quoted tendencies are similar to findings reported by Iván (1994) in an evaluation study concerning a trial project proceeding of Reform 94.

A recent comparative study (Bolam et al. 1996) called "The First Years of Headship in New Europe," based on an inquiry carried out within five European countries, including Norway, has charted the areas that newly appointed school heads see as challenging and problematic. This study points out that the upper secondary school has many different areas of study and, therefore, brings together teachers with various educational backgrounds, and experiences. This fact may often lead to definite subcultures. A climate of rivalry and lack of willingness to cooperate may be the result of such subcultures. To see the school as one unity and be willing to plan collectively may be difficult under such circumstances. Most of the answers given by the upper secondary school principals indicate their concern for getting teachers to accept Reform 94, the new employment agreement, and the need for new methods.

In his evaluation report, Bergli (1995), among other recommendations, suggests an adaptation and clarification of MBO principles. As to the prerequisites of the teachers, more competency building within a broad range of items in pedagogy and didactic is suggested. The teachers seem to have mixed attitudes toward the reform. Concerning the school as an organization, the fact that the schools have met great challenges necessitates that the consequences of the reform for management and leadership in the school organization be taken more into consideration. It is important, states Bergli, to deal with the new demands on the leadership function in the schools, and to consider the coherence between leadership and performance in the different levels inside the school.

The reform requires a renewal of the way the school is organized regarding the staff and use of time. Regarding the activities of the Ministry of Education and the county authorities, the report focuses on the relationship between two models to implement change—one, hierarchic, and the other, based on cooperation. The development process thus far is described as being too hierarchic. Changes in the school system, it is stated, are not a rational process in which the implementation goes steadily through different levels without problems. A cooperative model puts the school in focus and gives preference to developing an organization with a high degree of competence and autonomy.

The report prepared by The Work Research Institute (Blichfeldt et al. 1995) makes some concluding remarks and recommendations, which are referred in the following paragraphs.

According to this report, the implementation of the reform has been a process of profound organization development at the county and school levels which has taken place while central structures are also being changed. Therefore, uncertainty about lines of communication and decision making has occurred. At the school level, lack of motivation and engagement are creating problems for the reform implementation. The report recommends improving the flow of communication and revising central regulations relevant for aspects related to the economy and the staff. A more flexible use of the new employment agreement is recommended.

Lessons Learned from Reform 94

The main learning experiences drawn from the evaluation of the content issues of the reform indicate that leadership and management are key factors in the process, and it seems relevant to support leader training programs. The introduction of MBO necessitates greater emphasis on competency building at all levels. Skills for analyzing, interpreting, and putting the aims into practice seem to be insufficient. There seems also to be a need to review certain organizational processes in the areas of communication and decision making. Uncertainty and undefined roles and responsibilities exist, to a certain degree, at systems level.

Equality and Economy

As for the question raised in the early part of this article as to whether factors such as decentralization and delegation might lead to economic differences between communities and thus create inequality, due to the short time of implementation of Reform 94, it is not yet possible to make a final statement.

Due to economic reasons, strong opposition is being raised to the government's reform policies. Lately there has been a lively debate in the media which has focussed mainly on the inequalities among schools caused by different economic situations in the various communities.

In the latest issue of the teacher union's periodical, *Skolefokus,* the Minister of Education (Hernes 1995) "kicks the ball back to the teachers."

He draws attention to the role of the competent teacher as the most important and decisive factor for the students' performance. Referring to research, he claims that the "school of equality" depends on more than economic issues. In fact, a "school of equality" must be based on the equality of teachers' input.

Reforming one part of the educational sector affects the other ones. In the present period of change, it is now the teachers' turn. The focus of attention will be the coherence within the whole education sector, therefore steps are now being taken by the Ministry of Education to prepare a reform that will adapt the prevailing ideology of education to the content of teachers' training.

Keeping an Eye on the Process of Implementation

In addition to the information gathered through the evaluation program Reform 94 the Ministry of Education has arranged regional educational conferences all over the country to collect additional information regarding the reform's implementation process (for example, how the curricula and the guidelines are being used at the school level, to what degree the counties are complying with the law for meeting the needs of the principals, and other aspects of the reform) and to create an awareness as to the necessary steps to be taken in order to act in accordance with the planned strategies and aims of Reform 94. The overall aim of the conferences has been "learning through experience and exchange of ideas."

A limited number of school visits to meet the students and staff, and listen to their views and problems has also been among the means used by the Ministry of Education to get relevant and reliable information.

Steps Taken Toward Improvement

The Ministry of Education is now introducing new regional conferences, focusing this time on evaluation, both individually and systems-based. More guidelines based on the existing syllabuses are being produced to help the teachers in their work. A rather comprehensive teacher-training program continues and is being extended to the instructors of apprentices.

The government seems to have seriously considered various difficulties and problems pointed out in the reports, and rather drastic initiatives are being taken. Based on the LUIS program, a new curriculum for leadership training is now being designed but in a more condensed form. It focuses on the management of the learning processes, i.e., pedagogical leadership, and on the role of the school leader as a representative of the employers.

By acting so, the central authorities expect to get a firmer grip of the steering, attain more control, and make the leadership training more uniform all over the country—in short, secure a better reform implementation. The new training program is supposed to be integrated into the plans of the counties' school administrators, who shall put them into practice.

FINAL COMMENTS

There is much evidence pointing to the need to train the school leaders in the new roles brought about by the changes and challenges of Reform 94. Such training may also represent an adequate steering mechanism for the central authorities. However, certain additional conditions might need to be fulfilled as further explained.

The establishment of a proficient learning organization requires competent people able to handle the new classroom situation in which the students are supposed to take more responsibility and the teachers are expected to include them in the planning process. Under these conditions, it becomes important to look into the prerequisites of teachers and students.

The application of MBO principles by the Ministry of Education requires greater emphasis on the clarification and imparting of aims and objectives. In addition, a sharper follow-up of results is needed, accompanied by increased guidance and support. To raise the support for the reform and the motivation to carry it through, it seems almost imperative that the local institution be given the necessary freedom and internal independence for attaining proficiency of teaching. Finally, tensions and conflicts might to a certain degree be reduced if roles and responsibilities are clarified in the total system of education.

Will resistance to MBO develop until a new management practice is selected, or will an adequate training and adaptation result in its maintenance? Will Reform 94 turn out a success? Predictions about the future are difficult; only time will show. As it now stands, however, Reform 94 is likely to secure the quality of the upper secondary school of Norway. A basic condition, however, for a smooth and vital realization process is a dialogue-based steering and increased cooperation between the central and local levels.

REFERENCES

Bergli, Tor. 1995. "Reform og innsats 94/95—Evaluering av fire studieretninger" (Reform and Achievements 94/95, Evaluation of four branches of study). *Yrkespedagogiskedokumenter og rapporter, 20 C*, Høgskolen i Akershus.

Blichfeldt, Jon Frode, et al. 1995. "Evaluering av Reform 94, Underveisnotat II" (Evaluation of Reform 94—Progress Report II). *Work Research Institute*, Notat 7/95.

Bolam, Ray, et al. 1996. *New Headteachers in New Europe*. New York: Routledge.

Briseid, Ole. 1995. "Comprehensive Reform in Upper Secondary Education in Norway: A Retrospective View." *European Journal of Education*, no. 3: 255-264.

Fjeld, Svein-Erik. 1994. "From Parliament to Classroom—The Road from Legislation to the Good School." Statens Utdanningskontor i Hordaland.

Hernes, Gudmund. 1995. "På rov—eller på rømmen?" *Skolefokus*, no. 17.

Iván, Anne-Lise Thorenfeldt. 1994. "Mislykket og bortkastet—eller verdifull erfaringsbase for R'94?" (Ineffective and Timewasting—or Valuable Source of Experience for R'94?). *Schola*, no. 5.

Kirke-, utdannings- og forskningsdepartementet (Ministry of Education and Church Affairs). 1990-91. "Om organisering og styring i utdanningssektoren" (White Paper on the Organization and Management of the Education Sector). *Stortingsmelding*, no. 37.

Kirke-, utdannings- og forskningsdepartementet (Ministry of Education and Church Affairs). 1991-92. "Kunnskap og kyndighet—Om visse sider ved videregående opplæring (White Paper Concerning Aspects of Upper Secondary Education). *Stortingsmelding* no. 33.

Kirke-, utdannings- og forskningsdepartementet (Ministry of Education and Church Affairs). 1992. "Ledelsesutvikling i skol (LUIS)" (Development of

Leadership and Management in Schools Programme). *PEDLEX Norsk Skoleinformasjon.*

Kirke-, utdannings- og forskningsdepartementet (Ministry of Education and Church Affairs). 1992-93. "Om forholdet mellom staten og kommunene" (White Paper on the Relationship Between the State and Municipalities). *Stortingsmelding* no. 23.

Kirke-, utdannings- og forskningsdepartementet (Ministry of Education and Church Affairs). 1993. *Paper Outlining the Structure and Aims of Evaluation Procedures in Relation to Reform 94.* Oslo, Norway.

Kirke-, utdannings- og forskningsdepartementet (Ministry of Education and Church Affairs). 1994. *Reform '94—This Is Our Solution.* Oslo, Norway.

Kirke-, utdannings- og forskningsdepartementet (Ministry of Education and Church Affairs). 1994. *The Development of Education 1992-94—Norway.* National Report, International Conference on Education Forty-Fourth Session, Geneva.

Kirke-, utdannings- og forskningsdepartementet (Ministry of Education and Church Affairs). 1994. *Core Curriculum for Primary, Secondary and Adult Education in Norway.* Oslo, Norway.

Kirke-, utdannings- og forskningsdepartementet (Ministry of Education and Church Affairs). 1995. Arbeidet med læreplaner og bruken av metodiske rettlinjer og veiviseren (Conference Report: Experiences with Curricula and Guidelines). Nasjonal rapport fra regional konferanser i Drammen, Fredrikstad, Bergen og Bodø.

Kvist, Per. 1995. *Sentral styring og lokalt ansvar i utdanningssektoren— Erfaringer med ledelsesutvikling som nasjonalt styringsinstrument* (Centralized Administration and Local Responsibility in the Educational Sector—Experiences with Leadership Development as a National Management Tool). Statens utdanningskontor i Hordaland.

Kvist, Per, et al. 1995. *Reform-Ledelse—Skoleledelse mot år 2000, Ut redning om LUIS som styringsinstrument i reformarbeidet* (School Leadership/ Management Toward the Year 2000. Report on Leadership as a Means of Steering in Reform Work).

Monsen, Lars. 1995. *Evaluering av Reform 94* (Evaluation of Reform 94). Delrapport no. 2, Høgskolen i Lillehammer.

PART III

The Future

CHAPTER 11

The Future School Manager
Kah Slenning

INTRODUCTION

An interesting exercise in outlining future school manager competence is to rummage through the index of any modern book on management, listing words of positive qualities or abilities that could apply to a school manager. In *The Drama of Leadership* (Starrat 1993), the index, even with a strict reading, carries 71 index words indicating single points of competence within the range of a school manager's work. Just a few examples, from the beginning of the list: "Action, administration, authority, autonomy, ceremonies, charisma, commitment, communication, compassion, competition. . . ."

This chapter deals with the future competence demands on school managers in a ten-year perspective. The demands have been traced by creating scenarios about the development of society in general, followed by the development of school and education on primary and secondary levels, and on to the demands on school managers created by these developments.

Information has been gathered by carrying out a number of interviews with selected key informants, and by literature studies, mainly in the fields of futures studies, management, school development, economy, and social science.

The picture will be drawn, and the analysis made, from a national Swedish perspective and a general Organization for Economic Cooperation and Development (OECD) perspective in order to create guidance for recruiting and development of school managers by identifying fields of competence that need to be covered in training and focused in recruiting of new future school managers.

As stated by Block (1989), ". . .the task of future research is not to investigate the future—since it does not exist—but to map and arrange the tendencies in the present" (p. 23, author's translation).

THE NEED FOR DEVELOPMENT OF SCHOOL MANAGERS' COMPETENCE

Most Swedish school managers today have a teaching practice going approximately five to twenty years back in time. Few school managers have both teaching and managerial experience from the new decentralized system of free choice, with frequent evaluations, internal as well as external, with quality assessment and tightening economic conditions.

The school management itself has already moved from a basically rule-governed administrative work, to development of quality in a goal-oriented and decentralized system. Nygren et al. (1994) states: "Working in such an organization calls for greater personal responsibility. The company management must demonstrate clarity and induce enthusiasm in the employees. Basic ideas, goals and visions must be emphasized" (p. 13, author's translation).

Miron (1993) describes the situation thus:

> . . . sweeping educational reforms are taking place at a rapid pace in Sweden and minimal consideration has been given to the opinions of the various actors involved and little research is being carried out concerning this. Further, seemingly no consideration has been given to the experiences outside of Sweden. Finally, the outcomes and implications of the reform are uncertain and the proponents and opponents differ greatly in what they see as likely outcomes" (p. 1).

> While Sweden was rather late in introducing such reforms, they have surprised the world by quickly outpacing all others, at least in terms of legislation (ibid., p. 19).

Within the School Leaders' Working Environment (SLAV) project at Uppsala University, extensive analyses of—among other things—the working conditions of school managers have been carried out. A main issue is what is called "the invisible contract" between the local school manager and the teachers, providing a division of labor where the manager is "allowed" to handle administration and daily organizational routines as long as he or she does not interfere with the governing and shaping of the actual teaching, that is solely the right and responsibility of the teachers (Berg 1995, p. 102). This description offers a clear picture of the enormous task of actually establishing an effective management—one that is able to introduce and carry out radical alterations of both organization, contents and teaching methods of the Swedish schools.

In the near future, the capability of the school manager to handle this situation will have to be systematically included in a new professionalism.

THE CONCEPT OF COMPETENCE

One of the key concepts of this article is competence. Leion (1992, p. 125) defines "production competence" as the ability to create an increased value in one's work through raising the quality. He also focuses on the ability to handle "unusual situations," such as occurring problems in the organization, or rapid changes in it (ibid., p. 126). This last instance seems especially important to this study, since one of the key issues in the discussion of the competence of school managers will be how to handle change. What matters in school management are the results reached; as it will be seen, school management is a business of no excuses.

A Changing Society—and Education

> Pendulums move back and forth, back and forth. There is something nice and secure about pendulums: They do swing out, but they always return. Really, if one is not inclined to follow the journey of the pendulum, one can simply keep standing, and wait. Sooner or later the pendulum swings back. And everything does remain the same" (Kyndrup 1986, p. 124, author's translation from Danish).

The title of the chapter in which this ironical remark by Kyndrup is written, is "History Is Not a Pendulum." In many ways, and by many authors, this statement is underlined, either explicitly or in fact, through what is said about the present development of society (Dalin 1994a, p. 20; SOU 1992, p. 94, p. 85; SOU 1995, p. 71-72; IVA 1994, p. 53; Their 1994, p. 26-27; Dryden and Vos 1994, p. 37).

At the time of industrialization in Sweden, the demand was to build school houses, train teachers, and make the children attend compulsory school. At this time of post-industrialization, there is a need to alter the direction, attitude, and contents of the cultural reproduction.

As it will be stated in this chapter, one major point in the future development of school managers' competence is the need for a broad general orientation, in order to master changes in demands on education. The changes are manifold, and therefore only a brief account of the general development in society will be rendered.

Internationalism in trade and competition, concerning the mobility of goods, people, capital, and competence. Some claim that this results in "two worlds," the fast and the slow. In "the fast world," the organization of work will change. For example, for academics and specialists in certain professions, work will not be organized around the present security of steady employment. Rather, work will be organized in shorter terms, in projects, and in loosely connected groups of specialists selected for the task and will need a more varied competence (SOU 1995, p. 4; IVA 1994; Glans 1994).

Increasing speed of change, demanding a constant renewal of competence. Competence will no longer mean being able to apply what one knows. Of the utmost importance will be the ability to develop new knowledge and the ability to function in new forms of schools (Dryden and Vos 1994; Edgren 1990; SAF 1985; IVA 1993; IVA 1995; Leion 1992; Strandler 1989; Utbildningsdepartementet 1993).

A more sharply stratified labor market. The consequences for the labor market in a fast-paced, globalized, and increasingly competitive system may contain a division into "local" positions—demanding low qualifications and with low personal return and security—and positions for highly qualified experts, most frequently mentioned within technology and natural science-related occupations, and various cross-competence areas around these. The sectors of industrial production are diminishing when it comes to the number of people employed. The service sector, only a decade ago said to hold the work of the future, is appearing to shrink. What now? Information technology? The question at hand is if there will be enough work to go around. The restructuring of progressive branches of economy highlights the seriousness of the present lack of competence in Sweden. Will Sweden's present wealth, built on natural resources such as energy, metal, and forests, be of substantial importance in the future? (Lyttkens 1994; Naisbitt 1983; SOU 1995, p. 4; Toffler 1990).

Matters of the environment: In sketching a general background to future changes in society that will also affect education, it is obvious that matters of the environment will have to be mentioned. The changes that have so far taken place towards protection of the environment have concerned the technical systems at macro-level: energy and fuel, use of chemicals in industry and agriculture, etc., and mainly in the industrialized world. Few real restrictions have yet come to affect everyday life.

Decentralization and goal-steering. Traditional society depended on a high degree of centralism. In a changing system the regulating centralism cannot manage to govern development at the pace required.

With goal-steering and decentralization, evaluation of results becomes crucial, and the definition of competence becomes more operational: Competence will not be a question of a number of certificates and exams but of making the right things happen in an organization in order to reach the results formulated in the goals. (Hannaway and Carnoy 1993; Their 1994; Dalin 1994a and 1994b; Liljequist 1994; Starrat 1993; Möller 1995).

As one of many reasons for evaluation, accountability is mentioned as a driving force of the entire reform movement that is manifested in the decentralization and local responsibility. Winkler (in Hannaway and Carnoy 1993) mentions fiscal accountability, since, of course, school decentralization also has the purpose of increasing economic efficiency of education. Accountability in the sense of pedagogy, is jointly seen as a means of school improvement. This is one of the major points in the new Swedish curriculum as described in SOU 1992, p. 94. The accountability is driven by the responsibility of the local school for every individual student's achievement, i.e., the task of the school is not fulfilled unless every student has reached the minimum attainment targets.

Accountability in relation to the total outcomes of education is demonstrated in the OECD reports *Education at a Glance* (1995), and

Public Expectations of the Final Stage of Compulsory Education (1995). A good deal of the responsibility for adjusting education according to demands raised by outcome-accounting will rest on the school manager.

Free choice in all respects, and personal responsibility. In the system of decentralization and goal-steering, quality is seen as a key concept. The decentralized system is not just a different way of doing the same things more efficiently. Through the free choice of the individual, quality is thought to be stimulated, and competition between different units created (Miron 1993).

Demands on direct influence. The increased individualism, the many options of choice, and the demands on the individual in a more complicated, competitive labor-market are combined with demands from the individuals on direct influence. To the school manager this means that the individual is turned from being a passive consumer of social service into a "participant," or "co-creator." The manager thus becomes a balancing power between the students and their parents, other professionals, national goals, and local goals (Miron 1993; Starrat 1993; Glans 1994; Berg 1990; Liljequist 1994).

Mobility and multiculturalism: The former stability of local, regional or even national societies is eroding. To the individual, a multicultural society can give options of choice but also demands tolerance. In a dynamic multiculturalism, different values and traditions enrich the entity. To the school manager, the educational effects of muliculturalism cannot be overlooked.

The determining drive for competence: Sweden is faced with new demands of competence. In SOU 1995, p. 4—a document with a mainly economic profile on a national level—there is an outspoken fear of Sweden lagging behind in the total development of competence within the OECD countries, and, in a wider perspective, even newly-industrialized countries in, e.g., southeast Asia. There is fear of a substantial lack of qualified people within knowledge-intensive organizations, e.g., for tasks requiring cross-disciplinary competencies involving technology or natural science. It is clear that better educational achievement has to be reached. Part of this achievement is of the same principal dignity as the changing demands of any era, i.e., demands of mastering new contents of knowledge: In a small country like Sweden, knowledge of at least two foreign languages is seen as necessary. A basic ability to cope with theoretical knowledge within technology and natural science will be demanded from every student, but both technology and natural science will be seen within a humanistic and social framework. Finally, the handling of information technology will be part of everyday competence (SOU 1992, p. 94).

What seems more complicated is something that could be described as a "competence of attitude," an ability to adapt to changing values, changing circumstances, and the ability to re-learn. Problem-solving and analytical ability are also key issues (OECD 1995b; LR 1995). The Swedish Employers' Association, SAF, gives concrete examples of necessary new competences in a study covering the competence needs of 30 companies (Nygren et al. 1994). Interesting to note is that several representatives of companies—many of which have a distinct technical profile—do not stress simple factual knowledge as most important but, rather, stress issues like general attitudes, personality, ethics, and what might be called "employability." There is a concern over the attitudes of the young—except for the most highly educated—towards common values and towards work, education, and "life investments" in general. In this scenario, a complete change of attitudes is necessary, with new attitudes directed towards a more serious, "investing" and conscious lifestyle.

In the perspective of increasing pressure on individual competence and responsibility, schools may be left with a heavy responsibility to foster the young, since some parents are likely to pull away from personal responsibility.

A good professional was always one who did not only master his/her field intellectually but linked his knowledge to values and attitudes. The coming decade in Sweden will see a serious debate on values and attitudes, linked to "national competence." To a large extent, that will affect school management.

NEW TECHNOLOGY

New technology is becoming a precondition for other changes, such as the rapid movement and free flow of knowledge and capital.

Information technology, apart from being a precondition for other changes, is treated as a change in itself.

With the rapid technical development within Information Technology (IT) and within production and everyday life in general, we face a breakdown of old patterns in society. Access to information will not be a problem—there will be enormous amounts of information available. The problem will be to find and value information that can be put to good use—this could, in fact, be the practical meaning of "IT-literacy."

We have not yet seen any of the effects of the potential of change in schools—"computers" is just about to pass from a marginal "subject" studied by a few pupils (mainly boys!) to an awkward innovation taking up more space in the classroom than the slide projector. In the coming decade the entire organization of learning will need to be altered in order to make use of this delicate piece of technology. It is not even certain that this new organization will allow "schools" as we know them in a future perspective. The school manager will be the obvious catalyst of this change (Makrakis 1988; Textor 1982; Dalin 1994a; Toffler 1990; Naisbitt 1983; SAF 1985).

From IVA (1994), we quote: "The challenge lies in identifying the new possibilities created by information technology. One might, for example, ask: 'How would we build the organization if we started from scratch?'" (p. 48, author's translation).

The integration of IT with education may also create new problems that will make demands on school managers. A new form of literacy, and thereby also a new illiteracy, in relation to handling IT can result in new gaps of increasing differences in learning conditions between children.

Work and Education

Schools will even more than now lose their "knowledge monopoly," and learning will increasingly take place outside schools. All of Europe will be the scene for education of Swedish students, at least on secondary level, and all of the western world in tertiary education.

Education in itself will have to be immediately rewarding to young people. Because of the rapid changes in society, and the insecure development of the future, the reward cannot be postponed for too long—it as was the case for earlier generations. Education will follow the general life interests of the individual, not specific jobs.

Values and Social Relations

One concern in recent times has been the question of common values in society. On the one hand, there is a scenario in which a demise of consensus values in society becomes the overriding image, with more individual lifestyle patterns of consumption and demand. Within this image lies also an enlarged generation gap, in which the older generations will try to hold on to what they have managed to take, and younger generations will be shut out from the bulk of social and economic progress.

On the other hand, we may see a search for new values besides materialism and new common values in society as a response to a threatening dispersion of values. Existential matters and the shaping of life have to be discussed. Reflection will be counted as a value, not just reproduction. Reflection will actually be necessary to find new paths in the rapidly changing social organism—singular reproduction will become dysfunctional.

FUTURE DEVELOPMENT OF EDUCATION

The discussions in this chapter have given an image of the best possible school development in the next decade, which shall briefly be outlined here. This development can be seen as the syllabus of courses for the future school manager.

Organization of Human Development

The purpose of any change must be to create new opportunities for human development, which may have received too little attention, and too much to sheer and rigid organising, as if a change of organization would automatically bring about other changes of attitudes, practices, or results.

In the future, compulsory school in Sweden is likely to start earlier, and take advantage of children's natural curiosity. However, in a situation of greater flexibility and with a stress of lifelong and individual-based curricula, we may see other forms of formal demands on school attendance. These may come to be formulated more in terms of results and less in terms of physical age or birth date.

The adults perform their work at the schools in teams and in a project-oriented organization. The traditional weekly schedule and class cohorts have become obsolete. Some debaters give the image of total individualization, which does not leave much room for any kind of class-group organization. Others see dangers in this for younger students—up to early upper secondary school—in such a way that the present organization with class groups would need to be retained in some way to maintain social stability.

"Lessons," as we know them today, may be substituted by longer time-spans devoted to work with problem areas and projects motivated by the needs and the choice of the individual student. In general, schools will have abandoned the rigid structure of today and developed the capability of acting as "living libraries" to new needs of competence and also play a role as "competence consultants" for other parts of local society. In this perspective schools can also develop an effective apparatus to search and develop newly growing fields of knowledge. In the long-term, schools themselves may become more like any office or workshop.

The curricula are different, containing less details, possibly only a minimalist "basic competence." The student chooses problem areas to work with, not just subject courses.

Other professionals, besides teachers, are to be more active in the schools, in order to broaden the competence, both factually and socially. There is a tendency among professionals working in schools today of not being able to visualize other forms of organizing learning beyond the presently used forms of organization. This can be altered in what might result in a "de-schooling" movement. Also, more men will be involved, since education and learning in general will attain higher status. The teachers involved will have a broader competence, enlarged through recent reforms of teacher training, and cover a wider span of student age groups.

In upper secondary school, there may be a concentration on fewer areas of study for each individual. Selection to tertiary education will be done by testing, not by comparing marks from secondary school. Generally, different levels of education will become closer to each other, and there will be a closer attachment and cooperation between education and working-life.

Schools have regained their focus on education, in a broad sense, and have grown out of the "buying and selling" that followed the recent market-orientation reforms of school organization. A humanistic dialogue between the school and the users has replaced the seller-customer relationship.

In a national perspective, there will be a greater difference between schools in different municipalities. Differentiation, e.g., in the form of profile schools, has reached a national coverage, and is an option commonly available.

Schools are being operated by means of professional management. School managers are not only accepted but act also as true leaders of the activities. This means owning full legality and responsibility from above and full legitimacy from below. Above the level of sheer individualism, parents as a group become a true resource in school work.

In this organization, the management can effectively dispose the time and capacity of the school staff. Salaries can be used as an instrument to further develop quality, and create incentives for new initiatives. New agreements on working hours have come into effect, so that the teachers are actually present in school and not only during teaching and organized conferences.

School Culture

School, or learning, will be not only very important to the children but of high priority in society. Schools as organizations have a greater capability to play an influential role in society.

The school as an organization and the school staff as individuals have a very clear notion of their role and their mission. Thereby, the work of the school can be more highly appreciated in society. Effective evaluation is part of this work and a tool for a proper consciousness.

Good results should lead to high status, and can be rewarded. There is a sense of importance in investing in the future, seen both from the students' perspectives as well as from the adult society interested in promoting the young people. The "message" to the young must be that learning is rewarding. Good results also mean that basic demands are higher, and that the paradigms of technology and natural science are introduced on an early stage, not as subject specialization but as paradigmatic thinking and consciousness.

Direction and Style of Learning and Teaching

Schools develop creative people who shall maintain the urge to learn more when they leave school. The pupils individually are given the confidence of being able to affect the future.

The teachers have become tutors, and have acquired the skills to act as such. The role of the teacher can also be described as that of a coach. The students are trained to take responsibility for themselves. Learning will mean using more research and investigative methods, making the work in school more interesting.

As a general description, one can say that this reflects a shift from "an educating society"—a concept that implies a certain passiveness on behalf of the "object of education," i.e., the student, to "a learning society," which implies equal activity and initiative on all parts. Schools are still the last great remnant of pre-industrial and industrial society.

For the youngest children—younger than now, since school starts earlier—a more creative and playful pedagogy is developed.

"Values" in a general human sense are more important than local and specific matters. There is a need to instill hope and positive expectations of the future, to think freely, and realize the possibilities. Many threats to a good future life are present and readily available to the children through media and everyday life. Questioning traditions and values is also a part—though sometimes painful to the adults—of a vivid dialogue. The present lack of negative respect—fear—of authorities can be used as a constructive force of development.

The adaptation to the individual of the learning is coupled with a very clear sense of a general structure of what has to be achieved. This structure is thoroughly worked out from the earliest stages of kindergarten and throughout the entire training with a clear age progression of attainment and expectations. An investigative and imaginative search for knowledge will have to develop its own serious didactic—not just "go to the library and look it up."

OUTLINING THE FUTURE MANAGER

We don't need dictators—we need facilitators.

Background Experience

Opinions differ considerably about the background of school managers. Stakeholders within school often hold the opinion that the managers should have a teaching background because managers with a non-teaching background will face difficulties in gaining credibility and being regarded as legitimate leaders by staff groups. The reasons for this are arguments that an internalized experience of one's own is necessary for the understanding of the demands of school work, and for the correct and realistic perception of potentials and conditions of development.

Stakeholders outside school in many cases do not see a background as a teacher as a necessity for the school manager. In these instances, more emphasis is put on general skills of management. The reasoning behind this is that there will be enough teaching experience within schools, without the managers having to be experts on something that is not their job in the first place. Furthermore, the problem in school management is not that there has been a lack of teaching experience or skill; rather, the problem has been, and to large extent still is, that the management is unprofessional. Management is described as traditional, not knowledgeable about modern management techniques, without the level of coordination, the ability to set priorities, or the general awareness of the surrounding society necessary for progression and development of school work.

A teaching background can even be seen as a drawback. In this perspective, school managers with a solid teaching background are often unable to find new ways of organizing schools or to reconsider priorities in a tougher economic climate. The teacher managers are seen to be too firmly rooted in a certain way of thinking about "school," so that they may unconsciously restrict their ability to think freely in matters of development.

A special issue is that of the recruitment of managers—thus far mainly deputy managers—with pedagogic backgrounds other than teaching. Most often, this means pre-school teachers or other members of professions formerly within child care. Opinions differ considerably concerning the adequacy of recruiting managers from this group. On the one hand, they have—taken as a group—initially been known to run into trouble both in terms of actual skills—the ability to manage education—and of legitimacy, of not being accepted as managers by teachers. Both these problems could be explained as initial difficulties that will soon be overcome. However, there is also a fear that the actual academic level, which is normally lower in these professional groups, is a threat to the development of greater demands for theoretical standards within education than are now formulated.

Academic merits, theoretical knowledge in general and a specific ability to handle systems theoretically, are frequently mentioned as important. One important part of the theoretical knowledge concerns thorough insights into the missions of education formulated nationally and locally. It is likely that a background of humanistic or social science academic competence suits a necessary holistic view best, along with a consultative posture vis-à-vis the various specialists.

The manager does not need to be an expert in all technical fields of management. However, one "technical" field requires deeper insights. Information technology calls for special management interests.

Personal Skills and Characteristics

The making of a good manager is seen by many primarily as a matter of personality. In other words, it is more important to find the right personalities and then train them in specific technical skills—which is comparatively simple—than to recruit for technical skills and try to "train" personality.

Social skills are widely held as a basic feature of future school managers. This is often contrasted with the old civil servant managers. The manager also needs to have a personal philosophy—an idea of his or her own as to what management should lead to and what should be developed.

Social skills have often been described as an ability to handle people and deal with groups that often have contradictory interests. Since a general pattern, seen in the earlier descriptions of future demands on education and the general development of society, has been that of an increasing dependence for schools on other parts of society, the necessary social skills do not only relate to students and different staff groups but to a wide range of stakeholders in society. Maintaining good relations with stakeholders seems extremely important in order to ensure good working conditions and maximum development in a rather more informal and decentralized network organization of the local community.

One specific instance of social skill is the ability to create constructive dialogues. In order to instill new thoughts in the organization and among stakeholders, to develop, change, or even wind up parts of the organization, a constant dialogue is needed. The dialogue has many competence components, such as being able to handle the disappointment and frustration that may occur from groups or individuals disadvantaged by a change, being able to stick to the mission calls and being able to keep calm in conflict. A realistic self-conception and a reasonable self-confidence are crucial.

In relation to the future demands on the organization of education, the manager will need to be able to develop a greater diversity of competencies within the organization. Adding competencies may sound like an entirely positive action that would not create problems or conflict, but this addition will also create economic priorities in which the size of traditional competence will be challenged. Obviously, the manager would, in this perspective, also need a broad orientation and a wide network of contacts in order to identify and select crucial new competence.

"Handling people and groups" also means managing conflicts. The radical and rapid change foreseen for schools may not be possible without conflicts arising, either from individuals or interest groups. Individuals as well as groups will sense the threat of change or the negative side effects associated with changes. These conflicts must not be seen as evil per se but must not be allowed to get out of control and become destructive. In this balance, the social skill of handling conflicts would be found.

Closely linked to integrity is the courage to be a leader and a manager, to see what needs to be done, propose and create the conditions for it, and to face the conflicts that may arise. Courage takes a lot of knowledge and skill if it is not to become foolhardiness.

Values

It is all too easy to value oneself—and other people—according to specific fields of expertise; the school manager must not try to embody necessary competence himself but should find and utilize the competence needed in other staff members.

Professional ethics is mentioned by some people as a field that will be included in managers' professional skills, as a basic professional value, in the future. Compared to other professional groups such as of law and medicine, the professional ethics of school managers are not as well defined.

The manager's ability to create a sense of purpose and a feeling of participation and shared responsibility among staff, students, and other stakeholders is seen as very important. In a climate of rapid change, participation and positive expectations are crucial to successful development.

Training and Maintenance of High Standards

An initial training program for school managers, of whatever kind, cannot thoroughly cover the needs of competence development. The theme of recurrent training and stimulants is seen as increasingly important, along with the increasing pace of changes in surrounding society. Actually, the concept of a training program itself is frequently questioned.

Thus far, a standard procedure in creating a new school manager has been for an experienced and skilled teacher to become a manager, in some cases in a straight succession in the school where he or she has acted as a teacher. Initially, the work of this new manager has been defined by the traditions of the school, and after a few years the responsible municipality has offered a training program, containing discussions, some literature, case studies and field studies, and individual tasks in the field of school development. The training program is based on the manager's daily work—laden with traditions— and based on the accepted concept of how education is to be organized in our society. International outlooks, as well as orientation in the surrounding society, are not prominent features. After the training program, work goes on as usual.

As a contrast, the importance of continuous guidance and "refueling" has been stressed. There is no such thing as completed training that could result in a "legitimating diploma."

The strengthening of professional management in school calls for "proper" management training, e.g., jointly with newly appointed managers from other fields of enterprise. Continuous guidance could be used both for internal matters of organization and everyday management, in networks of fellow managers, and for external matters, e.g. to keep in touch with and develop cooperation with other stakeholders, research groups, etc. Attachment to research and scientific development is described as an important feature of continuous competence development.

In maintaining high standards among school managers, the status of the profession and the position is frequently mentioned. The future demands on a school manager—to some extent already in effect—will be those of an entrepreneur and a creator, but not an administrator. This also changes the character of the profession, and the level and scope of competence required. In order to recruit managers with a proper potential, a higher status is essential.

SUMMARIZING THE FUTURE COMPETENCE OF SCHOOL MANAGERS

The following components of a future school manager's competence seem to be those most frequently mentioned and emphasized:

Proper Background:

- Not necessarily a teacher but somebody with pedagogic insight and experience.

Socio-Cultural and Interpersonal Skills:

- Can handle individuals and groups within school and among stakeholders outside.
- Can handle conflicts, frustrations, and disappointments.
- Can understand and unite different cultures, professional, social, and ethnic.

A Natural Leader:

- Secure and self-confident but without the need for personal prestige.
- Interested in people and possessing a desire to understand them.

- "The first among peers," identified as an equal, but with a clear stature as a leader.
- Has well-considered ideas and goals of his or her own for the exercise of leadership.
- Makes priorities in a harsh economic climate and in situations of rapid pedagogic and organizational change.

A Catalyst:

- Helps in the transition of goals from the single school into general school practice.
- Creates accepted compromises between goals from, e.g., national and municipal agencies and conflicting aspirations from other stakeholders, e.g., parents and teachers' unions.

A Unifier:

- Communicates all important matters throughout school and to stakeholders: Purposes, directions, goals, results.
- Ability to create a common sense of purpose, shared values, and agreed-upon operational goals of the school.
- Ability to help everyone do their best, assume responsibility, and make their own decisions in accordance with goals.

A Systems Operator:

- Handles administrative systems to the advantage of the enterprise and is not ruled by them.
- Utilizes economy to the ends of the goals.
- Masters new information technology to the point of being able to inspire and plan for a broad use in school.
- Accepts and utilizes changes of organization made possible by new technologies.
- Brings in new competence needed for development and utilizes new technology.
- Has a well-developed reasoning capability in all administrative and economic matters without getting lost in details.

An Academic:

- Broad theoretical education on academic level, most suitably within humanities, social science, or political science.
- Can master one or more foreign languages.
- Broad orientation in the whole society, nationally and internationally—both theoretical and towards interpersonal relations.
- Specific knowledge of management in a wide perspective, not only related to managing schools. Contacts with business life.
- Research connections.

Controller, Initiator and Developer

- Masters and utilizes techniques of quality control.
- Utilizes results of quality control to initiate and carry out development.
- Performs or delegates economic controller functions.

Organizing the Development of School Managers

The Swedish national curriculum defines the roles and responsibilities of the school manager (SOU 1992, p. 94 p. 168-169); however, these requirements deal almost solely with the internal management of the school in an attempt to answer the question: "What, among everything that takes place inside a school, is the specific responsibility of the principal?" In the obligations, nothing is said about social skills and the broader orientation of "bringing the world into the school," that have been judged to be important for future competence.

Thus, future school managers will not only have to meet the requirements of the curriculum but go beyond them.

What Can Be Done?

Often, in discussing the competence of school managers, the conversation is restricted to training. This will be a too narrow view of competence development in the perspective of future changes. In the following sections an account will be given of initial training and recurring development.

Initial Training:

1. For the sake of professionalism, it seems proper to formulate an initial training program as compulsory and, at the university level, give academic credit points. This could add one or more additional terms to any academic education, covering broad issues of education and management.
2. Specific management training, not connected to school matters. It seems essential to introduce this kind of training, since the problem in developing education is not seen to be caused by a lack of "within-school" competence but rather of professional management. This training could best be carried out jointly with representatives from other enterprises in society.
3. Training for technical and administrative matters of economy, personnel management, law, and other connected areas, and, in particular, the use and development of information technology.

Recurring Development:

1. The present routine consists of a training program that runs for a few years, that runs parallel to newly appointed work at a school, after which the manager is left on his/her own for the rest of his/her career. This routine is not sufficient. Both work and training are time-consuming, and both suffer from this arrangement. In the perspective of lifelong learning, continuous and frequently recurring seminars, lectures, etc., should be included in competence development.
2. Monitoring and guidance, individually or in network groups are needed if the managers are to maintain a high standard and to deal with the inevitable problems. Network groups should consist of both school managers and managers from other enterprises. Keeping up with the evolution of society must be a central issue. The present tendency to use guidance mainly for psychological issues must not be the sole direction.

Contents of Training and Development:

Apart from what has already been accounted for, it has become obvious that the general direction of training and development will have to be directed much more towards external factors and issues. It seems as if the emphasis thus far on internal school matters has had the effect of preserving the organization of education. If the training and development of school managers is left to deal with the present form of schools, the "message" will be that this form is natural and just and that development is something that should go on within this organization.

In the context of the general development of society that has been sketched in this article, this "within" is precisely what should be avoided. The core of successful development seems to be to include what are now external issues.

REFERENCES

Berg, G. 1990. "Skolledning och professionellt skolledarskap..." (School Management and Professional School Leadership...) in the series *Pedagogic Research in Uppsala*, no. 92, Dep. of Pedagogics, Uppsala University.

Berg, G. 1995. "Skolkultur, lärare och skolledare..." (School Culture, Teachers and School Managers...) in the series *Pedagogic Research in Uppsala*, no 118, Dep. of Pedagogics, Uppsala University.

Block, E. 1989. *Ny framtidsmiljö för utbildning* (New Future Environment for Education). Södertälje: Askelin & Hägglund.

Carnoy, M. 1993. "School Improvement: Is Privatization the Answer?" In *Decentralization and School Improvement: Can We Fulfill the Promise?*, eds. J. Hannaway and M. Carnoy. San Francisco: Jossey-Bass Publishers.

Dalin, P. 1994a. *Utbildning för ett nytt år hundrade* (Education for a New Century). Stockholm: Liber Utbildning.

Dalin, P. 1994b. *Skoleutveckling Teori* (School Development Theory). Stockholm: Liber Utbildning.

Dryden, G., and J. Vos. 1994. *Inlärningsrevolutionen* (The Learning Revolution). Jönköping: Brain Books.

Edgren, J., ed. 1990: *Lära på jobbet* (Learning at Work), in the series "Competence 2000." Stockholm: Swedish Employers' Association.

Glans, K. 1994: *Vetenskap och teknologi efter murens fall* (Science and Technology after the Fall of the Wall). Stockholm: Ingenjörsvetenskapsakademien (IVA) (Academy of Engineering Science).

Hannaway, J., and M. Carnoy. 1993. *Decentralization and School Improvement: Can We Fulfill the Promise?* San Francisco: Jossey-Bass Publishers.

Ingenjörsvetenskapsakademien (IVA). 1993. *Företagsförnyelse inför 2000-talet: Visioner och vägledande principer* (Renewal of Companies Towards the Year 2000: Visions and Guiding Principles). Stockholm: Ingenjörsvetenskapsakademien (IVA) (Academy of Engineering Science).

Ingenjörsvetenskapsakademien (IVA) 1994. *Förändringen! Utveckling av verksamhet, ledarskap och medarbetare* (The Change! Development of Work, Leadership and Cooperators). Stockholm: Ingenjörsvetenskapsakademien (IVA) (Academy of Engineering Science).

Ingenjörsvetenskapsakademien (IVA). 1995. *Nya verksamhets-processer, Svenska erfarenheter av verksamhetsförändring i en ny IT-värld* (Swedish Experiences of New Processes of Work in an IT World). Stockholm: Ingenjörsvetenskapsakademien (IVA) (Academy of Engineering Science).

Kyndrup, M. 1986. *Det Postmoderne—om betydningens forandring i kunst, litteratur, samfund* (The Postmodern—About the Change of Meaning in Art, Literature and Society). Århus: Gyldendal.

Lärarnas Riksförbund (LR). 1995. *Synpunkten* (The Point of View). Lärarnas Riksförbund, no. 1.

Leion A., ed. 1992. *Den nyttiga kompetensen* (The Useful Competence). Stockholm: Timbro.

Liljequist, K. 1994. *Skola och samhällsutveckling* (School and the Development of Society). Lund: Studentlitteratur.

Lyttkens, L. 1994. *Arbetet som lyx* (Work as a Luxury. An essay of the Project "Technology and Future Work."). Stockholm: Ingenjörsvetenskapsakademien (IVA) (Academy of Engineering Science).

Makrakis, V. 1988. "Computers in School Education, The Cases of Sweden and Greece." *Studies in Comparative and International Education* 11. Institute of International Education, Stockholm University.

Miron, G. 1993. "Choice and the Use of Market Forces in Schooling: Swedish Education Reforms for the 1990s." *Studies in Comparative and International Education* 25. Institute of International Education, Stockholm University.

Möller, M. 1995. "Educational Management and Conditions for Competence." Master's Thesis, Institute of International Education, Stockholm University.

Naisbitt, J. 1983. *Megatrender* (Megatrends). Vänersborg: Timo Förlag.

Nygren M., et al. 1994. *Företagens kompetensbehov & kraven på skolan...* (Companies' Needs for Competence and the Demands on Schools...). Stockholm: Svensk Arbetet Forbund (SAF) (Swedish Employers' Association).

Organization for Economic Cooperation and Development (OECD). Centre for Educational Research and Innovation (CERI). 1995a. *Education at a Glance*. Paris: Organization for Economic Cooperation and Development.

Organization for Economic Cooperation and Development (OECD). Centre for Educational Research and Innovation (CERI). 1995b. *Public Expectations of the Final Stage of Compulsory Education*. Paris: Organization for Economic Cooperation and Development.

SOU. 1992. *School for Education* (Skola för bildning). Ministry of Education. Stockholm: Allmänna Förlaget.

SOU. 1995. *Långtidsutredningen 1995* (Long Range Analysis 1995). Ministry of Finance. Stockholm: Fritzes.

Starrat, R.J. 1993. *The Drama of Leadership*. Hong Kong: The Falmer Press.

Strandler, L. 1989: *Gymnasieskola 2000* (Upper Secondary Education 2000). Stockholm: Svensk Arbetet Forbund (SAF) (Swedish Employers' Association).

Svensk Arbetet Forbund (SAF) (Swedish Employers' Association). 1985. *En svensk "collegeskola," Regional samordning och förnyelse av utbildning inom teknik, ADB, handel och økonomi* (A Swedish "College School," Regional Coordination and Renewal of Education within Technology, Computing, Trade, and Economy). Stockholm: Svensk Arbetet Forbund.

Svensk Arbetet Forbund (SAF) (Swedish Employers' Association). 1992. *Flexibilitet i företag* (Flexibility in Companies). Stockholm: Svensk Arbetet Forbund.

Their, S. 1994. *Det pedagogiska ledarskapet* (Pedagogic Leadership). Mariehamn: Mermerus Ab Oy.

Textor, R.B. 1982. *Austria 2005, Projected Sociocultural Effects of the Microelectronic Revolution*. Wien: Orac Pietsch.

Toffler, A. 1990. *Maktskifte* (Power Shift). Höganäs: Wiken.

Utbildningsdepartementet (Ministry of Education). 1993. *Ingenjörer i livslångt lärande* (Engineers in Lifelong Learning). Agenda 2000, Rapport nr. 3, Ds 96. Stockholm: Utbildningsdepartementet.

Winkler, D.R. 1993. "Fiscal Decentralization and Accountability in Education: Experiences in Four Countries." In *Decentralization and School Improvement. Can We Fulfill the Promise?*, eds. J. Hannaway and M. Carnoy. San Francisco: Jossey Bass Publishers.

CHAPTER 12

The Comprehensive Schools in Norway: Challenged by a Changing Society

Içara da Silva Holmesland

INTRODUCTION

As the Western world approaches the year 2000, education is often the main theme of discussion in debates among politicians, policy makers, educationalists, and the public in general. The changes that have taken place in the past decade, both at the social level as well as at the level of transference of knowledge and information, have been very intense and have happened so quickly that they seem to be shaking several nations, no matter what their levels of development. Such turmoil is forcing many countries to re-think and, perhaps, re-direct their educational policies. Different nations are today scrutinizing their educational systems and carrying out reforms in order to improve their quality, increase their efficiency, and make them more responsive to the demands of their societies. Norway, in spite of its very well established public school system, is also being affected by changes occurring outside and inside its boundaries and is, therefore, also questioning the adequacy of its educational policies for meeting the demands of a changing society. Thus, the purpose of this paper is to discuss the comprehensive-compulsory school system of Norway, i.e., the public schools that are in charge of basic education in Norway and are attended by the population of youngsters between the ages of six and sixteen, having in view the present pressures for change.

There are three main reasons for my interest in examining the Norwegian educational system at this level. One of them is my concern as a parent—two of my children have just finished this level, and two others are still in the system, therefore I am very interested in following up its developments. A second reason is professional—I have been working in this school system in the past six years and have, thus, had the opportunity to observe it from a teacher's perspective. My third reason is plain curiosity from a research standpoint, which I will formulate in terms of the following question: "What kinds of predictions can one make about possible changes in the compulsory-comprehensive school system of Norway, considering the present trends in the society?"

The ideas expressed are based partly on information gathered from articles written about education in Norway and the results of studies considered relevant to the arguments here presented, and partly on my own perceptions and biases, heavily impregnated by previous experiences as an educator and researcher in Norway, Brazil, and the United States. As there has been no systematic analysis of data collected on the topic, this paper can, most likely, be classified as an opinion paper.

The paper covers three main themes. I start by presenting a brief overview of the historical developments of Norway's educational system. This part is directed mostly to readers not familiar with developments of the Norwegian comprehensive school system. Following that, some of the changes occurring inside and outside Norwegian boundaries which might have implications for its educational system are presented. Next, I bring forward results of research that identifies some important cultural dimensions that might have an effect upon schools and discuss the relevance of these findings for the Norwegian schools. Finally, some conclusions are drawn and presented in terms of changes that might be expected to occur in the Norwegian comprehensive school system.

EDUCATIONAL DEVELOPMENTS IN NORWAY

Norway has today a well-established public school system whose beginning dates back to 1739, when the first school law was written. Since then, the Norwegian school has gone through several reforms that led to the present structure and is known today as the unified or comprehensive school system.

If one examines the history of educational developments in Norway, it becomes evident that its educational system is deeply rooted in a society where the state has placed great emphasis on equality and social justice, with the interests of the collectivity considered above the interests of the individual. Equality, however, has not always been a feature of Norway's educational system. In its history one finds several descriptions of situations that point towards the opposite direction. It was mainly after World War II, as part of the establishment of the welfare state, that the political parties came to an agreement on the principles of equal education for all (Tjeldvoll 1996). These principles form the basis of today's Norwegian comprehensive school system. To give the reader a better idea of the educational developments in Norway, I will briefly refer to some changes that eliminated inequalities and led to the present structure of its unified school system.

The Separation Between Students

One type of inequality that existed in the past but has been eliminated with the establishment of the comprehensive school was the separation that used to take place after completion of the fifth grade in the elementary school. This separation caused great concern even in the beginning of this century and, as early as 1913, a report of the Comprehensive School Committee introduced the idea of the comprehensive school system and proposed linking the various types of schools in "an united and coherent educational system" (Andresen and Østerud 1982). That School Committee suggested, then, separation between students only after the 7th grade. The left wing parties were the strongest supporters of equal educational opportunities to all children, independent of their social level, and faced a lot of opposition to their proposals of unifying the educational system. In spite of the reactions against such ideas, an act of Parliament, in 1920, determined that "state subsidies should no longer be granted to secondary schools that were not based on a completed seven-year primary school" (Andresen and Østerud 1982, p. 15). As most of the Norwegian cities needed state subsidies for operating the secondary schools, this act was very decisive for the establishment of the comprehensive school and it became a law in 1936.

Rural and Urban Schools

Notwithstanding the 1936 comprehensive school law, inequalities continued to exist in Norway. Rural and urban schools, for example, were regulated by separate laws, which placed different demands on them. Students in the rural areas were offered less hours of instruction and often had to attend small classes in mixed age groups (Dokka 1986).

Because persisting inequalities continued to be a concern among the left wing politicians, the struggle to level off the differences in the society continued, finally succeeding, as already mentioned, only after World War II, when the socialist principles of equal education for all attained a high degree of consensus among the political parties (Tjeldvoll 1996).

The Nine-Year Comprehensive School

The main goal of subsequent educational laws passed in Norway was to offer a basic education of equal quality to all children, independent of geographical location, gender, ethnic origin, or social background. These laws included several regulations for increasing equality, among them provisions to offer an education suitable to children with special needs, handicaps, or learning difficulties (Special School Act of 1951) and to extend compulsory schooling to nine years (School Act of 1959). Beyond extending basic education to nine years, the School Act of 1959 united the urban and rural schools and established as an overall goal to educate the pupils to be good citizens, while taking care of their individual abilities and talents (Sennerud 1995).

Choosing the education policy as a social change agent for creating justice based on socialistic principles was part of the struggle to establish the Scandinavian model of the welfare state. According to Tjeldvoll (1996), despite the high costs for implementing a democratic educational model in a country whose population lives "spread along fjords, in between mountains, or on islands," most aims stated in the Norwegian educational policies were attained by the end of the 1970s. In the 1970s, the concept of "equality" was extended to "respect for inequality" (Telhaug 1992), which meant that handicapped students should not be segregated and were entitled to attend school together with non-handicapped students. However, the effectiveness of the educational policies towards equality has been questioned by authors

(Andresen and Østerud 1982) who claim that no matter how equal the educational opportunities were made in Norway, the groups with the best background were still able to make better use of resources. Thus, even though equality has been the main feature of Norway's educational policies, their effectiveness to attain this aim is questionable.

THE DILEMMA OF QUALITY VS. EQUALITY IN EDUCATION

When discussing the dilemma of quality vs. equality in education, one cannot avoid connecting it with the ideology of the welfare system, under which Norway's comprehensive school system was established. As the central idea of welfarism is to safeguard individuals from social evils (Heywood 1994) the same ideology was transferred to the school system. Therefore, everybody entering the school system has to be able to complete it, despite individual endowments and interests. Since the system is compulsory and nobody can be excluded, a midway position must be found and agreed upon. Although it becomes difficult to offer a high quality educational program under such conditions, this was the road selected in Norway to implement its democratic educational policies and, according to Tjeldvoll (1996), most aims of these policies were achieved by the 1970s when access to nine years of basic education became possible for all.

The decade of the 1970s was very special in Norway. Oil explorations in the North Sea had brought greater wealth, and it was not difficult, then, to find a well-paying job with nine years of basic education plus some additional training. In addition to business expansion, the petrodollars fomented intense immigration from both developed and less developed countries, making the Norwegian society more heterogeneous. One can perhaps state that many of the criticisms directed towards the comprehensive schools today are partly a consequence of changes that happened in Norway after the economic boom, which brought affluence and a greater heterogeneity to its society. Three specific facts that have probably increased the awareness in the population of the need for a higher quality education in Norway:
1. A shrinking job market made it more difficult to have a well-paying job with only nine years of formal education.

2. Technological transformations required a work force with far more intellectual skills and training in abstract thinking than in earlier times (Zuboff 1988).

3. Educational changes in other countries such as England, Denmark, and the United States in the end of the 1980s brought a wave of neo-conservatism or neo-liberalistic ideas which reactivated the debate on the level of knowledge at the lower secondary level (Telhaug 1992).

In 1987, the national curriculum was submitted to a revision which increased the academic demands at the lower secondary level. Despite the increase in the demand for knowledge in the new educational policies, it is claimed that the Norwegian school has not moved itself away from the ideals of the comprehensive school (Lauvdal 1994). This change, however, does not seem to have solved the main dilemma of the comprehensive school, which is still being discussed. Although the access to the lower secondary level has steadily been made more democratic, its content is often criticized. It continues to be difficult to offer an education that will meet the demands of two different groups of students—the so-called resourceful students and the less academically oriented (Tjeldvoll 1996). This author states that difficulties in mastering the content of school subjects, coupled with the situation of growing unemployment, seem to have had a negative influence on the motivation of less academically oriented students. At the same time, the technological changes in the job market demand the mastery of many complex skills (Zuboff 1988) which the resourceful students claim not to be learning. The schools, thus, seem to be frozen by the ideology of equality and not capable of satisfying the needs of the less ambitious as well as the more ambitious students. Just to illustrate this point, I would like to refer to a newspaper article "I Sosialmatriarkatets Støpeform" (In the Mold of the Social Matriarchy) in which Sandmo (1995), a graduate of the upper secondary level, expresses his discontentment with the comprehensive schools. In his criticisms, he points out several weaknesses of the comprehensive school system and reacts strongly to the pressures made in this system so that "all students will learn the same, in the same way and in the same amount of time, which means, according to the conditions of the weakest." He adds that the "Big Mother socializes each individual until all students have been pushed to the average and become ordinary." However, he claims to have been triumphant in not conforming to the pressures—during the years he went through the school system, nobody has succeeded in teaching him how to crochet!

These excerpts illustrate some of the criticisms made to the comprehensive schools and suggest a lack of fitness between the society and what the system is willing to offer. The changes that have occurred in the Norwegian society through the years, especially after the 1970s, seem to be subjecting the comprehensive school system to forces that are compelling it to alter some of its distinctive features of the post-war period. These pressures come from a population that has become increasingly more urbanized and heterogeneous.

Oil explorations in the North Sea have not only brought greater affluence to Norway but also a greater diversification of its society. Different ethnic groups are today present in the Norwegian society, contributing not only different skin and hair colors but also different languages, religions, cultures, and value systems. As these groups are heavily represented in urban areas, the schools in the larger cities, or their proximity, have been forced to adapt the teaching and the programs to the wave of foreign children. Extra resources have been allocated to teach children of immigrant families, sometimes in their own languages, until they are able to communicate fluently in Norwegian. These children have also the right to continue learning their mother tongue until they finish the 9th grade.

Other changes occurring in the society, which seem also to have had a negative impact upon students' performance and are a concern for education policy makers are the increasing numbers of single parents and of women participating in the work force.

Aware of these changes and having recognized that the student population covers a much wider spectrum of cultures than it did 30 or more years ago, the educational authorities have been adapting the educational programs to the needs of today's society. One of them is the earlier start in school, at six instead of seven, which has increased basic education from nine to ten years. The other is the extended school day from 8 A.M. to 5 P.M. for children attending grades K-3, an offer that has been welcomed by working parents. One can thus state that recent educational policies have increased the institutionalization of the Norwegian children (Telhaug 1992), with the school assuming some of the roles of the home. The purpose is to increase the level of knowledge by making better use of teenagers' learning capacity and, in addition, have more time to pass on cultural values (Telhaug 1992). The comprehensive schools have in this way accumulated more duties and responsibilities than ever. Being compulsory, the role it plays in society has become increasingly more influential.

CHALLENGES TO THE COMPREHENSIVE SCHOOL IN THE 1990S

The Academic Challenges

As we approach the year 2000, a question to be asked is whether the comprehensive school will be able to maintain the monopoly on knowledge and cultural values for a society that is gradually becoming more heterogeneous. Evidences of the difficulty of meeting the demands at the knowledge level already exist. Expressions of dissatisfaction with the academic level are often heard or read. Some groups have started claiming that a higher quality in education at all levels can be attained by means of private schools or the establishment of a voucher system (Norman 1994).

The acknowledgment of some of the academic weaknesses of the comprehensive school has led policy makers to adapt the curriculum and increase the time the students spend at school. A recent reform at the upper secondary level (Reform 94) has established a stronger link between lower and upper secondary education by ensuring access to this level. Happening at a time of enormous technological changes and of a shrinking job market, this reform serves two purposes: 1) to increase the educational level of the society, and 2) to keep the young people out of the job market.

The many efforts made thus far to adapt the comprehensive school to the demands of a changing society indicate that the Norwegian authorities still regard the public school as the best means for leveling off the differences in the society and most likely will continue protecting it from any threats. However, it seems that the new educational policies have moved a bit away from the more orthodox social democratic ideals and towards a more liberal view of education. In the words of Telhaug (1992), the Norwegian education is going through a "restorative" period in which the social democratic model is being adjusted to new demands in the society.

The Cultural Challenges

Besides the growing academic demands, another challenge to be faced by the Norwegian comprehensive school in the next years will be the transmission of a set of cultural values to a society becoming gradually more pluralistic. This, in fact, might be its greatest challenge due to the abstractness of the concept and the difficulty in defining what in reality is a cultural value. To support this statement, I will present some evidences of the already existing incompatibilities in Norway and present research findings that identify cultural dimensions along which it is possible to place different societies and characterize the behaviors of their members.

CULTURAL DIFFERENCES IN THE NORWEGIAN SCHOOLS

The multicultural character of the Norwegian comprehensive schools—especially those in urbanized areas—is a fact accepted by the educational authorities. The concern is not new and is expressed through educational policies which, faithful to the child-centered character of the Norwegian education, emphasize the need to facilitate the adaptation of children from other cultures. Such efforts indicate a genuine interest among educational authorities, teachers, and school personnel in general to make the public school an open space for cultural exchanges. In spite of these efforts, certain groups of immigrants have been attempting to establish their own private schools. In 1994, a request for establishing a Muslim school with support of public funds at the basic level (K-9) was rejected by the Parliament's educational committee, on the grounds that it could become a ghetto school, i.e., attended only by pupils from immigrant families, or a school for girls, who could, thus, be prevented from experiencing the challenges of a society that defends equality that the girls enrolled in the comprehensive schools enjoyed (Magnus 1994; Bleness 1994). Both arguments stressed the non-observation of the Norwegian laws of equality and of the comprehensive school. Subsequent requests for establishing Muslim schools at the upper secondary level have also been rejected by the government (Simenstad 1994; Muri 1995). These denials suggest that the establishment of Muslim schools is evaluated by different criteria than those used to judge requests from groups that profess the Christian faith, which receive public funds for running their own private schools. It appears that the government has a different standard for judging requests from Muslim groups. According to a member of the Parliament's school committee, the main reason for the denials is the fear that a private Muslim school could become a threat to the comprehensive schools. However, the real reason might have deeper roots. Perhaps it can be better explained by acknowledging that the school is a social system in charge of transmitting the values of the society in which it is embedded. Thus, the Norwegian school, like other public schools, has as one of its aims the transmission of the majority group values, which are not necessarily in agreement with the values of the minority groups. Certainly, this is not news, and the educational authorities have already established regulations to facilitate the integration of children of immigrant families. In spite of such efforts, there are still dissatisfactions! Why do some foreigners reject a public school system which is well established and very well organized and equipped? Are there any specific cultural incompatibilities that can lead to a rejection of the Norwegian comprehensive school? Perhaps some explanations can be found in research done about cultural diversity and the consequences for organizations. These studies are mentioned here because they not only acknowledge the importance of cultural differences but also identify important dimensions that can explain the behaviors, or expectations of behaviors, which might be sources for a lack of understanding leading to confrontations between groups of different cultures.

RESEARCH FINDINGS ABOUT CULTURAL DIFFERENCES

The importance of cultural differences in the environment of international organizations has received increased attention in the post-World War II period due to the growth in the number of large corporations that perform many business activities outside of their home countries. Because of the demand for increased knowledge in this area, there has been a greater interest in research on the influence of cultural differences on organizational behavior (Adler 1991). The results of a study by Hofstede (1991) in 1980 in 40 countries seem relevant to Norwegian reality. His empirical findings identified four cultural dimensions that can explain behaviors of people from different countries. Hofstede defines these dimensions as:

Individualism-Collectivism: Individualism distinguishes people from societies where the ties between individuals are loose and every person is expected to look after himself or herself, and his or his immediate family. Collectivism, on the contrary, pertains to societies in which people are integrated into strong and cohesive groups, which throughout life protect people in exchange for loyalty. Thus, in collectivist cultures, the members are controlled through external societal pressure—shame. In individualist cultures, control comes from internal pressure—guilt.

Power distance: This dimension is defined as the extent to which powerful members of institutions and organizations within a country expect and accept that power is distributed unequally.

Masculinity/Femininity: Masculinity is defined as the extent to which the dominant values in society emphasize assertiveness and the acquisition of money and things and do not emphasize concern for people. Femininity is defined as the extent to which the values in society emphasize relationships among people, concern for others, and the overall quality of life.

Uncertainty avoidance: The uncertainty avoidance dimension measures the extent to which people in a society feel threatened by uncertain or unknown situations and try to avoid them by means of written rules or rejection of deviant ideas and behavior.

CULTURAL DIMENSIONS AND THE SCHOOL ENVIRONMENT

The importance of cultural variables in the school environment is emphasized by Hofstede (1991, p. 3) because, as he states, the relationship between the individual and the group is established during the first years of childhood in the family where most people acquire their "mental software" from the elders with whom they grow up and by following their examples. These behaviors are later reinforced in the schools. A logical deduction is that the congruence or lack of congruence between values passed on by the families and those reinforced by the schools can be a strong determinant of the parents' acceptance or lack of acceptance of a school. A mismatch between such values can be a source of conflict. The study by Hofstede points out specific behaviors associated with cultural values that can be sources of conflict in the school environment and, therefore, should be recognized and understood by those working in the schools. The question here is whether there are such great differences between the cultural values in the Norwegian schools and those of the immigrant families whose children attend these schools. To make this analysis more objective, I will take the results of Hofstede's study and compare the cultural values of Norway with those of Pakistan and Turkey, according to the relative positions of these countries along the four dimensions previously described. The reason for selecting Pakistan and Turkey is that immigrants of these countries constitute the main group behind private Muslim schools. As the cultural values to be analyzed have implications for education, by means of a comparison I expect to gain some insights about specific cultural differences that might hinder the acceptance of the comprehensive school by immigrant groups.

Based on the scores obtained by these three countries along the four cultural dimensions, it is possible to state that:

1. Norway is a country whose society has a small power distance, is individualistic, has feminine values, and is weak in uncertainty avoidance.
2. Pakistan and Turkey occupy similar positions, and their societies are described in relationship to Norway as having a larger power distance, being more collectivist, having more masculine values, and being strong in uncertainty avoidance.

For reasons of comparison, I shall next consider the relative positions occupied by Norway, Pakistan, and Turkey along the four cultural dimensions and present Hofstede's descriptions of expected attitudes and behaviors of members of such types of societies in a school environment.

NORWEGIAN SOCIETY

In an individualist society with small power distance, Norwegian cultural values are favorable to an educational system that is student-centered and rewards student initiative. This system can, then, be described as one that accepts that students will argue with teachers and express disagreement and criticisms in front of the teachers and show no particular respect to teachers outside school. There is an expectation that the students will speak up in class. If a child misbehaves, the parents will often take the side of the child. The educational system is impersonal and encourages the students to be self-sufficient and self-reliant. Students are treated as individuals and impartially, regardless of their background. Group formations depend upon the task, friendships, and skills. Confrontations and open discussion of conflicts are often considered a healthy sign. Education is perceived as preparing the individual to meet unknown situations and to learn how to cope with new information. Therefore, it is more important to know how to learn than to learn how to do. The diploma in this society improves the holder's economic worth and provides a sense of achievement.

In this society the teachers do not expect to have all the answers, and intellectual disagreement can be seen as a stimulating exercise. Teachers try to get parents involved in their children's learning process and seek parents' ideas.

According to Hofstede's descriptions, feminine values are characteristic of welfare societies. Where feminine values are emphasized, the students will not be too eager to compete and mutual solidarity is seen as a goal. The average student is considered the norm, and failure in school is a relatively minor incident. When choosing a job, intrinsic interest in the subject plays an important role.

Teachers' friendliness and social skills and students' social adaptation are expected to be more important. In this type of society, the roles of men and women are mixed, therefore men should also teach younger children.

PAKISTANI AND TURKISH SOCIETIES

According to Hofstede's typology, members of these societies can be described as favorable to a parent-child inequality which is expected to be perpetuated by a teacher-student inequality. The educational process is expected to be teacher centered and does not reward student initiative. Students should speak only when invited to do so, and teachers are not to be publicly contradicted or criticized. When a child misbehaves, the parents are expected to be on the teacher's side and help to correct the child. In this type of culture the students remain dependent on teachers, and there might even be corporal punishment at school. Different ethnic or clan groups often form subgroups at school, and the family background might determine some preferential treatment. Confrontations and conflicts are not considered healthy and should be avoided so that the individual will not lose face. The purpose of education is to prepare the individual to be an acceptable group member. Education in these societies tends to emphasize learning how to do things in order to participate in the society. The diploma is an honor to the holder and entitles him or her to be a member of higher-status groups.

Having scored as strong in uncertainty avoidance, these societies are likely to expect teachers to be experts and have all the answers. Students of these cultures will most likely not express intellectual disagreements with their teachers because this can be understood as personal disloyalty. Parents might be brought in by teachers but only as an audience, as they are rarely consulted.

Both Pakistan and Turkey occupy a more masculine position than Norway along the masculine-feminine dimension. This suggests that teachers' brilliance and academic reputation and students' academic performance should play a more important role in these societies than in Norway. In a more masculine society, women tend to teach younger children.

If one compares the descriptions of the Norwegian culture with those of the Pakistani/Turkish cultures, it is possible to expect that these societies have quite different views concerning schools. These views most likely will be reflected in the parents', students', and teachers' attitudes and behaviors. A close examination of the described values of Norway, Pakistan, and Turkey points out many possible sources of incompatibilities in the environment of the comprehensive schools. Although the analyses here are just speculations about possible sources of disagreement, findings from studies about differences in organizational cultures (Hofstede 1991; Adler 1991) indicate that there is a pattern to the way that people think, feel, and act, which should be understood by those working in multicultural environments. Therefore, it is important that future studies dealing with the comprehensive schools in Norway focus on the identification of specific differences between the Norwegian culture and the cultural values of immigrant families.

CONCLUDING REMARKS

At the doorstep of year 2000, the Norwegian comprehensive school system faces a great challenge—to provide an education that will meet demands for higher quality, while maintaining social equality in a society that is becoming increasingly more heterogeneous, both academically and culturally.

For a period of about 30 years—between the 1950s and 1980s—the compulsory-comprehensive school system was widely accepted in Norway and praised as one of the main forces behind the efforts aimed at the elimination of social inequalities. During this time, Norway experienced also a great economic growth attached to oil explorations in the North Sea, which made it easier to invest heavily in education. Even though it appears that the egalitarian educational model adopted by Norway is the main force behind its economic development, one can wonder whether this country would have succeeded in implementing educational policies that emphasize equality over quality under an unfavorable economic situation. I raise this doubt based on the observation that with the worsening of economic conditions and rise in unemployment, the discussion about the need for more quality in education has been very often on the agenda of different groups in the Norwegian society. Although the discussion about higher quality in education can be connected to a new liberalistic wave in other countries (Telhaug 1992; Tjeldvoll 1996), one cannot ignore what is happening inside the Norwegian boundaries.

As a response to the criticisms directed towards the academic standards at the basic level, recent educational policies are aimed at preparing today's youngsters to enter a very competitive job market which, it is claimed, will demand more abstract reasoning skills in the near future. One of the strategies selected to implement the new reforms is to keep children longer in the school environment by means of lowering the age to start school (from seven to six years old), having longer school days, and making upper secondary education more accessible to all. Keeping children longer in the school environment, it is expected, will increase the knowledge level as well as facilitate the transmission of cultural values. These policies seem to be in accordance with the egalitarian model of education that has prevailed in Norway as well as other Nordic nations. Findings from research do not seem to support the belief that children will learn more by spending more time at school. It is surprising that the discussions do not deal more deeply with the quality of teaching the students will receive with increased school time. Under such circumstances, one can wonder if the result of the new educational policies will be a higher level of knowledge or more boredom, truancy, and discipline problems.

Another point refers to what is meant by "transmission of cultural values." This seems to be a touchy issue when one thinks about the different ethnic groups living in Norway today. Whose cultural values are these? As indicated previously in this paper, cultural values seem to play an important role in the life of organizations today. If the school organizations are to be run on the basis of Norwegian cultural values, one should not be surprised if different ethnic groups will react strongly to having their children spend more time in the public schools. If one observes the changes taking place in Norway as well as in other Nordic countries such as Sweden, for example, which is allowing market forces to determine the choice of public schools, one cannot but expect that market forces will also play an important role in Norwegian schools in the future, be the schools private or public.

REFERENCES

Adler, N.J. 1991. *International Dimensions of Organizational Behavior.* Boston, Massachusetts: PWS-KENT.

Andresen, H., and S. Østerud. 1982. "Studies on the Democratization of Education—Scholastic Success as Compared to the Pupil's Social Background." University of Oslo.

Bleness, C. 1994. "Frykt for muslimene" (Fear of Muslims). *Aftenposten (Oslo),* 5 August, weekend edition.

Dokka, H.J. 1986. *Reformarbeid i Norsk Skole* (Reform in Norwegian Schools). Oslo: NKS-Forlaget.

Heywood, A. 1994. *Political Ideas and Concepts: An Introduction.* London: The Macmillan Press Ltd.

Hofstede, G. 1991. *Cultures and Organizations: Software of the Mind.* London: HarperCollins Publishing.

Lauvdal, T. 1994. Pedagogikk, politikk og byråkrati (Education, Politics, and Bureaucracy). Doctoral thesis. Trondheim: University of Trondheim.

Magnus, G. 1994. "Nei til muslimsk skole" (No to Muslim Schools). *Aftenposten (Oslo),* 21 June, morning edition.

Muri, B. 1995. "Nytt nei fra byrådet til muslimsk skole" (Another "No" from the City Government to Muslim Schools). *Aftenposten (Oslo),* 13 September, morning edition.

Norman, V.D. 1994. "Privatiser Universitetenateat" (Privatise the Universities). *Dagens Næringsliv (Oslo)*, 3 September.

Sandmo, O.A. 1995. "I Sosialmatriarkatets Støpeform" (In the Mold of the Social Matriarchy). *Aftenposten (Oslo)*, 31 May, morning edition.

Sennerud, E. 1995. "A Comparative Study Between the Educational Systems of Norway and England." University of Oslo.

Simenstad, B. 1994. "Nei til muslimsk folkehøyskole" (No to a Muslim College). *Aftenposten (Oslo)*, 11 July, morning edition.

Telhaug, A.O. 1992. *Norsk og Internasjonal Skoleutvikling* (Norwegian and International School Development). Oslo: Ad Notam Gyldendal A/S.

Tjeldvoll, A. 1992. "Enhetsskoletanken Exit!" (The Exit of Comprehensiyve School Ideas). *Mercator*, November, Oslo.

Tjeldvoll, A. 1996. "Quality of Equality? Scandinavian Education Towards the Year 2000, Past and Future." In *Handbook of Development of Education, Past and Future*, eds. W. Cummings and N. McGinn. Buffalo: State University of New York (SUNY).

Zuboff, S. 1988. *In the Age of the Smart Machine: The Future of Work and Power*. USA: Basic Books.

CHAPTER 13

The Foes of Icelandic Vocational Education at the Upper Secondary Level
Jon Torfi Jónasson

INTRODUCTION

The main thesis argued in this chapter is that vocational education at the secondary level in Iceland is not a viable option in spite of a consensus among government agencies, many educational establishments, and representatives of various bodies in the labor market that it should be encouraged. Vocational education simply has too many serious organizational enemies that are hard to control. There has been and continues to be a strong emphasis on vocational educational programs in both developed and developing countries (see, e.g., Lauglo and Lillis 1988; Psacharopoulos and Loxley 1985; Ryan 1991). But a strange paradox is emerging. On one hand there seem to be compelling social, economic, educational, and political arguments (e.g., summarized by Grubb 1985, p. 527), for a very strong vocational educational component within an education system, some of which can be classified as common sense and some as theoretical. On the other hand there seems to be a disappointing dearth of evidence in support of these arguments in spite of serious searches. The economic arguments may be the most compelling, but it is difficult to disagree with an energetic analyst of the issue that "nearly every valuation of the performance of vocational education to meet the [needs of a modernizing economy] whether in developing or industrialized countries, has been negative" (Psacharopoulos 1987, p. 201). It is doubtful that this lack of empirical support for vocational programs will deter those who believe in their value and most likely "because of its inherently logical and simplistic appeal, vocationalism will be with us for years to come, and more countries will attempt, in vain, to tune their formal educational system to the world of work" (Psacharopoulos 1987, p. 203). This view is echoed by King (1988, p. 291) who maintains that the "vocational school paradigm may be dead in the view of many academics and researchers, but in the world of politics it still seems to have a good deal of life in it. . . ." In the present chapter a similar conclusion will be reached but for different reasons, thus attempting to add another dimension to the debate. The principal thesis is that even though various negative evaluations are ignored, vocational education has very little chance of surviving, nearly for various compelling organizational reasons; the forces at play nearly all work against vocational education, at least within the upper secondary school system. The evidence is collected within the Icelandic system, but many of the arguments will presumably transfer to a number of other economies, labor markets, or educational systems.

There has been "rivalry" between vocational and academic (liberal, general) education in Iceland most of this century, and we have witnessed a gradual takeover of academic education at the secondary level (see, e.g., Jónasson 1996a). This is contrary to expressed government policy during at least the latter half of this century which has put strong emphasis on vocational education at the secondary level (see, e.g., Gudmundsson 1993; Óskarsdóttir 1995). The main thrust of the present chapter is to show that these trends are influenced by strong external factors, some of which are impossible or very difficult to control. These are the enemies of vocational education, even though it might be conceded that some of the developments we have witnessed may in the long run be beneficial to society in general and the world of work, in particular (see, e.g., Psacharopoulos 1986 p. 562; Foster 1965). It will also be inferred that any counter measures by government will in the future only turn out to be short-term stalling maneuvers.

BACKGROUND

The compulsory part of the Icelandic school system covers ten years, extending from age six to sixteen. The secondary school system, which then takes over, can be divided into a number of categories.

1. Four years of academic programs, which conclude with "Studentspróf."[1]
2. Vocational programs, most of which conclude with a trade license and typically take four years, even though some programs vary in length.
3. Shorter vocational programs, some of which conclude with a license.
4. Shorter pseudo-vocational programs, which mainly feed into the four-year academic programs. These are normally within the comprehensive schools and are perhaps most akin to what is sometimes described as diversified curricula (see, e.g., Psacharopoulos and Loxley 1985).
5. Programs at the upper secondary level, which require some previous secondary preparation for entrance.

Categories 2-5 cover the vocational spectrum that is being considered in this chapter.

The Development of the Secondary System

The relative share of vocational education at the secondary stage has apparently diminished steadily but very gradually through the best part of this century, declining from around 50 percent of the secondary school population around the turn of the century to about 25 percent today (Jónasson, 1996b, Figure 1). However, the evidence for this may be disputed as the classification of many of the programs offered is difficult, especially within the present-day comprehensive system. There are two parts of the secondary school system that are often taken as representative of their respective classes of education. The first is education for the licensed trades, and the second is the second is university entrance examination (UEE). The former is a substantial part of vocational education at the secondary level and the latter the bastion of general education. Figure 1 shows how these two strands of education have grown over the last forty years, with a clear divergence evident from the early 1980s onwards.

**Proportions of 20-year cohort obtaining a trade license and taking
university entrance exams**

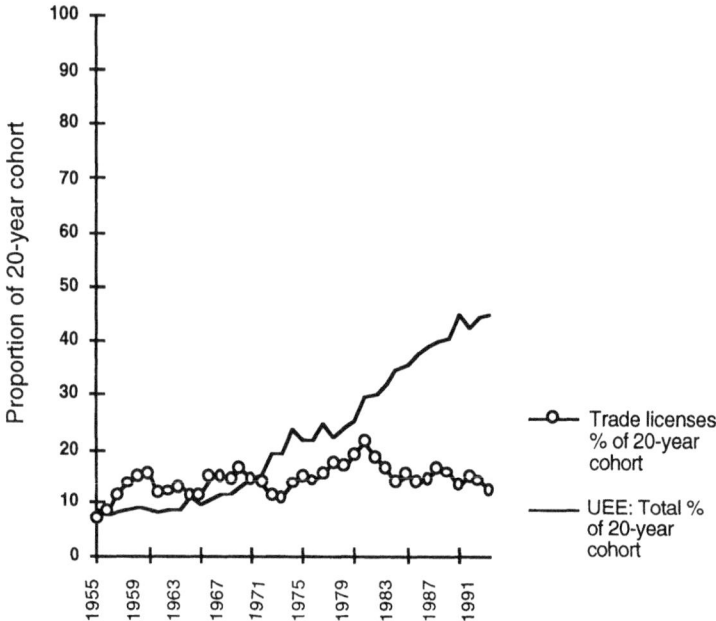

Figure 1. The proportion of the 20-year cohort obtaining a trade license (lower
curve) and university entrance examination, UEE (upper curve). Available
numbers for the trade licensees prior to 1955 may be unreliable and are
therefore not shown.

Government Attempts to Stem the Flow of Students into the Academic Tracks

It may be maintained that for the second half of the century there has
been a fairly continuous rhetorical effort made by the Icelandic
government to encourage vocational studies in the secondary sector and
in particular to stem the relative upsurge of students in the academic
tracks. The policy has had varied emphasis and has ranged from very
direct calls for the strengthening of vocational programs to a more
general vocational emphasis which is more akin to calls for
diversification within the secondary schools (see, e.g., Psacharopoulos

and Loxley 1985). In an attempt to reorganize the school system in 1946, a two-track set-up was proposed within the last part of the compulsory system, where one track was meant to be with vocational emphasis and the other of a more academic nature (Jónasson 1995). It was, however, up to the municipalities to decide whether to adopt this system, and many did not. Thus this attempt to underpin the vocational system at the secondary level did not succeed. Since then, the government has taken a substantial practical initiative—in 1955, by taking over the responsibility for, and financing of, the vocational trade schools, and in 1966, by allowing as an option that some of the previous apprenticeship training would be transferred into the schools. These two steps probably ensured the continued relative growth within the licensed trades by taking the training burden off the trades themselves. The third initiative was the establishment of the comprehensive system at the secondary level in the 1970s. The effect of these various steps has not been systematically studied, but a cursory inspection indicates that it has not been effective in enhancing or renewing vocational education in the long run, even though probably in all cases some signs of the desired influence can be detected.

In the past decade the rhetorical emphasis the government has put on vocational education has been especially consistent and strong. Several reports supporting vocational education in general have been published, and proposals, if somewhat diffuse, to enhance the share of vocational education at the secondary level have been put forward. Unfortunately the general criticism made by Psacharopoulos (1989) with reference to educational policies in several Third World countries probably applies here. This was that realistic financial implications had not been worked out and firm policies were not implemented. There have also been attempts made by several individual schools to strengthen and diversify their vocational programs. It is however very difficult to detect any substantial effect of this.[2]

THE FOES OF VOCATIONAL EDUCATION

In the following sections a number of the forces that contribute to the stagnation or even the relative demise of vocational education at the secondary level will be discussed and attempts made to produce the relevant evidence.

It is appropriate, however, to start with a brief description of what is meant by the term vocational education, even though definitional issues are taken to be among the foes of vocational education at the secondary level, and, therefore, this issue will also be discussed under a separate heading. In short, vocational education is taken to be any educational track or program which has as its primary aim to prepare a person for a particular field of employment. Preparation for further study or general educational aims is thus taken to be of secondary importance, even though these may be present in a vocational program. Apart from this very vague definition, there exists no consensus on a definition of vocational education. The spectrum of vocational programs covers both workplace-based and school-based programs, and these categories encompass a wide variety of programs (Lauglo 1983; Psacharopoulos and Loxley 1985, Figure 2.1).

The principal factors that may hinder the build-up of vocational education, in particular at the secondary level, are classified into the following groups which will be discussed in turn:

1. The labor market (industry, the world of work)
2. The education system
3. Financial constraints
4. Problems of definition
5. A changing society
6. The differential status of vocational and liberal education

THE LABOR MARKET IS INIMICAL TO VOCATIONAL EDUCATION

The labor market is the major enemy of vocational education. This may seem particularly strange as it is often thought that the various forces and bodies representing this sector are most appreciative of vocational education. They seem to put the strongest emphasis on its development within the education system and most emphatically claim that education should be much concerned with preparing the adolescent population for working life. If this is a somewhat self-serving attitude, it is, however, normally considered perfectly reasonable, understandable, and healthy.

But if one looks behind the scenes, a very different impression is gradually formed. The labor market ceases to be seen as the affectionate guardian of vocational education. In many respects, it turns out to be its enemy. This claim will be discussed and defended in the following sections by explaining and demonstrating the negative effect of the needs analysis movement and by demonstrating the lack of encouragement for vocational education given by the labor market as measured both by wage differentials and specific demands for vocational opportunities. It will also be done by demonstrating that the Icelandic labor market is composed of small firms, which makes it unable to tackle in-service training even for its own employees. Finally, it will be indicated that the economy dramatically influences the licensed trade vocational education, which is the strongest component of vocational education.

The Needs of the Labor Market

Many phrases in the educational discourse seem to be practically devoid of meaning or used as ill-advised slogans. The phrase "needs of industry" is in that category, probably near the top of the list. It is certainly widely used, and it is even claimed that it is of paramount importance that education cater to the "needs" of the economy, industry, labor market, or whatever. It is argued in Jónasson (1992a) that this phrase is ill conceived, and it almost certainly has a negative effect on the development of vocational education. It may be one of its most damaging but at the same time one of its most elusive enemies. Perceived needs of an industry or an employer are determined by what the known options are, by tradition, by the status quo, and by short-term problems or interests. This may have very little to do with the firm's, the sector's, or the industry's long-term interests. If these needs are influenced by a firm's short-term financial problems, ignorance about the available spectrum of competencies or developments in the field, unwillingness to diverge from outdated traditions, or simply the belief that changes are unnecessary, it might be surmised that the asserted needs may be an assortment of demands which only by chance coincide with the long-term interests of that particular sector of industry that the education was designed to serve.[3] If some kind of need analysis is used to determine the guidelines set for education, these factors would probably be overriding and incidentally undermine arguments based on vision, innovation, and dynamics. In what follows some indications of the interests, or in many instances the lack of interest, of the labor market will provide some underpinnings of these claims.

Lack of Encouragement

Despite rhetorical involvement, the labor market, or the world of work more generally has not been very supportive of the development of vocational education within the education system. Encouragement at the practical level has been distinctly lacking. Three lines of evidence, to support this rather harsh judgment will be presented.

Mixed Demands for Substantial Additional Vocational Opportunities

It may be argued that practically all vocational and professional education in Iceland that was built up in the nineteenth and the first part of the twentieth centuries originated from within the working population.[4] But as the state gradually takes over educational planning and finances, the initiative or encouragement given to the educational field from the various sectors of the labor market turns out to be marginal and seems to lack ambition, clarity, and force. To demonstrate this, three very important sectors of the Icelandic economy will be briefly discussed: the fishing industry, the tourist industry, and the "new" trade and services sector.

The fishing industry is by far the strongest sector in the Icelandic economy and has been the dominant provider of external revenue, above 90 percent for most of the century but has slipped down to around 75 percent (*Landshagir 1995*, Table 10.9). It is also the source of around 15 percent of the gross national income (*Landshagir 1995*, Table 14.5). In spite of this enormous strength, formal education for the fisheries workers has always been weak in relative terms, notably in the latter half of the century.

There are four schools exclusively concerned with education of specialized workers concerned with fishing or fish processing, and recently some comprehensive schools have offered various courses related to these fields. In the past decade or so, 4-5 percent of the secondary school population has registered in those courses.[5] The bulk of these students have been concerned with the mechanics of fishing (skippers and mechanics in the fishing and the commercial fleets) and only a minority with the mechanics of fish processing. Furthermore, a series of short courses has been organized by the fishing industry and the ministry of fisheries for in-service training, which make a very important contribution to the education of the work force on the factory floor. But compared to the importance of the sector, the effort put into educating the participants is minimal, certainly, in relative terms. There have been no emphatic demands by the fishing industry for the establishment of strong vocational schools or specialized courses covering various special fields within the industry to remedy this imbalance in the educational system.[6] In a recent collection of in-depth analysis of the "needs for education within the fishing industry," submitted by four "representatives" from within the fishing industry, they agreed that they were more or less satisfied with matters as they stood (*Fjörf fyrir menntun í sjávarútvegi* 1992). The conclusion expressed in the summary is "that the education of the industry's workforce satisfies its demands and that the industry has been alert and been responsive to changing demands" (p. 23). But the criteria used as a basis for this judgment are nonexistent or at best obscure. That document alone should suffice as a basis on which to seriously query the whole needs analysis approach.

Tourism has become a major industry in Iceland in the past ten years, contributing about 11 percent of exported goods and services and approaching 4 percent of GDP (Atvinnuvegaskrsla 1993, Table 5.8.1). There have, however, been no clear demands from this industry that education should be a substantial part of the infrastructure that needs to be built to foster the development of this sector. In several reports published in recent years on this issue, education is almost entirely absent from the discussion. The sector is either indifferent to education or satisfied with the status quo.

In most western countries a huge sector has grown that is often defined by the uninformative word "information." This is a fairly heterogeneous field, however, with some common features which seem to involve dealing with verbal or numerical information, quite often relying on computers (see, e.g., Williams and Yeomans 1994). Now it might be suggested that the traditional liberal education offered by the general education system stands beside the vocational ideal for this field and that explains why there have been no strong petitions for the enhancement of education within this domain on behalf of any representatives of the labor market. No concerted pressure has been put on the government to establish vocational schools in this field or to establish options within the existing schools. The practical initiative that has been taken probably stems largely from within the education establishment. To conclude, a cursory inspection of the formal indications, requests, or demands from three very important sectors of the economy demonstrates a lack of encouragement for serious vocational effort within the educational system. This state of affairs is both noteworthy and disappointing. In view of this evidence a list of positive examples would not suffice to counter the conclusion reached here.

Low Wages for Some Vocational Qualifications

The income of different educational groups may be the most important indicator of the value the labor market places on education. In a situation of full employment and perhaps often scarcity of labor the income distribution may be volatile and hence it may be difficult to obtain a clear picture. But at the same time, the market may be less constrained by formal agreements, notably salary contracts, and hence a more valid measure of how highly the market values education is obtained, than it otherwise would be, if unemployment had reigned for a considerable period.

A reliable income indicator is hard to find, mainly because of considerable overtime put in by a large proportion of the work force, which results in a significant departure from the basic rates in many sectors. Official wage tables are untrustworthy, and in fact no method exists for getting the "true" picture of how much people earn. One way of approaching the issue is to use surveys in which the respondents are asked about their basic earnings, their overall earnings, their basic working time, and their overall working time in addition to various background factors (Ólafsson 1993).[7] In order to get a realistic estimate of the earning differentials between various educational groups, two measures were used (Jónasson 1996c). One is the total monthly income and the other is the average hourly income.[8] Several inferences can be drawn from the data. First, that university education seems to be a very good bet, both when considering the total monthly income and the hourly return. Thus, it seems sensible from the financial standpoint to obtain a university education if it is at all possible. A careful cost-benefit analysis may, however, give a less favorable picture (Sigurjónsson 1988). Obtaining a UEE also seems to be a reasonably sensible option based on the "hourly return" indicator. Thus the academic track at secondary school, even as a waiting option, is a sensible choice. Second, a trade license seems to favor its holder with comparatively good total income even though it seems to cost him a fair number of working hours. The average hourly rate is not much higher than for those with commercial vocational training or the UEEs. The third inference of interest here is that several vocational courses are the equivalent of no vocational training at all. This holds true whether we consider the total income or the average hourly return. Thus there has been little incentive for young people to obtain vocational certificates, except when these are formal licenses, giving job monopoly. The implications of the above for the secondary student, if he has any inkling of this pattern, are clear. The academic track not only gives the broadest educational base and opens up the most avenues for eventual further study, but it also pays relatively well, at least on average, and thus seems to be a most sensible choice. Miscellaneous vocational education at the secondary level, on the other hand, does not make much financial sense, and it is difficult to see why it should be chosen. On the whole, academic education is still a good bet in terms of average long-term income, though this does not take into account the invested cost. Here we are not investigating the rationality of educational choice or the fairness of the labor market but only the signals the market gives. To what extent these signals are actually noted and then used or interpreted by the young is as yet not known. It is important to note that the state of affairs for the youngest age group gives a somewhat different impression from the older age groups. The trend there fits with the evidence presented by Óskarsdóttir (1995, p. 202), which shows that UEE does not result in higher initial salaries than dropouts obtain. But this pattern changes with the older age groups.

Little Concern for Education in the Hiring Process

Óskarsdóttir (1995) investigated the criteria used for hiring people who are starting their careers in three occupational areas—office work, service jobs, and production work—where trade licenses or tertiary degrees were not required. She concluded that formal education played a very minor role (p. 291) and also that those responsible for the hiring were not particularly well informed about the education system to put it mildly (pp. 321-324). This corresponds with Oxenham (1988) who concludes "that employers do not know what they want in the way of education, but simply take what is offered at prices they can afford" (p. 74). The general conclusion of this research is that the labor market is disturbingly indifferent to education and certainly does not give any special encouragement to vocational education.

What the Labor Market Needs

It has been claimed above that needs analysis is an inappropriate metaphor for determining the relationship between the world of work and the field of education. It was argued that some important sectors of industry seemed indifferent to the educational options available related to the sector, that the salary pattern in the labor market did not favor vocational education at secondary level in general and little emphasis is placed on education in the hiring process. This is in line with previous literature that shows little or very limited evidence for the relevance of vocational education (see above and, e.g., Wilms 1988, pp. 88-89).

The important question that remains is whether the labor market is justified in its basic attitude that is reflected in the indifference with which it treats vocational education or whether the market could simply be drastically wrong, not appreciating the direct and indirect benefits of vocational education? Is the labor market to blame for the apparent low interest shown in vocational education, or is vocational education itself to blame? Probably both.

The traditional view seems axiomatically to assume that the market is right and, in fact, knows what it is doing: "In competitive economies or private sector employment it is reasonable to assume that the earnings of graduates are a good proxy for their productivity" (Psacharopoulos 1987, p. 190). This fundamental premise needs, however, to be defended on empirical grounds, which is normally not done. Even though it may be possible on a macro level, it is doubtful that it can be done on a micro level (see, e.g., Bishop 1990). It is also doubtful that, except in very few industries, the employer has available the criteria, the monitoring devices, and the evaluation mechanisms to estimate objectively the productivity of each and every employee. Furthermore, if this is so, it is very unlikely that any effects of vocational education could be objectively discerned except perhaps with a very elaborate testing mechanism, which very few employers could afford, and sample sizes that are simply not present within individual enterprises. And even though this could be done to some extent, it is likely that other factors such as experience and perceived personal qualities would be considered far more important, the former in the short run and the latter in the long run, and hence be overriding factors when personnel is hired and rewarded. There are thus several *a priori* reasons to doubt both Psacharopoulos's premise and whether vocational education, or education *in toto* for that matter, has been positively valued within the labor market except, of course, when this is done by government regulations or labor agreements. But it must also be said, that even though there is a positive role played by the labor market at the rhetorical level, what counts is what happens at the practical level.[9]

But despite the verdict that the labor market is probably unable to appreciate good vocational education, it may also be the case that vocational education, on the whole, is not worth very much. Studies that explicitly relate increases in productivity to "traditional" vocational programs are hard to find, and there are reasons why a lot of vocational programs might be mistrusted. The main points of this chapter are, however, that the needs analysis paradigm is probably unduly conservative and, therefore, has a stifling effect on vocational education and that the labor market, justly or unjustly, gives little encouragement to the development of vocational education and gives very faint, if any, encouragement to young people to choose vocational programs.

The Effect of Small Enterprises

Vocational training does not, of course, have to be school based, and there is not only a strong tradition for apprenticeship training for many occupations but both pedagogical and economic arguments can be made for the advantage of on-the-job training. But this type of training is often very costly and in an apprenticeship system depends largely on the trainees' allowances. In the German dual system, which is often looked upon as a model for apprenticeship training, all the in-company training is borne by the companies themselves. It is estimated that this is about 60 percent of the total training cost, and the net cost per trainee borne by a company in 1980 was estimated around $1,400 per annum (Noah and Eckstein 1988, p. 61). The allowance paid by the German companies to the apprentices seems to be relatively low.[10] More generally the investment in training seems to be heavily dependent upon the size of firms. In France, firms with 10-19 employees spend 1.1 percent of their payroll on training, while firms with at least 200 employees spend some 4 percent (Drake 1991, pp. 224-225; see also Salomé and Charmes 1988, p. 64). Thus, it seems that only large establishments within a labor market can be counted on to take responsibility for vocational training. Nearly 60 percent of the labor force in Iceland are employed by establishments whose average size is near 15 or less full-time employees and 80 percent by establishments whose average size is around 50 full-time employees (based on Table 4.1 in Atvinnuvegaskrsla 1993). It is difficult to envisage small establishments having the financial strength to set up any type of independent continuing education infrastructure or having the capacity to invest in the training of a labile workforce. It needs to be established in the general debate about self-sufficiency in staff training and development or the role played by the labor market in an apprenticeship-type educational system to what extent the capacity of the market is dependent on the size of the financial unit concerned and thus the degree to which demands on a market such as the Icelandic labor market in these matters can be justified.

The conclusion reached here is that the structure of the Icelandic labor market does not seem to favor company-based vocational training when considered from this point of view. It is unreasonable to expect a market thus composed to carry a big share of the country's vocational system—even with some government support. In this sense the world of work is hostile to some forms of vocational training, even though it is of a purely structural origin and would not be directly detected.

The Influence of the Economy (and the Labor Market)

It may be assumed that the expansion of secondary education has been related to the strengthening of the economy. Figure 2 shows that the growth of the most prominent strands of the secondary system, when combined, has considerable affinity with the growth of the economy. This holds true in spite of the fairly dramatic divergence of these two major tracks in the 1980s (see Figure 1). Other certificates are not included here but would probably not alter the picture substantially. Even though the relationship seems surprisingly simple and strong, a causal link is not immediately obvious. It may, of course, just be the case that two very important features of a complex society both grow at a similar rate. The rise in the educational level of the workforce may also gradually contribute to the strengthening economy but with a lag of decades rather than years. Not only is this difficult to detect but a cursory analysis of the Icelandic economy suggests other more potent explanatory factors of increased GNP than education. The reverse relationship is more likely, i.e., that the developing economy allowed the increased educational spending required by an expanding education system or that the state of the economy in some way controlled the output of the secondary schools (as shown in Figure 2).

Growth of the economy and of the two major secondary sectors

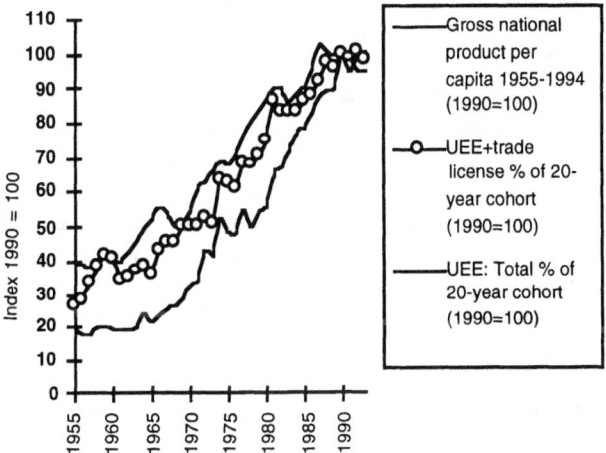

Figure 2. The growth of the economy (gross national product per capita) and of the two major secondary sector tracks—the university entrance examination and the trade license tracks—measured by the number of graduates. The measures are set at 100 in 1990. The bottom line shows the UEE on its own.

Apart from the general positive relationship between these measures, it is of interest to attempt to discern what direct influence, if any, the state of the economy has had on educational choices. This might perhaps be inferred by investigating the relationship between the fluctuations in the economy and those in the secondary school system. The most reliable and best-categorized data in the secondary sphere are the number of graduates shown in Figures 1 and 2.[11] The most parsimonious explanation of this close relationship is that economic expansion "allowed" an expanding educational system. Furthermore, an optimistic atmosphere in a reviving economy may encourage young people to seek further education, and their parents might then have the means to support them.

When apprenticeship is part of vocational education, the employer normally takes on considerable responsibilities when he takes on an apprentice. He has to pay him a salary that is 40-50 percent (75-95 percent for those who finish the school-based programs first) of that paid to qualified personnel, and he has to ensure training for the total training period. It might, therefore, be expected that the availability of openings for apprentices was dependent on the state of the economy, which normally determines the state of at least the larger industries. Thus the state of the economy may be thought to determine directly or indirectly the number of trainees in a particular vocational discipline. This has been clearly established by Jónasson (1996b). There, it was shown that there was no relationship between the fluctuations in the economy and the academic UEE, but a clear correlation between the economic fluctuations and the trade licensees, with the expected lags as tested by cross-correlation. The results of these tests are very clear. The output of the trade licensed vocational education is very sensitive to even minor fluctuations in the economy. The available evidence suggests that the controlling factors are in the labor market rather than in the student population (e.g., the interest shown by students in vocational training).

The Labor Market and Vocational Education: Summary and General Discussion

We have asserted that so-called needs analysis may not serve vocational education well. This is especially true in the instances in which there is no tradition for such education and new initiatives in the field are simply not seen as relevant. It was argued that some large sectors of industry are certainly not craving for more vocationally prepared manpower. The extent to which vocational education is rewarded is rather limited and confined to the licensed trades. The evidence suggests that little value is attached to education in the hiring process for large sections of labor market. Furthermore, it is suggested that the institutional structure of the labor market does not allow it to take care of vocational training, and the available evidence indicates that vocational education "on the job" is sensitive to year-to-year fluctuations in the economy. When this empirical inspection of some crucial aspects of the world of work is taken together, the general conclusion seems amply justified that this sector of society turns out to be inimical to vocational education despite its apparently genuine positive attitude at the rhetorical level.

The Labor Market as an Enemy of Vocational Education: Second Thoughts

Two important qualifications should be made when arguing that the labor market might be viewed as inimical to vocational education. The first is to remind the reader that the focus of the discussion is vocational education at the secondary level, even though some of the arguments may apply to vocational or professional education at the tertiary level as well. The second and more important point is that it has not been indicated that the labor market has intentionally been opposing the general build-up of vocational education at the secondary level. However, its functioning in general seems to have rather serious negative effects on any such development, and its indifference at the formal level has implicit negative effects. In a field where both implicit and explicit encouragement is sorely needed and expected, little is forthcoming. In this sense, one can call the labor market the enemy of vocational education at the secondary level no matter whether its indifference is justifiable or not.

THE EDUCATION SYSTEM UNDERMINES VOCATIONAL EDUCATION

There are a number of features in the development of the Icelandic school system that have been inimical to the strengthening of vocational education at the secondary level. Most of these are to be found within the secondary level, but it will also be argued that the development of the tertiary system has weakened the status of vocational tracks at the secondary level.

The Development of the Secondary School System

There has been a noticeable trend towards uniformity in the secondary system. There are a number of indications of this and a number of explanatory factors. Invariably this trend is towards the general education tracks and thus the vocational sections of the secondary system are gradually undermined, at least in relative terms. This is sometimes called the academic drift (see, e.g., discussion in Jónasson 1995; Raffe 1994, p. 151; Squires 1989, chapter 4). The relative weakening of the vocational sector was indicated already in Figure 2. In an extensive study of the cohort born in 1969 (Jónasson and Jónsdóttir 1992), it was found that over 80 percent of those entering secondary school enrolled in courses that have to be classified as general or academic (see Table 1, based on Jónasson 1994, Table 1).

Table 1. First registration in secondary school. Students born in 1969.

Traditional vocational education	15 %
Other vocational education	3 %
University entrance programs	82 %
Total	100 %

It was also found that of those who had obtained a degree or a formal certificate the year they reached the age of 22, only about 25 percent had obtained a vocational degree of some sort, with 11 percent occurring within the licensed trades, which is the sturdiest part of our vocational system (Jónasson and Jónsdóttir 1992, Table 4.1). The comparable figures based on the whole cohort are 11 percent and 5 percent respectively. It is, however, well known that the average age of those obtaining a trade license is above 25 years for many trades. At any rate vocational education within the secondary system is definitely not popular and has consistently become less so (see Figure 2). Some of the reasons for this decline of traditional vocational education within the secondary system may be found within the education system itself. Here we will consider some of the causes.

Uncertainty About the Role of the Secondary System

It has been interesting to follow the gradual change in the aims of the spectrum of secondary schools. During the first half of the century, one might be tempted to divide the secondary schools into two categories.

In the first category were schools with fairly well-defined principal aims. They were either concerned with preparation for university education (the UEE programs at the gymnasia) or some specific vocation (within specialized vocational schools). These specialized schools of either type were the dominant secondary schools during the third quarter of the century. The second category includes primarily schools at the middle secondary level with fairly general objectives: *gagnfræaskólar*, which are akin to *realschools* and *alfluskólar*, *hérasskólar*, which are related to the *folkehöjskole*. In the third quarter these were largely absorbed by the compulsory system. But in the 1980s the secondary system became dominated by the comprehensive system, and in 1988 a confirmation of the general character of the secondary system was passed by the Icelandic parliament. The law covers the whole of the secondary sector and contains a paragraph outlining a common objective for all schools. The new law allowed for the continuation of the dual system of gymnasia and vocational schools, but an important feature of the law was to confirm the existence of a large number of comprehensive schools that had been established in the previous decade. The new unitary objective of the secondary stage was threefold—to prepare students for participation in a democratic society by providing conditions for learning and development for all students, to prepare students for (qualifications in) different vocations, and to prepare students for tertiary education (the UEE).[12]

I have previously argued (Jónasson 1992b) that this apparently very sensible threefold purpose presents some problems for a system in transition. It is noteworthy that it has never been clear whether all schools should be obligated to cater to all the objectives for all students, or if they could select some of them and offer different selections to different students. The main point is that all schools within the system have the ability to shift emphasis, even from one principal aim to another. If this happens within a comprehensive school, which was originally established by merging vocational and general educational tracks, it might go unnoticed if only the loose legal criteria were applied. Such a shift would be squarely within the framework set by the law. Furthermore, a shift in the organization of vocational tracks in order to open channels into other tracks, notably the university preparatory programs, would not only be easy to defend on pragmatic grounds, they would fit very well within the web of the three different aims of the secondary system. Thus the system has formally become much more complex and diffuse. It must be more difficult to plan and direct an organization that has three grand (and presumably equally important) aims rather than essentially one. Apart from the general administrative problem this presents, it is suggested that it contributes to the undermining of the vocational emphasis in the vocational tracks. Having said this, it must be conceded that the present state of affairs has allowed a development of the system that may in some sense be "natural" (Jónasson 1996a) and, therefore, positive.

Mobility Between Different Tracks

One aim of the comprehensive system is to facilitate the flow between vocational and academic tracks. The implicit assumption was that a number of students who would not find the academic programs to their liking would transfer to the vocational programs. An investigation into the number of such transitions and their characteristics (Jónasson 1994) showed that only 17 percent of the students have transferred from one type of program to another, and of those more than half did so after a year or less of study. It is of particular interest to note that the group that turned out to be most mobile consisted of those who started their secondary education in the vocational tracks in the comprehensive schools; one third of them moved to the academic programs.[13] More importantly, there was a clear and significant positive correlation between the probability of transfer from the vocational track and academic performance at the end of compulsory school. Thus the drift of academically able students from the vocational tracks continues well into the secondary schools.

But there is an additional reason why the principle of transfer between tracks turns out to be inimical to vocational education. By insisting on good opportunities for transfer, education policy implicitly sets serious constraints on the planning of individual programs. Thus there is pressure to have initial courses be fairly standard (i.e., general) and to postpone the vocational courses towards the end.[14] This is in spite of some serious pedagogical reasons for starting vocational training with substantial practical experience and placing the more academic courses towards the end of the program. Thus organizational pressure on the structure of the syllabus undermines the pedagogical integrity of the vocational courses. The modular set-up that dominates the Icelandic secondary system allows considerable flexibility in the organization of the curriculum and thus makes it perhaps vulnerable to external pressure. In this sense the modular system can be said to facilitate the academic drift and reduce the vocational/academic divide (Raffe 1994).

Numerus Clausus (Explicit or Implicit)

In a number of vocational programs, there is explicit *numerus clausus*, and in some additional programs the *clausus* is only implicit.[15] The formal evidence relating to this question is scarce, but an indication of the general long-term effect may be obtained from the admission figures to the Icelandic College for Pre-school Teachers, which has operated a *numerus clausus* for a considerable time, and the number of applicants has frequently been far in excess of the number being accepted. The formal minimum requirement is two years of secondary schooling, but Figure 3 shows that the proportion of successful applicants who have finished the four-year university preparatory program has risen steadily in past decades. The chance for others of obtaining a place thus diminishes steadily. Thus even though the program is formally at the secondary stage, it is clearly moving up and out of it in practical terms.

Even though comparable data are not available for other vocations, a similar trend is discernible and thus it is debatable how the various vocations should be counted at the secondary level. The data show that nearly 50 percent of students in the first year (the basic year) in two of the largest vocational categories within the licensed trades are eighteen years of age or older, and 25 percent are twenty years or older.[16] The average age of those who finish these programs is between twenty-five and twenty-six years.[17] Thus the vocational part of the secondary school system seems to have moved out of the secondary arena, and it does not seem to be fair either to students who may be interested in these vocations or to the curriculum planning within these vocations to pretend that these are courses primarily designed for and taken by students who have just left the general compulsory curriculum.

Access to pre-school teacher training

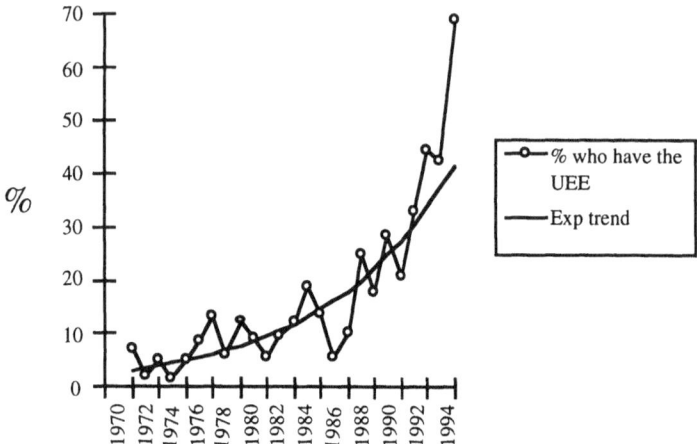

Figure 3. The proportion of those accepted to the three-year course at the School for Pre-school Teachers who have already obtained the university entrance certificate. The figure also shows the best exponential fit based on the years 1970-1994.

The Development of the Tertiary Level (University Level)

It is conceivable that the single most important factor influencing the development of the secondary system is the development of the next level—the tertiary system. In this case it is, however, singularly difficult to determine which comes first, the academic drift within the secondary system or the expansion of the tertiary system, largely dominated by the University of Iceland. This development is dealt with in some detail in Jónasson (1995), but two principal points will be made here. The first is that direct or indirect pressure on applicants to various degree courses to have passed the UEE when applying is steadily increasing within the education system. This can be seen by the steady and considerable rise in the number of institutions requiring this certificate or more importantly in the increase in the number of different courses offered at "university" level (Jónasson 1995, Figure 6). There are several indications that this trend will continue, i.e., the number of degree courses available at university level will continue to grow in the near future. This is reflected in the second point being made in this connection which relates to the number of students registering at university level, which, until recently, has been dominated by the University of Iceland. Figure 4 shows how this number has grown steadily during the whole of this century, and there are various reasons, e.g., increased competition for jobs or status, why this steady growth will probably continue. This will, in turn, maintain the pressure on students to pass the UEE and thus support the general or academic trend within the secondary system.

Students at the university level in Iceland

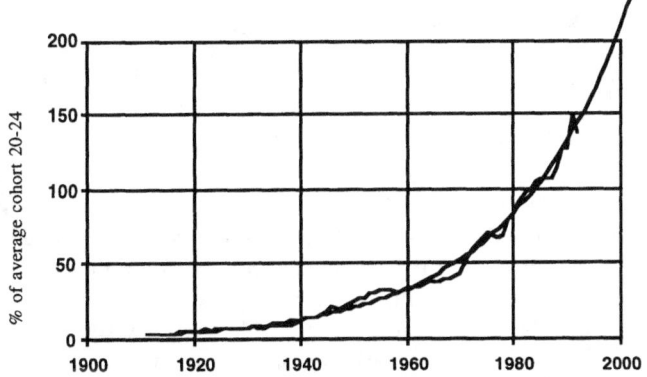

————All Icelandic students (combined Un+Stat.B) as % of cohort.
———— Exponential linear trend Ln. All Icelandic students (combined Un+Stat.B) as % of cohort.

Figure 4. The number of students at the university level in Iceland expressed as a proportion (percent) of the average cohort size 20-24. The exponential best fit is also shown extending to the turn of the next century.

Summary and Discussion of the Trends in the Education System

Thus there are several features in the character of the education system that together tend to undermine the status or relevance of the more traditional vocational tracks at the secondary level. The uncertain role of the system, the "lifting" of some of the major secondary vocational tracks out of the secondary system, and the development of the tertiary system, all push in the same direction, undermining a previously strong vocational bastion at the secondary level. Attempts may however be made to establish some vocational tracks partly in some "new" fields, partly perhaps of a remedial nature, but there are neither signs nor reasons why these can have the status the existing stronger vocational tracks have hitherto enjoyed within the secondary system. The pressure to establish new tracks will probably come largely from within the education system and from central authorities in order to solve administrative or general social problems and not from the labor market, which may, however, be coerced, or co-opted, to support these initiatives.

ACADEMIC TRACKS ARE INEXPENSIVE

In a world of scarce financial resources, the differential cost of competing programs may be a crucial factor. It is argued below that the relative high cost of vocational programs is certainly to their disadvantage. The common wisdom is that vocational education or training is more expensive than academic education, even though no established principle exists that allows a simple comparison (Cumming 1988). Is it very likely that vocational programs are undermined on financial grounds? In order to determine whether this might be so, some measure of relative cost must be obtained. As a very general guide it may be presumed that the teaching and recurrent cost of vocational subjects as compared to academic subjects is in the region of 1.5, with all the caveats concerning enormous variety between countries, subjects (Cumming 1988, Table 1; Psacharopoulos 1987, p. 193), and types of programs. The Icelandic case fits well within this norm. Individual courses in the trade vocations are roughly 1.5 times as expensive as a typical UEE course. The principal factors responsible for the difference between academic and vocational programs are teacher salaries, group sizes, and the cost of furnishing workshops. The variations in initial costs may be assumed to be in the same region. The differential cost can be further aggravated if the supply of students in the more expensive class of tracks is below optimum number, which is probably true in many cases in the Icelandic comprehensive system. From this vantage point the position of vocational education within the education system must be considered very weak in the long run, especially when the education sector faces either real or relative cuts. The facts are simple. If the education budget is not to be increased but the number of students rises, what options are there, given the relative high cost of vocational education and a lack of a real general incentive to retain its strength? The vocational programs will either disappear or be gradually transformed into fairly standard academic programs.

DEFINITION AND RATIONALE ARE UNCLEAR

Two rather innocuous philosophical factors within the sphere of vocational education turn out to be among its serious and elusive foes. One concerns the definition of vocational education, the other its rationale. Protecting a vocational program that has no clear definition is difficult, especially as it may be hard to discern its transformation into something else. A program may be classified rather whimsically as vocational or not, largely irrespective of its nature. Its classification may be moved between categories of programs simply by changing names. Similarly, if the rationale of a program is vague, it is very difficult to stick to or defend any of its characteristics; none may be deemed crucial. Consequently factors external to the program may to a large extent determine its structure, especially if the internal practical or pedagogical rationale is weak. It is hinted at below that both of these theoretical factors undermine vocational education in two ways. First vocational education gradually becomes academic partly because no one appreciates why it should be otherwise. Second, any practical or clinical parts of the programs are moved to the very end largely under external pressure for reasons of expediency, exactly opposite to what most pedagogical arguments require.

The Consequences of a Vague Definition

It was explained at the beginning of the chapter that vocational education is any educational track or program that has as its primary aim preparing a person for a particular field of employment. But behind this rather innocuous statement lie various tangled issues. The terminology is vague. It is not clear whether vocational education or vocational training are the proper terms. The purpose is vague. It is not clear whether vocational education refers to preparation for particular, narrowly defined jobs or to preparation for any gainful employment (see, e.g., Nilsson and Svärd 1991, p. 4). The content or characteristic is vague. It is not clear whether there are any necessary or sufficient ingredients that make a program vocational. At one extreme there are the apprenticeship-based programs in the industrial trades (where the apprenticeship seems to be the crucial part). At the other extreme there are the business programs that seem very similar to any general liberal education programs, with slightly more emphasis on bookkeeping and typewriting than is normally found in a general educational track, but otherwise substantially composed of general academic subjects with no apprenticeship component.

The definitional problem has several aspects to it. The first is the extent to which general education counts as a necessary ingredient in the preparation for a certain vocation. The second is how a vocation is defined and to what extent it is necessary to talk about vocational spheres or sectors rather than specific vocations or jobs. The third concerns the balance in the syllabus between actual practice at "on-the-job" tasks and more academic discussion about trends and issues relating to the nature of a specific vocation. The literature on these issues is growing, e.g., about what is meant by skills (see, e.g., Ashton, Maguire, and Sung 1991, pp. 233-236) but more on what skills may be relevant (see Gallie 1991 on the skill debate and Óskarsdóttir 1995, for a review of new vocational skills). In the present context, the only aspect of interest is the effect this uncertainty has on the standing of vocational programs, and it is suggested that the main effect is that the general (and academic) courses take over from the vocational programs. When there is financial pressure to reduce costly courses in practical training; when there are mounting problems with securing places and quality guidance within an apprenticeship system; when there is pressure from the mobility principle within the comprehensive system; when there are more problems of recruitment of qualified teachers within the practical as compared to the academic disciplines, then it seems relatively easy to accept gradually a higher percentage of general courses or modules within the vocational track—as a compromise, noting that there are convincing substantial arguments for it. This does not mean that there will not continue to be ambitious and temporarily successful attempts to maintain or even initiate vocational programs such as the national vocational initiatives in Britain and Norway or within individual disciplines (Williams and Yeomans 1994). However, the long-term fate of such efforts can be foreseen and it may even be possible to describe in some detail how they will operate.

Why Practical or Clinical Training?

The rationale for the practical, clinical, or apprenticeship part of vocational training is at least threefold. First, and probably most important, is the pedagogical necessity of being able to relate theory to practice. This pedagogical factor has both a motivational and a cognitive dimension. Another rationale is the necessity to learn to apply any academic ideas or practical skills in practical situations, where the student encounters genuine working atmosphere and conditions. This requires practice on the job or perhaps partly in a practical class to be ongoing throughout the vocational course. These may be termed student-centered arguments and are very important for the quality of the vocational course. They demand that fairly intensive practical training or at least practical experience be placed early in the vocational program and subsequently remain an integral part throughout. The third rationale for any type of "clinical" practice is the necessity to learn skills that are very job specific. This training may come at the end of the vocational period, or, as is of course more reasonable, at the beginning of a new job. This rationale is often related to the direct financial interests of the prospective employer and is of considerable importance in an economy dominated by small firms and probably for small firms in whatever economy (Grubb 1984, p. 451). If these three arguments for vocational training are not clearly understood by those in charge of the program and most importantly if their differences are not appreciated, then even though some general feeling for the importance of practice may be present, it is easy to succumb to several forces that push the on-the-job training to the very end of the vocational program, where its value as a potentially crucial pedagogical ingredient is minimized. Two additional reasons for maintaining a strong apprenticeship system should be mentioned in this context. One is access to cheap labor (Elbaum 1989 p. 342) and the other is an indirect method by which the labor unions might attempt to control the number of qualified additions to their labor market (p. 349). Only the former might coincide with the need to organize practical training as an integral part of the whole vocational program.

A FAST-CHANGING SOCIETY HAS ITS EFFECTS

The economic infrastructure of many western societies is changing and this is also the case in Iceland. And this change is probably perceived by many young people, who face selecting a career, to be occurring rather rapidly. Many employers probably also have the same feeling. Whether such an attitude or feeling could be justified is, however, not at issue here. But the consequences are. There are at least three reasons why a fast-changing society, or rather the perception of this change, is a serious enemy of what we normally mean by vocational education at the secondary level and probably at the tertiary level.

The first reason is that students may be reluctant to choose a vocation at such an early stage in the system, if they have an alternative option, as there may be several signs indicating the insecurity of jobs in many fields. They may even be interested in a particular vocational program but prefer to get some kind of insurance by finishing secondary school and passing the UEE. The second reason why a changing society undermines traditional types of vocational education is that there is no tradition for vocational education in the new fields, and such trends may be very difficult to establish. It is noteworthy that substantial practical training exists principally within vocations where it has built up over a long time. In more recent disciplines, the practical or clinical experience is often minimal and superficial. Elbaum (1989) notes, however, that the apprenticeship tradition was adapted in new disciplines in the nineteenth century if there was a clear economic benefit. The third reason is the uncertainty on behalf of employers and educators alike as to what skills are most desirable in the coming decades. The colorful spectrum of skills that has been suggested in recent years (see, e.g., Levin and Rumberger 1989, pp. 235-236) shows vividly the practically impossible situation curriculum developers find themselves in.[18] If the educational establishment attempts to go along with these suggestions the result is bound to be equally colorful, diffuse, and non-vocational. Note here that UEE does not result in higher initial salaries than dropouts receive as discussed earlier, though graduates presumably possess some of the new skills desired.

THE STATUS OF VOCATIONAL AND LIBERAL EDUCATION

It is often said that the academic schools have a higher status than the vocational schools and, therefore, attract keener students. The establishment of the comprehensive system was meant to counter this apparent problem of differential status. No domestic study has a number of important confounding factors, many of which have been specifically addressed here, but indications that such factors exist are discussed above. Most of the forces at play seem to direct the students towards the academic programs, independent of their immediate interests. A survey conducted among students at two comprehensive schools in Iceland asked how interested they were in a number of options open to them, but they did not, however, have to rank the options (Bílddal 1993). Nearly half of the sample, 45 percent, said they were very interested in obtaining a vocational trade certificate but over 80 percent of the same group said they thought it very important to pass the university entrance examination. It is thus clear that the young people have to choose, and it is clear what they end up selecting.[19] In a study among Icelanders born in 1969 who had not finished a secondary program by the age of twenty-two, 68 percent said they were more interested in practical than academic subjects (Jónasson and Jónsdóttir 1992, Table 5.3.2); more than 80 percent wanted to complete school (Jónasson and Jónsdóttir 1992, Table 5.4.4), and a large portion, at least 60 percent, expressed keen interest in some vocational program (Jónasson and Jónsdóttir 1992, Table 5.4.5). This fits reasonably well with the rather positive attitudes to practical or technical jobs reported in Lauglo and Närman (1988, pp. 248-249) and makes clear how some relevant industrial education enhances this attitude.

It might be conjectured in light of the scant evidence available that a large fraction of those who select the academic tracks do so for reasons other than keen interest. One reason may simply be an attempt to delay a vocational choice; another may be strong parental pressure, or a difficulty in getting an apprenticeship.[20] Many select the academic track as a default or a negative option.

In view of the previous chapters on the enemies of vocational education, it seems sensible for many students to make the general or academic choice even though they could well envisage a vocational choice. It is not the case that the relatively dwindling registration in the "secondary" vocational programs is a true reflection of the interest students may have in entering the vocations in question. The students themselves should therefore *not* be counted among the enemies of vocational education.

GENERAL DISCUSSION

Vocational education at the secondary level faces two classes of problems. One is that it is difficult to show empirically its relevance, at least in general terms. Second, there are several forces at play which seriously seem to undermine all genuine or ostensible attempts to strengthen vocational education at the secondary level. It is not clear how strong these forces are or whether they can be annulled. They appear to be both forceful and resilient, if somewhat elusive, especially as most of them seem to come into play inadvertently. Apparently the most damaging come from within the labor market and the education system itself. It is doubtful that any measures can be taken which would suffice to reverse or even halt the eradication in the long run of anything but nominal vocational programs at the secondary level. Whether such measures are sensible in view of the scant empirical validation of vocational programs at that level is another question.

These forces come from sectors that consider themselves to be favorable to the vocational enterprise. This holds true especially for the labor market but also for important sectors of the education establishment. Needs analysis is detrimental to vocational education; the salary structure in the labor market does not encourage vocational education generally; the apprenticeship system seems to control licensed trade education unduly and the size of enterprises is not conducive to on-the job vocational training. Similarly several features of the secondary education system complicate the build-up of vocational education or camouflage its transition into general academic programs. The tertiary system has grown so strong and has such a wide spectrum of programs that it seems to be a somewhat poor option for any student who might have a chance by not opting for a university entrance certificate. In addition to these rather formidable groups of deterring factors, there is the lack of a definition to vocational programs, allowing practically anything to be counted as vocational and a lack of consensus about the rationale of vocational education, which again means that there is no defence against a smooth transition of any vocational program into an academic one. An apparently fast-changing society encourages a student to defer any final educational choice and gives an additional reason for choosing the general academic track at the secondary level. The question of status may have some influence in this respect but probably less than might be expected, given the overwhelming numbers selecting the academic program. The cost of vocational programs as compared to academic ones certainly does nothing to counter this development.

It thus seems to be of paramount importance to those who still believe it makes good sense to maintain or to develop serious vocational options at the secondary level to reconsider their rationale very seriously, and if they are convinced that such programs hold up to close scrutiny, plan their actions so as to counter the hindrances discussed above.

NOTES

1. These may be called university preparatory programs, UPPs, which conclude with a university entrance examination, UEE, which awards a university entrance certificate, UEC. Cf. the French "baccalaureate," the German "Abitur," the Scandinavian "student prøve," etc.

2. The positive effects of work experience programs are difficult to assess (see, e.g., Watts 1983). Furthermore even though the surface characteristics seem to be right, vocational programs seem to be difficult to maintain (see, e.g., Evans and Davies 1988, pp. 43-46).

3. Documented cases of short-sightedness of industries may be scarce, but see, e.g., Gospel and Okayma 1991, p. 21; and McKinley 1991, pp. 93-111.

4. We do not discuss the extent to which the driving force should be exclusively attributed to certain individuals within each sector rather than the sector as a unit (see, e.g., Nilsson and Svärd 1991, p. 5, on the initiative in Sweden). This becomes of crucial importance if someone wants to argue that industry should be given control over vocational education on the assumption that this would encourage its initiative.

5. Based on data made available by the Icelandic Statistical Bureau in May 1995.

6. The representatives of the industry have of course, when invited by the government, taken seats on a number of committees set up to propose educational initiatives and the individuals concerned have, without doubt, played an important role in molding the proposals made.

7. The data were collected in ten independent telephone surveys by the Social Science Institute of Iceland in the years 1993-1995 with the total number of respondents about 10,000, of which 7,500 received a salary. The sample on which these numbers are based, including the ages between twenty and seventy, is around 5,800.

8. It is assumed that inadvertent or conscious relative bias is independent of the groups being investigated, and thus the pattern obtained is trustworthy, even if the absolute numbers may not be.

9. Such initiatives are exemplified by Salomé and Charmes 1988 in an analysis of five newly industrialized countries in Asia, p. 73.

10. In the metal working sector in 1989, British apprentices received 73 percent of the pay of skilled workers, whereas the German apprentices received 35 percent (Marsden and Ryan 1991, Table 11.3).

11. It is problematic to extract the number of new entrants into the academic and vocational tracks from the centralized database available, except for the last few years.

12. It is also of interest to note that in an explanatory note following the proposed law for secondary education, it is stated that these three aims should be woven together as not to be seen as unrelated aims. In a regulation set subsequently the number of aims is increased and the formal problem of selecting between them or following all of them is further enhanced.

13. In absolute terms the picture is different because over 80 percent of the students entering secondary education register in tracks that must be termed academic or general.

14. There are other forces pushing in the same direction. The sheer logistical problem of placing a huge number of beginners in "on the job training" or in practical classes (many of which may drop out of the program) is often formidable. Prospective employers also almost certainly prefer to train their potential new employees towards the end of their studies.

15. It is implicit if it is required to obtain an apprenticeship contract at some stage in the study, and it is very difficult to obtain such a contract even though in principle there is said to be no limit on the number of students who could go through the program in question. The *clausus* is also implicit if it is known that a very high proportion of students will not pass vital exams in the program.

16. Based on data from the Icelandic Statistical Bureau, Hjalti Kristgeirsson, personal communication 19.5.95.

17. This is data made available by the Ministry of Education (May 1995) and is deduced from the three largest vocations: house building industry, electricity, and metalwork. These are fairly feeble indicators, however, because the pressure on those who are actually in a program to finish is often fairly low and thus an older completion age does not necessarily reflect an older starting age.

18. This is a very old dilemma, and there is an abundance of references to literature from the previous century and the early part of the twentieth century

to demonstrate this. See, e.g., Nilsson and Svärd 1991, p. 6, on the Commission on Rationalization in Sweden, which started work in 1936 and wanted to emphasize intellectual skills in vocational education.

19. Thus when Wright (1988, p. 130) reports that the proportion of students wishing to go to college or university ranges from 38-86 percent, he may be underestimating the independent interest in vocational education, as he only seems to allow one choice.

20. There is an abundance of anecdotal evidence supporting these different reasons for not selecting a vocational track, which may be of primary interest to the student. It has not been possible to substantiate it with solid Icelandic data.

REFERENCES

Ashton, D., M.J. Maguire, and J. Sung. 1991. "Institutional Structures and the Provision of Intermediate Level Skills: Lessons from Canada and Hong Kong." In *International Comparisons of Vocational Education and Training for Intermediate Skills*. ed. P. Ryan. London: The Falmer Press.

Atvinnuvegaskrsla 1993. 1996. *Report on the Status of Icelandic Industries in 1993*. Reykjavík: fjóhagsstofnun.

Bailey, A. 1990. "Personal Transferable Skills for Employment: The Role of Higher Education." In *Industry and Higher Education: Collaboration to Improve Students' Learning and Training*, ed. P. Wright. Buckingham: Open University Press.

Bengtsson, J. 1993. "Labor Markets of the Future: The Challenge to Education Policy Makers." *European Journal of Education 28*, 3, pp. 135-157.

Bílddal, S. 1993. *Hugmyndir nemenda um nám og störf* (The Ideas Students Entertain about Jobs and Study. Research project in educational studies. Unpublished.

Bishop, J.H. 1990. "The Productivity Consequences of What Is Learned in High School." *J. Curriculum Studies 22*, pp. 101-126.

Cumming, C.E. 1988. "Curriculum Costs: Vocational Subjects." In *Vocationalizing Education: An International Perspective*, eds. J. Lauglo and K. Lillis. Oxford: Pergamon Press.

Drake, K. 1991. "Interventions in Market Financing of Training in the European Community." In *International Comparisons of Vocational Education and Training for Intermediate Skills*, ed. P. Ryan. London: The Falmer Press.

Dunn, J.A. 1988. "The Future of Secondary School Vocational Education: Curriculum Reform or Retrenchment—Basic Academic or Technical Skills." *Journal of Studies in Technical Careers* 10, pp. 372-383.

Elbaum, B. 1989. "Why Apprenticeship Persisted in Britain but Not in the United States." *The Journal of Economic History* 49, 2, pp. 337-349.

Evans, J., and B. Davies. 1988. "The Rise and Fall of Vocational Education." In *Education, Training and the New Vocationalism*, eds. A. Pollard, J. Purvis, and G. Walford. Milton. Keynes: Open University Press, pp. 35-51.

Fjörf fyrir menntun í sjávarútvegi. 1992. *On the Need for Education in the Fishing Industry*. Reykjavík: Menntamálaráduneytid og Sammennt.

Foster, P. 1965. "The Vocational School Fallacy in Developmental Planning." In *Education and Economic Development*, eds. C. Arnold Anderson and M.J. Bowman. Chicago: Aldine, pp. 142-166.

Gallie, D. 1991. "Patterning of Skill Change: Upskilling, Deskilling or the Polarization of Skills?" *Work, Employment & Society 5*, 319-351.

Gospel, H.F., and R. Okayma. 1991. "Industrial Training in Britain and Japan: An Overview." In *Industrial Training and Technological Innovation. A Comparative and Historical Study*, ed. F. Gospel. London: Routledge.

Grubb, W.N. 1984. "The Bandwagon Once More: Vocational Preparation for High-tech Occupations." *Harvard Educational Review 54*, 4, 429-451.

Grubb, W.N. 1985. "The Convergence of Educational Systems and the Role of Vocationalism." *Comparative Education Review 29*, pp. 526-548.

Gudmundsson, G. 1993. *Tróun starfsmenntunar á framhaldsskólastigi* (Development of Vocational Education at the Secondary Level). Reykjavík: Menntamálaráduneytid og Sammennt.

Jónasson, J.T. 1990. *Menntun á Íslandi í 25 ár, 1985-2010* (A Forecast about Various Aspects of Education in Iceland for the Years 1985-2010). Reykjavík: Framkvæmdanefnd um framtídarkönnun.

Jónasson, J.T. 1992a. "Vöxtur menntunar á Íslandi og tengsl hennar vi atvinnulíf" (Growth of Education in Iceland and Its Relation to the World of Work). *Í Menntun og atvinnulíf*. Reykjavík: Menntamálaráduneytid og Sammennt, pp. 54-83.

Jónasson, J.T. 1992b. "Tróun framhaldsskólans: Frá starfsmenntun til almenns bóknáms" (The Development of Secondary Education: From Vocational Education to General Education). *Uppeldi og menntun*, 1, pp. 173-189.

Jónasson, J.T. 1994. "Skipt um skodun" (On the Movement of Students Between Different Tracks in Secondary Education). *Uppeldi og menntun*, 3, pp. 63-82.

Jónasson, J.T. 1995. "Er skólakerfi a springa? Um flróun háskólastigsins á Íslandi" (Is the Education System Bursting? On the Development of Higher Education in Iceland). In *Rannsóknir í félagsvísindum*, ed. F.H. Jónsson [Research in the Social Sciences]. Reykjavík: Social Science Research Institute.

Jónasson, J.T. 1996a. The Resilience of an Academic Programme. An Account of Eighty Years of Steady Growth of the Student Population Passing the Icelandic University Entrance Examination (UEE).

Jónasson, J.T. 1996b. The Relationship Between Trade Licences and the Economy. Manuscript.

Jónasson, J.T. 1996c. The Relationship Between Education and Income in Iceland. Manuscript.

Jónasson, J.T., and G.A. Jónsdóttir. June 1992. *Námsferill í framhaldsskóla*. Reykjavík: Félagsvísindastofnun. (A research report on the educational development of the cohort born in 1969, prepared by the Social Science Research Institute of the University of Iceland for the Ministry of Education).

King, K. 1988. "Evaluating the Context of Diversified Secondary Education in Tanzania." In *Vocationalizing Education: An International Perspective*, eds. J. Lauglo and K. Lillis. Oxford: Pergamon Press.

Landshagir 1995. 1996. *Statistical Yearbook of Iceland*. Reykjavík: Hagstofa Íslands.

Lauglo, J. 1983. "Concepts of 'General Education' and 'Vocational Education' Curricula for Post-Compulsory Schooling in Western Industrialised Countries: When Shall the Twain Meet?" *Comparative Education* 19, pp. 285-304.

Lauglo, J., and K. Lillis. 1988. *Vocationalizing Education: An International Perspective*. Oxford: Pergamon Press.

Lauglo, J., and A. Närman. 1988. "Diversified Secondary Education in Kenya: The Status of Practical Subjects and Their Uses after School." In *Vocationalizing Education: An International Perspective*, eds. J. Lauglo and K. Lillis. Oxford: Pergamon Press.

Levin, H.M., and R.W. Rumberger. 1989. "Education, Work and Employment: Present Issues and Future Challenges in Developed Countries." In *The Prospects for Educational Planning*, ed. F. Caillods. Paris: UNESCO: IIEP.

Marsden, D., and P. Ryan. 1991. "Initial Training, Labor Market Structure and Public Policy: Intermediate Skills in British and German Industry." In

International Comparisons of Vocational Education and Training for Intermediate Skills, ed. P. Ryan. London: The Falmer Press, pp. 251-285.

McKinley, A. 1991. "'A Certain Short-Sightedness': Metalworking, Innovation, and Apprenticeship, 1897-1939." In *Industrial Training and Technological Innovation. A Comparative and Historical Study*, ed. H.F. Gospel. London: Routledge.

Nilsson, A., and B. Svärd. 1991. "The Quantitative Development of Vocational Education in Sweden 1950-1990." *Lund Papers in Economic History* 12.

Noah, H.J., and M.A. Eckstein. 1988. "Business and Industry Involvement with Education in Britain, France and Germany." In *Vocationalizing Education: An International Perspective*, eds. J. Lauglo and K. Lillis. Oxford: Pergamon Press.

Ólafsson, S. (1993). "Variations Within the Scandinavian Model: Iceland in a Scandinavian Comparison." In *Welfare Trends in the Scandinavian Countries*, eds. J. Hansen, S. Ringen, H. Uusitalo, and R. Eriksson. New York: M.E. Sharpe.

Óskarsdóttir, G.G. 1995. *The Forgotten Half. Comparison of Dropouts and Graduates in Their Early Work Experience—The Icelandic Case*. Reykjavík: Social Science Research Institute and University Press, University of Iceland.

Oxenham, J. (1988). "What Do Employers Want from Employment." In *Vocationalizing Education: An International Perspective*, eds. J. Lauglo and K. Lillis. Oxford: Pergamon Press.

Psacharopoulos, G. 1986. "The Planning of Education: Where Do We Stand?" *Comparative Education Review* 30, pp. 560-573.

Psacharopoulos, G. 1987. "To Vocationalise or not to Vocationalise? That Is the Curriculum Question. *International Review of Education 33*, 2, pp. 187-211.

Psacharopoulos, G. 1989. "Why Educational Reforms Fail: A Comparative Analysis." *International Review of Education 35*, 2, pp. 179-195.

Psacharopoulos, G., and W. Loxley. 1985. *Diversified Secondary Education and Development.* Baltimore: Johns Hopkins University Press.

Raffe, D. 1994. "Modular Strategies for Overcoming Academic/ Vocational Divisions: Issues Arising from the Scottish Experience." *Journal of Education Policy 9*, 2, pp. 141-154.

Ryan, P., ed. 1991. *International Comparisons of Vocational Education and Training for Intermediate Skills.* London: The Falmer Press.

Salomé, B., and J. Charmes. 1988. *In-Service Training. Five Asian Experiences.* Paris: Organization for Economic Cooperation and Development (OECD).

Sanderson, M. 1993. Vocational and Liberal Education, a Historian's View. *European Journal of BHMR-tíindi.* 1 (2), pp.10-12.

Sigurjónsson, B.B. 1988. "Ævitekjur og ardsemi menntunar." *European Journal of Education* 28, 3, pp.159-175.

Squires, G. 1989. *Pathways for Learning. Education and Training from 16-19.* Paris: Organization for Economic Cooperation and Development (OECD).

Standert, R. "Technical Rationality in Education Management: A Survey Covering England, France and Germany." *Education* 28, 3, pp.189-196.

Watts, A.G. 1983. "The Effectiveness of Work Experience." In *Work Experience and Schools,* ed. A.G. Watts. London: Heineman Educational Books, pp. 84-98.

Williams, R., and D. Yeomans. 1994. "The New Vocationalism Enacted? The Transformation of the Business Studies Curriculum." *The Vocational Aspect of Education 46,* pp. 221-239.

Wilms, W.W. 1988. Captured by the American Dream." In *Vocationalizing Education: An International Perspective,* eds. J. Lauglo and K. Lillis. Oxford: Pergamon Press.

Wolf, A. 1993. "Some Final Thoughts: Vocational Education Policy in a European Context." *European Journal of Education* 28, 3, pp. 241-243.

Wright, C.A.H. 1988. "Curriculum Diversification Re-examined—a Case Study of Sierra Leone." In *Vocationalizing Education: An International Perspective,* eds. J. Lauglo and K. Lillis. Oxford: Pergamon Press.

CHAPTER 14

Comprehensive Schooling at the Intersection of Market, State, and Civil Forces: Two Swedish Case Studies

Holger Daun

INTRODUCTION

Large-scale transformations of the Swedish society have taken place during the past decades, some of them initiated by the state. Behind and within these changes we may find certain parameters. An analysis along these parameters may not only help us understand the societal and educational changes that have occurred but also forecast the probable educational changes within the near future. Recent educational changes in Sweden may be termed "restructuring." Papagiannis, Owens, and Easton (1992) take this concept to mean decentralization, introduction of choice, and/or privatization. The background to the restructuring and probable future changes in primary and lower secondary education in Sweden will be described and interpreted with the help of a conceptual framework. Three schools will be used as examples.[1]

THE SOCIETAL CONTEXT

The Swedish government was, during the 1930s, already determined to eliminate poverty through economic growth in society and to achieve equality through "state-directed" interventions. Investments in education and research were prioritized elements in these efforts

(Husén 1988). Industrialization had started 80-90 years earlier and it accelerated after World War II. More than half of the Swedish population left agriculture and the countryside for employment in factories and offices localized principally in urban areas. These areas increased their population figures while many rural areas were left with only elderly people. Later on, the public sector grew and hundreds of thousands of jobs were created in the service sector. The labor force that was needed for this project was recruited principally through stimulation of immigration to Sweden and mobilization of women working at home.

These changes resulted in geographical disparities and inequalities despite the efforts made by the state to equalize the living conditions of people. Another implication of these efforts was the standardization of local cultures, even though it was unintended (Frykman and Löfgren 1979).[2] A good illustration is what happened to the same ethnic group in Sweden. In order to benefit from the material wealth provided by the Swedish welfare state, it had, to a large extent, to sacrifice important elements of its culture (Paulston 1980).

The economy had become increasingly export-oriented and dependent on changes in the world system. With the worldwide recession, the economy started to stagnate in the middle of the 1970s. It became apparent that it was not possible to maintain the public sector intact. Two principal measures were taken: 1) Decentralization of administrative bodies and decision-making to lower levels in the state apparatus (from central to provincial level or from ministries to national or provincial agencies, for instance); and 2) privatization of public companies and service units for reducing public expenditures (Montin 1992).

Historically, the state machinery in Sweden has been "double." Besides the central government structures, there are also locally elected municipality parliaments, governments, and boards. World War II and then the construction of the welfare state required initiatives and coordination at the national level, and this resulted in the reinforcement and centralization of the bodies at this level.

Also the municipalities have the right to tax the population. The general frame of action for the bodies at the municipality level is, however, circumvented by central laws, which define their degree of autonomy and competence, and by the national budget system. The national government generates taxes that are then partially reallocated to the municipalities according to their financial situation and needs. The manner in which the municipalities might use the subsidies received from the central level is formally defined by very specific laws. A large portion of these subsidies can be earmarked for various purposes (they might have a "special destination"). Some of these laws have been gradually abolished, since decentralization efforts started in the end of the 1970s. The central state now distributes lump sums more often than before. This change is evident within the educational domain (Odin and Åhs 1985).

The Social Democrats governed the country (alone or in coalition) from the beginning of the 1930s until 1976, but the majorities in many municipality parliaments varied from one province to another and from time to time. In municipalities where the Social Democrats had ruled for a long time, alone or with the support from the Left party, child care and education were more developed than in municipalities where the non-socialist parties had been in majority. This fact mirrored more the cleavage in "social paradigm" and social policy that existed between the two party blocks than the economic situation of the municipalities (Johansson 1982).

With the massive internal migration and urbanization, many rural areas lost their base; they were left with a large portion of elderly people who were not active and did not pay taxes but instead demanded public care. The national government introduced a specific policy for stimulating investments in these scarcely populated areas, but it was not enough for the maintenance of the 4,000 municipalities that existed in the beginning of the 1950s. On two occasions, the municipalities were merged, and in the 1980s, their number had decreased to less than 300.

In the processes described, we find certain parameters that have influenced the education system. In addition to this, we have to look at the discourse area and at the policy area. The former contains the issues that are debated in public (mass media, the national parliament, and so on), and the latter includes the policies that are implemented *de facto*. What policies are probable and their degree of implementation are to a large extent influenced by the combination of societal parameters (Dahllöf 1984; Marklund 1984).

Apart from the educational discourse and policies, it is necessary, at least in the case of Sweden, to look at three other areas if we are to understand present or future educational processes: social policy, regionalization policy, and immigration policy. They have a direct impact on education. The social policies defined after World War II may be seen as active, collective, and prioritizing equality. They are active as preventive measures and on a broad scale (subsidies to all children regardless of their parents' income, for instance). A large portion of the needs are defined on a collective level, which means that the individual himself or herself does not have to prove his or her needs in order to get support (Johnston 1990). Finally, the social policy should provide not only a minimum material level of living for all citizens but also equality.

The regionalization policies were introduced when the negative geographical and social effects (regional disparities and imbalances) of the focus on economic growth became evident. Elements of these policies are, for instance, subsidies to companies in rural or scarcely populated areas and dispersion of public authorities and administrative bodies from the capital to other cities around the country.

Immigration policies were not explicitly formulated until the end of the 1960s. This is due to the fact that immigration had until this period been on a very small scale. With the economic growth, the companies could not find sufficient manpower within the country and had to recruit actively from Southern Europe. This fact coupled with the increasing number of refugees in the world changed the situation completely. The few immigrants who had arrived previously were expected to be assimilated in the Swedish society. With the new policies, the immigrants received the opportunity of economic and political integration into the society, at the same time retaining the right to preserve their culture. The key concepts for this new policy were "Equality, Freedom of Choice and Cooperation" (Widgren 1982). Some instruction in the language used at home was also guaranteed to immigrant children.

Sweden has a long tradition of democracy and participation. During the past century, popular movements (labor, free church, consumer, temperance) emerged from the grassroots level. The local groups of each movement joined and created national voluntary organizations. Some of the organizations were interest oriented; their aim was to improve the material life conditions of their members. Others were value oriented; they wanted to make society function according to moral values, mainly connected to the Protestant religion (Boli 1989; Daun and Fägerlind 1991; Paulston 1980).

The popular movements established national offices in the capital, and their members began to have an influence, especially on education, via three channels: 1) in the National Parliament, where members of these movements were for a long time over-represented; 2) in committees appointed by the parliament or the government, including representatives of the movements who were assigned to study certain problems and suggest solutions; and 3) through the system of remittance, according to which various organizations can express their points of view.

With the migration and urbanization, the popular movements became more and more centralized, and, with the mentioned involvement in state affairs, tendencies of symbiotic relationships between them and the state emerged. These tendencies were still more reinforced by the state subsidies that the organizations came to receive for their activities. Revenues from member quotas or other types of contributions came to be proportionally less important and state subsidies more important in the budgets of the organizations. To the processes of centralization and corporativism should also be added the secularization of the Swedish culture that has taken place from the beginning of the twentieth century.

A high percentage of the Swedes are organized as members in voluntary organizations and are taking an active role in politics. This fact has sometimes been termed "Organizational Sweden" (Elvander 1968). However, membership and degree of participation have decreased since the 1960s. The spontaneous movements, like the Vietnam movement and the ecological movement, have to some extent become the channels through which intentions, desires, and demands from the civil sphere are manifested.

Except for a few cases, such as free churches, the popular movements never demanded more liberal rules and laws to facilitate the establishment of non-public primary or secondary schools. On the other hand, adult education of two types has been an important issue for the these movements ever since they were created: 1) study circles, and 2) folk high schools (Boli 1989).

Since World War II, the civil sphere of the Swedish society has become state owned. This means that the state sphere and the production sphere have conquered space in the civil sphere and in people's privacy. Since the beginning of the 1980s, incentives, moral values, and so on, in the civil sphere have also become impregnated by concepts, ideas, and perceptions originated in the production sphere.

EDUCATIONAL CHANGES

The educational reforms decided upon immediately after the war may be seen as an important ingredient in the construction of the welfare state: All children were to receive nine years of compulsory education in comprehensive schools. This project required central decision-making and redistribution of resources from the national level. The new education was tested in a number of municipalities before it was implemented on a national scale in the beginning of the 1960s.

It was more or less taken for granted that the state should continue to be in charge of and guarantee education. Previously, the schools had been following a national curriculum, but no national assessments or evaluations had been made. The schools were inspected by provincial officers working under the National Board of Education. All pupils followed the same curriculum and programs with the exception that certain options could be made in lower secondary (grades 7-9). With the introduction of the comprehensive school a national grading system was implemented and "standardized tests" were periodically given to the pupils. Central criteria for teacher training and teacher competence were also established. The regulations did not give much space for school choice or establishment of free schools. A pupil could enroll in a school other than the one he or she had been assigned to only if special reasons existed. Therefore, very few pupils attended a school outside their designated area. At that time, private schools received very small subsidies. The result was that less than 1 percent of primary school pupils attended free schools at the end of the 1980s. Most of these schools were of the Waldorf or Montessori type (Isling 1984).

Immigrants had to attend public schools, where the language of instruction was, and still is, Swedish, but they also were guaranteed of having a certain amount of hours per week of instruction in their own mother tongue. Where there existed large and homogeneous groups of immigrants, it was possible for the schools to organize classes in mother tongue instruction, but in areas that had a large number of different immigrant minorities, or had few immigrants as in many rural municipalities, it was not possible to do so.

Minor curriculum changes were made in 1969 and 1980. A government committee was appointed in the middle of the 1970s to investigate and suggest how internal improvements of school activities (SIA) could be accomplished. The reforms that had been made were perceived by the teachers and their unions to be "external," i.e., mainly dealing with the structure and the organization and not touching on the many problems that existed in the schools. One of the principal results of the proposals made by this committee was a "relaxation" of the budget procedures and more autonomy for the municipalities and schools regarding decisions over the use of the subsidies coming from the central state level. In short, the municipalities and the schools began to receive lump sums related to the number of pupils and some other criteria. In reality, this implied that the schools were given a lot of freedom in relation to the means used in achieving the goals established centrally (Odin and Åhs 1985).

In the beginning of the 1990s, the Social Democratic government abolished the National Board of Education and its provincial antennae. The responsibility for the schools was decentralized to the municipalities. That is, the praxis that emerged from the SIA decision was formalized, and important aspects of the educational evaluation and inspection were left to the municipalities themselves. Many municipalities made administrative changes so that the organization would better correspond to the new conditions granting more autonomy. The school activities now came to be judged more in relation to goal achievement than to how rules and regulations had been followed.

The degree of consensus in educational and social policy matters has never been large, but it was—until the beginning of the 1990s—a tacit rule that matters concerning national security and education should be as broadly "anchored" as possible.[3] The Conservative Party has traditionally been against all reforms aiming at equalization and, consequently, rejected the comprehensive school as well as other reforms pointing towards this direction.

Considerable changes were implemented by the Conservative-Liberal coalition government that came to power in 1991. These changes, however, were neither preceded by consultations with, nor "anchored in," the labor movement, research society, and teachers' unions. Decentralization continued and strong subsidies were transferred to free schools. Money should "accompany" the pupils by means of a voucher system through which the schools chosen by the pupils would receive a sum equal to the average cost per pupil. Private or free schools were to receive 85 percent of the average cost for a pupil in the public system of the municipality where they were located. The most important result of these changes was the establishment of hundreds of free schools (but whose enrollment is still less than 2 percent of all primary school pupils). School fees could now be charged to the parents.

A new type of dynamics emerged among public schools as they were to make their own plans of action and present them to the parents and others in the local community. The schools had to market their own profiles. In some urban municipalities the competition between the schools became very strong. The same effects, however, were not observed in rural areas, where the distance between the public schools is very large.

It should also be mentioned that applications for opening free schools were to be decided upon by the National Agency for Education. If this agency approves an application, the municipality has to execute the order, even if it implies that an additional (free) school will make the expenditures exceed the budget established by municipal authorities.

The Social Democrats returned to power in 1994, but no significant changes have been made in the education system. School-based management continues and the range of possibilities is maintained, but the level of subsidies to free schools is under debate. In 1995, a state committee proposed that the municipalities should decide about the level of subsidies to free schools. If this proposal is accepted by the National parliament, each municipality is free to choose to what extent public subsidies should go to free schools. A consequence of such a decision might be that municipalities in which the Social Democrats are in majority will probably lower the subsidies to a level which will make it very difficult for free schools to exist, while municipalities with a Conservative majority will use public money for the entire cost of every free school.

STRATEGIC EDUCATIONAL CHANGES

Societal changes and state policies determine the functioning of education systems. More specifically, the policies are materialized in some strategic variables which have to do with the types of control, regulation, and finance. From a macro perspective, various combinations of different aspects such as the type of control and regulation, the type of regime/governance, the type of finance, and the place for teaching and learning processes make some types of schools more probable (Edwards and Whitty 1992; Raywid 1985, 1989, 1992). Table 1 lists some of the effects of the 1991/92 decision to restructure the education system.

Buildings: The standardized requirements were and are established centrally and their fulfillment is a requirement for receiving subsidies. The location of the schools is decided upon by the municipal authorities. Formerly, state subsidies were earmarked for investments in buildings, but nowadays this money is included in the lump sum sent to each municipality.

The catchment area was established for each municipality by its own authorities. In the beginning, education decisions in one municipality applied only within its geographical area. This meant that each school was required to accept all eligible children living within the area defined by the municipality authorities, and school officials were not allowed to recruit pupils living in other school districts or municipalities. With the change in 1991/92, the school is still required to accept all pupils within its district but is now allowed to recruit pupils regardless of their place of residence, if openings are available. The first condition mentioned does not apply to free schools, as these schools can recruit their pupils from wherever they want, because the costs are covered by the money that "accompanies" the pupil.

The school age is established centrally, but schools are free to accept younger children. Even though the compulsory school age is seven to sixteen years, parents have the right to a place for a six-year-old and the municipality has to provide it if the parents request it.

Teacher training and competence are still defined centrally, but in reality a portion of non-trained teachers function in the schools, and sometimes teachers might teach subjects for which they do not have the formal training. The recruitment of teachers was, until 1991, a task for the municipality; however, it has now been delegated to the school level.

Curricula and programs: Before 1980-82, detailed regulations determined what, how much, and when various elements were to be

Table 1: Educational Changes in 1991/92

	CONTROL AND REGULATION			
	Public Schools		Private Schools	
Physical				
Buildings	Yes, central	Yes, central	Yes, central	Yes, central
Geographical localization	Yes, local	Yes, local	No	No
Students:				
Catchment area	Yes, local	No	No	No
Age	Yes, central	Yes, central	No	No
Socio-cult.	No	No	No	No
Teachers:				
Training and Competence	Yes, central	Yes, central but . . .	Yes, central but . . .	Yes, central but . . .
Recruitment	Yes, local	Yes, local	No	No
Academic:				
Curricula, programs	Yes, central	Yes, core central and local	Yes, central	Yes, core central
Evaluation, examination	Central and local	Central and local	Central and local	No
Marks, diploma	Central	System central but school decision	Central	System central but school decision
	SUBSIDIES			
Buildings	Central and local	Lump sum	Lump sum	Lump sum
Teacher salaries	Yes, central	Lump sum	Lump sum	Lump sum
Equipment, textbooks	Central and local	Lump sum	Lump sum	Lump sum
Bussing	Central and local	Lump sum	Lump sum	Lump sum
School meals	Central and local	Lump sum	No	Lump sum

taught. Since 1991, there is a less defined core curriculum, and the schools, or teachers, have a high degree of autonomy in regard to the unspecified subject matter. National examination tests are given in the core subjects in certain grades, and they should function as reference points for the distribution of the marks. A new system for the marks was implemented in 1995, and it implies still more autonomy at the school level.

Subsidies were until 1980-82 very regulated and earmarked. Since 1991, each municipality has been receiving a lump sum from the central level. It covers a certain portion of educational costs, while the remaining portion has to be provided by the municipality's board. Each school district then receives a lump sum allocated centrally and by the municipality. The school district has a high degree of autonomy in relation to the distribution of the expenditures on various types of items.

Regarding the catchment areas, regulation of enrollments, and admission of pupils, Sweden has moved from one extreme to another—from a high degree of regulation to almost none. In a comparative perspective, this is a very drastic measure, since no quotas regarding, for example, ethnic or linguistic background are applied (McLean 1989; McLean and Voskrensenskaya 1992). This means that certain schools in a densely populated area can be made up of all pupils of Swedish origin, while other schools in the same area can be made up of

Table 2: Catchment Areas and Types of Regulation of Enrollment and Admission after 1991/92

Admission	School type	Catchment Area		
		One school district	Across school districts	No limitations
Regulated	Public schools	(1)		
	Public and private schools			
Unregulated	Public schools			
	Public and private schools			(2)

pupils belonging to immigrant families. The Swedish system has moved from the combination mentioned in (1) to the combination presented in (2), as shown in Table 2. With this description of the national context, some preliminary findings from three case schools will now be reported. The Swedish system has moved from the combination mentioned in (1) to the combination presented in (2) as shown in Table 2.

THE THREE CASE STUDIES[4]

Two of the schools are situated in the urban municipality of Dala[5]—a public school (DP) and a free school (DF)—and the third school is a free school in the parish of Oden in the Frej municipality, which is a scarcely populated rural area. Some basic information about the context of the three schools is presented in Table 3.

Table 3: Basic Information About the Case Areas and Case Schools

	Dala Municipality	Frej Municipality	Oden Parish
Inhabitants in 1994	68,800	57,400	470
Area		3,174 sq. km.	
Inhabitants per sq. km.		18	
Percent immigrants	29	1	< 1
Distance to case schools	0.5 - 11 km.	--	0.5 - 7 km.
Distance from case school to nearest school	1 km.	--	5 - 15 km.

Dala Municipality and the DP and DF Schools

Two of the schools—DP and DF—are situated in Dala, a municipality near Stockholm, the Swedish capital. Until World War II, this area was dominated by agriculture and small-scale industry. Some smaller urban agglomerates existed in the midst of agricultural activities. With the massive urbanization and immigration during the 1950s and 1960s, immigrants were channelled to urban areas in or around the big cities. Dala became one of the biggest municipalities in the country partly because it received many immigrants. In 1994, 29 percent of the inhabitants were born outside Sweden. The population increase is shown in Table 4.

Table 4: Population Figures for Dala Municipality, 1940-1992 (selected years)

Year	1940	1950	1960	1970	1980	1992
Inhabitants	13,948	22,638	30,614	58,946	66,834	68,840

There are more than 100 nationalities represented in the population. The municipality itself does not have many large workplaces (industry or service), but a large proportion of the population either have jobs in the capital or are unemployed.[6] The immigrants are concentrated in the northern part of the municipality; in some quarters, they constitute 90-95 percent of the population.

Dala has 25 comprehensive public schools (grades 1-6). The two case schools are situated in the northern part. The fact that the majority of the pupils were immigrants or had parents who were born outside the country created a large number of cultural, linguistic, and pedagogical challenges for the schools and their teachers. Other challenges resulted from changes in educational policies and reductions in educational budgets. Decentralization (mainly school-based management) was implemented and followed by choice and reinforcement of free school establishments. Budget reductions were to be made not only at the national level but also in the municipality of Dala (Möller 1995).

Confronted with the decision made in the municipality's educational board to reduce expenditures, the director of the DP school decided in 1993 to close one of the older buildings and concentrate the pupils in the newer buildings. Some of the teachers protested and suggested other ways to decrease the expenditures but without success. They were also prepared to start a (public) school within the existing DP school, but this proposal was also rejected by the director and the municipality's school board.[7] They then took the initiative to establish a free school in the building that was to be closed. Most of their pupils accompanied them and enrolled in the free school. Since a large proportion of these pupils were immigrant children, the free school came to have a large group of immigrants. Some pupils from other classes, mainly of Swedish origin, also enrolled in the free school.

Fifteen percent of the pupils attending the public school enrolled in the new free school, 22 percent of them being of Swedish origin and 13 percent belonging to immigrant families. This meant that the public school lost three whole classes plus some pupils from other classes. There are indications that the DP school also lost pupils (mainly of Swedish origin) to other public schools situated in the areas where the majority of the inhabitants are of Swedish origin. The number of pupils and the percentage of pupils of foreign origin in the DP and DF schools are presented in Table 5.

Table 5: Percentage of Pupils with at Least One Immigrant Parent

	1992/93	1993/94	1994/95	1995/96
DP: public	64%	84%	87%	---
Total number	437	304	317	312
DF: free	---	47%	44%	51%
Total number	---	139	148	221
Both schools	437	443	465	533

In 1994/95 and 1995/96, more pupils left the public schools and moved to the free school. They came mainly from other public schools in the Dala municipality, but a few of them came also from other municipalities.

The free school started as a foundation (*ekonomisk förening*)[8] with the two directors and some of the teachers as members. Later, it was transformed into a joint-stock company with the two directors (former teachers in the DP school) holding the large majority of the stocks and the other teachers owning the remaining stocks. Although the parents are not stockholders, they can still exert some influence through the School-Parent association.

Apart from pedagogical/methodological differences between the DP and DF schools, the cost per pupil has to be lower in the free school. It receives 85 percent of the average cost per pupil in the whole municipality and it is not allowed to charge fees to the parents. Various measures have been taken to keep expenditures at a low level. One example is the cost for cleaning work; the pupils themselves clean classrooms, and other spaces in the school are cleaned by the parents. The money saved is, according to one of the directors, used for excursions.

Frej Municipality: The Two Parishes and the Oden Free School

Frej is a sparsely populated rural municipality. The active population earns its living from agriculture, the public sector, and tourism. Since industry is of little importance, a large proportion of the population had to migrate to urban areas (the biggest cities of the country) when the economic growth became more rapid and industrialization advanced during the 1950s and 1960s. The service sector did not start to expand until the 1970s, and, thereafter, the migration from the municipality became less extensive. Less than 1 percent of the population are immigrants.

The area which is now Frej municipality consisted until 1950 of more than 90 municipalities (each with its own board) that corresponded to the 90 parishes that already existed in the Middle Ages. Each parish had its church, municipality board, and school. With the emigration, the number of inhabitants became too small to maintain the secular political and administrative structures. Therefore, the 90 municipalities were merged into 14 in 1950, and these were then merged into one in 1970.

Due to the large proportion of people owning farms or working in agriculture, the Center party has always had a strong position in Frej.

Each parish has now from 50 to 1,200 inhabitants. From the 1950s to the 1980s, more than half of the primary schools were closed so that in 1995, there were 35. Oden and Tor are two parishes from which pupils to the Oden school were recruited.

Table 6: Population in the Frej Municipality and Two Parishes Enrolling Pupils in Oden School

Frej municip.	1940	1950	1960	1970	1980	1992	
No. of inhab.	58,500	59,000	55,000	53,800	55,300	57,400	
Oden/Tor Parishes	1956	1968	1973	1986	1991	1992	1993
No. of inhab.	789	617	571	552	544	554	555

The number of pupils in the Oden school decreased steadily from the 1950s to the 1990s. It was a small school which did not receive very much attention from the municipality administration or school board. After demands from the Parent-School association and from the local committee of the Center party, the municipality's technical board decided in 1988 to renovate the hall that was used for serving school lunches and use it also for sport activities.

Due to bureaucratic inertia, this decision still had not been executed in 1991, when financial resources of the local state bodies both at the national and the local level became scarce. When all municipal authorities were forced to make cuts in their budgets, the educational authority found that money could be saved by postponing the renovation of the Oden school. Furthermore, in the general review of the economy, the director of the educational authority found that the number of children in the Oden school had become so small that there was a risk that state subsidies would no longer be paid to this school.[9] He suggested the case be reviewed. After receiving the findings from the review, the director of the educational authority proposed to the politicians in the school board that the Oden school be closed. The pupils could attend another school, located 7-8 kilometers away from Oden. When this fact became known to the population in Oden, intensive activities started. The Parent-School Association and the local committee of the Center party sent letters to the board, arguing for the reinstatement of the Oden school. However, the board followed the director's proposal. The population then formed a special action group for the "maintenance of the Oden school" and made its own investigation of the case.

It sent an appeal to the board asking for a renewed consideration of the case. The argument was that the authorities had not made a correct calculation of the costs for maintaining the school or for bussing the pupils to another school. The appeal was, however, left unheard by the board: the school was to be closed. The parents then formed a special committee for the preparation of an application to the National Agency for Education to establish a free school.

The application was approved, and the Ecological School of Oden was established in the existing school building. An economic association made up of all parents and some other inhabitants in the municipality assumed responsibility for the school. Two teacher positions were announced, but none of the teachers who had previously worked in the building (when it was a public school) applied for the positions. Instead, they found employment in other schools in the Frej municipality. During the first year, the parents provided a lot of idealistic and non-paid work, however, a continuous need for parental input in the school still exists.

During the first year, the school had 34 pupils altogether in grades 1-6. All pupils from the former public school were enrolled, and some additional pupils from parishes at a longer distance were admitted. Due to the general reductions made in the educational budget of the municipality, the Oden school received smaller subsidies in the second year than it did during the first year.

The Schools in Their Contexts

The educational changes that have taken place may be studied by comparing them against the background provided by certain parameters, which are situated within three principal areas of analysis. These parameters also control the educational policies and implementations during the years to come. The areas are: 1) society, 2) policy, 3) types of regulation and control of and subsidies to the educational system.

Society may be seen as consisting of three spheres: the state sphere, the production sphere, and the civil sphere. The state sphere includes structures, functions, activities, and discourses that emerge from the project to create, maintain, and develop a nation and nationhood within a certain territory. It also includes efforts aimed at legitimizing the state machinery and the production sphere, from which the state derives its resources. The state also mediates between various, and sometimes conflicting, interests in the society. The state machinery may function at various levels in society. In Sweden, for instance, there is a central state apparatus but also more than 200 municipality parliaments, which also belong to the state sphere. A large portion of the activities in the state sphere are guided by bureaucratic rationality and bureaucratic rules and incentives and by the tendency to treat individuals in a standardized way. Since education systems are financed by the state, they are, thus, state apparatuses (Apple 1980; Dale 1989).

The production sphere includes structures and activities for the production of goods and services for sale. It is governed by the market principles and incentives.[10] That is, in the production sphere, individuals act primarily for material, or utilitarian, reasons.

The civil sphere consists of structures and activities that derive from incentives that are based on individuals' intentions, ideals, and morals. Value-based popular movements, for instance, belong to the civil sphere. The same applies to interest-based popular movements (trade unions, for instance), but as soon as they deal with material benefits, they enter into the production sphere. Around the world, the civil sphere of each society has become more heterogeneous in some aspects, due mainly to migrations and revitalization of local cultures (ex-Yugoslavia and Canada are just two examples).

There are transactions and exchanges between the three spheres, and a large share of these take the form of ideological and symbolic influences. During the past decade, metaphors, ideas, morals and incentives from the sphere of production have been applied to or have come to guide actions and phenomena not only within the state sphere but also in the civil sphere. Marketization and commodification of leisure time activities is just one example (Johanek 1992).

There are also interactions between every individual society and its spheres, on the one hand, and the world system, on the other hand. Exchanges take place not only between the production spheres of various countries but also between European Union (EU) bodies and national government as well as between civil spheres in various countries.

The education system does not only have a strategic position in the intersection between these spheres, but it is also in direct interaction with them. It has to fulfill certain requirements from and tasks for the three societal spheres. The strategic position of the education system in the national context and the principal features of restructuring education are presented in Figure 1.1.

Position of the Educational System in the National Context

(1) THE STATE SPHERE	(2)THE PRODUCTION SPHERE
Decentralization of and within the state sphere: school-based decision- making, school-based management, shared decision-making, and so on.	(a) Pseudo-market (possibility of choice) (b) Real market (complete choice, vouchers, fees)

Freedom of choice:

Within the public sector only   *Public and private sectors*

Education System

(3) CIVIL SPHERE

Figure 1.1 Three societal spheres and strategies of restructuring education

Decentralization of various types implies a movement from more central levels to lower levels within the state sphere. This movement is always in the direction towards the civil sphere, while what is commonly called privatization is a movement from the state towards one of the other two spheres. However, a move towards the production sphere (the creation of a school for profit motives) and a move towards the civil sphere (the parents and teachers establishing a free school, for instance) may have completely different implications for the participants (school staff, parents, and pupils) (Weiler 1989). A transfer of ideas or metaphors from the production sphere to the educational arena, or vice-versa, may be of two types: (a) rules, incentives, and so on from the production sphere are applied to education as if the educational domain were a marketplace, or (b) the essential aspects of the production sphere are directly applied within the educational domain. Logically, we could also find movements from the civil sphere to the other spheres, but empirically, such cases are not mentioned in the literature on restructuring. The policies are a zone between the state sphere and the other societal spheres. It includes various types of policies, educational policies among others, and these are conditioned by changes in the relationships between the three spheres as well as ideological streamlines and "waves" in the world system. In regard to education and social policies, three principal paradigms and a large number of policy issues may be distinguished (Boyd 1992; Chubb and Moe 1990; Colclough 1990; Daun 1993). Each of the paradigms has one principal orientation:

1. Market orientation
2. Welfare and needs orientation
3. Popular orientation

The market-oriented paradigm has been used for analyzing politics (see, for instance, Downs 1957), and it is related to some theoretical approaches in sociology and social psychology (Homans 1961, for instance). It is also consistent with the behaviorist psychology (Townsend and Burke 1962). It is the base from which ideas of privatization and choice have been derived (Daun 1993). Society is perceived to be constituted by a sum of individuals who want to maximize their own utility rate. Ethnic diversity is seen as a mosaic of various free individuals or groups (Gordiani 1993). Education is principally an individual and societal investment that should contribute to material growth.

The welfare orientation is related to basic human needs and human resource development ideas. Basic education is seen not only as an instrument for achieving welfare but also as a welfare item in itself, a human right. Society is perceived to be made up of socio-economic classes and contradictory interests. The state is there to guarantee distribution of welfare (Cornia et al. 1987, UNDP 1991). The welfare orientation dominated social and educational discourse and social and educational policies during the 1960s and 1970s and was then more or less replaced by the market orientation.

The popular orientation has not materialized anywhere, but it is an important ingredient of utopian socialism, anarchism, and populism (Johnston 1990; Woodcock 1962). It implies that people themselves act freely and create their own organizations and institutions without interference from the state sphere or the production sphere.

Discourse (educational or other) derives from the paradigms and the interaction between the societal spheres. Policies are the more concrete manifestations of the paradigms and discourses. The education discourse and education policies may also be analyzed in relation to various dimensions of equality (Ball 1990; Daun and Löfving 1995).

Table 7: Educational Equality and Some of Its Dimensions

Pupil Characteristics	(a) Equal Access	(b) Equal Opportunity	(c) Equal Outcome
(1) Socio-economic class	1a	1b	1c
(2) Sex	2a	2b	2c
(3) Handicap	3a	3b	3c
(4) Ethnic / linguistic affiliation	4a	4b	4c

Equality of access, regardless of socio-economic class and sex (1a and 2a), was the principal theme not only in Sweden but also in other industrialized countries during the first period after World War II. The same applies to education in relation to handicapped persons (3a). When practically everybody had access to primary and lower secondary education, equality of opportunity and outcome (1b and 1c and to some extent 2b and 2c) also entered into the education and research discourse. With the economic recession and the hegemony of the market orientation, equality came to lose some of its space in discourse and policy or came to some extent to deal more with equality in relation to cultural characteristics (4a and 4b). However, this latter area of equality is not as pertinent in Sweden as in Canada or Belgium, for instance.

The mentioned relations between the societal spheres place the education system between contradictory demands in regard to cultural and linguistic sensitivity. Some of these contradictions are:

1. cultural affiliation versus class affiliation
2. local culture and local identity versus European culture and European identity
3. assimilation versus integration
4. mother tongue as a family issue versus mother tongue as the language of instruction in the school

The whole cultural/linguistic problem has been articulated during a period when two other societal forces affect the school: 1) the economic recession and demands for effectivity and 2) the European Union (EU) ambition to create a European identity (Collot, Didier, and Loueslati 1993; EU 1994 a,b).

Apart from the societal spheres and educational paradigms, discourses, and policies, the types of existing parties and power relations influence what is taking place within the educational system.

ANALYSIS AND TENDENCIES FOR THE FUTURE

At the macro level, the societal conditions of a shrinking economy but increased production of "messages" such as migrations, cultural secularization, commodification of culture, revival of sub-cultures, and so on, are similar for the three case schools. The schools also function within the context of decentralization of the state machinery (and, consequently, of the school system) and budget reductions. In addition to this, the changed policies (the state control, regulations, and subsidies, in particular) made the establishment of the free schools possible. In Frej, many other schools of the same size as the Oden school had been closed before the policies changed due to the decreasing population and the reduction of educational expenditures. The populations protested but did not have the financial and legal means for creating alternatives to the closed schools.

For the first time in the history of Frej, the Social Democrats, in alliance with other parties, came to have the majority in the municipality parliament and boards after the elections in 1994. More schools are planned to be closed in Frej, but the decisions to do so have been delayed, evidently because the municipality school board and municipality government do not want to have more free schools established. The existence of such schools contradict the welfare paradigm as it is interpreted by Social Democrats in Sweden, and it is also more costly; the subsidies to free schools may be more expensive than having the pupils taught in larger public schools.

For the population in Oden, the closure of the public school was seen as something more than a measure to save public money. Many estimates were presented to the school board by the Parent-School Association, the action group, and various local bodies of the Center party. These estimations showed that no money was to be saved by closing the Oden school, providing more space in another school, and busing the Oden children to this school.

In a letter to the school board, the local committee of the Center party writes that ". . . the estimations (made by the school board) are embarrassingly incomplete and made in haste. . . ." The budget for the first year of the Oden ecological school was smaller than what had been estimated by the municipality school board. That is, the amount of money to be saved by busing the children to another school would not be as large as estimated.

The decentralization process did not affect the possibility of establishing free schools, since the competence to make decisions concerning the number and localization of schools is not delegated to the school districts but is determined by the municipality's school board. These decisions can be changed only by the municipal parliament. It means that the director of the school district in which the Oden school is situated did not have the right to let this school continue as a public school. In Dala, the suggestions coming from a group of teachers were rejected by the municipality school board. If the suggestion to create a school-within-a-school had been made by a politician, it would have had to be handled at the highest level of the municipality, and it could (theoretically) have been accepted.

The two free schools were created for completely different reasons, but what provoked their creation was the reaction from the municipal bodies on the proposals coming from the civil sphere. The initial idea in this sphere was in none of the cases to take over from the state sphere. The contrary is very evident at least in the case of the Oden school. There was, paradoxically, a struggle between the civil sphere and the state sphere over the fact that participants in the former felt that participants in the latter did not maintain the space that the state had and did not guarantee the welfare that was expected.

An action group was formed out of the Parent-School Association and its purpose was to convince the municipal authorities that the Oden school should be maintained. The parents saw it as a self-evident duty of the state to guarantee education for their children in the local community itself. Letters from the action group to the school board indicate this:

We work and pay taxes. . . . We are the foundation of this society. . . .
If you want cooperation and consensus, then you should skip all arm-

chair constructions and use all local conditions and advantages that
already exist...

In another letter, sent in the last days before the decision to close
the school was to become final, the action group argued from the same
point of departure—that schooling is a welfare issue that has
traditionally been guaranteed by the state and should continue to be so.
In the last moment, it seemed possible to save the school, either by
giving it a new profile within the public sector or by establishing it as a
free school. In both cases, a plan and a program for the "new school"
had to be presented to the school board:

> ...We need time... postpone the decision to August.... The enemy
> forces us to write a plan for an activity that has existed for a long
> time.... Who is the enemy... and why do we have an enemy....[11]

Participants in the (civil) local community now have come to perceive
participants in municipality authorities (state) as enemies.

The conditions for the two schools differ in another important
aspect related to the civil sphere. The Oden parish does not have any
immigrants, while these constitute a large proportion of the population
in Dala. There are indications that pupils of Swedish origin move from
public schools that are "immigrant dense" to public or free schools that
are not.

What will happen within primary and lower secondary education in
the future is conditioned by macro factors such as economic growth or
stagnation and processes in the world system (requirements from the
European Union, for instance) and power relations between the parties
in the National parliament and the national government. According to
Eide (1992) the Scandinavian educational policies and systems differ
from those on the continent in that they are more welfare oriented. Is
this "tradition" going to be broken?

It is also evident that a minor change in the policies such as
changed regulations and subsidies can have far-reaching consequences
for the free schools as well as for the choice possibilities. If the decision
concerning the amount of subsidies to the free schools is delegated to
the municipalities (as suggested by a government committee in 1995),
the parameters for choice and the survival of free schools will vary
from one municipality to another. The present majorities in both of the

municipalities studied here will probably decrease the subsidies considerably. Then both free schools will be closed.

On the other hand, the loose system of regulation and control of admission and catchment areas (see Table 2) that was introduced by the Conservative Party seems to be in direct contradiction to the welfare paradigm and educational equality of access and opportunity. It is hard to understand why a Social Democratic government maintains this system when it evidently allows pupils of Swedish origin to leave schools that have a large proportion of immigrant pupils. Does this indicate that the welfare policy is becoming more and more influenced by the market paradigm?

In the middle of the 1980s (before the consequences of the economic recession were fully perceived), Dahllöf (1984) and Marklund (1984) discussed the likelihood for various types of educational reforms to occur in different countries. The restructuring that was implemented after the change of government in 1991 was not possible to predict from the parameters they discussed. It seems that many decisions made from the end of the 1980s on are rather independent from and contradictory to the social and cultural forces in Sweden. In short, the governments and national parliaments seem to have become able to make decisions, the results of which cannot be predicted solely from the relationships between the societal spheres of society. If we also add that there are influences from the world system, it becomes evident that it is difficult to foresee what educational changes will probably take place in the future.

NOTES

1. The three schools are being studied in a current research project on restructuring education. See Daun and Miron (1994), *Restructuring of Education in Europe: A Research Programme*. Stockholm: Institute of International Education.

2. It may be unintended but, on the other hand, some governments in the world see certain lifestyles as indicators of cultural deprivation and make efforts to compensate the pupils for this deficiency (see, for instance, Connel 1994).

3. Traditionally, the following political parties have existed in Sweden: The Social Democratic Party, the Center Party, the Liberal Party, the Conservative Party and the Communist Party. Later on, two other parties

emerged and played an important role in politics since the middle of the 1980s: the Green (Environmental) Party and the Christian Democratic Party. All reform committees have had representatives from at least the four largest political parties and the larger interest or voluntary organizations. *Förankra besluten* (anchor the decisions) is a typical expression mirroring the efforts to have a broad base guaranteed before decisions are made and implemented.

4. Since the research project was still going on at the time of publication, preliminary findings from only three of the four case studies are presented here.

5. Pseudonyms are used for all municipalities and schools involved in the study.

6. In Sweden, urban areas or cities of this type came to be called *sovstäder*, which in English means "bedroom community."

7. In the United States, school-within-school is one established type of restructuring. It implies that the minor school stays under the administration of the major school and in its building but it retains its own budget and its own pedagogical style. See, for instance, J. Nathan (ed.) (1989), *Public Schools by Choice, Expanding Opportunities for Parents, Students and Teachers*. St. Paul, Minnesota: The Institute for Learning and Teaching.

8. An *ekonomisk förening* is an association of economists in which the members pay an initial fee or quota. The aim of the association is to fulfill defined tasks in the interest of its members, but it is not allowed to make a profit in the same way as stock companies.

9. There are certain requirements for the municipality to receive subsidies from the state. One of them is a minimum number of pupils in the school. If the number of pupils falls below the established minimum, no state subsidies are paid by the central level.

10. In their pure form, the market principles may be formulated in the following way: 1) All individuals have an incentive to act in their own interest and aggressively in order to maximize the utility for their own sake; 2) There is a large number of producers/sellers and consumers/buyers, who act independently from each other; 3) All producers/sellers try to maximize their profits; 4) There is free circulation of goods and services; 5) All sellers and buyers have perfect information concerning available goods and services, as well as about their prices; 6) Extraneous factors, such as obstacles to transactions and exchanges or costs related to these, do not exist; 7) Every actor is free to enter into or exit from the market arena; and 8) When all consumers can choose, the quality of what is offered will increase. For this summary of the market principles, see Colclough 1990; Cookson Jr. 1991, 1992; Doughartty and Sostre 1992; Krashinsky 1986; and Levin 1991.

11. Skrivelse 30.8.93 till Gotland Kummun fran Aktionsgruppen foer Oden sholas berarande (Letter 30.8.93 to Gotland municipality from the Action Group for maintenance of the Oden School).

REFERENCES

Apple, M. 1980. *Education and Power*. London: Routledge & Kegan Paul.

Ball, S.F. 1990. *Politics and Policy Making in Education. Explorations in Policy Sociology*. London: Routledge.

Boli, J. 1989. *New Citizens for a New Society. The Institutional Origins of Mass Schooling in Sweden*. New York: Pergamon.

Boyd, W.L. 1992. "The Power of Paradigms: Reconceptualizing Educational Policy and Management." *Educational Administration Quarterly* 28, no. 4.

Chubb, J.E., and T. M. Moe. 1990. *Politics, Markets and America's Schools*. Washington, D.C.: The Brookings Institution.

Colclough, C. 1990. "Structuralism versus Neo-Liberalism: An Introduction." In *States or Markets? Neo-Liberalism and the Development of Policy Debate*, eds. C. Colclough and J. Manor. Oxford: Clarendon Press.

Collot, A., G. Didier, and B. Loueslati. 1993. "La société interculturelle: projets et débats: Introduction." In *La pluralité culturelle dans les systèmes éducatifs européens*, eds. A. Collot, G. Didier, and B. Loueslati. Lorraine: Centre régional de documentation.

Connel, R.W. 1994. "Poverty and Education." *Harvard Educational Review* 64, no. 2, pp. 125-49.

Cookson Jr., P. 1991. "Private Schooling and Equity. Dilemmas of Choice." *Education and Urban Society* 23, no. 2, pp. 185-99.

Cookson Jr., P. 1992. "Introduction" (to special issue on *The Choice Controversy*). *Educational Policy* 6, no. 2, pp. 99-104.

Cookson Jr., P. 1992. *The Choice Controversy*. New York: Corwin Press, Inc.

Cornia, G.A., R. Jollby, and F. Stewart. 1987. *Adjustment with a Human Face*. Oxford: Clarendon Press.

Dahllöf, U. 1984. "Contextual Problems of Educational Reforms: A Swedish Perspective." In *Educational Research and Policy. How Do They Relate?*, eds. T. Husén and M. Kogan. Oxford: Pergamon Press.

Dale, R. 1989. *The State and Education Policy*. Milton Keynes: Open University Press.

Daun, H. 1993. *Omstrukturering av skolsystemen. Decentralizering, valfrihet och privatisering. En internationell översikt* (Restructuring School

Systems. Decentralization, Choice and Privatization. An International Research Review). Stockholm: National Agency for Education.

Daun, H., and I. Fägerlind. 1991. "SIDA Educational Policy and Basic Education in Tanzania. The Swedish State, Basic Education in Sweden and the SIDA Policy." Paper presented at the NASEDEC conference in Hornbaek, Denmark, October.

Daun, H. and A. Löfving, 1995. "Likvärdig skolgång" (Equalized Schooling). In Skolverket: Likvärdighet i skolan, en antologi (Equity in School, An Anthology), eds. H. Daun and A. Löfving. Stockholm: National Agency for Education.

Daun, H., and G. Miron. 1994. Restructuring of Education in Europe: A Research Programme. Stockholm: Institute of International Education.

Doughartty, K.J., and L. Sostre. 1992. "Minerva and the Market: The Sources of the Movement for School Choice." Educational Policy 6, no. 2, pp. 160-79.

Downs, A. 1957. An Economic Theory of Democracy. New York: Harper and Row.

Edwards, T., and G. Whitty. 1992. "Parental Choice and Educational Reform in Britain and the United States." British Journal of Educational Studies 40, no 2, pp. 101-17.

Eide, K. 1992. "The Future of European Education as Seen from the North." Comparative Education 28, no. 1, pp. 9-17.

Elvander, N. 1968. Intresseorganisationerna i dagens Sverige (The Interest Organizations in Contemporary Sweden). Lund: Gleerups.

European Union (EU). 1994. "Europe at School." Le Magazine no. 1.

European Union (EU). 1994. "School failure and social exclusion." Le Magazine no. 1.

Frykman, J., and O. Löfgren. 1979. Den kultiverade människan. Lund: Liber.

Fullan, M.G. 1991. The Meaning of Educational Change. New York: Cassell.

Gordiani, T.J. 1993. "École, identités nationales, identité européenne." In La pluralité culturelle dans les systèmes éducatifs européens, eds. A. Collot, G. Didier, and B. Loueslati. Lorraine: Centre régional de documentation.

Homans, G. 1961. Social Behavior: Its Elementary Forms. New York: Harcourt, Brace and World.

Husén, T. 1988. Skolreformerna och forskningen. Stockholm: Verbum Gothia.

Isling, Å. 1980. Kampen for och mot en demokratisk skola (The Struggle for and Against a Democractic School). Stockholm: Sober.

Isling, Å. 1984. Grundskola för allmän-mänsklig kompetens (Comprehensive School for General Human Competence). Stockholm: Sober.

Johanek, M. 1992. "Private Citizenship and School Choice." *Journal of Educational Policy* 6, no. 2.

Johansson, L. 1982. *Kommunal servicevariation. Rapport från Kommunaldemokratiska forskningsgruppen.* DsKn 1982:2 (Variation in Municipality Service. Report from the Committee for Research on Municipal Democracy). Stockholm: Kommunaldepartementet.

Johnston, B.J. 1990. "Considerations on School Restructuring." *Educational Policy* 4, no. 3, pp. 215-31.

Krashinsky, M. 1986. "Educational Vouchers and Economics: A Rejoinder." *Teachers College Records* 88, no. 2, pp. 163-67.

Levin, H.M. 1991. "The Economics of Educational Choice. A Reply to the West." *Economics of Education Review* 10, no. 2, pp. 171-75.

Marklund, S. 1984. "Effects of Educational Research on Educational Policy-Making: The Case of Sweden." In *Educational Research and Policy. How Do They Relate?*, eds. T. Husén and M. Kogan. Oxford: Pergamon Press.

McLean, M. 1989. "'Populist' Centralism: The 1988 Education Reform Act in England and Wales." *Educational Policy* 3, no. 3, pp. 233-44.

McLean, M., and N. Voskrensenskaya. 1992. "Educational Revolution from Above: Thatcher's Britain and Gorbachev's Soviet Union." *Comparative Education Review* 36, no. 1, pp. 71-90.

Montin, S. 1992. "Privatiseringsprocesser i kommunerna—teoretiska utgångspunkter och empiriska exempel" (Processes of Privatization in the Municipalities—Theoretical Points of Departure and Empirical Examples). *Statsvetenskaplig tidskrift,* no. 1.

Möller, M. 1995. "Educational Management and Conditions for Competence." Master thesis. Institute of International Education, Stockholm University.

Nathan, J., ed. 1989. *Public Schools by Choice. Expanding Opportunities for Parents, Students and Teachers.* St. Paul, Minnesota: The Institute for Learning and Teaching.

Odin, B., and K. Åhs. 1985. *Den dolda styrningen. Skolpolitisk intention—pedagogisk verklighet* (The Hidden Steering. Intentions of Education Policy—Pedagogical Reality). Lund: Studentlitteratur.

Papagiannis, G.J., J.T. Owens, and J.T. Easton. 1992. *The School Restructuring Movement in the USA: An Analysis of Major Issues and Policy Implications.* Paris: UNESCO.

Paulston, R.G. 1980. "The Same (Lapp) Ethnic Movements." In *Other Dreams, Other Schools: Folk Colleges in Social and Ethnic Movements,* ed. R.G. Paulston. Pittsburgh: University of Pittsburgh.

Raywid, M.A. 1985. "Family Choice Arrangements in Public Schools: A Review of the Literature." *Review of Educational Research* 55, no. 4, pp. 435-67.

Raywid, M.A. 1989. "The Mounting Case for Schools of Choice." In *Public Schools by Choice. Expanding Opportunities for Parents, Students and Teachers,* ed. J. Nathan. St. Paul, Minnesota: The Institute for Learning and Teaching.

Raywid, M.A. 1990. "Successful Schools of Choice: Cottage Industry Benefits in Large Systems." *Educational Policy* 4, no. 2 pp. 93-108.

Raywid, M.A. 1992. "Choice Orientations, Discussions and Prospects." *Educational Policy* 6, no. 2, pp. 105-22.

Telhaug, A. O. 1990. *Den nye utdaningspolitiske retorikken.* Oslo: Universitetsforlaget.

Townsend, E.A., and P.J. Burke. 1962. *Learning for Teachers.* New York: The Macmillan Company.

United Nations Development Programme (UNDP). 1991. *Human Development Report 1991.* New York: Oxford University Press.

Weiler, H.W.N. 1989. "Education and Power: The Politics of Educational Decentralization in Comparative Perspective." *Educational Policy* 3, no. 1, pp. 31-43.

Widgren, J. 1982 . *Svensk invandrarpolitik* (Swedish Immigration Policy). Stockholm: Liber.

Woodcock, G. 1962. *Anarchism.* London: The World Publishing Company.

CHAPTER 15

From the Mass to the Elite: Structure, Limits, and the Future of Scandinavian Educational Systems

Osmo Kivinen and *Risto Rinne*

INTRODUCTION

In many countries, egalitarian educational policies adopted after World War II have recently come under question, and in the Scandinavian countries, where Finland and Sweden are reorienting themselves from their status on Europe's geopolitical periphery to full membership in the European Union (EU), similar challenges have been made against the characteristic "social democratic" model of welfare. With the opening up of educational policy toward new kinds of opportunities, what should be the relationship between elite and mass education? Which countries and which models might offer appropriate paths for developing alternatives to traditional State-centralized educational systems? In a "post-Fordian" society, how can the link between school and work and a new division of labor be organized? In the following pages, we shall be looking for answers to questions such as these. We shall consider educational systems elsewhere in the postindustrial world as alternatives to schooling as it has evolved in Scandinavia; we shall be looking closely at alternative interpretations of "egalitarian educational policies," with reference to their historical applications in the Nordic countries and especially in Finland. We shall also ask what the tasks of education are and how they are shifting in a changing society. Finally, we shall consider the problems posed by over- and underutilization of education on the labor market and in the lives of individuals.

SCANDINAVIA AND INTERNATIONAL EDUCATIONAL MODELS

If the process of preparation for employment is examined on a comparative basis between different countries, four basic patterns can be discerned. In the Nordic countries such as Finland and Sweden, vocational education is for the most part provided in purpose-built institutions. In the United States, most people learn their job on the job, and vocational colleges as such play a minor role. In Germany, the prevailing system of vocational education is the dual apprenticeship, consisting of clearly differentiated periods of general education and of vocational training. Finally, in the fourth model, vocational education in France is largely carried out within the general school system (Blossfeld 1992: 172-178).

The American model is currently attracting considerable interest in Europe. Its hierarchy of educational pathways, clearly status differentiated but open to market pressures, presents a serious challenge to the Nordic pattern of education. However, it will not be easy to steer Scandinavian egalitarian educational policy into the paths of market-driven competition.

Within Europe, the recent expansion of the European Union has reawakened a struggle between Berlin and Paris for the intellectual leadership of the continent as might be exemplified by their very high investments in cultural projects currently underway in both cities. In the future, the realistic role available for the smaller countries on the European periphery might merely be to decide which pool to ally themselves with. From the perspective of Berlin, capital of a reunited and increasingly powerful Germany, Finland has for centuries been a "good pupil" (whether the homework was Luther, Hegel, or Marx), and the few Finns who have so far boarded the Eurotrain are more likely to step off in Berlin than in Paris. Moreover, it has been suggested that the passengers on the Eurotrain travel in different classes: Osmo Pekonen (1995), for example, predicts that in the Brave New Europe the number involved in making important decisions will be in inverse proportion to the scale and importance of the decision. An appropriate slogan for the emergent United States of Europe, it seems, could well be: "Elites of the world, unite!" and in that case, it may be doubted whether Nordic representatives will stand much chance of a grasp on the handles of EU power.

Elitist thinkers such as Pekonen (1995) have warned that the opportunities for influence within the European Union (one of the factors which swung the vote in the Finnish and Swedish membership referenda) will remain an empty promise unless the national school systems can rapidly cultivate the kind of elite which the self-confident mandarins educated at the elite schools of Western Europe can acknowledge as their equals. Otherwise, the role available for Finland and Sweden, with their predominance of engineers and narrow experts, will be limited at the most to the negotiation of technical details. This "civilization gap" is seen as the outcome of an obsessive egalitarian thinking deeply rooted in the Nordic school system, too great to be overcome by crash courses in diplomacy; what is called for is a fresh approach in educational policy to the relationship between equal treatment for all citizens and the needs of the elite.

If we really wish to influence the course of events in the EU, it is thus argued, the Nordic member states will need their own "Euro-elites," capable of operating in the incredibly complex decision networks on equal terms with, for example, the French elite. In France, the elites have their own schools, which are demanding in standards, harshly competitive, and ruthless in weeding out the weak, and where the pupil is no "spoilt petty king whose whims are exempt from discipline" (Pekonen 1995). In the top schools, pupils are required to produce concentrated, sustained work. French society acknowledges the existence of social hierarchies, and their reproduction is indeed one of the central functions fulfilled by the school system (cf. Bourdieu 1988). The elite schools offer a dazzling crystallization of Gallicism at its best and at its worst. The educational model is a centralized and elitist one characteristic of a historically imperialist nation; it has its roots in medieval feudalism and in the hierarchical-cooperative social order promoted by the Roman Catholic Church (Ringer 1992). While it displays in some respects similarities with the strict hierarchical patterns of the American model, it is less open to market influences. For society in the Nordic countries, however, thoroughly permeated by the Protestant ethic and constructed around egalitarian models of citizenship, an elitist school system of this type is of little use. In small countries, the promotion of an aristocratic-type elite education for the few, at the expense of furthering the talents of the nation as a whole, would both undermine the general level of civilization and lead to social and economic decline. If the alternatives are concentrating resources on the education of the brightest elite or maintaining a good general level of education for the population at large, the choice is not difficult. Is it possible, however, in small societies like those of the Nordic countries, to combine an elite education for a select few while maintaining a high standard of general education for the population as a whole?

EGALITARIAN MODELS OF EDUCATION

The recent history of all the Nordic states (Denmark, Finland, Norway; and Sweden) since the World War II is characterized by the pursuit of reduced social differentiation, low income differentials, and a high level of social security. As a consequence of policies pursuing the well-being of the entire citizenry, the state regulated public sector has expanded enormously. Openness of social mobility and the equality of all citizens are two of the fundamental principles which have underlain the "Social Democratic" policies characteristic of the Nordic states. Educational policies aiming at equality of opportunity have been seen as the spearhead of social policies for the promotion of a fuller democracy (Esping-Andersen, Rohwer, and Sørensen 1994; Jonsson 1987).

It is not only in the Nordic states that the expansion of education has been seen in the twentieth century as one of the pillars of a democratic society. Unqualified trust in the omnipotence of education, however, has gradually faded. Even by the early 1970s, many investigations were beginning to demonstrate the failure of education to fulfill its more ambitious promises, and not even the achievement of "greater equality of educational opportunity" could be taken for granted. The OECD recognized that the enormous expansion in educational expenditure during the 1950s and the 1960s had actually brought about only marginal alterations in equality of opportunity, and optimism and expansionism partly gave way to pessimistic scepticism (cf. Neave 1976, pp. 60-61). With the abandonment of inflated expectations, it has become possible to recognize the relativity of "equality of opportunity" slogans, and the conflicting interests associated with them. Even twenty years ago, Guy Neave (1976, pp. 60-66) drew a distinction between three separate models of educational opportunity found in post-World War II educational policies: the elitist, the socially oriented, and the individually centered. All of these can readily be recognized in Nordic educational policies.

In the elitist conception, intelligence is perceived as inherited and measurable, and individuals can be classified on the basis of psychometric tests. Once the individual has passed a particular phase of development in early adolescence, tests are believed to predict his/her level of ability as an adult and thus his/her prospects in later life. From this perspective, equality of opportunity implies the removal of financial obstacles to the educational progress of the gifted: opportunities for high-powered education should be restricted to a specified percentage of highly intelligent individuals. Equality of opportunity would thus be determined during primary and secondary education, and secondary education in particular should serve above all as a filter for the determination of educational careers and pathways, by separating the gifted from the less able. The role of schools in social mobility would thus be akin to that of Darwinian natural selection. The best senior high schools would then channel the most able students into the elite universities and thence into elite professions and status. Ultimately, the entire educational system could then be evaluated on the basis of the achievements of university graduates.

In socially oriented models of equality of opportunity, however, the emphasis is placed upon the determination of intelligence by the individual's growth environment: home and family, parents' expectations and influences. While intelligence is recognized in principle as being measurable, it is not considered as remaining constant irrespective of environmental influences. Consequently, an individual's prospects of scholastic success and future career cannot be directly predicted on the basis of early achievement. The educational system should be able to offer all children equal education and focus compensatory measures in primary and secondary education on children from environmentally disadvantaged families. By delaying the beginning of educational specialization and selection procedures, it is expected that equality of opportunity will be enhanced. The success of the educational system can then be evaluated on the basis of the proportion of students who proceed with education voluntarily after completing their compulsory education.

The individually-centered model of equality of opportunity places the emphasis upon seeing intelligence as a cultural phenomenon. Since intellectual capacity is culturally conditioned and dynamic in nature, it cannot meaningfully be measured. The key concept for educational policy is differentiation. Equality of opportunity cannot be evaluated on the basis of qualifications achieved or student flows but on the basis of how far individuals are able, in a manner appropriate for themselves, to access and utilize information. An educational system can only be evaluated on the basis of how far it is capable of generating benefits for the multiple and diverse needs of all classes and all individuals.

In Finland, as in the other Nordic countries, educational policy before the 1950s and 1960s had been strongly elitist, imposing restrictions on the expansion both of the universities and also of the selective senior secondary schools. Binary school systems proceeded from a decisive bifurcation carried out after merely four years of initial elementary schooling. Gradually, however, this elitist model succumbed to pressure: first in the five-year junior secondary school, and subsequently in the three-year senior secondary school leading to the matriculation examination. The effective thrust behind this shift did not, however, come about as a result of abandonment of elitist conceptions of hereditary intelligence but rather because rising standards of living allowed increasing numbers of families to allow or insist on their children acquiring a fuller education in the expectation that this would ensure them better conditions than their parents.

By the 1970s, consequently, the Nordic states had adopted clearly socially oriented models in educational policy. In Finland, higher education was drastically expanded, with the establishment of new institutions to serve both the outlying provinces and new fields. Schools were reorganized around a nine-year comprehensive "foundation school,"[1] where extensive compensatory measures were to be made available for children coming from disadvantaged family environments. Particular attention was paid to ensuring that everyone would have access to nationally standardized curricula, irrespective of locality, gender, or wealth. Educational specialization was postponed as long as possible, though in practice the comprehensive school did incorporate subtle mechanisms of occupational guidance.

In Finland, the 1990s have seen a shift toward a more individually-oriented model in educational policy, perhaps slightly later than in other Nordic societies. Even though statements of curricular objectives have laid nominal stress on individualism since the 1970s, it is only on the brink of the twenty-first century that "consumer-driven" curricular concepts are being introduced. In practice, this means a dismantling of centralized controls, decentralization of curricular decisions, relaxing of standards, and an emphasis on individual differentiation. This shift in educational thinking is closely linked to a re-evaluation of the Nordic welfare state in general. The 1990s recession has provoked a powerful neoliberal critique of the enormous burden on the public sector generated by cost-free welfare services. In consequence, the concept of equality of educational opportunity is once again taking on stronger Darwinian implications, with the promotion of individual competition in the education and labor markets, unhampered by equalization measures (Kivinen and Rinne 1995).

REDEFINING THE TASKS FOR NORDIC EDUCATION

As in other countries, the roots of the educational institutions in the Nordic countries date back to the nineteenth century. At that time, Finland was an autonomous Grand Duchy under the Russian Tsar. Under legislation passed in 1866, elementary schools were set up to "civilize the common people" and teach them due obedience to authority, whereas the middle orders were educated in the secondary schools, and the public officials and clergy at the one university in the country (originally established in Turku in 1640). Following the achievement of independence in 1917, compulsory education legislation was passed in 1921, though its implementation took several years. The decades following World War II, when standards of living rose steadily, saw a rapid expansion in education as the children of wider and wider sections of the population opted for a longer education. Within a few decades, the mean duration of schooling rose from five to twelve years. This expansion of education in the Nordic states is not drastically different from that in other Western countries, though in Finland, like other features of social change, it happened more abruptly. Possibly as a relic of the authoritarian mentality of the Tsarist state, Finns have internalized an unusually firm trust in the blessings of education. The general education offered in the comprehensive school, which has steadily been lengthened, is seen as providing one of the basic requirements for success as a civilized nation, while the provision of postcompulsory vocational training for wider and wider sections of the population has been encouraged as the motor of efficient industry and effective services, thus ensuring the nation's capacity to compete successfully on international markets. Similarly, the proliferation of higher education institutions (both in terms of disciplines and geography) has been seen as promoting scientific and technological progress and also as consolidating the national graduate elite expected to boost national self-respect.

The nine-year "foundation school" (*peruskoulu*) system introduced in Finland was an imitation, even in name, of its Swedish counterpart, the *grundskola*: a homogeneous model, with largely universal standardized curricula, and pupils proceeding through in annual cohorts. In practice, there was virtually no room for internal differentiation. The teachers were trained according to a standard pattern, the curriculum was national, and budgetary and other legislation was detailed and precise. It is only since the end of the 1980s that the homogeneity of the system has been opened up to differentiation, curricular flexibility, and decentralization and deregulation of legislation. Within the "foundation school," previously standardized for all, there are now moves to (re)establish classes for gifted children, and there has even been discussion about setting up independent schools with market funding.

Following the foundation school, the academic alternative is the senior high school, a three-year course leading to the nationally uniform Matriculation Examination. Senior high school is currently attended by slightly over half of the age group. In recent years, increased scope for differentiation has been introduced: there are schools with a special emphasis (e.g., sports or natural sciences or music); in addition, the principle of annual cohorts is being replaced by a modular curriculum, which can be completed over a period of 2-4 years. Notwithstanding these changes, the range of subjects taught continues to reflect traditions stretching back into the nineteenth century, largely isolated from the social environment and taught by means of a highly traditional pedagogy.

Moreover, the status of the senior high school in society today is utterly different from what it was when these schools were established. Originally, the matriculation examination was the entrance examination for university, but with half the population achieving a pass of some level, universities have introduced their own *numerus clausus* selection procedures, while many students who have completed their matriculation then proceed into vocational further education rather than academic higher education. On the other hand, in addition to its function of academic and intellectual selection, the senior high school currently also fulfills a significant function in keeping otherwise unemployed young people off the streets.

The Finnish vocational education system is highly school-like and has typically been criticized for being too remote from the world of work and for failing to provide the real skills and abilities needed at work. In recent years, serious attempts have been made to find solutions to the gulf between work and school, and among the educational reforms in the 1990s; the most drastic are probably those in the field of vocational education. At the tertiary level, Finland is in the process of establishing a binary system, with vocationally-oriented *Fachhochschulen* (*ammattikorkeakoulut*)[2] based on the German or Dutch model to complement the universities and fine arts colleges. The aim is gradually to develop vocational education to university status. Evidently vocational education will become slightly longer in duration than at present. What changes these reforms will in reality achieve in the relations between school and work remains (despite the promises and rhetoric) to be seen; many in the universities suspect that the *Fachhochschulen* will in fact achieve only an exterior upgrading of status.

In the continental tradition, the traditional primary task of the university was to produce public officials. After World War II, when the welfare state was being developed, public sector jobs increased at such a rate that eventually two-thirds of Finnish university graduates were finding permanent employment with the state. As a consequence of the drastic shift in public policies occasioned by the 1990s recession, however, it is anticipated that in the future only one-third of university graduates will be able to find work in the public sector. If this prediction proves valid, it will generate powerful pressures for wide-reaching changes in the nature of higher education; already the prevailing rhetoric is of enterprise and self-employment.

Currently both the Swedish and the Finnish governments are refining their plans for greater efficiency and rationalization in higher education. University policy is thoroughly permeated by the rhetoric of productivity and efficiency. The outcomes of higher education are under constant evaluation, and intensified competition is being promoted between individuals and institutions. Nordic higher education policy, on the brink of the twenty-first century, breathes the ethos of competition, enterprise culture, and performance management.

In social and educational policy texts, however, the slogans persist that "in the future, as the labor force ages and contracts, the maintenance and expansion of welfare will increasingly depend on levels of education and skills." The availability of highly trained manpower is to be ensured both by expanding formal education in the postcompulsory stage and by investing in adult education. Business and industrial interests, especially, speak of crucial choices facing this little country on the periphery and of the need to adopt strategies based either on high skills or on low wages. The high skills option, which is heavily reliant upon education and training, implies heavy ongoing investment in promoting and maintaining the level of skills in the labor force. The low wages option, on the other hand, with an extensive use of cheap immigrant labor and reduction of expenditure on education and training, would shift Finland into the category of low-wage countries, characterized by simple patterns of mass production and falling standards of living (KTM 1993: 58-59).

FROM THE PURSUIT OF LEARNING TO KEEPING SURPLUS LABOR ON HOLD

In official documents on educational policy, the central function of education is usually seen as the task of equipping young people with the knowledge and skills required of full citizens and workers. In this interpretation, a good broad-based general education trains people in civilized behavior and equips them with skills in literacy and numeracy, and with the ability to cope in one or two foreign languages. Vocational education, on the other hand, equips people with the skills required for specific occupations. In addition to these functions of providing qualifications and socialization, education is also inevitably linked with processes of societal selection. The pathway through universities leads to prestigious jobs, while vocational colleges recruit into the working class. The conversion of societal selection processes into processes of separating individuals runs ineradicably through all levels of education from primary to postgraduate.

In modern society, organized around the principle of wage labor, school institutions have increasingly taken on the tasks of social surplus storage and crèche. When the labor market has no pull, young people and adults cannot be offered meaningful work; for children there is nothing worth doing; consequently, the school takes over as the Great

Storehouse. In an age of mass unemployment, all educational institutions from primary to university find themselves functioning more and more as waiting rooms and crèches. In this situation, education no longer concentrates on its traditional primary objective of enhancing citizens' knowledge and skills. The institutions themselves become increasingly mass-oriented in nature and have to content themselves with, somehow, maintaining positive expectations among young people who are watching employment and other opportunities steadily recede out of sight. Yet, even when unemployed and idle, humans search for meaning. Education—even in its new, strange function—ought to set out and make people happy. For a generation accustomed to the luxury products of the entertainment industry, however, the school is hard put to turn out a competitive show.

In the twenty-first century, the media environment will be capable of delivering most of the qualifications traditionally supplied by the school. On the other hand, as education duration becomes longer and longer, the task of the school becomes increasingly that of a crèche, and it will be futile to expect the school to fulfill the pedagogic functions once assigned to it. In that case, the sensible educational policy for the twenty-first century would be not to lengthen but to curtail the duration of schooling. A similar conclusion is indicated also by signs that the school does not serve very well as a crèche. The majority of young people have in any case always found life at school a boring and tedious alternative to the school of life (Jackson 1968).

BENEFITING FROM HIGHER AND HIGHER QUALIFICATIONS

As work is reshaped in the post-industrial society, many traditional occupations are disappearing, others are being radically reorganized, and completely new occupations are making their appearance. The fundamental question is, therefore, how a school institution originally designed for the needs of a nineteenth-century agrarian society can adapt to the needs of the flexible labor market of the twenty-first century. Without in any way underestimating the value of a general education, it must be pointed out that the smaller nations on the northern periphery, in their harsh environments, have succeeded only through hard work. In the future too, under intensifying international competition and without natural resources to fall back on, they will need to survive on the basis of their citizens' skills.

The different ways that learning for a job is organized in different countries reflects different social background expectations. If it is assumed that important occupational experiences cannot be replicated in the classroom but only at the workplace, then effective training for the job needs to be arranged on the job itself. If, on the other hand, it is assumed that in the future individual workers will need a more flexible command of general skills, then vocational education can be arranged to promote general skills apart from the job, in general schools (Blossfeld 1992).

On the dimension of occupational hierarchy, what matters is how far education differentiates between the unskilled and semiskilled workers on the one hand and the occupationally trained on the other. It is also a question, how far the system allows opportunities for skilled workers to climb the job ladder. If certification is trusted as a definition of working skills and if the promise of career advancement is seen as the best motivating force for workers, then what we need is a German-type life-scale system with certification of working skills. If we do not trust certification or stress the dynamism of career ambition, what we need is the French dead-end career vocational school of the American uncertified on-the-job training system. The good thing about the German dual system is that it enables a large proportion of young people to transfer smoothly from the schoolbench of the general education school on the labor market into work, since this type of training for occupational life feeds the young straight into places of work. The dual system is specifically constructed on the partnership of the educational sector and of industry, with industry in the dominant role (Blossfeld 1992: 175; Pritchard 1992).

When educational trends in Western Europe and the United States are compared, the conclusions are often contradictory. Three trends, however, are usually emphasized (Goldthorpe 1985; Blossfeld 1992): First, a powerful shift away from manual and productive jobs into non-manual service and administrative jobs. Second, the biggest drop has occurred in semiskilled and unskilled workers, while for skilled workers the drop has been less. The third claim is that the major increase in non-manual employment has occurred not in unskilled non-manual but in skilled commercial and administrative positions, skilled services, the semi-professions and professions. Blossfeld, for instance

(1992: 169) draws the conclusion that "there has been an upward shift in the skill structure of jobs; modern society needs skilled and highly skilled labor more than ever," and he predicts that this trend will continue.

It is, of course, true that high-tech jobs are increasing relatively fast. In many occupations, technical progress and the complexity of tasks have genuinely increased the need for formal education and training. In terms of the occupational structure of society, however, the numerically significant increase in jobs created as a result of the spread of new technology is taking place within highly traditional fields (Forester 1987; Kutscher 1987; Wirth 1987). In Levin and Rumberger's (1989: 211) forecast of the occupational structure in the United States in the year 2000, although the fastest relative growth is predicted for various semi-professional occupations and for certain occupations in information work, in absolute quantitative terms the biggest increases will be in the numbers of sales assistants, waiters and waitresses, nurses and cleaners.

The concept of over-education has typically been deployed to refer to situations with a marked decline in the labor market status of the highly educated, due to a mismatch between supply and demand for educated people (cf. Kivinen and Rinne 1993). This may result in graduate unemployment and in the placement of highly educated people further down the professional hierarchy than has previously been the case (see Freeman 1976). Rumberger (1987: 92), for instance, argues that personnel who are overqualified for their tasks will be discontented and that their productivity will be lower than that of others engaged in similar tasks but without formal training (see also Silvennoinen, Kivinen, and Rinne 1992).

The question of over-education is closely linked to that of credentialism (see Collins 1979), i.e., the weight placed on credentials—educational qualifications and certification—in connection with the recruitment of labor and with promotion. Over-education can even constitute a barrier to employment; it is in employers' interests to keep wage costs to a minimum, and over-education can raise the cost of labor above the market value of the work performed (Bills 1988).

Over-education has commonly been defined in at least one of the three following ways (Tsang and Levin 1985: 97; Tsang 1987: 239):

1. as a decline in the economic position of educated individuals relative to historically higher levels
2. as under-fulfilled expectations on the part of the educated with respect to their occupational attainments
3. as the possession by workers of greater educational skills than their jobs require, that is, under-utilization of workers' education.

On each of these definitions, there is evidence for the current occurrence of over-education. The question is, however, not as simple as this. Since an educated person can in one sense never be "over-educated," the problem can rather be seen in terms of a person's education being "under-utilized" at work (Bailey 1991), where a narrow definition of tasks, and the infelicitous organization of work, may block workers from finding rewarding outlets for their skills (cf. Tsang and Levin 1985: 97).

Action against the problems posed by over-education may be taken by individuals, by employers, or by governments. Individuals, for example, may realign their resources away from education. Companies may prefer to base their recruitment policies on criteria other than high levels of education, e.g., by reducing the length of training requirements. It was found by David B. Bills (1988), for instance, that work experience was by far the most significant criterion used by employers, both for recruitment and for promotion policies, with the focus placed on applicants' "suitability," rather than on the extent of their formal education and training. Bills comes to the conclusion that the function of educational qualifications is to "get you in the door." In discussions of over-education, it is often overlooked that workers are in many cases recruited not in order to carry out specific tasks but to fill a specific slot in the hierarchy, and if the hierarchy has any flexibility, it should be possible for individuals to gravitate upwards to an appropriate level (Bills 1988: 92-93).

The entire problem of over-education or under-utilization takes on a completely different aspect if educational credentials cease to represent strictly locked doors. Flexible production, with new modes of organization, places in question the entire conventional educational system, with its rigid forms of organization, starting from the fact that the rational design of education and training can no longer be based on a specified occupation but rather on flexibility.

TOWARD A MORE DEMOCRATIC EDUCATIONAL SOCIETY

As has been pointed out by Ulrich Teichler and Barbara Kehm (1995), however, despite the predominantly negative reactions that mass higher education arouses, in the right conditions it can also act as a catalyst towards a more democratic society. The expansion of higher education in universities, polytechnics, and *Fachhochschulen* creates the circumstances for a more rational and appropriate division and distribution of tasks in society. Inappropriate hierarchical structures at work and in society in general which depend upon irrelevant status differentials can, through education, be overthrown.

There is an urgent need for scholars scrutinizing the relationships between education and work to introduce more adequate models of interpretation and complement their traditional narrow conception of demand by paying attention to the push effects of education (cf. Teichler and Kehm 1995). Unfulfilled expectations of "jobs appropriate to qualifications for everyone" need to be replaced by more honest appraisals of the relationships between work and training. In European conditions, at least, there is an urgent need for new kinds of focus. A style of professionalism, which admires a high degree of formal education and professional status, promoted by professional organizations, will not easily be able to reconcile the unprecedented challenges presented by the changing working environment, with employers' demands for comprehensive flexibility. What will be needed in the future is workers with high skills in their own specialism, capable of flexible collaboration with their fellow workers, and unafraid of tasks falling outside their normal field of know-how. In this way, the fashionable cry for lifelong education could actually mean something.

In a society composed of highly educated individuals, there is no sense in trying artificially to maintain formal differentiation between the heavy demands of further education and higher education. As the school system opens up for the gifted reserves in the people at large, it is not necessary at work to cling to traditional conceptions of the scarcity of professional skills and qualifications. There is in fact no shortage of human resources, of potential wise men and skilled workers. The real problem resides in the bottlenecks that have been built into life at work, which block more and more people from being able to demonstrate their skills and develop their skills and talents.

NOTES

1. The official English translation used by the Finnish educational authorities for this term is "comprehensive school," but this is potentially misleading (at least for readers familiar with the British system) since in the UK the term "comprehensive school" refers to nonselective schools specifically in the secondary stage, whereas the Finnish and Swedish systems conceive the first nine years (ages seven to sixteen) as a common "foundation school" for all (even if divided into a "junior stage" and "senior stage" which in practice closely correspond to primary and junior high schools in many other countries). This foundation then leads into differentiated further education (the "middle stage") and higher education.

2. The English-language term officially adopted by the Finnish Ministry of Education for these institutions is the (ironically now discarded) British term "polytechnic"; the Finnish term *ammattikorkeakoulut* is however a direct calque (translation) of *Fachhochschule*. Whether the Finnish institutions succeed in evolving into high-prestige vocationally-oriented institutions like their German counterparts, or as a "II Division" of universities as happened in the UK, remains to be seen. It should be noted, however, that their curricula are all specifically vocational, and offer humanities, social sciences, or natural sciences, for example, only for instrumental purposes (e.g., language skills, social studies for the care professions, or applied mathematics for engineers).

REFERENCES

Bailey, T. 1991. "Jobs of the Future and Education They Will Require: Evidence from Occupational Forecasts." *Educational Researcher* 2:11-20.

Bills, D. 1988. "Credentials and Capacities: Employers' Perceptions of the Acquisition of Skills." *The Sociological Quarterly* 3:439-49.

Blossfeld, H.P. 1992. "Is the German Dual System a Model for a Modern Vocational Training System? A Cross-National Comparison of How Different Systems of Vocational Training Deal with the Changing Occupational Structure." *International Journal of Comparative Sociology* 33, 3-4:168-81.

Bourdieu, P. 1988. *Homo Academicus.* Oxford: Polity Press.

Collins, R. 1979. *The Credential Society: A Historical Sociology of Education and Stratification.* New York: Academic Press.

Esping-Andersen, G., G. Rohwer, and L. Sørensen. 1994. "Institutions and Occupational Class Mobility: Scaling the Skill Barrier in the Danish Labor Market." *European Sociological Review* 10, 2:119-34.

Forester, T. 1987. *High-Tech Society: The Story of the Information Technology Revolution.* Oxford: Basil Blackwell.

Freeman, R.B. 1976. *The Overeducated American.* New York: Academic Press.

Goldthorpe, J.H. 1985. "On Economic Development and Social Mobility." *British Journal of Sociology* 36:549-73.

Jackson, P. 1968. *Life in Classrooms.* New York: Holt Rinehart & Winston.

Jonsson, J.O. 1987. "Class Origin and Educational Attainment: The Case of Sweden." *European Sociological Review* 3, 3:229-42.

Kivinen, O., and R. Rinne. 1993. "Educational Qualifications and the Labor Market: A Scandinavian Perspective." *Industry and Higher Education* 7:111-18.

Kivinen, O., and R. Rinne. 1995. *The Social Inheritance of Education. Equality of Educational Opportunity among Young People in Finland.* Statistics Finland. Helsinki.

KTM. 1993. *Kansallinen teollistumisstrategia.* Kauppa-ja teollisuusministeriö. Helsinki.

Kutscher, R. 1987. The Impact of Technology on Employment in the United States: Past and Future. In *The Future Impact of Technology on Work and Education*, eds. G. Burke and R. Rumberger. London: Falmer Press.

Levin, H.M., and R.W. Rumberger. 1989. "Education, Work and Employment in Developed Countries: Situation and Future Challenges." *Prospects* 19, 2:205-24.

Neave, G. 1976. *Patterns of Equality.* Windsor: NFER Publishing Company Ltd.

Pekonen, O. 1995. *Ranskan tiede.* Jyväskylä: Gummerus.

Pritchard, R. 1992. "The German Dual System: Educational Utopia? *Comparative Education* 28, 2:131-43.

Ringer, F. 1992. *Fields of Knowledge: French Academic Culture in Comparative Perspective, 1890-1920.* Cambridge: Cambridge University Press.

Rumberger, R. 1987. "The Potential Impact of Technology on the Skill Requirements of Future Jobs in the United States." In *The Future Impact of Technology on Work and Education*, eds. G. Burke and R. Rumberger, pp. 37-84. London: Falmer Press.

Silvennoinen, H., O. Kivinen, and R. Rinne. 1992. "New Educational Strategies in Finland: Managing Structural Change on the Labor Market." In *The Educational Strategies in Finland in 1990s*, eds. O. Kivinen and R. Rinne. Report nr. 8 of the Research Unit for the Sociology of Education. University of Turku, pp. 37-84.

Teichler, U., and B. Kehm. 1995. "Towards a New Understanding of the Relationships Between Higher Education and Employment." *European Journal of Education* 30,E 2:115-32.

Tsang, M.C. 1987. "The Impact of Underutilization of Education on Productivity: A Case Study of the U.S. Bell Companies." *Economics of Education Review* 6, 3:239-54.

Tsang, M.C., and H. Levin. 1985. "The Economics of Overeducation." *Economics of Educational Review* 30, 2:93-104.

Wirth, A.G. 1987. "Contemporary Work and the Quality of Life." In *Society as Educator in an Age of Transition,* eds. K. Benne and S. Tozier. Chicago: Chicago University Press.

Contributors

Holger Daun is a senior researcher at the Institute of International Education (IIE), University of Stockholm.

Kjell Eide is a senior researcher at the Institute for Studies in Research and Higher Education, Norwegian Research Council, Oslo.

Peder Haug is a senior researcher at the District College of Møre and Romsdal, Department of Education, Volda, Norway.

Jens Hoff is an associate professor at the Institute of Political Science, University of Copenhagen.

Içara da Silva Holmesland is a senior researcher at the Educational Leadership International Network, Oslo.

Torsten Husén is professor emeritus at the Institute of International Education (IIE), University of Stockholm.

Anne-Lise Th. Iván is senior consultant at the Norwegian Ministry of Education, Department of Secondary Education, Oslo.

Jon Torfi Jónasson is professor of education, Faculty of Social Science, University of Iceland, Reykjavik.

Osmo Kivinen is a professor at the Research Unit for the Sociology of Education, University of Turku, Finland.

Jon Lauglo is professor of comparative education, Department of Sociology and Political Science, Norwegian University of Technology and Science, Trondheim.

Gary Miron is a researcher at the Institute of International Education (IIE), University of Stockholm.

Mina O'Dowd is a Ph.D. student at the Institute of International Education (IIE), University of Stockholm.

Reijo Raivola is professor of education at the University of Tampere, Finland.

Risto Rinne is a professor at the Research Unit for the Sociology of Education, University of Turku, Finland.

Kah Slenning is a Ph.D. student at the Institute of International Education (IIE), University of Stockholm.

Arild Tjeldvoll is professor of comparative education, Institute for Educational Research, University of Oslo.

Index

REFERENCE BOOKS IN INTERNATIONAL EDUCATION

EDWARD R. BEAUCHAMP, *Series Editor*

EDUCATION IN THE PEOPLE'S
REPUBLIC OF CHINA,
PAST AND PRESENT
An Annotated Bibliography
by Franklin Parker
and Betty June Parker

EDUCATION IN SOUTH ASIA
A Select Annotated Bibliography
by Philip G. Altbach, Denzil
Saldanha, and Jeanne Weiler

TEXTBOOKS IN THE THIRD WORLD
Policy, Content, and Context
by Philip G. Altbach
and Gail P. Kelly

TEACHERS AND TEACHING
IN THE DEVELOPING WORLD
by Val D. Rust and Per Dalin

RUSSIAN AND SOVIET EDUCATION,
1731–1989
*A Multilingual Annotated
Bibliography*
by William W. Brickman
and John T. Zepper

EDUCATION IN THE ARAB GULF
STATES AND THE ARAB WORLD
An Annotated Bibliographic Guide
by Nagat El-Sanabary

EDUCATION IN ENGLAND
AND WALES
An Annotated Bibliography
by Franklin Parker
and Betty June Parker

UNDERSTANDING EDUCATIONAL
REFORM IN GLOBAL CONTEXT
Economy, Ideology, and the State
edited by Mark B. Ginsburg

EDUCATION AND SOCIAL CHANGE
IN KOREA
by Don Adams
and Esther E. Gottlieb

THREE DECADES OF PEACE
EDUCATION AROUND THE WORLD
An Anthology
edited by Robin J. Burns
and Robert Aspeslagh

EDUCATION AND DISABILITY
IN CROSS-CULTURAL PERSPECTIVE
edited by Susan J. Peters

RUSSIAN EDUCATION
Tradition and Transition
by Brian Holmes, Gerald H. Read,
and Natalya Voskresenskaya

LEARNING TO TEACH
IN TWO CULTURES
Japan and the United States
by Nobuo K. Shimahara
and Akira Sakai

EDUCATING IMMIGRANT CHILDREN
*Schools and Language Minorities
in Twelve Nations*
by Charles L. Glenn
with Ester J. de Jong

TEACHER EDUCATION IN
INDUSTRIALIZED NATIONS
Issues in Changing Social Contexts
edited by Nobuo K. Shimahara
and Ivan Z. Holowinsky

EDUCATION AND DEVELOPMENT
IN EAST ASIA
edited by Paul Morris
and Anthony Sweeting

THE UNIFICATION OF
GERMAN EDUCATION
by Val D. Rust and Diane Rust

WOMEN, EDUCATION, AND
DEVELOPMENT IN ASIA
Cross-National Perspectives
edited by Grace C.L. Mak

For Product Safety Concerns and Information please contact our EU
representative GPSR@taylorandfrancis.com
Taylor & Francis Verlag GmbH, Kaufingerstraße 24, 80331 München, Germany

www.ingramcontent.com/pod-product-compliance
Lightning Source LLC
Chambersburg PA
CBHW062122280526
45788CB00001B/23

* 9 7 8 1 1 3 8 9 6 8 3 8 7 *